THE
WANT
MAKERS

INSIDE THE
WORLD OF ADVERTISING

ERIC CLARK

PENGUIN BOOKS

PENGUIN BOOKS
Published by the Penguin Group
Viking Penguin, a division of Penguin Books USA Inc.,
40 West 23rd Street, New York, New York 10010, U.S.A.
Penguin Books Ltd, 27 Wrights Lane, London W8 5TZ, England
Penguin Books Australia Ltd, Ringwood, Victoria, Australia
Penguin Books Canada Ltd, 2801 John Street,
Markham, Ontario, Canada L3R 1B4
Penguin Books (N.Z.) Ltd, 182–190 Wairau Road,
Auckland 10, New Zealand

Penguin Books Ltd, Registered Offices:
Harmondsworth, Middlesex, England

First published in Great Britain by Hodder & Stoughton Ltd. 1988
First published in the United States of America by Viking Penguin,
a division of Penguin Books USA Inc., 1989
Published in Penguin Books 1990

1   3   5   7   9   10   8   6   4   2

LIBRARY OF CONGRESS CATALOGING IN PUBLICATION DATA
Clark, Eric, 1937–
The want makers: inside the world of advertising/Eric Clark.
p.   cm.
Reprint. Originally published: New York: Viking, c1988.
Includes bibliographical references.
ISBN 0 14 01.1777 6
1. Advertising.   I. Title.
HF5821.C557   1990
659.1—dc20   89–23228

Printed in the United States of America
Set in Times Roman
Designed by Sarah Vure

For Raymond Hawkey

CONTENTS

ACKNOWLEDGMENTS

Hundreds of individuals and organisations in a number of countries have helped me in the preparation of this book. I am grateful to all of them – whether in agencies (where they ranged from chief executives to copywriters), client companies, media corporations, research organisations, academic institutions or lobbying groups.

They are far too numerous to mention individually (and some, in any event, would prefer anonymity).

However, some must be singled out. Like anyone who writes about advertising, I was grateful for the existence of the two premier trade magazines, *Campaign* in the UK, and *Advertising Age* in the United States. The latter seems to me to be as near a perfect example of a specialist magazine as it is possible to produce. Among advertisers themselves, one must be mentioned. Procter and Gamble has a world-wide reputation for secrecy and non-co-operation, but its vice-president in charge of advertising, Robert Goldstein, met with me and answered every question I asked him. Tragically, he died in August 1987 in a river accident. Among academics, I am especially grateful to Professor Kim Rotzoll of the University of Illinois at Urbana Champaign for giving me access to his working papers on advertising and ethics. I am also grateful to the Advertising Association Library (and in particular its information officer, Philip Spink), Ann MacDonald, Rachael Clark, Nigel Lloyd, Callaghan O'Herlihy and Robert Heller. Finally, I acknowledge the help of the Phoenix Trust in researching material in the United States.

I should note that when individuals are quoted or mentioned their titles and agencies are as they were at the time of interview.

E. C.

INTRODUCTION

There is a famous Edgar Allan Poe story in which frantic searches are conducted for a missing letter. Furniture is dismantled, cushions are probed with fine, long needles, carpets are removed and floorboards examined under microscopes. All the time the letter is standing in full view on a mantelpiece, hidden by its very obviousness.

Advertising is like that missing letter. As it has become more insidious, more persuasive, more a part of our everyday life, so it has become largely invisible. Its images are taken for granted. Advertisements have achieved a natural quality.

Yet it is not totally invisible, because we continue to absorb the messages, like it or not. As *The Times* put it, 'Advertising works – without our knowing that it is working on us. Good advertising works – with still greater stealth.'

Here lies the irony: the more we are bombarded by advertising, the less we notice, and yet, almost certainly, the more we are affected. Not us *personally*, of course. Asked about the power of advertising in research surveys, most agree that it works, but not on them. Alone, it seems, they are immune. Some groups, like doctors, believe this with passionate conviction. Only the professionals responsible for the advertising know differently: after all, they see the results.

There are many theories about advertising and how it works. One, formulated by Dr Herbert Krugman, who was head of research for General Electric's corporate advertising for many years, argues that the special power of advertising lies in the fact that we *don't* give advertising much attention. In consequence, we're unwary; we don't put up our normal defences. We may not notice anything, but the messages are being taken in and stored, ready to be triggered into action at the right moment. As Krugman puts it, 'The effects of advertising on the individual are modest, but they are powerful in the mass and over time. Like erosion caused by shifting tides, little change occurs at any one moment, even though clear-cut effects appear eventually.'

Today advertising is vast, increasingly global and more and more 'scientific' in its methods. Its domination over the kind of programmes we watch, the contents of the newspapers and magazines that we read, grows each year. It helps determine the politicians we elect, the medicines we are offered, the toys our children demand, and the sports that are to thrive or decline. All of this is new in its size and its range, its implications and its dangers. Election appeals have become interchangeable with Coca-Cola commercials; products themselves are no longer simply sold by advertising – increasingly they *are* the advertising. Over a wide range, from jeans to beer to medicines, advertising has become the only real difference that exists. Its growth in recent years has been staggering. Worldwide advertising expenditure in the twenty years to 1985 rose six-fold, the greatest growth coming outside the United States. It topped $225 billion by 1988, more than the gross national products of Denmark, Finland, Ireland, Israel and Kenya added together. Robert J. Coen, of McCann-Erickson Worldwide, an acknowledged expert on advertising expenditure, expects it to reach $1 trillion by the year 2000. America's advertising expenditure has been described as 'the largest information budget in the world'.

Figures themselves, however, are largely meaningless except to experts. It is when the vast sums are translated into actual advertisements that they take on significance. America leads the way: radio can consist of forty minutes of commercials every hour; the *New York Times* Sunday edition sometimes has 350 *pages* of ads; by the time he or she leaves High School, the typical American has seen over a quarter of a million TV commercials; the film *Superman* was introduced with 6.5 *billion* messages through radio, TV, magazines and newspapers in addition to the separate promotions for more than 1,000 Superman-related products.

But America is no longer unique. To varying degrees others now follow. Advertisements devised in New York or London or Paris or Tokyo for goods made in as many countries emerge on TV in Hong Kong, on mobile cinema screens in Kenyan clearings, or in breaks created on video films in Saudi Arabia. Advertising has taken a toehold on the streets of Moscow where Pepsi-Cola ads adorn the sides of buses. It has penetrated further into communist China, a vast continent coveted by international agencies as 'the world's largest untapped advertising market'.

World events, like the Olympics, become world advertising events. At the World Athletics Championships the bibs on the athletes' chests carry the names of advertisers to TV viewers in about 160 countries; film is preserved for future commercials; and important customers occupy free seats handed out by the advertisers concerned.

There is advertiser-financed opera, poetry and yachting, sponsored school crossing patrols and classroom notebooks. Escaping ads becomes increasingly impossible. The toilet? Advertising space is already being sold on the back of public lavatory doors. In taxis or buses? They've already been invaded by audio, even video messages. In hospital? Video screens loom over some waiting rooms, disgorging two-hour doses of programme and commercial.

A visual equivalent of Muzak has been devised to provide a kind of video wallpaper in public areas such as bars and hotel lobbies to reach travelling businessmen. The head of a company creating what he called 'ambient Video' told the magazine *Advertising Age* that ten years before, in 1975, people would not have tolerated electronic advertising in taxis as they do today or inflight ads or commercials on baseball and football scorecards. But today's consumer had come to understand that if you could catch him, he was fair game. 'And catching him, he believes, is the videogame of the future.'

What today's advertiser has above all is the capacity to be all-invasive. Kim B. Rotzoll, Professor of Advertising at the University of Illinois, Champaign, has put it well. Advertisers, he wrote, do not 'have the power to *compel*, no matter how vast their promotional efforts. They do, however, have the power to *prevail* – prevail in our magazines, newspapers; prevail in our radio and television programmes; prevail on the shelves and in the store windows; ultimately, prevail in our priorities.'

Advertising reigns so supreme that trying to define it might seem superfluous. Webster says it is, 'Any form of public announcement intended to aid directly or indirectly in the sale of a commodity, in securing employment etc.' Jeremy Bullmore, chairman of J. Walter Thompson, London, says, 'An advertisement is a paid-for communication intended to inform and/or influence one or more people.' Rosser Reeves, the great American advertising man, called it, 'The act of moving an idea from the head of one man into the head of another.'

There are less objective and embracing definitions, many of them stemming from the fact that whatever it is, advertising is *not* journalism but salesmanship and as such finds no compunction to tell all sides of the story. Nicholas Samstag, former director of promotion for *Time* magazine, said, 'The half truth is the essence of advertising.' Truman W. Eustis III, senior attorney for the *New York Times*, expressed a similar sentiment slightly differently, 'All advertising is inherently misleading. That's how you sell things.' H. G. Wells reckoned it was the art of teaching people to want things.

Advertising exists to inform – but even more so to persuade. It sells goods and services by turning them into images and dreams. As a discipline, it is a curious mixture. It is not really an art, nor a science, although it has something of both. The science is there, in the form of research, but it is science with a small 's', although the 's' is growing larger, helped by huge computer data banks and electronic developments. Nor can it truly be called an art, although many of its practitioners would vehemently dispute that. But art is an end in itself; art-in-advertising is simply a means to an end. There is, however, a strength in the mix. As one advertising man has said, it allows the best ads to combine 'the passion of Patton and the cunning of Rommel'.

As an industry, advertising has power way beyond its size. In a list of Britain's biggest companies by sales, compiled by the magazine *Business* in 1987, the largest advertising agency – Saatchi and Saatchi – was only at number forty-seven. In a *Business Week* list of America's top companies by stock-market valuation, in 1986, the top agency group, Interpublic, which embraces such agencies as McCann-Erickson, did not appear until 643.

Nevertheless, advertising has claims to be regarded as *the* industry of the 1980s and 1990s. It is an industry tailor-made for what has been dubbed 'the Me-generation'. It is a generation which advertising men insist actually *likes* to be advertised to (although this claim has to be reconciled with the fact that the industry is preoccupied with stopping the same generation from 'zapping' out ads from pre-recorded TV programmes). 'This,' argues one advertising man, 'is the age of *visual* literacy.' Advertising is in the vanguard. 'It is the popular art form of our age.'

More prosaically, we are in an age when an ever-increasing number of goods are dependent on advertising, partly due to the plethora of choice. In the mid 1970s the average American supermarket offered its customers an average of 9,000 items, by 1985 it was 22,000: in one month alone, 235 new items were introduced onto the American market.

Today there's almost universal acceptance by sellers of everything from hotel rooms to computers, detergents to motor cars, that advertising is an integral part of the package. Ed Ney, former chairman of the giant American agency, Young and Rubicam, points out that as recently as the mid seventies many companies still 'used to have furious discussions, should we advertise or not?' Those days are over. It has happened, Ney says, because 'it's a proven success that advertising works.'

The advertising man has also become more and more important as the payer of bills. Much of the media is now not so much subsidised by the advertiser as in existence by leave of and for him. It is a cliché to say we are on the edge of a global communications revolution, with untold channels beamed direct to homes, but few have realised the implications. Real power is likely to lie with those who can afford to pick up the tab for the programming. Who are they likely to be? The big advertisers and their agencies are in no doubt.

Given the real, and increasing, power of the advertiser and the advertising professionals it is surely vital that we should know more about the men and how they work. Its practitioners argue that their work is a mirror of society, not a creator of images or values. Advertisements do no more than pick up what already exists. Its critics, they argue, are really criticising society or revealing an élitist attitude to selling; they feel an unease about a world in which one company offers thirty-four varieties of popcorn while people starve. They transfer their feelings to (highly visible) advertising.

As for selling, as far back as 1848 *Punch* urged, 'Let us be a nation of shopkeepers as much as we please but there is no necessity that we should become a nation of advertisers.' David Bernstein, one of the UK's leading advertising men, says, 'To make things is respectable: to sell them somehow unclean and underhand. And advertising is the most visible part of selling.'

In the event, the advertising men complain, adopting an approach that they frequently extend to products, what is wrong is their image. In consequence, in America and other countries the industry has been creating ads to try to change it. Thus, in the United States, ads seek to convince that advertising helps you 'make the right choices' or that 'Without advertising even the best ideas take ages to catch on.' The tagline reads, 'Advertising – another word for freedom of choice.' Australia's campaign included a TV commercial in which a middle-class home was gradually stripped of all its belongings while a voice intoned, 'They don't have advertising to annoy them in some countries.' Canada's carried the theme, 'For your information – it's advertising.' In Europe campaigns began in Belgium and Switzerland. There was said to be especial need in Italy where the number of commercials rose from 45,000 to 400,000 in two years. This 'explosion' was thought likely to lead to 'adverse consumer reactions'.

It is not necessary to be anti-advertising, however, to believe that more is wrong than misunderstanding and a consequent false image. The dichotomy in poor countries between the realities of life and the dreams being pushed is real enough. Billboards selling unrealistic hopes and temptations loom over desolate urban scenes. The International Advertising Association met in Turkey in 1985 so that advertising men, including Turks, could discuss such areas of interest as computer shopping from home – this in a country where huge numbers simply struggle to exist.

Nor do you have to be anti-advertising to believe that some of the time the advertiser aims at those least able to cope. 'Halve your monthly payments with one simple loan', urges an English advertisement, suggesting that the borrower can then pay off all his debts. The target is obviously someone already well into debt. Then there is 'hidden advertising' of the kind found in a (now withdrawn) dental advice kit prepared for children. The advice appeared to underplay the role of sweets in causing tooth decay – something perhaps more understandable when you realise the kit was provided by Mars.

Advertising has an impact beyond its power to persuade. Because potential customers must be captured in the first few seconds of every programme, television programmes that are to attract the advertiser must be fast paced from the opening seconds so as not to lose viewers, which is why even the fastest paced British TV series and dramas are too slow for the American networks. Dramas are written with 'breaks' or gaps are created forcibly: Franco Zeffirelli tried, unsuccessfully, to sue a Milan television station which he claimed had ruined his film *Romeo and Juliet* by interrupting it for advertisements eighteen times.

Advertising has given us new words – 'wash 'n' wear', 'flashcube', 'fast back', 'B.O.' (body odour) and 'film' (for dental plaque). It invented the term 'athlete's foot' and it was advertising professionals who turned bread, pickle and cheese, the 'ploughman's lunch', into a staple of the English lunchtime and tourist diet. Equally, it has virtually destroyed some words by devaluing their meaning. Words like 'real' and 'natural' have become whatever the advertiser wants them to mean. There's 'all natural' spray deodorant (from Weleda); chocolate chips (from Hershey) with 'all natural' ingredients; 'all natural' cosmetics for little girls (from Granny's Girl).

Many things about advertising are changeless despite all the recent growth and developments. What advertising men are dealing with is people's hopes and fears, and as William Bernbach, one of the true greats of the business, said, 'Human nature hasn't changed in a million years.' John Caples, the noted American copywriter, commented, 'Times change but people do not change. Words like *free* and *new* are as effective as ever.' An ITT marketing director, Rod Mimpress, has said, 'Fear, envy, vanity, health, utility, profit, pride, love and entertainment. If you ever spend money it will be for one of those reasons.' But a lot *is* changing, and all the signs are that the changes are ones that will make advertising more potent a force in all our lives.

Among the characteristics of advertising men there are two that should be mentioned. The first is that they mainly believe that those who criticise advertising are an untypical, wet minority, if not downright anti-capitalist, and certainly not to be confused with the 'ordinary people'. This is a convenient and easy way out. It should, and must, be possible to criticise advertising without disputing either its existence or the need for it in modern society. To paraphrase, advertising has become far too important to be left to the advertising men. Yet that, by stealth, is what is happening.

The second is something that advertising men rarely admit: almost alone among the public *they* are an élitist minority in that they hardly ever watch advertisements. Or rather, to be strictly honest, they hardly ever watch advertisements other than in unreal work situations. This is true both of the advertisers who pick up the bills and the professionals who create the ads. In 1986, when the average adult in the UK was watching about twelve hours of commercial television a week, most business executives were seeing less than a quarter of that, and a fifth of them no commerical TV at all. A singular lack of rapport with their targets was shown in another piece of research. At the height of the debate on whether the BBC should show commercials, 199 marketing and sales directors were selected randomly from Dun and Bradstreet's Key British Enterprises and were approached for their views. As marketing or sales directors, the majority were in favour of ads on the BBC. However, asked the same question 'as a member of the public and a TV viewer', most were very much against the idea. The point is, of course, that they were quite happily in favour of other people being submitted to something they would rather not have to face themselves.

As for agencies, they watch ads in their offices on video – companies exist specifically to record and package such commercials for them.

It surely follows that the people who receive the product have more right to examine, and criticise, than those who produce but rarely watch. John O'Toole, a leading American advertising figure, pointed out in *The Trouble with Advertising* that it had been estimated that Americans were exposed to 1,600 advertising messages a day. 'If anything is following you around that doggedly, you're better off knowing what it is up to.' This book is an attempt to answer those questions – 'what it is up to' and 'how and why it works'. It comes from a TV viewer, a newspaper reader, a product buyer and a parent who is neither anti-capitalist nor anti-advertising. It started as primarily an examination of how the industry is organised and who runs it. It soon became obvious that more vital was the industry's practices – how, behind the glossy exterior, it sets out to try to make us do what *it* wants.

Advertising is a vast subject, and although I have spent four years interviewing hundreds of people from copywriters to researchers to heads of mega-agencies, this book makes no attempt to embrace it all. What I have done is to concentrate on those areas where, it seems to me, there should be most concern and vigilance.

Advertising in the developing world is a subject in its own right. I have touched upon it in individual chapters, but this book is primarily about the Western world. I have concentrated on the United States and on Britain because, together, they seem to me to present a comprehensive picture of what is happening now, with a significance that extends beyond their own boundaries.

Advertising has a number of close relatives, notably direct marketing, sales promotion and public relations, all growing in range and size. With the exception of references to the first, I have considered them outside my parameters. I have, however, included within my gaze areas of what might be called 'hidden advertising' – sponsorship, often used to overcome bans on advertising as with, say, cigarettes, and the placement of branded products within television programmes and movies.

The advertising industry is one of great cycles. Among them is the industry's own public attitude to its power. Depending upon the time, and the particular circumstances, it is apt to claim either a lot of power or a little. Either they are the Great Persuaders or no more than simple salesmen whose approaches tend to do no more than mirror society. In recent years it has become commonplace to belittle the power of advertising, a viewpoint encouraged publicly (though rarely believed privately) by agencies and advertisers anxious not to attract unto themselves more restrictions as they expand.

I began my inquiries with an open mind. I am still pro advertising. The alternative seems to me to be untenable. However, to use a comparison, you do not have to be anti the motor car to believe in speed limits, seat belts and a prohibition on drinking and driving.

Advertising is far from impotent or harmless; it is *not* a mere mirror image. Its power is real, and on the brink of a great increase. Not the power to brainwash overnight, but the power to create subtle and real change. The power to prevail.

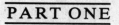

PART ONE

THE
MACHINE

1

The Advertising Industry

'If I were starting my life over again, I am inclined to think I
would go into the advertising business in preference to almost
any other.'

President Franklin D. Roosevelt

In the spring of 1986 Pepsi-Cola concluded what by any standards
was an extraordinary business deal. The company agreed to pay the
twenty-seven-year-old pop singer Michael Jackson nearly $15 million
to appear in two of its television commercials and to provide creative
consultancy on a third. For 180 seconds of screen time, plus the advice,
Jackson was to earn five times as much as Marlon Brando could
command for a full-length movie. Furthermore, Jackson would not be
shown holding, let alone drinking, Pepsi. It is widely known that, as a
Jehovah's Witness, he would never touch a drop of the product.

The $15 million was just a starter. Production added something over
another $2 million a commercial (nearly twice as much as it cost to
make the award-winning *My Beautiful Laundrette* and almost three
times as much as the equally highly acclaimed *Letter to Brezhnev*). Then
there was the cost of television time, perhaps another $50 million
worldwide. In total, over $65 million. All to sell a carbonated soft drink
that, whatever its merits, millions of its customers probably cannot tell
from rival colas but for the name on the bottle.

But *that*, in fact, was the point. Pepsi-Cola, like its arch rival Coca-
Cola, is primarily its image. It is what millions of customers *think* it is,
or what they associate it with. There may be little that is rational about
it (although the decision to spend that kind of money is made on very
logical grounds: the carbonated soft drink market is worth an estimated
$65 *billion*), but the decision to buy something or to choose 'A' rather
than 'B' is rarely made on grounds of reason. That, in itself, is not new.
Anyone selling anything has known, and acted upon it, since the first
sale. What is new is that advertising has now moved on from being the
creator of the image that *helps* sell the product. Today, advertising *is*
the product. What people are buying, whether it's drink, jeans, medicines, or electronic gadgets, is the perception of the product they have

absorbed from advertising and it is that perception that can make the difference between success and failure in the market place.

Mike Detsiny is managing director of The Creative Business, a London advertising agency, and former group marketing director for Allied Breweries where he had four lagers under his control. He says, 'The many competitive brands are virtually identical in terms of taste, colour and alcohol delivery, and after two or three pints even an expert couldn't tell them apart. *So the consumer is literally drinking the advertising, and the advertising is the brand.*' (My italics.)

Such an approach extends beyond products between which there is little or no real difference. Often, even where such differences exist, it is better to sell the image. The reason for this is simple: the product can easily lose its real edge if a competitor comes up with something better; it cannot lose its image because it is not dependent on any actuality.

Dr Stuart Agres, director of strategic planning at Marschalk, New York, explained, 'With rapid technological advances in manufacturing methods, a product doesn't hold its advantage for very long. Any product advantage can be ripped off very quickly. If you sell purely on rational needs, the next manufacturer can not only duplicate those factors, but can make a feature of one upmanship. In the fifties and sixties detergents got clothes white. Then it was white and bright. Then it was white, bright and fresh. Then it was white, bright, fresh and soft . . .'

Today's advertiser tries to make his product timeless in its appeal. Scotch Videotape, from 3M, the $8.5 billion US conglomerate, provides a striking example. With a booming video recorder market in the UK, a number of major brands battle for tape sales. They would all like to be able to say that their tape has a quality not found elsewhere.

Wight Collins Rutherford Scott, the agency given the task of advertising Scotch Videotape, found that the tape could re-record more than 500 times without losing picture quality. There was, however, a slight problem. All quality tapes can do the same thing. In the agency's own words, 'the risk with this proposition was obvious – it wasn't unique. Competitors could easily upstage us'. 3M also had a policy of replacing all tapes with no quibbles, but so too did many of its competitors. The agency's solution: give the tape a lifetime guarantee, illustrating it with ads that showed a 'cuddly and nice' skeleton called Archie still using the same tape he bought back in the 1980s. Thus consumers gained the *feeling* that Scotch offered something no other manufacturer did. As the case history went on to point out, the beauty of the advertising was that once customers were aware of Scotch's message, 'Any competitive activity would only enhance the position as the first, the original and the best'. Scotch quickly spent £1.9 million to get over its new message. It succeeded spectacularly. Within two months of the launch the tape became the brand leader.

3M's advertising was fun to watch, often a sign that what is being sold hasn't very much special to offer. 'A lot of the more entertaining advertising is produced for products that don't have any particularly distinguishing characteristics,' said John Salmon, chairman of Collett Dickenson Pearce, a London agency. It handles Heineken beer, where the tongue-in-cheek advertising has a theme that the beer 'refreshes the parts other beers cannot reach'. It is, says Salmon, 'based on the idea of Heineken being unusually refreshing. There is no basis for this. It is just as refreshing as any other lager.'

Advertisers have long sought to attach special auras to brands, thus giving them an added undefinable value. Charles Revson, founder of Revlon, is often quoted as saying, 'In the laboratory I make cosmetics, in the store I sell dreams'. Products that are mundane and prosaic may become imbued with colour, glamour, imagery: a sweet carbonated British drink made out of apples (Babycham) turns girls into Cinderella at the ball; chocolate mints (After Eights), mass produced and cheap enough for children to buy with their pocket-money, speak volumes of luxury.

Advertising men call it 'the brand property'. Barry Day, vice-chairman of McCann-Erickson Worldwide, defines it as the element that is 'unique, memorable and indissolubly linked to that brand and no other'. The 'brand property', he says, 'lies not in what the product *is* but what it does and what the advertising suggests'. Thus Martini's 'brand property' is the teen and twenties fantasy world created in its slick, jet-set commercials. Coca-Cola's starts with the bottle shape; the basic feeling of the advertising conveys that this is *the* American soft drink.

The brand image may be priceless. Carl Hixon, a consultant, formerly of the agency Leo Burnett in Chicago, told a conference of a fantasy he has in which he asks to buy the Philip Morris Company and is told the price is $850 million. He then makes an offer to buy one part of the Morris empire, the rights to manufacture his own cigarette with the name Marlboro and to use a cowboy to market the brand. This time the price is $45 billion! When Ronson, a company famous for cigarette lighters, shavers and electrical products, collapsed, its name was acquired by others who then licensed it to manufacturers of various products. One was a cigarette; 'Ronson has fantastic recognition as a brand name,' said the cigarette company's managing director. In the United States, Fruit of the Loom and Stetson are two companies that do not make anything. They allow the use of their image-laden names in return for royalty payments. In such a way products are endowed with some *apparent* difference.

Keeping brands thriving has always meant constant modification: in the thirty years after it was launched Tide soap powder received fifty-five significant changes. But today, when a brand *is* its advertising, modifications to them are often made not so much to content but to image.

In 1983, Guinness, probably the world's most famous brewery name, had problems, not the corporate difficulties that were to erupt later but the more specific ones of the famous drink itself. Although the dark stout was still selling 7 million glasses a day in 140 countries, its sales had been falling for a decade. Some felt that Guinness's problem was very simple: the drink was out of date in an age of lighter or less potent tasting drinks. As one trade magazine, *Drinks Marketing*, put it, 'The cynics still claim that the famous stout, which has been brewed for some 220 years, has been overtaken by changes in consumer taste and should be allowed to die gracefully.'

That, of course, is all right unless you own the brewery. What Guinness did, with the aid of psychological research, was to mount a new campaign to try to change the image from something drunk by old ladies in stale-smelling bars to a drink fit for macho young men. The commercials, playlets revolving around the word 'Guinnless' (someone who hasn't had a Guinness) were hardly the stuff of Oscars, but the decline was halted and sales actually began to rise. The product was the same; the image was different.

Cars have always had image as an important selling ingredient but real differences have also been stressed. According to automobile marketing men, those differences are vanishing because of global sharing of technology and management techniques. The National Automobile Dealers' Association meeting in Las Vegas in 1987 were told by one expert, 'The quality difference is closing, and in another five years all [car makers] will have to be over the threshold of world-class value in order to compete.' Product quality was thus ceasing to provide a major, real difference. The expert's advice to the executives, therefore, was 'spend time creating an image that will carry you through the 1990s'.

This and other factors – such as a deluge of new products and the need to open new markets as ones at home become saturated – make advertising one of the great growth industries of our time. To build demand for a product, the amount spent on advertising may equal the anticipated income from sales. Seemingly ridiculous sums are spent to develop markets for tomorrow – Victor Kiam (the entrepreneur who so liked the razor he bought the company) ploughed $4 million into his advertising in Germany in 1984, twice as much as the total sales revenues of the previous year. All this means more, and even more skilled, advertising. This, in turn, requires vast sums of money and an enormous amount of talent. Advertising can call on both in abundance: for money from the product and service suppliers; for talent from the agency men, the professional persuaders.

Advertising is an expensive business. Between them the rival soap powder giants Procter and Gamble and Lever Brothers spend nearly £80 million a year in the UK alone battling to convince us to use their products. Pedigree spent over £30 million persuading us to feed our pets with its brands, Imperial Tobacco over £25 million encouraging us to smoke Embassy and John Player rather than Silk Cut or Senior Service.*

In America, with its bigger market-place, figures are even more startling. General Motors and Ford spend nearly $1.4 billion each year in their advertising battles, Pepsi and Coke over $860 million in theirs. McDonald's earmarks $550 million to advertise its hamburgers, and Anheuser-Busch just a little less to promote its beers.*

The money spent on actually *making* the advertisements may seem small compared with such astronomic figures, but it is hardly small change. Set beside the money, time, energy and talent that goes into the thirty-second commercial, most major feature films pale in comparison. 'By screen time per pound commercials' productions on the whole still make *Heaven's Gate* look positively cheapskate,' declared Alan Parker, who turned from making commercials to such films as *Midnight Express* and *Fame*.

British Airways' Manhattan Landing commercial – in which a symbolised New York flies – is reputed to have cost £600,000 to make. The Apple 1984 commercial, from Chiat/Day, cost $500,000 and (at the time of writing) has been shown only once. A Diet Coke commercial shot at Radio City Music Hall was reputed to have cost $1.5 million. In the UK, a 1986 Barclays Bank commercial from the trendy advertising agency, Yellowhammer, cost a reported £750,000.

All of this makes commercials far and away the most expensive items on film. Miner Raymond, a Cincinnati-based communications consultant, pointed out that in 1988 the average American commercial was costing twenty times as much to make per running minute as a prime nighttime programme like *Hill Street Blues*. By that year the average cost of producing an American TV commercial was $230,000. In Britain, it was widely accepted to be 'only' £75,000. Mike Townsin, media director of Young and Rubicam, London, estimated it could cost as much to make one commercial as the commercial television companies were spending on ninety minutes of programmes. 'If they spent money at the same rate we really would have the best television in the world.' It is little wonder that directors like making commercials and that the medium has attracted a host of famous names from Joseph Losey to Federico Fellini. It is not just the fees, but the opportunity it allows for achieving perfection, albeit in a small – some would say trivial – world.

Soaring costs are a perennial source of conversation among clients who swap horror stories with all the morbid curiosity of hospital patients exchanging details of their operations. Miner Raymond tells of an art director who rejected a dining-room table scheduled to be used in a commercial. Reminded that the table would be covered by a cloth, he

* The figures are for 1985, as are others in the book unless stated otherwise. UK figures come from *Campaign* and American from *Advertising Age*.

responded, 'But *I* would know what's under the cloth and it wouldn't be right.' Anne Birnhak, an English woman who models her hands, tells of a two-day shoot (at £35 an hour) for Marigold rubber gloves. 'I wore the gloves for the entire two days. They might as well have used a gorilla.'

To the ad maker, though, it's all – or mostly all – necessary. Peter Levelle, head of television at the London agency Collett Dickenson Pearce, said:

> Everything has to be perfect. In a feature film you might have a scene of two men talking in a bar over a glass of beer. If you turn that glass of beer into a product the approach is different. What does the beer look like? Is it being shown to its best advantage? Is it the right colour and is there the right amount of head on it? Does it look fresh? It must be the perfectly pulled pint.

If, as the cliché claims, genius is the capacity for taking infinite pains, then the making of a commercial must surely be such an act. Take just two examples. The commercials for Heineken lager have become an English institution. With the aid of a glass of Heineken miraculous things happen. In one commercial Heineken makes it possible for Wordsworth to write the poem 'Daffodils' after several earlier attempts fail. The finished film shows the poet surrounded by daffodils. There are, in fact, 6,000 of them, and they were all shipped from London to the Lake District in two pantechnicons and planted on the hillsides especially for the film. Or take a French commercial designed to sell HOM sportswear. In this ad a helicopter flies over Greenland. A man strips and leaps from it, clad only in his briefs, hitting the water between the towering ice floes. He swims to a dinghy, clambers inside, the camera goes into close-up on his face and the words 'Sportswear HOM' come onto the screen, the first indication of the product. Many things are possible in film, but it does not look faked. I sat beside Jacques Séguéla, whose Paris agency made the commercial, at a presentation he was giving to fellow advertising men from all over the world. 'Did he actually do that, Jacques?' whispered a fellow adman as the film faded. 'Yes, he risked his life.' Later, on the rostrum, Séguéla reiterated the point: 'For the first time in the history of advertising a man risked his life to promote a product,' he proclaimed.

The ingenuity and effort that does go into ads is truly awesome. Cars are shipped from the UK to Canada to recreate scenes meant to depict winter in Yorkshire; Bordeaux, France, is combed in the search for just the right wine cellar in which to photograph a wine box (this one was finally shot in Britain after the searches were regarded as having failed); innumerable commercials are photographed in Venice or the Greek Islands or the Bahamas to get just the 'right light'. In an attempt to film wolves baying at the moon for a British cigarette commercial, a film crew camped out for three weeks in a heavy duty wire mesh 'hide' in a Scottish wildlife park that held six Canadian wolves. (That attempt also failed. The scene was finally shot in Slough, using 'pet' wolves belonging to the wife of a stockbroker; sky shots were done separately; everything was then reassembled in the studio.)

For those who believe with Raymond Chandler that advertising is the great waster of human talent, the shooting of the Renault Alliance commercial for Grey Advertising, New York, must rank as a classic.* It is impossible not to be impressed with the logistics of the operation. The final film showed New York's Park Avenue with cars flooding out from cross streets, leaving Park Avenue deserted but for 300 cars, each of them a Renault Alliance.

As a first stage in putting together the commercial the agency and the production company plotted cars on a model of the avenue. It was decided that thirty cars would be enough to achieve the effect: the thirty could be turned into 300 in the processing room afterwards. The city of New York was then approached and permission was given for four blocks of Park Avenue and all the side streets off to be closed for ten-minute shooting intervals between 10 a.m. and 3 p.m. for three days. Scaffolding, for a camera, was erected at the junction of Park Avenue and 92nd Street; a guard was mounted to make sure it wasn't moved. Precision drivers were recruited in California and flown in from the West Coast. Parking was found for the thirty cars (and six spares) and they were then wrapped in plastic and also placed under guard. During the actual shooting, drivers, directors and the cameraman kept in contact through walkie-talkies. The cars had to be driven at exactly the same speed as each other so that the film could later be doctored to give the effect of 300 vehicles. People living and working in Park Avenue were asked not to use their front entrances; other people were asked not to walk across the street.

The number of companies that can provide the money for such extravanganzas is comparatively small. Although vast numbers of companies advertise, just a few industries and some individual corporations dominate, often across the world. A breakdown of the top 100 advertisers in the US in 1985 shows that ten groups spent over $1 billion: the automobile industry, food, alcohol, confectionery and soft drinks, drugs and remedies, entertainment and amusements, retail, toiletries and cosmetics, travel and hotels and resorts, and business services.

Throughout the world kinds of advertisers and even specific names are remarkably constant. Eighty-seven of America's largest 100 advertisers are multinationals. The main advertisers in Australia include Unilever and Philip Morris; in Brazil, BAT and Ford; in Canada, the Government and Procter and Gamble; in France, IBM and Renault; in

---

* Chandler said, 'Chess is about as elaborate a waste of human intelligence as you could find anywhere outside an advertising agency.'

Japan, Toyota and Matsushita; in Germany, Volkswagen, Procter and Gamble and Henkel; in the UK, Procter and Gamble, Mars and Kellogg; in Italy, Fiat and Alfa Romeo.

It is not necessary to be very cynical to conclude after a look through the names of major advertisers and products that the less obvious the need for any item the greater its dependence on advertising. As Norman Goluskin, of the New York agency Smith/Greenland, put it, 'If I discovered a cure for cancer I could say it in a ten-second commercial. If I don't have anything exciting or important to say I have to beat you over the head a few times.'

Traditionally, the big advertisers are the producers of what are known as FMCGs – Fast Moving Consumer Goods, in other words smallish items that frequently have to be rebought such as cigarettes, confectionery, potato chips, and soap powder. Many of America's and Britain's giant advertisers are such companies: Procter and Gamble, Kellogg, General Mills, Nestlé, Mars and Pedigree Petfoods.

However, advertising has spread beyond its historic users. Today the list includes more and more disparate groups. It embraces companies trying to sell political philosophies, unions recruiting workers, Jews persuading the Russians to 'Let my people go', and the beleaguered Austrian wine industry attempting to recapture its markets after the scandal of anti-freeze being found in some wines. The Boy Scouts Association of America uses advertising. So does the Dow Chemical Company to polish an image battered by its manufacture of napalm and the defoliant Agent Orange: in one of that company's advertisements a proud father can barely stifle his tears of happiness when he learns his son is going to work for the company. In its attempt to turn American public opinion against President Reagan's 'Star Wars' plans, the Soviet Union has advertised in the *New York Times*, reproducing a *Pravda* editorial. In spring 1986 Britain's largest union, the Transport and General Workers' Union, became the first in the country to advertise its services on television. Even the BBC in its fight to stave off having to take advertisements to solve its financial problems chose an advertising campaign to proclaim itself 'The finest broadcasting service in the world'.

The range of those advertising their commercial wares has grown to take in not only doctors and lawyers and other professional men to whom advertising was once an anathema, but also those selling cemetery plots and even coffins. The unlikeliest products are given the adman's full treatment. Razor Ribbon, a barbed wire 'designed to inflict maximum injury', from the American Security Fence Corporation, is advertised as being available 'in several attractive colours'.

Companies advertise not only to sell their products but to persuade people how wonderful they are. Shell presents itself as caring of the environment: tough and efficient IBM tries to convince that it also has a human face. Advertising has become an integral part of takeover battles; in one three-month period in 1986 the *Financial Times* carried 100 pages of such ads, compared with three to four pages a year before. Charities, in competition for money just like makers of products, use the same techniques and professionals. The Church of England Children's Society even changed its name to the Children's Society on the advice of its new advertising agency, Yellowhammer, which felt the name was 'a stumbling block – it smacked of the wrong Victorian values'.

Government is a major, and growing advertiser. The British government's spending in 1987 was over £88 million, ranging from £96,000 spent by the Historic Buildings and Monuments Commission to over £14 million to promote National Savings. In Britain and France vast sums have been spent selling state-owned industries. In three months in 1986 British Gas put enough into its share-offer campaign (£21 million) to outspend all other advertised brands for the whole of the year. In the United States, government in 1986 spent over $300 million, making it the twenty-ninth largest advertiser. In the three-year period to 1986 spending on advertising by the Spanish government rose from 1.5 billion pesetas to 6 billion pesetas.

Governments urge their citizens not to drink and drive, to use state-owned railways, to buy government bonds, not to use drugs and to help prevent the spread of AIDS. The South Africans, arguing they need to counter 'unfair' media coverage, have run image-improving campaigns in Britain and the United States. One typical ad devoted about a third of its space to a picture of happy and prosperous-looking blacks shopping, the rest to text detailing the 'facts'.

Advertising is attractive to both the government and the agencies. For the government it allows it to project the image it wants. Whether an advertising campaign against heroin use is the best way of spending the money is debatable, but it allows the government to be *seen* caring. As for agencies, there's the money, of course, but even more, it is high profile, and because normal checks as to effectiveness (via extra sales) don't apply, agencies are often allowed their creative heads.

Despite these developments, the world's largest advertiser remains a traditional FMCG company, Procter and Gamble. The scale of its advertising, and its consequent impact throughout the world, is truly awesome. During 1987 it spent nearly $1.4 billion on advertising and promotion in the United States alone. It is the biggest single advertiser in many countries, including Britain.

P & G's main businesses are detergents, dentifrice and diapers and, since the takeovers of Richardson-Vicks and G. D. Searle, it is also America's leading marketer of over-the-counter pharmaceuticals. It markets eighty-three brand name items in thirty-eight product categories in the US and 140 foreign countries. Among them are Camay, Ivory and Zest soaps, Pampers diapers, Head and Shoulders shampoo, Crest toothpaste, Jif peanut butter, Duncan Hines mixes and cookies, Vicks cold remedies and Vidal Sassoon products. Its brand names are so great a part of modern international currency that in Singapore plants have been set up to manufacture and market to Arab countries products with names like Tibe, Tike, Tile and Tipe, all designed to fool buyers into believing that they're getting genuine Tide.

Procter and Gamble recognised the importance of advertising almost from the beginning and in 1913 the company was the US's top advertiser.

It was Harley Procter, the son of one of the co-founders, who brought the first marketing brilliance to the firm. In 1878, after years of experimenting, Procter and Gamble developed a white soap, to be called P & G White Soap. Harley argued that scores of companies were marketing a white soap; what the company's new product needed was a distinctive name, well advertised.

Thomas Barratt, of Pears Soap in Britain, reportedly said, 'Any fool can make soap. It takes a clever man to sell it.' Harley Procter knew how to *sell* soap. The right name came to him as he listened to the minister reading a psalm at the Mount Auburen Episcopal Church one Sunday morning: 'All thy garments smell of myrrh and aloes and cassia, out of the ivory palaces whereby they have made thee glad.'

In the words of *Eyes on Tomorrow*, a company-blessed history: 'There Harley abruptly stopped following the minister's reading. His eyes and thoughts focused on the phrase, "out of the ivory palaces". *Ivory!* Ivory was white and hard and long lasting. The word evoked an image of purity and luxury. Harley left church that Sunday morning excited and exuberant. *Ivory soap!*'

Harley then decided to have the soap analysed for purity and to advertise it as '99 and 44/100ths pure', a slogan still thriving a hundred years later. And much was made of the fact that Ivory Soap floated. Advertising can, without malice, be defined as the art of speaking the part-truth, and Ivory's floating ability is a near-perfect illustration. The reason that it floats is that it contains a lot of air. (The legend is that a workman went to lunch forgetting to switch off the soap stirring-machine.) The customer, it might be argued, is paying for more air, less soap. But he gets a product that pleases him and which is different.

Over the years, other products have followed, and so has the advertising. By the beginning of the eighties, Procter and Gamble was already buying anything from 18,000 to 20,000 thirty-second commercial spots on American TV alone. But Procter and Gamble's influence does not stop there. The wrapping around its messages is as important as the messages themselves and the company also produces 1,000 daytime hours of its own TV each year plus mini-series such as *The Holocaust* and *Marco Polo* that have filled screens throughout the world. In the words of the *Cincinnati Enquirer*, 'For better or worse, Procter and Gamble . . . has spent more money and more time on the air injecting itself into the American consciousness than anyone else'. And because both Procter and Gamble and television are universal, that statement can be applied to a lot of other countries.

By coincidence I experienced such an injection the night before I visited the company. Settled in my room at the Westin – built thanks to a $2.6 million loan from Procter and Gamble, repayments not to start until profits are made – I found myself watching the first part of *A.D.*, starring Ava Gardner and James Mason. At a cost of $30 million, it is the largest advertiser-supported mini-series since television began. This twelve-hour-long series is a part of Procter and Gamble's plan to be a major player in network prime time programming. The following morning the programme attracted good reviews. More crucially it also registered a thirty-two Nielsen share of the audience. Later, analysts explained to me that once again P & G had got things right.

Procter and Gamble makes television programmes for the same reason it does everything else – to sell more of its products in the most cost-efficient way. *A.D.* is (in the words of a trade magazine) 'a lean, expertly tailored marketing machine' for forty-one of the company's brands. The mini-series contains space for eighty-four minutes of commercials. Procter and Gamble takes sixty-eight minutes of that time itself. The analysts explained that it then becomes a matter of simple arithmetic. If Procter and Gamble were advertising on NBC in prime time that week, the average cost would be around $130,000 for each thirty seconds. Because of its enormous clout, P & G would not have to pay this much,* but it would have had to hand out considerably more than *these* commercial breaks cost them – below $100,000 each. NBC, however, has guaranteed to rerun *A.D.* within two years. On that occasion, P & G's cost for showing its commercials will really fall.

None of this will be known to the millions of people who will later watch the series abroad. What they will see is a highly professional, handsomely produced, mildly entertaining slice of historical hokum that should help pass a few evenings relatively contentedly but which will certainly not offend, stimulate or excite anyone. It is bland communication out of the *Reader's Digest* school, with all the virtues and vices of such. When Stephen is stoned to death, the only sign on his body of the enormous hail of rocks that we have watched hurled at him is a few discreet spots of blood on his face.† It is the world according to the advertising needs and values of the American Midwest.

Procter and Gamble's involvement with programme content is far from new. The company invented the soap opera as a vehicle for its commercials. 'Procter and Gamble virtually built daytime radio for the networks,' wrote Oscar Schisgall in *Eyes on Tomorrow*. 'Women listened while they did their housework. According to the letters they

* Exactly what it pays is a secret as closely guarded as the minutes of the Soviet Politburo.

† In the UK, the *Guardian*'s television reviewer wrote, '*A.D.* is in the purest and bubbliest sense of the phrase a soap opera.'

sent, they sometimes wept for the characters. When they went to the grocery stores they remembered what they had heard in commercial messages, and for Procter and Gamble business boomed.'

Procter and Gamble's headquarters lie in Cincinnati, one hour fifty minutes' flying time from New York, and, perhaps appropriately, in the heartland of the United States. The company has been attacked for its arrogance and insularity, praised for its fierce loyalty and dedication to getting everything right. It is said to be so loaded in talent that the overflow, according to Hercules Segalas, an analyst, had in 1982 provided the presidents or chief executive officers of forty-seven major US corporations. Personalities, though, are played down. Gordon Wade, a management and marketing consultant in Cincinnati, said, 'the whole theory is that when people die, the corporation lives on'.

It is also one of the most secretive companies in the world. Reportedly, office managers conduct regular checks to ensure desk drawers are locked. Outside, staff are warned not to talk business in aeroplanes or trains, restaurants, elevators or other public places. The company expects such security to extend to its advertising agencies. When Procter and Gamble parted company with Young and Rubicam, their agency for thirty-four years, four men were sent immediately to the agency's London offices to remove the thousands of papers relating to company business. Fifty packing cases of files, letters, and research documents were taken away in an operation that took most of a day.

The vice-president in charge of the company's advertising is Robert V. Goldstein, and as such one of the most powerful men in the business, his name known wherever there is a major agency or media company. He never worked for anyone other than P & G. He began as a brand assistant (P & G started the practice of what is known as 'brand management' whereby managers take overall responsibility for individual brands just as though they are companies in their own rights), rose steadily and took his present job in 1979.

We met on his forty-ninth birthday. At 8.30 a.m. he was already at work, standing jacketless near his eleventh-storey window against the backdrop of the glaring concrete of the new and not very beautiful Cincinnati. The eleventh floor is high-executive land. The corridor carpet was expensive soft green, the panelling dark wood. The walls were hung with portraits of former chairmen and presidents. Open doors showed executives silently at work in large offices. All of them seemed to have computer consoles. There was one in Goldstein's office, accommodated on a second desk behind his main one. Facing the desks were shelves of memorabilia including photographs of his family – the wife he married when he was twenty-one, and three sons.

A cut-out of the 'Mr Clean' liquid detergent character stood in a corner – the brand was twenty-five years old that year. There was also a framed sign which said, 'The eye will remember what the ear will forget.' Goldstein explained that he heard it spoken by a consumer during a research session: 'It really encapsulates what will make a TV commercial work.'

He was welcoming. I had been told that, like Procter and Gamble itself, there were those who 'hate and fear' him. For several hours he answered my questions courteously, only occasionally showing (controlled) anger when the talk turned to such arguments as advertisers as pre-empters of competition or manipulators of media values.

Procter and Gamble's philosophy about advertising, he said, was very simple:

> If you make a better product for meeting consumer needs you ought to tell them about it. Over the years we have found that the most efficient and effective way to do that is mass advertising for the kind of goods we sell. The average-cost TV commercial in the most expensive part of the day in the United States will deliver a message for under one and a half cents a household. You certainly couldn't mail a letter or postcard for that . . . When you get down to looking at it, it is a very efficient method of selling. If there was a better or cheaper way we would not be advertising.

Nor, despite the vast money and talent employed and the wide use of research techniques, did Goldstein believe that the basic practice had changed much in over 100 years. 'I don't think the advertising creation process is dramatically different from when the first Ivory Soap ad was made in eighteen-something or other. The advertisements today look a lot more glamorous and fitting to our eye. My sense is that if I look at an ad today versus an ad of thirty years ago, it is more pleasing. But that's simply because my eye has changed. It's all relative to what else is going on.' He added later, 'The role of advertising is to sell the product. There is a great variety of ways, but basically only one objective.'

Goldstein pointed out that less than 10 per cent of all new products launched in America are still around three years later. 'If we were so damn smart, we wouldn't have any failures.' Nevertheless, the research backup both for products and for the way to advertise them is staggering. The company claims that to learn what consumers think of products they use and what kind of improvements they seek, it has over 2 million contacts with them every year. The research set-up is one of the world's largest. Goldstein said that he 'figures that if it was a separate company it would be the fifth or sixth largest market research company in the world. We spend a lot of money, an unbelievable amount, which is just plain talking to the consumer. Asking questions and getting answers.' Procter and Gamble has been computerising its data for twenty-five years. 'Obviously we can get a lot more out of the data. I think we can profile them [consumers] more accurately – but I have to say, "More accurately than what?" More than the man in the store where they talk every day? No! More than we could twenty years ago? Yeah – I think it's possible.'

Procter and Gamble works closely, very closely, with its advertising agencies. Goldstein said there is daily contact with all of them. Periodically, agency executives are flown into Cincinnati for conferences that have been likened to 'indoctrination' sessions. All agencies who work for Procter and Gamble know they will have to work within close confines and under constant scrutiny. But, in return, the rewards are very real: big budgets, new product assignments and a rare loyalty. The magazine *Marketing Week* estimated that the *average* tenure of a Procter and Gamble agency was thirty-seven years. Five of P & G's dozen agencies in the US each had over $100 million worth of P & G business in the fiscal year 1985-6: Leo Burnett; Grey; Wells Rich Greene; Saatchi and Saatchi Compton; and (a staggering $197 million) D'Arcy Masius Benton and Bowles.

Goldstein said that in relations with agencies there were 'no holds barred, no secrets'. He detailed a 'typical situation'. 'We agree there's a need [for a new campaign] – say a new product. Say we come up with an idea for a Duncan Hines cookie made out of bananas and oatmeal.' The product is developed and tested (with researchers getting reactions of potential buyers). An advertising strategy is conceived. The agency puts together ads. They are discussed with Procter and Gamble, and also tested on consumers. 'They then come in with the results and say, "These look like the two best." We might pick one.' The product and the advertising are tried out in a test market-place – 'That's a miniature version of the world.' While the product is being evaluated as to how well it sells and how people regard it, so is the advertising: people will be asked whether they remember it, how they react to it. Then, unless it is all a failure, the product – and the advertising – will become national.

Advertising agencies who work on Procter and Gamble business may be very well off financially but they have to face the sneers of their 'creative' brothers. Procter and Gamble style advertising, with its reliance on safety and research testing (such as Day-After Recall where an ad is judged by whether people *remember* it) may help sell products but it is hardly admired. In Procter and Gamble formula ads, women demonstrate cleansers or laundry detergents to neighbours, tell simpering small daughters that washing-up liquids are mild to their hands, and stand-up presenters deliver capsules of advice. Detractors in advertising say it is such ads that give the business some of its odium. It is an area where Goldstein became sensitive, and it is true that the company's advertising has recently become – comparatively – more adventurous. 'We don't have a single style of advertising,' he protested. 'We have advertising that's musical and advertising that's not. We have real people and glamorous celebrities. Advertising that is basically heavily demonstration and advertising that is very cosmetic and selling dreams.

That is contrary to public impressions but it is true.' He slipped a video into the machine so we could watch the latest batch of commercials made by different agencies for different brands. In the Pampers ad real women are being recorded by a hidden camera; Wondra has a hard-sell testimonial; Downy has a slice of life (it looks pure Americana but it was made in Germany); Jif has children and singing; Bounce shows towels in a washing machine ('This one I hate but it's hard sell'); Duncan Hines muffins shows close-ups of children eating ('charming'); New Hope shows a woman washing her hair; there are lots of bubbles ('Here we are selling sex appeal and dreams . . .').

At the end, he said, 'The point is fairly evident. There is not one style. If I hired a salesman to sell a product to hundreds of different clients, would you expect him to use the same selling everywhere?'

Procter and Gamble is a jealous client, expecting total loyalty from its agencies. Goldstein volunteered he had 'lost or fired more [agencies] than anyone in the history of the company. Until five years ago the only ones we ever lost had been agencies that went out of business. I have parted company with three in the last five years.'

The reason in each case was that Procter and Gamble saw a conflict of interest with another account its agency was handling. The company line on conflict is a hard one. 'Conflict means *conflict of interest*,' said Goldstein, stressing the last three words hard.

Do you want a lawyer who represents you also to represent the other party in a lawsuit? Do you want a business adviser who is working with you with long-range-plans information if he is also advising a competitor? I am asking rhetorical questions. I don't think anyone would. Would you want the manager of your buying department to be also the owner of the firm selling materials to you? I would say you wouldn't want those things.

After a spate of big mergers among agencies, Procter and Gamble reassigned millions of dollars' worth of business to avoid conflict but also, according to agency observers, as a sharp reminder to its agencies of its power as the holder of the purse. The company even studied the possibility of buying its own agency, but discounted it. Despite the problems of conflict and management changes as agencies merged and merged again, Procter and Gamble had obviously concluded that there was no substitute for the advertising professionals.

As the English adman David Bernstein has pointed out, it is the ability to create ideas that differentiates the agency from the advertiser. Clients may think they know all about advertising, but at the end of the day it's the people from the agencies who come up with the ideas.

Advertisers and their agencies are staffed by people who could be from different planets. They may need each other, but theirs is rarely a love match. 'The average advertiser,' says Geoffrey Palmer-Moore, who runs a London company that helps clients choose an agency, 'is a pretty sensible, level-headed, commercial-orientated businessman.' Many agency people, in fact, see them as dull, solid and boring. For their part clients regard agencies as strange places staffed by odd characters. 'For many chairmen, the world of advertising is an enigma,' said Michael Cox, marketing director of Matthew Clark, the UK drink distributor. 'Advertising is a necessary evil, an expensive waste, or, alternatively, an opportunity to boost the corporate ego. But if the world of advertising is a mystery, the agencies that create this world are peopled by the bizarrest of creatures pretending to be what they are not.'

Many clients watch the cavorting and the continuous flux of the agency world with bemusement. They stare upon agency births and deaths, acquisitions and mergers, breakaways. Names of companies change and change again. Thus a footnote to an agency listing: 'Pritchard Wood and Erwin Wasey Ruthraef merged to become Wasey Pritchard Wood. Later became Wasey Campbell-Ewald. Then taken over by Lowe Howard-Spink to become Lowe Howard-Spink Campbell-Ewald.' (It has changed again since!) One London agency, circa 1987, boasts the name Still Price Court Twivy D'Souza.

As for individuals, 'The agency world, as we all know, is a world of gypsies,' said Keith Monk, advertising adviser to Nestlé. 'They come and go as quickly as you can change shirts.' Fred Turner, chairman of McDonald's hamburger chain, described advertising and marketing executives in general as 'bullshitters'. In England, Malcolm Parkinson, marketing director of B & Q, the country's leading DIY chain of stores, accused agencies attempting to gain the company's £4.6 million advertising business of 'trying to treat us like hayseeds, up from our offices in Southampton. They think they will bamboozle us with the bright lights.' Agency salaries frequently stun them. John Harvey-Jones, the former head of ICI, was once quoted as saying that he earned less than the chairman of one of his smaller advertising agencies.

Nevertheless, need them they do. The United States has about 10,000 advertising agencies, Japan has nearly 3,000, France 2,500, Brazil 1,400, and the UK just under 1,600. It is a truly global industry. 'I don't think there's a country on earth where there's not an advertising business,' said Robert Jenkins, a much-travelled advertising man now with his own agency in London. 'Even in places like Papua, New Guinea, there are advertising agencies.'

If there is business of any size, the global agencies will be there too. Ed Ney, former chairman of Young and Rubicam, New York, explained, 'All you have to do is look out for a middle-class economy. Whenever you see one, you know there's an amount of advertising going on. We follow it. Sometimes we try to go ahead. The great interest now is China. The ramifications are just beyond belief in terms of advertising.'

Agencies vary in size from the small like Jenkins' (five staff and freelance help) to the huge like Young and Rubicam (4,000 employees in New York alone, and handling nearly $5 billion worth of business a year).

The professional advertising man owes his existence to the Industrial Revolution. Manufacturers needed to create national sales for their goods; furthermore, advertising was a way of shifting power from the seller to the manufacturer – it encouraged people to demand specific items that retailers were thus forced to stock.

Early advertising agents were media brokers. The American agency, N. W. Ayer, founded in 1869 and still very much active today, revolutionised the business by acting as the representative not of the media selling space but of the advertiser buying it. In return it took a fixed commission, 15 per cent of the media budget, a system that remains in use today (although increasingly lower percentages or set fees are now charged instead, much depending on the clout of the client).

The next major development was for agencies to become involved in actually putting together the ads, something at first undertaken only on sufferance. Fulltime copywriters did not emerge until the end of the century. One of them, John E. Kennedy, a former Royal Canadian mounted policeman, changed the direction of advertising. The story goes that Albert Lasker, one of the giants of advertising (he built up a fortune of $52 million), was handed a note in the office one day which read, 'I am downstairs in the saloon, and I can tell you what advertising is. I know that you don't know. It will mean much to me to have you know what it is and it will mean much to you. If you wish to know what advertising is, send the word "yes" down by messenger.' The note was from Kennedy, by then a copywriter for Dr Shoop's Restorative.

Until that time advertising was designed to keep a name before the public. Kennedy changed this. His definition was 'Advertising is salesmanship in print'. Lasker hired Kennedy for the staggering salary of $28,000 a year. Within two years he was earning $75,000.

John O'Toole, who went on to head Lasker's agency, has written:

It seems so simple and obvious today. But what this definition did in 1904 was to change the course of advertising completely and make possible the enormous role it now plays in our economy. For, by equating the function of an advertisement with the function of a salesman who calls on a prospect personally, it revealed the true nature of advertising. For the first time, the concept of persuasion, which is the prime role of a salesman, was applied to the creation of advertising.

Although the advertising industry was hit by the depression of the early thirties it recovered quickly and grew steadily from 1935. The real growth came after World War II when US companies began to move aggressively into foreign markets. By the early 1960s most large agencies were 'full service' agencies, that is they offered a whole range of services including research, media analysis and placement, and areas relating to developing new products including packaging and brand name advice.

Like many industries, advertising has gone through its phases. Today, it is the age of the mega-agency and (conversely) the small, breakaway 'creative' agency, determined to offer something different from the 'faceless' products of the big. The big get bigger and the medium size get squeezed harder. New giant companies have been formed by mergers and takeovers. Three major American agencies, BBDO, Doyle Dane Bernbach and Needham Harper, joined in 1986 to become the world's biggest, to be displaced only a month later when Britain's Saatchi and Saatchi took over the Ted Bates agency, creating a company with $7.5 billion worth of business.

The mega-agencies have operations spanning the world. The American Interpublic Group, (a holding company which includes the agencies McCann-Erickson Worldwide and Lintas:Worldwide), has a world map on which outposts are marked with green circles, red triangles and black squares depending on the individual agency involved. Green circles run through Central America like stepping stones, black squares decorate India. An alphabetical list underneath runs from Argentina to Zimbabwe. Both Taiwan and mainland China are included. It reminds me of another map I was once given, that of the US State Department showing diplomatic and consular posts. Or, but for its modern graphics, it could be a page from an old English school atlas, showing the British Empire at its height.

Other agency maps could be drawn and would look as impressive: the world according to Young and Rubicam with its forty-one American and 125 overseas offices; or Ogilvy and Mather (sixty US and 209 foreign); or J. Walter Thompson (seventy-three and 130). 'JWT colonised South America shortly after Columbus,' goes an industry saying.

As business expands and becomes more international, the march goes on. In the three years to 1986, Foote, Cone and Belding (Lasker's old agency), made seventeen acquisitions outside the United States increasing by sixteen the countries in which it operates and so making it 'larger, stronger and truly international'.

As with the advertisers (whom they usually follow), the same names recur constantly, J. Walter Thompson is the top agency in Argentina, Chile, Ecuador, Greece, India, Spain and Venezuela; second in Britain, Columbia and Malaysia; third in Canada; fourth in the Dominican Republic, Hong Kong and Italy. McCann-Erickson is first in Italy, second in Chile, the Dominican Republic, Ecuador, Finland, Mexico, and Singapore.

By 1987 over a fifth of the world's advertising was being handled by the top seven agencies. Of the ten largest agencies in the world in 1987 eight were American, one Japanese, and one British. The largest agency holding company in the world was Saatchi and Saatchi.*

The story of the Saatchi brothers, Charles and Maurice, is well known. They started their empire with a stake of £25,000 and a tiny operation in a rented office when they were twenty-seven and twenty-four respectively. They have always shown a flair for gaining publicity, not least by the well-used gambit of embracing personal seclusion Howard Hughes style. One of the agency's key developments was the reverse takeover of an old-established public agency, Garland-Compton, cautious and traditional but twice Saatchi's size, and with blue-chip clients including Procter and Gamble. The other, in 1978, was when the agency was chosen to handle advertising for the Conservative Party. When the Tories won the election, the advertising was given much of the credit. Suddenly everyone had heard of Saatchi and Saatchi.

The agency attracts strong admirers and detractors. Both agree that it has a pragmatic approach to the business. John Salmon, chairman of Collett Dickenson Pearce, told me that, 'Charles Saatchi once said to me, "If our clients don't like our work, I show them some of the rubbish and say, Would you like that?" '

In 1979 it became the largest agency in Britain, overtaking J. Walter Thompson. Three years later acquisitions were being made at the rate of one a month. Its method of financing takeovers is brilliantly simple. An initial downpayment is followed by years of deferred payments linked to meeting future profit targets. Buying agencies gives Saatchi new accounts. Assuming that these accounts grow, the agency is soon covered for its extra outgoings.

Saatchi's takeover of the American agency, Ted Bates, stunned the American advertising business. Ted Bates fills a very special place in US advertising. First, right from its start, in the late 1940s, it has been involved in mass-market products, the kind everyone buys. It was the agency which talked to Mrs Iowa. It also gave advertising the most famous letters in the business – USP, Unique Selling Proposition, coined by Rosser Reeves, co-founder of the agency with Bates. During the fifties Reeves hammered out a disciplined approach to advertising which, he claimed, could result in the creation of a USP for every product, company or service. Thus out of Bates and USP came Anadin's 'Fast, fast, fast relief', which Reeves boasted increased sales from $17 million to $54 million. For Mars' M & M Candies, 'Melts in your mouth, not in your hands'. For the Navy recruiting, 'It's not just a job, it's an

* The world's largest agency was the Japanese Dentsu, followed by Young and Rubicam. Saatchi and Saatchi Advertising Worldwide, Backer Spieluogel Bates Worldwide, Ogilvy and Mather Worldwide, McCann-Erickson Worldwide, J. Walter Thompson Co., Liutas: Worldwide, and Hakuhodo International. Among holding companies, after Saatchi and Saatchi came the Interpublic Group and then the Omnicom and WPP Groups. Of the top ten holding companies in 1987 four were British, one French, one Australian and only three American.

adventure'. And for Bic, 'It writes the first time, every time'. Its takeover had considerable emotional significance but, more importantly, confirmed Saatchi's to be right at the forefront of the age of global advertising.

Ever-increasing internationalism is one of the dominant features of the advertising world in the eighties. It is possible to step off an aeroplane in any nation in the world and see the effect. Pick up a paper in Turkey, say, and odds are that there will be an ad for Marlboro or Lowenbrau; switch on the TV and the commercial may feature Mercedes or Mitsubishi.

Such a development is being driven by many factors. With markets at home sated, manufacturers are forced into more and more new areas to sustain growth. If products can be internationalised, there are economies of scale (including ones to be made in advertising). These developments go hand in hand with some in the media. The *International Herald Tribune*, for example, publishes in Paris but by 1986 was printing in eight centres around the world; satellite beams the same TV programmes across continents.

A drinks advertiser ran through products that were now 'international': jeans, T-shirts, sports shoes, soft drinks, power tools, credit cards, fast food . . . He suggested to me that we noted down as many individual brands as came to mind in five minutes. The list was formidable: Colgate toothpaste, American Express cards, Ariel washing powder, Bacardi, Ballantine's whisky, Canada Club, British Airways, Canon Cameras, Coke and Pepsi, Ford Escort, Heineken beer, IBM computers, Kellogg's Corn Flakes, Kodak film, Marlboro cigarettes, Mars bars, Nescafé instant coffee, Persil, Philips, the Fiat Uno, the Volkswagen Golf, Lego Toys, McDonald's hamburgers . . . You could walk into any town certainly anywhere in Europe and find such words were part of the everyday currency, and their advertising part of the routine advertising.

Companies operating internationally have the choice of three approaches. They can standardise, adapt, or produce something different for overseas customers. The same choices apply with regard to advertising.

There has been a trend for major international companies to consolidate their advertising in the hands of fewer and fewer companies. Kodak cut the number of agencies handling its business from fifty to just two. The leading American adman, Ed Ney, said, 'The truth is that world advertisers are choosing agencies of some size, some structure and geographically pretty much cover. They are going to be the winners. It's easier to manage for huge companies. And they have much more leverage against two or three agencies. When something goes wrong in Caracas, they call me up or Bill Phillips [chairman/CEO of Ogilvy and Mather] or Bill McKay [of J. Walter Thompson], and say, "Hey, we are working with you in twenty-five countries; you are screwing up; get it fixed." And, believe me, you get it fixed.'

Agencies without an international network have found themselves increasingly vulnerable. In defence, they argue that although the world may be shrinking, differences are real and vital, and therefore mega-agency advertising is lowest common-denominator advertising. David Bernstein recalls being one of thirty middle management men from the Interpublic empire being called to New York to watch a presentation for Coca-Cola. 'The fast talking presenter screened pictures of ten pretty girls, each a Coke model from a different country. We had to guess which was from which. None of us did very well. This pleased the presenter, but the prospect of lowest common-denominator woman-hood saddened a few Europeans.'

Jacques Séguéla further argues that that denominator will be American:

> Now there is no democracy in advertising because America is domi-nating. The English play a bad game in this battle. They fight first for themselves. Saatchi and Saatchi became an American [style] agency, not a European one. Advertising is our roots because our children learn life with advertising. They spend more time with television than with school. In ten years we will be not the centres of Bordeaux and of beer, but of Coca-Cola. For me the third world war has begun; it is not a missile war but a communications war on TV, newspapers, cinema and signs.

The anti-globalists have ready stores of anecdotes to illustrate cultural differences that, allegedly, negate trans-border advertising. Seguela tells of an African advertisement for a brand of battery. The opening sequence showed it being placed in an aquarium. The second scene a week later: the battery was withdrawn from the water and placed in a radio which worked first time. Sales of batteries were a fiasco. Re-searchers found out why. Potential customers had read the ad as meaning that the battery *only* worked if it was submerged in water first.

In Taiwan, Pepsi's 'Come Alive with the Pepsi Generation' was reportedly translated on billboards as 'Pepsi will bring your ancestors back from the dead'. In Brazil, an American airline advertised that its planes had 'rendezvous' lounges, not knowing that 'rendezvous' in Portuguese means a place to have sex. In French Canada, Hunt-Wesson attempted to use its 'Big John' brand name by translating it into French as '*Gros Jos*', a colloquial French phrase that denotes a woman with huge breasts.

Dr Jean-Bruno Bouée, a Frenchman who applies Jungian psychology to advice on international trading, tells of a Western shampoo that was advertised on Japanese television. The commercial showed a man's hand caressing a girl's hair. A sample of thirty Japanese men and women were asked to imagine what happened next. All but one said that the man produced a sword and severed the girl's head! The ad was withdrawn.

The globalists like the stories as much as anyone, but say that all they really show is that the people devising the ads didn't do their homework properly.

Ads *can* cross borders, they say. With Impulse, a perfumed all-over deodorant from Elida Gibbs, the basic scenario is used everywhere from South Africa to South America: a man rushes to bestow flowers on a girl wearing the spray. (The actual men may differ, however: in South America and Italy older men are used; women in the UK, it is said, would find such men 'too threatening'.) The campaign for Ballantine's whisky appears unchanged in forty-six markets. Henry Pomeroy, the director of advertising for Hiram Walker, explained, 'Wherever a consumer goes he sees Ballantine's positioned with the same message. He boards a plane in Hong Kong and sees a Ballantine's message that is consistent in the departure hall, the duty free shop, on board, in the international magazines that he reads on board and on posters when he arrives at his destination.'

A commission set up by the International Advertising Association had no doubts as to how the future would go: 'It [global marketing] is the breakthrough marketing look of the eighties,' it concluded, 'and it's going to transform the advertising and television industries in the decades to come.' Why now? it asked, answering: because of television developments such as cable and satellite.

Believers point to other factors. People's desires and needs are the same. Erik Elinder argued twenty years ago in the *Journal of Marketing*, 'The desire to be beautiful is universal. Such appeals as "mother and child", "freedom from pain", "glow of health", know no boundaries.' Today there is an increasing convergence of tastes, habits, activities, and lifestyles. Even food tastes, always regarded as among the most national of characteristics, are said to be taking on some uniformity. Nestlé sells frozen mousaka in France, muesli is widely eaten in the UK, the Italians are buying tomato ketchup, and yoghurt and mineral water are found everywhere. 'We're moving towards uniformity in food tastes, if not across the globe, then certainly in Europe,' said Michèle Pougny, of the Research Institute for Social Change in Paris.

Advertising agency men who don't like the mega-world of the big agencies have a solution, of course: they can quit and set up their own operations. Constant start-ups is one of the features of the agency business that makes it exciting – today, a telephone and a room, tomorrow . . . In one recent boom period new agencies were opening in London at the rate of almost one a week. (They can close just as quickly. In the US, six out of every ten are estimated to go out of business within five years.) Starting a new agency is easy. All it needs (given a talented individual or two) is an office, a telephone and enough money to operate until the cash comes in. Small agencies draw a disproportionately large number of the most talented creatives who see the big agencies as advertising machines.

One factor that should prevent any single agency becoming too big a presence, and thus ensure the continuation of a wide variety of agencies, is that issue of clients not wanting their agency to handle the work of a rival. This means, in practice, that the biggest agencies can only take a finite amount of the market available. A conflict of interest may not be immediately apparent to the outsider. Hallmark Cards, moved its $40 million worth of business from Young and Rubicam because the agency had won the business of AT & T Communications international long-distance account. The conflict: that on 'special' days, like Mother's Day and Christmas, there was a clash between telephoning and deciding to send a card from Hallmark.

Whatever happens, the situation can only help the smaller agencies (though probably not the medium size). It can also, especially in Britain, lead to the bizarre situation where the big agencies sometimes clash head on with the very small for the same account. It is almost as though the Bechtel Corporation and a group of Irish navvies were fighting for the same contract to build a new stadium. The difference is that in the world of advertising the Irish navvies sometimes win.

Today there are three major centres of advertising in the world: New York, London (generally regarded as the centre of 'creativity' in advertising) and Tokyo (home of Dentsu, the most powerful advertising agency in the world).

No one could deny that New York is the spiritual home of advertising. In many ways, it still dominates. The United States absorbs almost half the world's advertising expenditure, spends the greatest percentage of its GNP on it,* and the largest number of big agencies still operate from its shores. To many people, Madison Avenue is New York advertising. In reality, agencies are now strung out over the city. The American Association of Advertising Agencies has well over 100 members in New York but not many more than a dozen with a Madison Avenue address. Many big names are elsewhere. J. Walter Thompson is on Lexington, Ayer on Sixth, Ogilvy on 48th Street, Grey on Third. A number of agencies have moved completely away from midtown Manhattan to downtown. The areas they chose, around lower Park and Fifth Avenues, they dubbed 'Madison Avenue South'. The prime motive for moving here and even further south to Hudson Square was price, but the areas became more than a cheaper alternative to Madison Avenue. They began to represent an escape, a freedom from the suit, tie and calculator environment of the traditional Madison. They were colourful, artistic, the stuff of a creative business. But Madison as a symbol remains.

* At 2.4 per cent of the Gross National Product, advertising is way ahead of organised crime, which *Fortune* has estimated to be running at 1.1 per cent.

'If Wall Street is one image of American capitalism – dark, grey, granite-cold, calculating,' wrote Michael Schudson, an American sociologist, 'Madison Avenue is its upbeat counterpart – steel and glass, jazzy and fast talking, more cynical than serious, more pressed than pressurising, grinning but terse.'

London has no equivalent to Madison Avenue. Many flocked to Covent Garden in the seventies; a decade later the area was written off as 'too establishment' and new agencies began to nest in Soho. Many of the best-known names, however, are located elsewhere: Boase Massimi Pollitt (probably London's most admired all-round agency, voted both the adman's and the client's favourite shop) in converted warehouses at the rear of Paddington station; J. Walter Thompson in solid, respectable eighteenth-century Berkeley Square, as befits an agency that has been described as the Ministry of Advertising; Lowe Howard-Spink in Knightsbridge.

Unlike New York, London's agency world has a closeness that verges on the claustrophobic. There's a trade magazine, *Campaign*, that thrives on chat and gossip: 'In America, advertising is business-business, here it's show business,' said its ex-editor, Bernard Barnett.

Outside America, London is now the major advertising centre of the world. Eight of the largest London agencies in 1987 were American but the US agencies have been steadily losing out both in real terms and status within the business. An *Advertising Age* survey showed that in the four years up to 1984 their share of the British market fell from 43 to 36 per cent. *Campaign* has commented, 'The facts are that the Americans just aren't cutting it any more; no one in the first division wants to work for them.'

London regards itself as the centre of creativity in advertising. Martin Boase says, 'There's no question that the Athens of advertising was New York throughout the sixties. There's also no doubt that it shifted here in the seventies and is still here.' The view is not insularly British. Jacques Séguéla jokes that the happiest man in the world is one with 'an English advertising agency, an American salary, a French cook and a Chinese wife'. Vincent Daddiego, a writer at Young and Rubicam, New York, also teaches advertising and shows English ads to students. 'English commercials are the Grail,' he says.

Boase believes there are a number of reasons for Britain's pre-eminence. First, there is the British attitude to salesmanship: 'We find it embarrassing to indulge in overt salesmanship. Persuasion has to be covert.' Second, there is more scepticism about the power of advertising from the advertisers themselves. And, third, says Boase, Britain as a country is just the right size, big enough to have budgets large enough to enable agencies to employ reasonable people, but not like the US, 'so gigantic that it can only lead to a master-servant relationship'. The way commercials in the UK and the US have developed historically is also a factor. In the US, the earliest commercials aped radio and repetition of brand names was the central feature. In Britain, on the other hand, TV commercials became smaller versions of cinema commercials. Many were short films.

Britain's class system and rigid union structures have also, more surprisingly, contributed to the country's high advertising creativity. Jay Chiat of Chiat/Day, one of America's most creative agencies, believes that advertising has attracted good young people in England because it provides a way for them to break out of the 'caste system. It's a glamorous, well-paying career. And one does not have to be high born or go to the right school to get in. As a result, young people come in young and hungry, bringing a passion to their work that doesn't seem to exist any more in the young creative people here – at least not in the ones we've been interviewing.' Robin Wight, in London, agrees. 'Young working-class talent is finding its outlet in advertising,' he says. 'It is a great class accelerator. Many professions cut themselves off from the whole of this talent – think of banks and lawyers.'

The single most powerful advertising agency in the world, however, is neither in New York nor London, but in Tokyo. Its position within Japan is illustrated every New Year's Eve when Dentsu throws the country's most spectacular party for 5,000 guests. Competition for invitations is heavy; armies of highly paid Ginza girls wander through elaborate sets spread over two floors of reception rooms at the Imperial Hotel.

As an advertising market, Japan is second in size only to the USA; annual gross advertising expenditure by 1986 was over Y 3.5 trillion ($22 billion). Dentsu spends about a quarter of this (and the second largest agency, Hakuhodo, about 9 per cent). Japan is a market-place controlled by the Japanese agencies. The situation is a unique one. Japanese agencies were originally and primarily media-selling agencies. There are complex interlocking shareholdings between agencies, newspapers and television stations in Japan. Most of the agencies either own a section of the media or are substantially owned by them. What it all means in practice is that agencies, and in particular Dentsu, hold important chunks of newspaper space and television time to hand out as they feel fit. Advertisers thus need to have several agencies. They have to go to a certain agency to gain access to particular TV time slots or newspaper pages.

Enormous power thus resides within the agency. Dentsu claims to work for almost every motor manufacturer, for example. Dentsu's views on programmes are thus very important: when it likes one it can buy a great deal of advertising. The agency has also bailed out faltering newspapers by giving them ads.

Dentsu claims to be able to avoid conflict between its various clients by operating in fifteen separate account divisions, all physically divided and each with its own director. The main headquarters building is an imposing grey-colour twenty-storey block in Tokyo's Ginza district. Significantly, Dentsu's art directors and copywriters are located in another block a short walk away. Creativity isn't a major internal function at Japanese agencies: much work is farmed out to local 'hot shops' and many big advertisers, such as Suntory, the drinks giant, handle their own. The two big functions are media, and account direction; the account executives are expected to keep in *daily* contact with the clients they handle.

Training is then formal by Western standards. At Hakuhodo newcomers go to the company's school of advertising for lessons in marketing, copywriting and running accounts. After three months they are posted to a division.

Dentsu's staff are exhorted to work to 'Dentsu's Ten Spartan Rules' that were laid down by Hideo Yoshida who took over as president two years after the end of the war and built Dentsu up into a true power. They include: 'Once you start a task, never give up – complete it, no matter what . . .' And 'Don't be afraid of friction. Friction is the mother of progress and the stimulus for aggressiveness. If you fear friction, you will become servile and timid.'

Television is the biggest advertising medium in Japan, with newspapers next. Commercials are short – fifteen seconds – and they occur every ten minutes. The pressure, therefore, is insidious. There is no escaping an advertiser. Major advertisers will use all five commercial channels simultaneously. The commercials themselves, perversely, are the softest of soft sell, appearing sometimes, in fact, to be selling nothing at all. Junji Imaki, of Hakuhodo, showed me a series of his agency's commercials. Many were charming and calculated to make you feel nice for having watched them, a feeling meant to be remembered when you shop. In one especially striking one, a toy fireman painstakingly climbs a ladder to the top of a skyscraper where he extinguishes a cigarette. The ad is for National batteries. I'm not sure whether they are any better than other batteries but I suspect faced with a choice of batteries when I needed one I'd feel a heel if I didn't reach out for the National brand. 'The approach to the consumer is very emotional,' explained Mr Imaki. 'People in Japan want commercials first to be beautiful. I think some from abroad are not beautiful. They explain the product rationally. There's no excitement for the audience . . .'

There is one in which a naked woman swims in a pool. The water is yellow at one end, purple at the other. She briefly reveals one breast. A voice intones, 'Water is gentler than men. Parco.' Parco is the name of a fashionable department store. In a Suntory spot for whisky, a puppy is shown having various small adventures as it wanders around the city in the rain. The commercial switches to a closing scene of one hand passing a tumbler of whisky on ice to another hand. The voice-over says, 'There are all kinds of ways of living. Take care. Anyhow, take care. Everyone take care.'

Wherever they are, whether they are enormous international agencies or small, local ones, agencies have much in common. They employ the same sort of people with the same kind of talent, they're organised in roughly the same way, and they're offering the same kind of product. 'When you get down to brass tacks, at the end of the day we're selling ads to clients that they hope to sell to punters,' Bert de Vos, chairman of D'Arcy Masius Benton and Bowles' London operation told me.

Agencies grow and live or wither and die on whether or not they win new business. Louis Hagopian, chairman of N. W. Ayer, New York, said, 'The way you get an account is to convince a client that you've performed some magic for others, and he'll give you the stage to do it for him.' Not surprisingly, agencies pursue clients assiduously. An advertiser can find he is wooed as ardently as any desirable woman. One advertiser who agreed to visit the offices of Allen, Brady and Marsh, a UK agency known for its show-biz downmarket approach, told me he was met at a railway station by a chauffeur who had memorised his face from photographs. Then, as lunch unfolded, it became obvious that the agency had researched his every taste in food with infinite care.

Agency executives swarm to conferences at which clients will be present. Potential clients are targeted and pursued over years if necessary. Account executives are said to join clubs and organisations whose members include target clients. One of the largest agencies is said to have encouraged an executive in England to move into a village where his normal activities would bring him into regular contact with a major advertiser who was of the same, minority, religious faith.

A hint that a client is unhappy will produce a flurry of activity. When Woolworths in the UK fired its agency, another agency, Gold Greenlees Trott, placed a forty-eight-sheet poster where the store's marketing director would see it on his way to work each day. It carried his name in huge letters with under it the words 'Don't just go to the same old shops' together with the agency's logo and telephone number.

In choosing a new agency advertisers often ask agencies to take part in what is known on Madison Avenue as 'the creative shootout', more prosaically called 'speculative presentations'. Selected agencies are 'invited' by the advertiser to prepare ads as though they already had the account. The industry has mixed views about them. Advertisers, in the main, like them. Most of the large, coveted clients insist on them. Agencies, with exceptions, are against them as unfair, costly (in staff, time and cash) and demeaning. However, they are a fact of life. In the UK alone there are 500 or more each year, involving between 1,500 and 2,000 competitive presentations. Money gambled by the agencies taking part can be large: those competing in America for the Hallmark account were said to have spent over $500,000 each in putting together commercials. In Britain especially, small compete against large. The owner of one confessed that entering creative shootouts with the big agencies was like 'sitting down to play poker with $50 and having to bluff all the way'. But small agencies usually welcome them – after all, they've the chance to make an impact.

New agencies, of course, are lean and hungry. 'Obviously you get fanatical enthusiasm from people building a new business,' said Peter Kirvan, soon after he and two partners opened a new London agency. 'The only way you can make your way in this market is to attack.' In the previous three months, Kirvan's company had pitched nine times, winning four accounts and losing two. It was still waiting for the results of the other three. It is a pace that he says could not be continued indefinitely. 'We couldn't pitch thirty-six times a year. It means working from eight in the morning until eight at night and weekends, and hoping that you won't have to do it next year.' Next year, of course, some other new agency will be there, willing and keen to work just those hours.

Chasing new business brings out the show-biz side of advertising. Stars are paraded: during the fight to win Hallmark in which Ogilvy and Mather were competing against Young and Rubicam, Foote Cone and Belding, and Leo Burnett, David Ogilvy himself happened to turn up in Kansas City. Boase Massimi Pollitt dressed up people in yellow page-boy outfits to pitch for Yellow Pages. Geer, DuBois hired Liv Ullman to be the agency receptionist for the arrival of important executives from *People* magazine whose account was up for grabs. Young and Rubicam preceded its bid for the Kentucky Fried Chicken account by sending out executives to work in fast-food restaurants. The chairman of British Rail arriving at the offices of Allen, Brady and Marsh was, according to adland legend, met by staff who parked him in a dirty room and took no notice of him until, finally, someone deigned to serve him tea in a cracked cup. About to walk out, he was stopped by Peter Marsh who appeared like an actor on cue and explained the whole thing was a charade, meant to show the railway chairman the image the public had of British Rail.

Admen occasionally help perpetuate the image many businessmen have of them. Jerry della Femina, long dubbed the wildman of Madison Avenue, reportedly presented for the Alitalia account much against his will. At the presentation he apparently disliked the airline men as much as he had hated the whole idea. The highlight was a demonstration of how well the agency had handled the account for a vaginal deodorant called Feminique. The client interrupted and said, 'You must understand, Mr della Femina, Alitalia is not another Feminique.' 'Yes,' della Femina replied, 'but it's got a better destination.' He said later, 'That remark cost me the account. But given the choice between getting millions in billing and saying that, I'd prefer to say that. It proved to me that I was still me, and not influenced by the kind of billing that was at stake.'

In London, David Abbott, about to present for the Metropolitan Police account, apparently muttered loudly 'Hello, hello, hello' as Sir

Robert Mark, the commissioner, entered the room. Mark, never noted for a sense of humour, turned and left.

There is no way of knowing how rarely or how frequently dirty tricks occur. A few surface. Attempts were made to prevent Grey Advertising winning the Saudi Airlines account by 'reminding' the airline that the agency in New York was run by Jews. On a different level, but with the same end in view, Leyland Trucks was apparently fed false information about the British agency Cogent Elliott after it got onto a short-list. Bernard Barnett, editor of *Campaign*, claimed in 1983 to know of one case when an agency left a pile of cash in the back of a prospective client's car for him to find after the presentation. 'To those who suggest that such things are part of the bad old days of adver-tising patronage, I can only say that the incident happened two weeks ago.'

One agency's gain, of course, is usually another's loss: they've been fired for some reason. The American Association of Advertising Agen-cies has said that the average relationship between an agency and client is eight years, with ten years the norm at the largest agencies. However, a lot of breakups do take place. *Advertising Age* figures showed that in just one year a staggering $1.4 billion worth of advertising moved from one agency to another. In the UK, a five-year survey, published in *Campaign*, looked at accounts spending £100,000 and over, and found that 53 per cent of those established during the period had switched agencies, some of them as many as three times. Ironically, perhaps, there seems to be wide agreement in advertising that when accounts are lost, when the divorce does come along, 'bad work' is much less a factor than a host of minor irritations. That is why so much stress is placed on maintaining a good relationship with the client. Whatever the size, agencies usually have three basic divisions: creative (made up of the people who devise the ads), media (which places them) and the account men, who deal with the clients and are responsible for keeping them happy.

Known as 'the suits', the account men are 'the business types' of the industry. They can (and frequently do) cross over to the client side. Historically they are the men in grey-flannel suits, the archetypal glad-handers in button-down shirts. They act as the bridge between the advertiser and the men who create the ads, explaining one side to the other. They are well versed in the special language of advertising, which is constantly changing. ('Let's run it up the flagpole and see if it salutes' is 1950s). There is much military terminology: 'target' audiences, 'shotgun approaches', 'breakthrough campaigns', a 'blitz' on competitors. And sporting: 'game plan', 'touch base', 'run with it', 'see if it'll fly'. Ideas are not good, they're 'big', and if an advertising campaign lasts it 'has legs'. What account executives like to see is a 'cash cow' that the client can 'milk' for years. If he has nothing to say, it can be disguised with phrases like 'we're hitting the norms'.

Until about twenty years ago the account man was generally king. Vincent Daddiego, a Young and Rubicam creative, recalls entering the business about that time: 'In many cases the account guys used to create the advertising.' The top people at the largest agencies have mostly (but not entirely) risen from the ranks of account men. As a breed they are strongest when advertising is most client dominated. Clients and account executives often play tennis or golf together, even share holidays.

Today an upsurge in 'creative'* ads – ones that intrigue and entertain to beguile viewers into watching – has given the 'creative teams' of copywriter plus art director more power within agencies. Throughout its modern history, advertising has alternated between periods in which the creative or the hard-sell approach has predominated. Hard-sell may be an actor/salesman waving his arms and delivering his patter, or an actress/housewife holding up a garment to show her neighbour that her washing is whiter. Creative is more likely to be a piece of mini-entertainment – humorous, like Pepsi's archaeological dig set in the future where no one knows what a Coca-Cola bottle is, or intriguing, like Chanel No 5 where a garden becomes piano keys which in turn become sky.

At present creativity – and, thus, 'creative' admen – is 'in' because, in an age of too many ads chasing customers, it seems to work. Even agencies not known for their creativity have rushed to embrace it, with varying degrees of success.

'It is easier to write ten passably effective sonnets than one effective advertisement,' Aldous Huxley, a former copywriter, once said. Those who can write – or scheme or direct – the ads have seen their worth increase, as agencies compete for the best talent. Reuben Mark, head of Colgate-Palmolive, is said to have urged all his staff who deal with agencies to make the admen *want* to work on the Colgate account. 'He said to me that he knew the best creative people can choose what they want to work on,' said Len Sugerman, of Foote Cone and Belding, one of the Colgate agencies. 'That's true. In the end creative people is what this agency is about. It takes a very special kind of talent to come up with a breakthrough idea to order and then have the craftmanship to make it work. People who can do it are in very short supply, earn a lot of money and are in great demand. If you force them into something the danger is that they will leave.'

The creatives are often regarded even by their fellow advertising men as strange creatures. All agencies give them some latitude. An (anonymous) agency chairman told *Campaign*, 'They are like babies, all totally naïve. They have to be because they are talking to other babies [the rest of the creative department] about what is essentially

---

* The great Creative Age was the 1960s when William Bernbach was creating ads like 'You don't have to be Jewish to love Levy's' with black boys and Indians biting into rye bread, and the famous Volkswagen commercials.

trivia. Can you imagine anyone remotely adult composing, "Hey, Tosh, Gotta Toshiba?" '

A creative team does not start with just a completely blank piece of paper and a rough set of thoughts (like, say, a novelist or scriptwriter). They are presented with what is known as 'a strategy'. This is a document derived from research which spells out in some detail what the advertising is meant to achieve, including just what is being sold and to whom. The team are expected to produce within these confines.

What creatives do at that stage is read, interview, talk, think. They become experts on subjects for brief periods. David Abbott has written sixty print ads for Sainsbury, the British grocery supermarket chain. 'For two weeks,' he told me, 'I am an expert on cheese or pink champagne. I write the advert and move on to the next thing.' Like many creative men, he likes 'the fact that it is a comparatively short attention span'. Neil Patterson, as creative director of TBWA in London, 'piled into medical bookshops and libraries', visited hospitals and special units to research anorexia for nursing recruitment ads – 'I even took an anorexic to lunch'.

Vincent Daddiego reckons that there is a breed of admen who create instinctively. He recalls the first assignment he ever handled. He was twenty-three, and it was to create a series of spot commercials for Playtex's '18-Hour' Girdle. 'What in the name of bleeding Jesus do I know about girdles?' he asked himself. But he says that he knew that whenever the family came home from visiting, his mother would invariably say, 'My girdle is killing me!' He worked his campaign around that cry. One showed an opera soprano and tenor taking their curtain call. Both were smiling broadly and as the camera moved in viewers heard the soprano mutter through her smile, 'My girdle is killing me!' Another portrayed a very attractive woman in an evening gown playing a beautiful melody. She turned to camera, smiled and whispered the same phrase. Daddiego says that his campaign 'was responsible for increasing sales of products faster than the girdles could be manufactured'. In devising it, he says, he only did 'what the old huckster will do. A huckster is just an individual who senses what will turn consumers on to a product.'

Bob Pritikin, a San Francisco writer, fits Daddiego's definition of 'huckster'. He wrote his favourite advertisement early in his career for a company called the Pureta Sausage Co. Trying to find his Big Idea for advertising the company's hot dog, he was told on a plant tour that the whole cow – except 'scuzzy parts like the eyeballs and nostrils' – went into the mincer. The headline, he recalled, came to him like a bolt of lightning: 'Pureta – there's a T-bone steak in every frank'.*

* There is a sad ending to this story. The Food and Drug Administration objected to, and stopped, the ad, though not until the campaign had run for months and sales had soared.

In the 1930s, an advertising man called Obie Winters solved the problems of a manufacturer of a horse linament named Absorbine whose sales were falling. Winters had the linament laboratory tested and found it worked on ringworm of the foot. His genius, though, lay in creating a wholly new name for ringworm that would sell his newly-targeted product to the general public – 'athlete's foot', a term that is now in the dictionary and in such wide usage that its derivation has been forgotten.

The legendary Claude Hopkins, described as 'the greatest copywriter who ever lived', noticed grains for puffed wheat and puffed rice being steam exploded in containers resembling cannons when he toured Quaker Oats, and immediately coined the phrase, 'Food shot from guns'. Some thought it 'the idea of an imbecile' but it increased sales and was still being used seventy years later. For Pepsodent toothpaste he invented the term 'film' (for plaque) in ads that appeared in seventeen languages. Hopkins' agency, Lord and Thomas, also persuaded Americans to *drink* oranges: until that time, 1916, they were only eaten. A classic ad headed 'Drink an Orange' began, 'Orange juice – a *delicious* beverage – is healthfulness itself'. A man was hired to invent a juice extractor (shown actual size in the ads) which sold through grocers at 10 cents. More than 3 million were distributed virtually overnight. Hopkins was paid a staggering $185,000 a year.

Ideas can take weeks – or be instantaneous. In the 1960s, a team wrestled for weeks for an idea to illustrate the reliability of the Volkswagen in winter. Eventually they agreed that a snowplough driver would make an excellent spokesman. The breakthrough came a week later when one of the team wondered aloud, 'How does the snowplough driver get to his snowplough?'

More recently, Ian Potter, creative director of FCO, a London agency, recalled the birth of a campaign for Araldite. He was given a brief for five black and white press ads 'to say little more than "this glue can stick anything to anything". I went to see Richard [French, agency chairman] and asked what he thought. He asked what I had in mind. I just turned round and said, "How about sticking a car to the poster?" It was as easy and as hard as that.' The campaign opened with a Ford Cortina stuck to a poster.

Advertising on the agency side is a freebooting profession. There is no recognised way in, no set qualifications. You succeed only by succeeding. Entering advertising is not easy. In a good year, for example, there will be about 120 vacancies in the UK. Competition is intense. Boase Massimi Pollitt claims to receive applications from about one in every thirty-five of the students who graduate from university each year. In the US there is specialist undergraduate training: around ninety colleges in forty-two states offer a programme in advertising, and nearly 5,000 students graduate.

Advertising, however, is one of those areas where employers back hunches and rate samples of work higher than qualifications. Perhaps the highest quality wanted is the sheer determination to get into advertising. 'Advertising is about selling things – anyone entering it ought to be able to sell themselves,' one agency told me. Thus students who parade with sandwich boards or dress up as Superman usually get interviews at least.

J. Walter Thompson, New York, took an unusual recruiting step. It advertised in the *New York Times* inviting would-be copywriters to complete an eight-point copy test. Question 6 said, 'You've heard the story about the man who made a fortune selling refrigerators to Eskimos. In not more than 100 words, how would you sell a telephone to a Trappist monk, who is observing the strict Rule of Silence? (But he can nod acceptance at the end.)' Question 7 went, 'Design/draw two posters. One is for legislating strict gun-control laws. The other is in support of the NRA.'

One big draw is that although advertising may be a tough business it is also a fun business. 'Advertising is the rock 'n' roll of the business world,' said Tom Manahan, of a Boston agency LMS. Fun and success are pursued with equal dedication. Offices are often personalised with fruit machines, juke boxes, cartoon figures, life-size models, fullsize galvanised brightly painted dustbins, jokes (a hat with an axe buried in it), as well as more serious – and expensive – items, like specially designed desks or wall displays of varying kinds of expensive ephemera. Cars are important, both as a part of a pay-and-perks package and as status toys. In the mid 1980s, the most common high-perk car in London was probably the Porsche (various models costing up to £35,000-plus) although there were Ferraris too (up to more than twice that) as well as other high luxury models such as the Aston Martin.

Admen everywhere are regarded, justifiably, as the biggest lunchers of all. They defend the practice – people contacts are so important, it allows them to spread themselves . . . The fact is that in London, for example, it is likely that at least three of the city's most renowned eateries would be up to 75 per cent empty if all the admen walked out: Langans, L'Etoile and the White Tower. One new breed adman, Dave Trott, said contemptuously that advertising is only the third most important thing in many agency men's lives: 'The first two being lunch and dinner.'

There is also, seemingly, enormous effort invested in such areas as organising the best parties and producing the best Christmas cards. Thus Boase Massimi Pollitt throws a Christmas party in Madame Tussauds with 150 staff wearing masks in a likeness of Martin Boase and 150 in the likeness of John Webster, the executive creative director. A creative director at another agency, KMP, is forty, so a helicopter picks him up and takes him to an English seaside resort for a seaside café lunch. Abbott Mead Vickers has a novel idea for its Christmas card – Santa's sleigh being clamped for parking in the wrong place. The photograph, outside the agency's offices, only involves live reindeer and 500 gallons of foam to simulate snow.

Ah, say adland's defenders, all this may be true, but it's only the gloss. What people do not see is the adman working long nights and weekends, dedicated to the clients and the product. What is more, it is frequently added, most who do it are less concerned about the money they earn than about the final ad. And that, indeed, may be true. This is not to say, however, that admen do not care about money. Alfred Politz, a dominant force in advertising research in America in the 1950s and early 1960s, recalled that when he first arrived in the US from Germany to start a new life he asked himself, Which profession makes the most money with the least intelligence? 'The answer was "advertising".' Philip Dusenberry, executive creative director of BBDO, said, 'I have always believed that writing advertisements is the second most profitable form of writing. The first, of course, is ransom notes . . .'

The men at the corporate top in the ad world are far from badly paid. In 1987 Philip Geier of Interpublic earned $1.4 million and Ed Meyer of Grey Advertising an estimated $1.3 million. In the UK, 1988 figures showed the latest earnings of Maurice and Charles Saatchi to be £500,000 each and Robin Wight and Peter Scott of WCRS £250,000 each plus bonuses. But they are big men in big business. It is, perhaps, more interesting to look at pay lower down the scale. In the mid 1980s, big agencies in London were reported paying upwards of £150,000 for top people. In the US, *Adweek* told of a thirty-year-old copywriter making close to $90,000 who said, 'The phone never stops ringing. I probably get five solid offers a week to jump, and each one contains an exciting compensation package. Agencies will pay almost anything if they want you.' One headhunter alone, Judy Wald, placed over 30 creatives at over $150,000 each plus perks in 1987, notwithstanding the fact that it was a year of redundancies because of a flurry of takeovers. A survey the following year showed UK agency account men earning considerably more than client counterparts.

Perks can range the whole gamut of ingenuity – cars, country club membership, personal expenses, mortgage payments for a country house, children's education and holidays. Stock option schemes and bonuses can become 'golden handcuffs'. A bonus at an agency riding high can apparently be as high as 50 per cent of salary, perhaps a staggering $150,000. Winston Fletcher said, 'You can live off the company by having your food, motoring, travel and flat in town all paid for so that your salary is really pocket-money.'

Some admen will argue that in part the salaries and the perks are compensation not only for a talent shortage, but for the high risks. Stress is rated as high: certainly it is a business of deadlines with rewards for meeting them successfully, retribution for failing to do so. There is also a blurring between work and home, and the strain of having to project much of the time.

Professor Cary Cooper, of the University of Manchester Institute of Science and Technology, conducted a detailed survey into occupational stress. Advertising notched up a score of more than seven on a ten-point stress scale, putting it into the top bracket – although also there were dentistry, mining, the construction industry, acting, police, airline pilots, prison warders and journalism.

Another survey showed that over 90 per cent questioned admitted to drinking way above the recommended 'safe' level (equivalent to eighteen measures of spirit or glasses of wine a week for men or twelve for women). Mrs Denise Larkin, general secretary of the National Advertising Benevolent Society which helps advertising people who are sick or unemployed, said there was a drink pattern: Because a man was working to a deadline he found he had to work overnight. Then he couldn't relax, so he had a drink. The next day he couldn't work, so more drink followed . . . Creative admen may wake up and find they have lost their skills, she said. 'They are very highly strung anyway. The kind of person who makes a good advertising person is also a person given to difficulties when things go wrong. I suppose they have to be prepared to take chances. They are generally risk takers.'

Account losses and agency mergers mean job losses. Mrs Larkin says unemployment is an especial problem because advertising men are used to living well and usually 'spend without accumulating'. She said, 'The moment they are told they are to be promoted, they move on to the next lifestyle – a new house, a new car, private school. One of them told me, "People who live within their means lack ambition." '

Advertising men link age and risk. Advertising, they say, is a young man's business. An anonymous creative head told *Design and Art Direction*, 'It's a dangerous business, for God's sake. As you start pushing forty you figure you have maybe ten years left; no one really knows what happens because agencies are comparatively young.' One of the most striking facts about the advertising scene in London especially is how young much of it is. It is very easy to justify this rationally in terms of ads. Advertising people need to be preoccupied by what is new. It is a business of fads and fashions. That is not meant to be derogatory. Advertising takes and uses from all around it. A young man is more likely to be more attuned.

A paper prepared for J. Walter Thompson, London, in 1976, entitled 'Old Men in Advertising', concluded that:

it would seem that with few important exceptions older people won't contribute effectively. So they won't enjoy themselves in advertising. Thus it is in an employee's as well as management's interests to recognise that advertising is unlikely to offer many of them a lifetime's career. The prospect of finding a second career is not as horrid as it might seem. Though the specific skills of advertising are of limited use elsewhere, it is an excellent stepping off point for very many other jobs, even at the age of forty or more.

Some argue that when older men leave it is sometimes less because they cannot handle the business any more than that they have 'matured' out of it. They simply find it intellectually intolerable. Shepherd Mead, author of *How to Succeed in Business Without Really Trying*, was creative head of Benton and Bowles in New York until he was forty-one and quit to write fulltime. He said, 'Copywriting is a form of intellectual prostitution. No advertising creative man will stay in advertising when he can afford to get out. Who would write about soap powders when he could be writing his own novel?'*

The majority do stay. A large number would, in fact, prefer to write about soap powders than novels. They like the mix of fun and money, thrive on deadlines and applause. They do not think about the final product, except in terms of personal success or failure, and the reactions of their professional peers. It's not so much the end justifying the means (which might be an advertiser justification), but that the means is justified within itself. John Caples, the advertising man who wrote such classics as 'They laughed when I sat down to play the piano', has pointed out that two forces are at work in an adman's prospects: scepticism and the desire to believe. The good adman is content to concentrate his all on overcoming the first and flaming the second.

Nearly eighty years ago, a textbook advised advertising men, 'Above all else, in planning an advertisement that will catch the public, *aim low* . . . the great mass of people, rich or poor, have simple minds, and you must talk to them in a simple way.' Today's advertising man will still do that – but only if he is convinced it will work. Nothing should disguise the fact that glitzy though the advertising scene may be, no matter how pleasant and personable its individuals, what the business is all about is results.

Joe Bensman, a sociologist who spent eight years in an agency, wrote that advertising is not the place for anyone 'kind, gentle, ethical or religious . . . Advertising requires strong defences, toughness, nerve and the willingness to exploit oneself and others.' Or as Jerry della Femina, an agency head himself, put it, 'When you think of advertising, don't think of Rock Hudson manipulating Doris Day. Think of H. R. Haldeman [one of the Watergate conspirators and an ex-adman] trying to screw up some tapes, because that's closest to what large-agency advertising men are about.'

* Other writers who have worked in advertising and got out include Sherwood Anderson, John P. Marquand, Eric Ambler and Scott Fitzgerald (whose work included 'We keep you clean in Muscatine', written for a laundry).

Research and Researchers

'Advertising people who ignore research are as dangerous as generals who ignore decodes of enemy signals.'

David Ogilvy

Isolated in a small darkened booth situated in a suite of rooms in a Florida shopping mall, a volunteer is staring at pages of *Playboy* magazine projected onto a small screen in front of him. A few minutes before, he had been buying cigarettes; now, persuaded to take part in an unspecified piece of market research, he sits in Suite 521, Altamonte Mall, his chin balanced on a rest. By pressing a button, he can advance the pages himself, thus working through the magazine at his own pace.

What he doesn't know is that an invisible beam of infrared light, being focused on his eyes, is making it possible to record direct onto computer tape the position of his pupils every sixtieth of a second. At the end of the session, the researchers can play back the tape linked with a video in such a way that they will see the pages of *Playboy* in the way his eyes followed them. A bouncing ball of light maps exactly where his eyes are focused. If he dwelt for a long time on the shots of Dana 'the new princess of porn' but skipped the wordy captions, dipped the Party Jokes but disregarded a review of new rainwear, that's what the researchers will see, too. They will be more interested, though, in what his eyes did with the Lord Calvert Canadian whiskey ad or if they lingered on the brand name in the double-page pitch for Jeep or in how much attention he devoted to the long copy for RCA tapes.

For this is serious ad business. This man, together with other similar volunteers at five other testing centres located from New York to Dallas, is helping advertisers and their agencies devise the best way to sell their wares 1980s style. The particular magazine he has been asked to scan through happens to be *Playboy*; it could equally have been *Newsweek* or *Business Week*, *Cosmopolitan* or *Sports Illustrated*. Or, instead of a magazine he could have been shown a series of different advertisements, some still in their evolving stage. This particular company, Perception Research Services, New Jersey, tests about 40,000 people a year – twenty every day at every centre – in the pursuit of whether an ad seizes and holds attention. Or, to phrase it another way, whether in the words of Elliot Young, the company's president, the ad has 'stopping power'. If the eye-tracking research concludes it has not, it may be changed: the (expensive) star in one liquor company's ad attracted no more attention than a regular model. The company changed the ad, getting rid of the celebrity.

At the end of the day there is a record for every published – and embryonic – ad. 'When a person goes through a magazine one of three things happens,' says Young. 'The person may never look at the ad – he may look left, never right. If he looks, he may give it a quick glance. Or, third, he may work on it.' Young helped develop the eye-tracking technique around 1969 when he was a researcher at the Interpublic Group. Perception Research began life in 1972 as an Interpublic subsidiary: Young and four co-workers bought it four years later.

Young's clients are advertisers, publishers and agencies, big names that include Seagram, Du Pont, Eastman Kodak, Kellogg, *Reader's Digest*, *New Woman*, *People*, McCann-Erickson, J. Walter Thompson and Young and Rubicam. They are all people who want to know how best to put together ads that will be lingered over. They also want to know where best to place them: Young's researchers indicate, for example, that although *Playboy* is loaded with liquor ads its readers are happy to absorb ever more of them. Perhaps not altogether surprisingly, it also shows 'that the performance of an ad will depend to some extent to what is on the facing page. If it were a centrefold model – and *Playboy* doesn't operate that way – an ad's invitation would be ignored . . .' With advertisements in their testing phase, target ads are mixed together with others chosen purely to add 'clutter' or to disguise the real object of the exercise. Researchers then note whether the particular ad or series of ads attracts and holds attention.

The tests have limitations. The most obvious one of all is that they only show what someone is *looking* at, not what he or she is thinking or feeling at the time. The person might be staring in the direction of an ad but thinking that he has forgotten to post a letter. (Young's organisation tries to overcome this by following up the tests with interviews in which people are asked about what they saw.) There's also the not inconsiderable fact that the test setting is far removed from the real world. All that conceded, there are still many advertisers and their agencies who believe – to the tune of paying $5 million a year for the results of Young's tests – that the knowledge they gain gives them some edge in advertising to their potential customers. Young's company is not alone in the eye-tracking field. Nor is the practice confined to the US. It is being used in Australia, Canada, Japan, and many western European countries.

There are even more bizarre methods of trying to construct advertisements that will make people want to buy: in other testing places, volunteers are linked to devices that measure their brain waves, while countless others are questioned by psychologists, observed by anthropologists, or asked to model in clay what they think of named branded goods. All this in an attempt to find out what potential buyers really feel deep, deep down. Why not, you might wonder, simply ask them? Well, literally millions *are* asked every year. The answers they give continuously swell the mass of data available to the marketing and advertising men. But it's not enough for a lot of reasons: people often lie; even when they don't do so consciously, the argument goes, they don't really know what they want. That requires researchers to probe below the surface. Consumers are asked to sit back and peel away the layers, revealing their desires, drives, weaknesses, ambitions, dreams, so that, in time, the advertisers may use that knowledge to sell their jeans or perfumes or cars.

The works of psychiatrists, psychologists, anthropologists, sociologists are raided and their theories adapted. Computers are used to collate and cross reference a mass of sometimes seemingly disparate information, making it possible, for example, to find common links between people who buy dehydrated cooking sauce and pot plants!* Researchers gathering views and information call into play machines that dial random numbers automatically in order not to miss consumers who are unlisted. They may use devices that purport to measure the degree of stress levels in voices so that questioners can gauge the truth of answers.

All is designed to help the advertising men answer one question: how do you put together an advertisement that the reader or viewer will notice, absorb and – the real goal – that will persuade him to go out and buy, whether it is Colgate Toothpaste instead of Crest, or a hi-fi outfit the buyer didn't even know he wanted or could afford or owed to himself until then? It is about reaching the people who might want to buy your product, and then making them want it and no other. 'Advertising,' said Herbert Zeltner, a New York marketing consultant, 'has a dual role: one part is to make people want a product, the other is to tell them it is available and where it can be found. The first role is the most interesting to advertising people.'

Today's advertisers have special problems. The first, which we have encountered before, is that the real difference between competing products is frequently no longer significant. Therefore, what the advertiser has to sell – in his ad as well as off the shelves – isn't self-evidently more worthy of the customer's money. The second is that in the stores, on television and in print it is increasingly hard for a product to stand out. The first task of ads, getting noticed at all, becomes more difficult every year. With more and more ads, there is ever-greater competition for the attention of the viewer and the reader. In the US between 1967

---

* Spillers Foods in the UK were able to use this information: they promoted their Homepride Cook-in-Sauce and Classic Curry Sauce ranges with an offer of free plants.

and 1982 the number of print and broadcast ads increased by 103 per cent. There was a similar growth in the UK and it was forecast in 1985 that by the end of the century the number of ads would double again. It is not only that there is more television to accommodate ads, but more individual commercials are crammed into the available time. After over a decade in which the thirty-second commercial was standard, America began to receive the fifteen-second ad in the 1980s; in the UK by 1985 twenty-second commercials were accounting for about a fifth of all commercials.*

In the 1980s, every advertiser was having a tougher time persuading his targets even to watch or read his ad. Steve Fajen, media director at Saatchi and Saatchi Compton, New York, in the midst of a lengthy talk about his work, reached for some research material and began, 'We don't show many clients this. But this is fact.' 'This' was research material on how many of the expensive ads beamed at Americans were actually getting anywhere. His figures began with the average number of hours Americans watch TV each week – forty-seven. This consists of forty-three and a half hours of network, local independent or cable TV, two and three-quarters hours of playback of recorded video, and fifty minutes of prerecorded rented or bought video. Those figures apply to the average home in the average week, though as Fajen adds it involves 'a lot of averaging'. Out of that time, TV provides seven and a half hours of commercials and the two and three-quarters hours of taped programmes thirty minutes. 'How much is truly seen?' asks Fajen, with the air of a conjuror about to reveal the rabbit. It emerges that because of zapping – fast forwarding the ads on video – or people talking or going to the bathroom and doing all the other things people do when the commercials come on, the seven and a half hours falls to one hour twenty-seven minutes of commercials actually seen. Of the thirty minutes (with the greater incidence of zapping on taped programmes) only three minutes is watched. That means, says Fajen, that each individual sees about 120 television ads a week. 'Now, the networks average about 4,000 commercials a week. Yet only 120 are seen by the average viewer. That's scary. Suppose you are my client, Eric Clark Inc, and I tell you that all this marvellous creative stuff we've created will reach 75 per cent of the public . . . All I'm really telling you is that the *programmes* will be seen by 75 per cent . . .'

Research carried out in the UK by the Post Office produced a similar picture. It showed that more than a quarter of the people who had watched an edition of *News at Ten* had seen *none* of the commercials. Of these, 26 per cent simply hadn't paid attention, 21 per cent had made a drink, 20 per cent left the room, 11 per cent were preoccupied

---

* Many advertising men don't like the idea of fifteen-second ads; one, Marshall Karp, executive creative director at Marschalk, New York, described them as 'advertising without foreplay'.

with other things, 8 per cent switched channel, 6 per cent went to the lavatory and 5 per cent talked to someone.

It doesn't stop there. Fajen is talking about the commercials that people *see*. What happens – or doesn't happen – even then is another matter. The majority of the ads that are seen never 'break through'. The human mind cannot give weight to everything that comes its way; the brain decides not to bother with most ads at all or, if it does, it rapidly forgets them. According to *Consumer Behavior*, an industry textbook, 'Only about one-third of those commercials a person is exposed to make any active impression in memory. Of those which are attended to, only about half are correctly comprehended and fewer than 5 per cent are actively recalled for as long as twenty-four hours.' Even this doesn't end the admen's problem: advertisements may need to be seen and noted if they are to work, but additionally they have to persuade people to take some action, which is something else again.* In all, it calls for a kind of warfare: the brain puts up its protective barrier: the people who create the ads have to come up with a way to get round, over, under or through it. It is like storming a castle: the invaders stand a better chance of success if intelligence (in this case, research) has found out whether it is more sensible to rush the gate, scale the walls, dig a tunnel, or creep inside in disguise.

The battalion of researchers that provide the backup for the admakers is vast and constantly growing. Overall, the amount spent worldwide on marketing, advertising and public-opinion research was estimated in 1987 at nearly $4 billion, the bulk of it in the US and in Europe. In pursuit of why and how people are prompted to buy, millions of consumers are constantly watched, quizzed, divided and examined in almost every conceivable group and subgroup. Their circumstances, beliefs, habits and behaviour are continuously measured and pored over. Trends are continually charted and analysed to help determine which products are likely to become ripe for selling. A Doyle Dane Bernbach survey, for example, showed widespread underlying concern among people about social isolation and rejection. From this, the agency decided there was a bright future for what it called 'social supporters' – health clubs, vacations, games and telecommunications – and for 'social surrogates' to help people along, such as video games and computers.

In creating new products and new advertisements, research is involved every step of the way. In practice, it means that virtually nothing appears from a major advertiser or agency until it has been opinion-polled, test-marketed or copy-tested, submitted on the way to panels of consumers whose words have been turned into statistical tables or analysed by psychologists.

---

* Though there is the theory that advertisements work on people on a kind of drip principle without conscious attention being given to them.

Some advertising industry veterans recall a world, not that many years ago, when 'research' meant that a copywriter would leave his office, find a 'real consumer' – perhaps a relative or a neighbour – and ask that person what he or she thought about the product the advertising man was about to try to sell. The 'insight' he gained might then be incorporated into his copy. Equally, of course, it might not. Many admen believe that the mark of the truly creative ad-maker is that he knows instinctively what to say. Much of the history of modern advertising is the struggle between the researchers with their models and tables and formulas about how advertising works and the creative admen who *know*.

Robert Benson, chairman of the famed S. H. Benson agency (Dorothy L. Sayers was at one time one of its copywriters), said of research, 'I never forget that there was once a Provost of Oriel who said, "show me a researcher and I will show you a fool". A little hard. A little unnecessary but I think I know what the man meant.' Albert Lasker, who has been called the 'father' of modern advertising, defined research as 'something that tells you a jackass has two ears'. 'After thousands of experiences,' he also said, 'the advertising man comes to know the real selling point in a commodity or proposition.' Bill Bernbach's view was, 'Research can tell you what people want, and you can give it back to them. It's a nice, safe way to do business, but who the hell wants to be safe . . . Anyway, advertising isn't a science, it's persuasion. And persuasion is an art.' According to legend, when he was told that the projected campaign for Avis being number two and trying harder would fail, he retorted, 'Get some other research'.

Others take different views. John O'Toole, chairman of Foote Cone and Belding, believes, 'Research provides the stuff that ads are made of: information. Thus it is the most important function of all. Without research the campaign would be empty. Research in our broadest sense is also our point of contact with the consumer, our lifeline to reality.'

The anti-researchers find reinforcement in the jargon of researchers. This is the opening sentence of an article published in the US *Journal of Advertising Research*: 'This research examines relationships between scaled attitudinal reactions to television commercials and viewers' demographic characteristics, their product usage and brand preferences, and interview situational variables.' Or what of a paragraph that begins, 'It should be reiterated that the diagnostic charts are ancillary to the principal evaluative measure dealing with posttest purchase point assignment (with pretest point assignment serving as a covariate)'? Much more outlandish examples could have been quoted. The point about these short examples is that they are so 'normal' that any researcher reading this will have difficulty in understanding why others should find them worth mocking.

Sceptics might say that the jargon helps hide the inexactness of the science. To paraphrase, many believe that there are lies, damn lies and research. Iain Murray, an English commentator on marketing matters, has defined the First Maxim of Market Research as 'whoever controls the research comes out of it rather well'. Others point out that what researchers are really trying to do is not so much work out how advertising works, but how the human brain works. Viewed that way, it is perhaps not surprising that even a believer can admit (albeit somewhat extravagantly) in print that although people have developed partial theories about advertising and how it works 'so far there has not been developed a conceptual system that can be compared with those of Newton or Galileo.'

There is the fact, too, that research theories come and go: today's 'solution' is tomorrow's discard. Like so much else in advertising, research goes in and out of fashion, not only in the importance attached to it but also as to what precisely the industry wants it to do. When times are tough and the economy bad, almost certainly it will be called upon to help produce safe, workmanlike ads; when times are better it will be seeking to help the copywriters and art directors produce more 'creative' ads.

Much of ad-related research takes place away from the agencies in specialist organisations ranging from the giant Nielsen company to single experts. But there are major research departments at most large agencies – Young and Rubicam, J. Walter Thompson and Leo Burnett, for example, all have staffs of over 100 in their US head offices alone. There is an enormous backup of published research that the researchers can draw upon in their quest to understand and persuade. Its vastness can be appreciated by considering the fact that two men writing in the *Annual Review of Psychology* reviewed 790 articles that had been published on advertising research in just two years.

Research is an attempt to turn advertising into a science of sorts, or as ad researchers themselves are fond of saying 'science with a small "s"'. Dr Johnson thought it had been achieved over 200 years ago: 'The trade of advertising is now so near to perfection that it is not easy to propose any improvement,' he said in 1761. Sixty years ago, in 1925, Claude Hopkins, as an insider, opined, 'The time has come when advertising has reached a science. It is based on fixed principles and is reasonably exact. The causes and effects . . . have been analysed until they are understood.'

The ad industry began enlisting fairly basic research in the very early days of modern advertising. The New York agency of N. W. Ayer conducted some as far back as 1879. A firm of manufacturers wanted a list of newspapers in areas where threshers were sold. The agency wired telegrams to state officials and publishers around the United States and in three days put together a survey of the market. Ayer then offered the information to the manufacturer in return for being given the account.

There were significant developments after World War I. In 1918

Daniel Starch, a marketing professor at Harvard, began studying recognition methods of testing advertisement copy. O'Toole in *The Trouble with Advertising* says it was in the 1920s that the market research industry really began. Quoting a conversation with George Gallup, he ascribes its development to Albert Lasker. According to Gallup, Lasker's agency, Lord and Thomas, was handling a canned evaporated milk account. When the product was introduced in a test market in Indiana, sales at first were excellent but then dropped to almost nil. Lasker sent members of his staff to the area to knock on doors in an attempt to find out what was wrong. The problem, it emerged, was a slight almond taste that buyers disliked. It was corrected easily. 'And so another industry was born,' writes O'Toole. The real turning point, though, he claims, was when Lasker 'arrived at a conclusion that . . . must have raised eyebrows if not hackles in the luncheon clubs of New York and Chicago in the twenties. He asserted that the advertising agency is not really the representative of the manufacturer to the consumer but vice versa.' This is a view that is proclaimed strenuously by researchers today, and it is true to a point but only to a point. At the end of the day the work of the agency or the researcher is aimed at helping the client to sell what he has to offer, even if they persuade him to make alterations to it, real or – more likely – cosmetic.

Gallup, himself, started the first formal agency research department – for Young and Rubicam – in 1929. A statistical professor from Indiana, Gallup went to New York at the behest of Raymond Rubicam. The work that Gallup and Daniel Starch did during the twenties provided the basic concepts of copy testing that still exist – the extent to which they are read and understood.

The thirties witnessed more developments. In 1933 Gallup, Elmo Roper and Archibald Crossley began experimenting with 'random selection techniques' which would make opinion polls more accurate. Polling itself was originally conceived as journalism. In 1824 the *Harrisburg Pennsylvanian* took a straw poll to see whether citizens of Wilmington, Delaware, wanted John Quincy Adams or Andrew Jackson as President. Polls were common from the beginning of the twentieth century, but they used vast numbers of respondents. The breakthrough was the use of the small, scientific sample which opened the way for companies and advertising agencies to check people's wants and views relatively simply, cheaply and quickly.

Around the same time, the A. C. Nielsen Company, today the world's largest research organisation, began surveying drugstores. The company had started in 1923 as a firm of engineering consultants, but took its new step in response to an approach from a client. This led, almost by accident, to a decision to establish a permanent panel of drugstores representative of the country as a whole. They measured product movement and market size, and established the concept of products holding a percentage share of the market – a concept which preoccupies marketing men today. While Nielsen was asking stores what they were selling, J. Walter Thompson decided to ask people what they were buying. The agency formed its first Consumer Purchase Panel in 1939, a sample of households chosen to be representative of the nation. The panel reported monthly on purchases of grocery, certain toiletries and items of clothing and other commodities in which JWT had an interest.

A major shift developed in the 1950s. Advertising generally was firmly product-orientated until well after World War II, but in the 1950s it began to be directed increasingly towards people's desires, needs and wants. Marketing as a separate discipline had its greatest growth period in the competitive boom economies of the fifties and sixties. As its practitioners developed skills in understanding people's needs and wants, they turned to trying to create them. The sixties saw the birth of what was called 'the romance of the computer age'. Computers made it possible to play about with vast numbers, and researchers rushed to use the capability. They juggled with the mass of information collected on people and divided them into more and more groups. Problem-solving models were devised, disregarding the fact that in too many places the models needed information that just didn't exist. The researchers then 'solved' this problem by getting specialists to construct the missing information from what was known and from their own expertise.

Computers still disgorge vast amounts of research material; the desk top terminal is to an advertising researcher's office what a pot of pencils is to a writer's or art director's. But the romance has faded a little; the research pendulum has swung increasingly to trying to find out less about numbers and more about what people want, how they tick – and how to capitalise on it.

Psychologists were first recruited by the admen in the period following World War I. The then new approach of Behaviourism was seized upon by advertisers and agencies who saw no bounds to their capability to engineer desires to sell their goods. More than sixty years later, Joel S. Dubow, communications research manager of Coca-Cola USA, in 1984 nominated one of the Behaviourist leaders, Ivan Pavlov, as 'the father of modern advertising'. Speaking to an advertising research workshop organised by the Association of National Advertisers, he explained, 'Pavlov's unconditioned stimulus (UCS) was a spray of meat powder which produced salivation . . . But if you think what Pavlov did, he actually took a neutral object and, by associating it with a meaningful object, made it a symbol of something else; he imbued it with imagery, he gave it added value. And isn't that what we try to do in modern image advertising?'

A book published in New York in 1919 provides a picture of what the good agency expected to gain at that time with the help of the psychologist. The book, *Advertising: Its Principles and Practice*, devoted a major section to 'Psychological Factors in Advertising', in which it listed 'chief instincts that can be appealed to in advertising'. Paying tribute to psychology, it noted that several concerns now had a psychologist on their staff, and many others 'resort to the psychological laboratories for the purpose of having special researches and tests planned and conducted, either in the laboratory or in the field'.

'Just as the manufacturer is utilising the expert services of the chemist, the electrician, the physicist, and the engineer, so the advertiser is utilising the expert services of the psychologist.' Claims for a scientific basis were sweeping: 'In our own day, experiments have shown in quite definite ways the relative strength of various appeals which can be used as selling points in advertising copy. The experimental methods have been checked up by the analysis of actual advertising campaigns and the detailed results of particular pieces of copy. Time and again this has been done, especially in the laboratory.'

The problem then, as now, was to put together an advertisement that would attract initial attention, hold it in an interesting way, bring about an association or impression which would have permanence or memory value, and 'convince, persuade or induce; and, finally, to suggest and lead to specific response'.

Millions of man hours have been occupied by researchers, agencies and advertisers trying to wrestle with that problem since then, but the authors in 1919 were sure they knew the answer. They suggested taking various values and giving them a rating from 0 (the lowest) to 100. The highest five were healthfulness (92), cleanliness (92), scientific construction (88), time saved (84) and appetising (82). The lowest were imported and beautifying, both with 10. The way the system worked was simplicity itself. The advertiser was recommended to choose the highest attribute that could be attached to the particular product he was selling. These then became the points to stress. In the case of jewellery, it suggested, the top three would be quality (72), modernity (72) and reputation and guarantee (58).

It was basic, unsophisticated stuff (and the order of ratings, it should be noted, depended on purely subjective values, and allowed no variation depending on product). What is interesting, though, as the authors expound their theories, is that they make clear the conviction even then that, whatever consumerists may argue, man and woman do not choose by reason alone (or at all). These words could have been written today:

One of the striking tendencies of human beings is to act, judge, believe or vote on strictly instinctive, emotional grounds, and then, after the act is committed, to try to justify it or defend it by intellectual or logical reasons . . . Men buy automobiles in the same way. I buy my car because my neighbour has one, because it will gratify my vanity or satisfy my pride. Then having bought the car, I look about for logical justifications which I can give for my conduct.

With a tone of some pride, the authors added:

> The advertising man is beginning to understand this human tendency, and frequently advertisements will be found which begin with a distinctly emotional, short-circuit appeal, thus persuading and seducing the reader. Then, at a later point, the writer hastens to add a series of logical reasons, which probably exercise but little influence on the prospect's own decisions, but they fortify him against the objections of his mother-in-law, his employer, his banker and his conscience.

It was not until a quarter of a century later, after World War II, that the admen and their researchers really turned their attention to trying to tap people's dreams and fears. The reason was a very practical one. In the US, companies emerged from the war with a greater capacity to produce goods than the market would absorb. Marketing thus became more important than production. To sell more, the advertiser and his agency professionals needed to know a great deal more about the consumer's motives and behaviour. The move away from product-orientated, 'reason why' ads was encouraged by the growth of television as a major advertising medium. By its nature, television is better able to convey images than facts. The development of advertising regulation was a further stimulant – advertisers unable to make actual statements of detail about products found they could still get their messages across safely by using playlet techniques.

As a result of all this, what might once have been called an information industry (albeit one stressing only the points the advertiser wished to stress) has become an all-out persuasion industry. By the mid 1970s less than half of American television commercials could be regarded as informative even using the very generous definition that they contained just one of fourteen different information criteria including price, quality or performance. Only one in a hundred of them was offering information in three or more categories. By the same criteria, 14 per cent of magazine ads contain no information at all.

'Advertising,' believes Marcel Blenstein-Blanchet, veteran French adman and founder of the agency Publicis, 'translates desires that already exist in us.' Professor Hugh Rank, a critic of advertising, agrees but adds, 'If advertisers are often accused of peddling dreams, we must recognise first that they are *our* dreams: they are all genuine human desires; they are the benefits we seek.' David Bernstein, a well-known English creator of advertisements, believes that all the promises that advertising makes can be classified under one or more of: self-preservation, love for others, self-expression, envy, sloth, lechery, gluttony, pride or covetousness. 'There is no product that can't make an appeal to the majority of those nine drives.' But which particular dreams, which desires, which drives at any time? And how to tap them?

In the fifties, the ad industry turned to aspects of Freudian theory for the answer. Psychologists probed for the hidden motivations that made consumers act as they did; the power of symbolism was emphasised – a car failed to sell not because of the way it performed, nor because of its price, but because it had a blunt bonnet. And because a car is a phallic symbol, this car lacked potency and penetrating power!

The guru of the new age of 'motivation research' was Dr Ernest Dichter, whose name was to become known worldwide, thanks largely to the exposé of his work in Vance Packard's book, *The Hidden Persuaders*. Dichter's impact was international. 'His research,' wrote Blenstein-Blanchet, 'provided advertising with a kind of radar to find its way through the darkness of the collective subconscious.' Soon, recalled one insider, every agency had to have its resident 'motivation' expert: 'You'd got all these psychologists and psychiatrists doing depth interviews and making recommendations. They'd come up with brilliant ideas in Viennese accents. They'd tell you the Freudian significance of your product. These guys could charge many thousands of dollars for a single appearance.'

Today's advertising men often downgrade motivational research; like so many things in advertising they prefer to regard it as part of the alien foreign land of the past or as a wayward black sheep of the family no longer to be spoken of in polite company. Motivation research, says the textbook *Consumer Behavior*, was an 'invasion' that 'generated more heat than light' dismissing it to research history. But as David Bernstein points out, 'the very people who knock Ernest Dichter are the people who use his ideas, albeit in a modified form.' In fact 'motivation' research – and its impact on the persuasion industry – is as alive as ever. Because it is not politic to say so, it has simply changed its public face.

Dr Ernest Dichter is in his study on the telephone speaking to a newspaper reporter. With the caller's permission, he has switched on a loudspeaker so that I can hear both sides of the conversation. 'This might help you,' he murmurs, cupping the mouthpiece. Dichter is a believer in self-advertisement. The reporter is asking Dichter about the machinations of supermarkets trying to tempt shoppers into buying more than they intended. 'Let's put it this way,' the doctor says in an accent that is still unmistakably Viennese. 'Every shopper is potentially a gourmet. If you don't make it easy for her . . . The basic idea is that human desires are limitless . . .'

The room, in his sprawling ranch-style home/office in New York's Westchester County, looks out on trees. Dichter himself, plump, cherubic, with receding curly hair and glasses, is at his desk, feet resting on a huge sheet of plate glass that protects the carpet. On two walls books reach to the ceiling. Shelves are labelled *Management*, *Marketing*, *Abnormal Psychology and Diagnosis*, *Child Psychology*, *Consumer Motivation* . . . There is a TV, three radios, a computer, as well as all the paraphernalia of the workaday office such as filing cabinets and a dictation machine. There is also African art, lots of small plants and a balcony with a bird feeder. Below are the rooms where the research assistants work, including the archives and a 'focus room' with its one-way mirror.

One of the research assistants, Kurt, enters, flops into a chair, listens, smiles and whispers, 'He works three times as hard as someone half his age.' Both men are wearing sports shirts, perhaps their one concession to the fact that it's Good Friday and in New York, an hour away, most offices are deserted.

The interview isn't going well. Dichter is answering all the questions, but it's obvious the reporter isn't getting what he wants: Dichter's replies aren't provocative enough. The reporter's exasperation is getting through to Dichter. The conversation ends. Two hours later it still rankles. Dichter repeats several times that the reporter had described his answers as 'only common sense'. You can say almost anything about Ernest Dichter, except that what he says is '*only* common sense'. It is as if Merlin had been dismissed as a mere 'conjuror'. Or, perhaps, whispers a voice inside me, it's like the boy who failed to see the Emperor's new clothes.

Ernest Dichter, three months off seventy-eight, back just a few days from giving consultations in Vienna and London, is the father of motivational research. Over the years, he's been 'exposed', attacked, laughed at, consigned to research history, and survived to find himself and his work accepted and acceptable. 'He has won his battle to get people to accept motivational research,' said an *Advertising Age* article in 1984, which he hands me together with a mass of other literature about his work. More telling are the framed addresses and certificates I study on his walls: the Market Research Council in 1983 making him a member of the Hall of Fame 'in recognition of Contributions of Outstanding and Lasting Value to the practice of market research'; the American Psychological Association's making him a fellow in 1980; the American Marketing Association's Induction into 'AMA Attitude Research Hall of Fame'.

'Once you are a guru you are assumed to know the answers to all problems,' he says. 'All the big names are dying out – Gallup. Politz* . . . I'm the last of the Mohicans. I have the advantage now of all those years of experience. Like a good physician I can diagnose very quickly.' He runs through some of the projects he has on hand: for a bank in

---

* Alfred Politz: Physicist turned influential market researcher and a great rival of Dichter in the fifties.

Arizona, he's researching what people will want in their homes, offices and factories in the future; for a packaging company, there's a study on the difference between milk drinkers and non-milk drinkers. There is the launch of a new cream, said to remove wrinkles: 'I don't question the veracity.'

His company, Ernest Dichter Motivations Inc, is trying to find out why some people save shopping coupons and some don't: 'What's behind it? Are coupon users more of an anal character or are non-users afraid of being identified with cheap money grabbing? Coupon Saver – Greed or a sign of love?' Someone else wants to import armbands. 'It is interesting – the armband comes from slavery. Maybe a man giving an armband means, "You are my slave now."' Kurt interjects, 'I heard the same thing about wedding rings.' It has the authentic Dichter stamp: a company wants to sell armbands and he puts its potential customers on the psychoanalyst's couch.

For Heublein, the giant liquor company, Dichter is being asked to advise on which of two advertising approaches the company might adopt for its Black Velvet whisky. Both feature women. One woman wears less than the other and is more overtly sexy. She is accompanied by the slogan, 'Felt any velvet lately?' The other Dichter calls a 'more traditional' woman. Her slogan is, 'Only one Canadian feels like velvet.' Dichter has done some initial research with groups of men, but he obviously feels it is only a start. The first big question he wants answered is how much Heublein wants to spend: 'Twenty-five thousand, thirty thousand? I gave him [the Heublein man] a little candy – as an advertising person I should be able to advertise myself. I said, "Maybe the new-look sexist one is more honest. The other one's waspish – she's the one who'd make a lot of pretence." I gave them a possible reversal – I told them they may have built in some porn. Maybe the one's saying, "Felt any pussy lately?"'

Kurt nods agreement. There's an air of unreality building in the room. If he goes ahead with the research, Dichter wants to stage psychodramas involving men and women playing the roles of the kinds of women depicted in the ads. Then there will be one-to-one interviews ('Women as well, which they never thought about') and then 'maybe 100 structured questions developed in a more quantified fashion'.

He's doing something similar for Alberto Culver's VO5 shampoo, a shampoo that he says has an old image and which Alberto are trying to revitalise. So far they've been attempting to do so with new ingredients such as Evening Primrose, Vitamin E and Henna, he says. Alberto Culver hired him to go to England to investigate one particular aspect. There is a shampoo called Timotei from Elida Gibbs which, says Dichter, 'has taken the market by storm. The client hired me to find out what Timotei is doing right. And if we can apply it to our product in the UK and possibly the US.'

Alberto Culver's UK advertising agency had already studied the situation. 'They investigated all types of women and somehow over-looked the fact that 50 per cent are working women,' says Dichter with an air of triumph. 'They didn't think about it. It happens often: a big advertiser and a big advertising agency and they hadn't thought of it. That was my key concept: what about working women?'

Mothers and daughters were lined up in suburban Purley for Dichter to interview. Timotei sells itself ostensibly on the promise that it's so mild that users can wash their hair as often as they like. Dichter, not surprisingly, doesn't think it is as simple as that. He thinks that some women may see it as 'somehow a more virginal kind of product'. Timotei's bottle has a distinctive dot as part of the letter 'i'. There's a Timotei bottle on the desk in front of Dichter and from time to time he pauses to stare at it. 'That "i",' he muses aloud, 'may hold a secret . . .'

Dichter studied psychology in Vienna. A year before Hitler marched into Austria he moved to Paris where he set about trying to get a US entrance visa for himself and his wife, Hedy. For a long time he was unsuccessful. Eventually a vice-consul asked him what he would do in America if he did get a visa. Dichter outlined his ideas on applying psychology to marketing, voting and political problems: 'Something snapped in him and he sent a cable to Washington supporting my application.'

Once in America, Dichter called the Compton agency among others and became involved with Ivory Soap. He told the agency that bathing wasn't just about getting physically clean but was also a psychologically liberating ritual. Thus the slogan, 'Be smart and get a fresh start with Ivory soap . . . and wash all your troubles away' which he developed, he says, using his anthropological knowledge. 'I knew bathing was a ritual. You cleanse yourself not only of dirt but of guilt.' He muses, 'I didn't charge them very much. It was probably the first study using motivational research. Compton are still clients.'

In his book, *Strategy of Desire*, Dichter explains that his aim is 'to go back to the reality of human behaviour'. There are, he wrote, two phases in motivational research. 'One is to find out why people behave as they do. The second is to prescribe a remedy and to determine how people might be motivated.' He added, 'It is the second phase which critics refer to when discussing the ethics of persuasion.'

Dichter's next piece of research was to become infamous, an investigation into car-buying habits for Chrysler in which he came up with the equation that convertibles are mistresses, sedan cars are wives. The open car, he reported, was the symbol of youth, freedom and human dreams; the sedan was sedate, conservative and practical.

He worked as a propaganda specialist during the war before becoming a consultant. His 'big break', he volunteers, was *The Hidden Persuaders*, the best-seller by Vance Packard in which his works featured heavily. The book was an exposé of Dichter and his 'manipulation' of people. However, says Dichter, 'PR is very funny. As long as they spell your name right . . . I was on every programme. I got invitations from all over the world.' He opened a dozen offices. One was in London. He told the British their high consumption of sweets and chocolates was a major outlet for their suppressed emotions. 'People canalise their vicious tendencies into candy-eating. That's why the British are the biggest sweet-eaters in the world.' His home became 'a castle' with twenty-six rooms. He adds matter-of-factly, 'I had a heart attack which was inevitable.' He's twice sold out his business only to take it back, apparently when the buyers found it lost value without his personal presence. He still keeps offices in Zurich, Frankfurt and Paris, and says the demands for his services flow in. 'I haven't been selling myself for quite a few years . . . Clients do bargain [over money] but not very much.' He says he still reckons to make $150,000 a year.

He hands me a Dichter company brochure. Over 120 clients are detailed from, alphabetically, Affiliated Advertising Agencies International to Zentralspakasse, Vienna. Many of the big names are there: agencies like Burnett and Young and Rubicam, advertisers like Coca-Cola, General Foods, Sears Roebuck and Westinghouse, media companies such as CBS, *Esquire* and the *New York Times*. 'I never know from one day to the next what may come in.' He mentions more ongoing studies: 'I'm just trying to give you a feeling of the field – sometimes I get frightened myself.'

Not all are concerned with marketing or advertising commercial goods or services. He's done work for the Red Cross on how to get people to donate more blood, for the American Cancer Society on how to get people to stop smoking. He has done a study for the Israeli government on what creates impact on TV ('They have a secret TV station in Lebanon'). The conversation leaps about – pieces of information, ideas, thoughts, asides emerge like machine-gun fire. It is easy to see why companies are happy to pay him $5,000 just to spend a day talking to a group of their executives. It is a one-man brainstorming session. He's also been asked about promoting peace. His first thought is that the Americans and the Russians have the procedure misnamed. 'Disarmament is the wrong word. No one wants to be disarmed. Call it something else.'

Dichter is still important for two reasons. First, his own work illustrates the lengths to which the advertisers and their agencies go to try to persuade or manipulate the customer. Second, he also represents, albeit sometimes at its extreme, one school of research very much in its ascendency, which largely determines the content of an increasing amount of advertising.

Research can be divided up in several ways, but one way is to split it into what are generally called 'quantitative' research and 'qualitative' research. The first has been defined as 'counting noses'. It is the information that can be gathered by observation (what products are being stocked in the shops, which are selling), experimentation (what happens to our brand if we advertise here and don't advertise there), and from the answers to surveys. To interview a hundred people about an ad that was on TV last night and find that fifty-three remembered it is a piece of 'quantitative' research. The amount of quantitative material available to advertisers and agencies is vast almost beyond comprehension. Much of it is continuous and pours into offices every day of the week.

'Qualitative', on the other hand, has been defined as 'getting into people's heads'. In qualitative research, potential customers are encouraged to 'reveal' their 'real' thoughts and feelings. Behind such research lies the belief that it somehow yields more of the 'truth'; in so doing it will therefore provide the insights that will guide the ad-makers in their attempt to hit the right spots. Dichter's term for it is 'interpretative' research. He illustrates the difference between the two with an example of a suit manufacturer. The man needs to know how many suits the average man has in his closet and what colour they are. That can be determined by quantitative research (or, as Dichter calls it, 'descriptive research'). 'If, however, he wants to effect change in this area, to cause the average male to purchase one more suit than has been his average until then, he must know the motivation behind suit purchases, he must know how to appeal to the needs, drives and desires in order to raise this average. Interpretative research is the only tool which will enable him to acquire this knowledge.'

Dichter says that the way he does this is not unlike the method used by a physician in diagnosing a patient's condition: 'When I came here [to the US] I was baffled by the fact – and it's still being done – that market research tried to find the answers by asking people why they are doing what they're doing. It's like some asinine author going to New Guinea and sitting down and asking people why they do this funny thing. The answer might be interesting but if it's taken at face value it's not very good. A physician doesn't take a patient's answer as his diagnosis.'

I asked Dichter how he would describe himself and he answered without hesitation, 'A scientist.' His approach, he says, involves first asking himself what are the possible answers to a problem. Like a medical researcher, he then sets up a number of hypotheses which he tests. 'I just try to use a modern, correct, scientific approach.' Interpretative research 'has to start with hunches, guesses and hypotheses'.

In questioning people, this means 'we have developed modern approaches that clinical psychology uses'. He gave me an example, in politics. Polls asked people their voting intentions. People gave a definite answer although 'the largest number would say they were all mixed up if they were honest'. For this reason, he argued, polls were increasingly inaccurate. The Dichter approach? Get at what people really feel. Take the contest between Mondale and Reagan for the presidency. 'I'd ask, "If Mondale was an animal what kind would he be?" I would have got back answers that he would be a tame rabbit, maybe a mouse. Reagan would be a jaguar, a fox, a much more aggressive animal. Now, if you know that today's voters are looking for a father figure, that they would like a dictator . . .' He waved his hands, leaving the conclusion unspoken.

At the heart of the work of Dichter and all those who have followed him is the assumption that many of a person's decisions are governed by motivations over which he or she not only has no control but of which that person is probably unaware. People behave irrationally and furthermore they may not want to admit the real reason.

One Dichter case illustrates this claim especially well. A company assumed that the way to advertise its baby food was to promise mothers that the product would help make their children healthy. Dichter claims that after 300 interviews he discovered that what mothers most wanted was that feeding their children should be more convenient and pleasant for *them*. The way to advertise, therefore, was to say that the children would enjoy eating the baby food – but also to stress that feeding time would be shortened, an appeal to a much less elevated motivation.

Another client, an oil company, asked Dichter how he could persuade the English to install more central heating. Dichter claims to have found a deep reason for an English reluctance: 'A fear of breaking with the English tradition of toughness, a fear of becoming soft.' The answer:

We made fun of the hardy Englishman who would rather freeze than give up his illusion of ruggedness. We pointed out how fireplaces were also forms of central heating, although inefficient ones. We further provided the necessary rationalisation for the potential customer, convincing him that central oil heating would permit him better health and thus enable him to participate in rugged outdoor sports more often than if he had the sniffles. While most Englishmen now use central heating, they still try to avoid the American-type 'overheated' homes and offices.

Dichter says he still has a problem with some clients: they become frightened by his ideas even though they have engaged him. There is, for example, a seed company which is concerned that many people don't garden. The answers people have given in surveys include such obvious ones as they haven't time or space or it is cheaper to buy fruit and vegetables than grow their own. However, Dichter claims to have found a deeper, more important reason. He reckons part of the problem is that the company's advertising shows the fruit and vegetables looking *too* perfect. People, expands Dichter, are afraid to grow their own tomatoes because they know they can never compete with the ones shown. He is trying to persuade the company to change its illustrations next time to make their products look less perfect. He confesses it may not happen; 'for them it goes against the grain'.

Dichter argues that ads should always leave readers and viewers with something to do themselves:

> Although it may seem like a farfetched comparison, in a study of ketchup ads, we found that when we put a scientifically measured correct amount of ketchup on hamburgers in the ad, it deprived the potential buyer of the feeling that he could complete the action himself. Practically speaking, then, the poster that only begins the action of pouring the ketchup but does not finish it presents a chance for the viewers' creativity because it permits more participation.

Dichter has been accused, with some justification, of overinflating the power of what he preaches. His record is impressive, however, and his clients are obviously convinced by the efficacy of his work. Asked about success, Dichter points out that they 'keep coming back'.

Researchers like Dichter defend their work by saying, in effect, that all they are doing is showing things the way they really are. 'What we are trying to do with motivational research and motivational thinking,' Dichter says, 'is to go back to the reality of human behaviour.' He apparently finds it impossible to understand why so many people have found his work frightening. 'Why are we so afraid of being influenced, of being persuaded?' he has written. He argues that the only real debate is over the *purpose* to which persuasion is put.

> Is it moral to help convince people of the beauty of a new car, to make them spend the $3000 or $4000 which they could have used for something else? And if it is immoral, where shall we draw the line? Do you really need the fireplace in your home when you have automatic oil heating? Was it right to buy the garbage-disposal unit which flushes into the sewer valuable food residues which might have been put into the compost heap for the organic garden?

In the event, Dichter has argued, the end product of motivational research need not be solely commercial. Dichter instances work for the Cancer Society to see how people can be persuaded to attend for regular check ups. (It seemed that half were afraid the test would be positive, and the other half that nothing would be found and they would have wasted money and would feel foolish.) But none of it seems wholly convincing. Frequently, the researcher comes across as a hired gun: as long as there is someone to pay him he'll do what's necessary, no questions asked. There is a strong whiff of this when Dichter writes, 'We have used clinical material on cigarette smoking, based on the reactions of the neurotic to smoking. This approach has proved very helpful in arriving at an understanding of the guilt feeling in smoking, a fact that may determine the acceptance or rejection of actual health claims.'

There is another defence – that the researcher acts as a bridge between the buyer and the seller. The consumer benefits, goes the claim, because pressure is put on the manufacturer to satisfy the consumer's real needs. Robert Worcester, managing director of the UK research company MORI, says, 'Research means representation. I am paid a substantial amount of money for shouting in the ear of people things they don't want to know.'

Perhaps the most famed example of this is the well-known story of the Betty Crocker cake mix. When the product was introduced to the market, all buyers had to do was add water and bake. It was not a success. A clever researcher set out to investigate the reason. He did this by showing women two shopping lists, one that included the mix, one that substituted flour. The women felt that those who used the first list would be lazier women. Using the mix, it was concluded, produced a guilt feeling. The company amended the formula so that an egg had to be added, thus giving the housewife the fiction of feeling she'd actually cooked the cake. Sales increased. The example may seem hardly earth shattering. But it *is* important if you are in the business of selling a new cake mix or are one of thousands of employees dependent on the company succeeding. And, as one researcher says, the man who came up with the right answer has probably saved an awful lot of women an awful lot of drudgery.

As early as the 1960s there were claims that motivational research had seen its 'best days'. It is true that a shift in power from researchers in advertising agencies (which favoured motivational research) to client companies (whose research managers tended to come from backgrounds that stressed economics and statistics) had an important impact. The new fashionable research involved the computer and reducing marketing problems to mathematical formulas. One mathematician made a speech forecasting the day when advertising copy would be written by electronic machines!

What actually changed, though, was not so much the 'motivational' researcher but the way he amended his reports so they sounded less Freudian, more prosaic and pragmatic. In other words, less dotty.

Today's 'motivational researchers', although they shun the name arguing it does not apply to them, are far from a dying breed. They call themselves 'qualitative researchers', and, like Dichter, they purport to uncover the real thoughts and feelings through encouraging people to reveal what goes on inside them. The central point of their world is the 'focus group', apparently so-titled because the attention of an entire group of people, gathered by the researcher, is focused on the product, concept or strategy being evaluated. Groups may also be encouraged to act out situations, and there will be 'depth' interviews.

If it all sounds familiar, then the techniques are – though the researchers, adaptable to their clients, will frequently report in prosaic, businesslike terms rather than Freudian analysis. Sue Robson, of the Qualitative Consultancy, London, believes that the reason for qualitative research's impact today is that at a crucial time 'qualitative researchers stopped being closet psychoanalysts and became pragmatic, marketing oriented members of an advertising team . . .'

There is no doubting the influence of 'qualitative' research on advertisements that are produced. This is especially so in the UK but increasingly ·so in the US where, for example, the toy marketer Mattel interviewed 70,000 children and adults in one year alone. Examples, from Britain and America, illustrate such research in practice. In Britain, the London office of Leo Burnett called in qualitative researchers to review its campaign for Perrier. For two years the advertising had consisted of a series of puns based on the French for water, *eau*. Thus one ad said 'H2EAU'. The researchers reported that the drinkers of Perrier cared much less about the water itself than its distinctively shaped container – the bottle was the most important part of Perrier to its customers. As a result, the ads began using visual puns showing the bottle, such as 'Picasseau' in which the bottle was broken into separated shapes.

In the United States, General Electric needed to project a radical new image to promote its range of youth-oriented audio goods. Focus groups helped it come up with a commercial showing adventurers in a fantasy land, using a GE radio to free a princess. They also persuaded Elizabeth Arden to advertise the 'secret ingredient' of a new product as Primilin II (instead of Primilin I!) and guided Kronenbourg on how to communicate a masculine image to drinkers (show the beer spilling out over the table). Perhaps more potentially disturbing, they were also used by the White House to determine how best President Reagan could 'sell' Americans his summit meetings with Mikhail Gorbachev, and in preparing the President's State of the Union speeches. Such groups before President Reagan's 1988 Moscow summit helped determine what he said publicly and some of the actual phrases used.

Groups are sometimes encouraged not only to talk, but to act, to play, even to paint or to model. They are urged to pretend to be salesmen or creators of adverts, or even to be the brand itself which has sprung into walking and talking life. They may be asked to finish stories that begin with openings such as 'X [the name of the brand] went to a party one day and . . .' Consumers may be asked to link brands of products with pieces of music or pretty pictures. It is all in aid of what one agency research specialist calls 'being one jump ahead of the consumer'.

This is one research session in the UK: A group of housewives are standing in a room. One woman starts to advance on another only to be met with protests: 'Go away, you rotter. You'll scratch me, upset me . . . Ooo! Ugh! You're paining me. It's like rape! Go over there (pointing to another woman). She'll love it.' She turns to another woman. 'I want you,' she says, beckoning her. 'Mmm, lovely. Smooth me. Caress me.'

These women have been stopped in the street and persuaded to reveal their innermost feelings about kitchen cleaners. In this particular part of the session, they are gameplaying. The woman doing the protesting and then making loving noises is playing a kitchen sink! The objects of her words are women acting out the parts of two competing brands, one of which she obviously does not like.

The man who organised this particular piece of research is Peter Cooper, once an academic lecturing at Manchester University and now head of a research company with clients who include Mars, Lever Brothers and Rowntree Mackintosh. According to Cooper and Judie Lannon, head of research at J. Walter Thompson in London, material that emerges from such sessions 'is a rich source of thoughts, language and creative ideas' when presented to advertising creatives.

Cooper claims that a major difference between today's qualitative research and the motivational researcher of the sixties is that now it's recognised that consumers are not passive objects. They are informed, in the UK at least they like advertising, and there is an interaction between ads and them. Motivational researchers of twenty years ago did not see the consumer as a thinking person. 'He was like a rat in a puzzle box. Our classic Freudian person was moved by forces he didn't understand, and clever advertising men realise those forces.'

Cooper, though, is obviously just as interested in trying to tap hidden layers, a point made clear in a paper co-authored with Judie Lannon. At the top, they say, there are 'conscious factors' which are 'accessible to structured questionnaires'. Next come 'private feelings and language' which 'need a sympathetic interview structure'. Below them are said to be two more levels: 'intuitive associations' – needing 'non-verbal play' techniques. And 'unconscious factors' – calling for 'projective interviewing (and observation, deduction). Spontaneous, uncensored reactions.'

This 'model', they say, 'is similar in some respects to the motivational ideas of the 1950s and early 1960s in pointing to unconscious-repressed and embarrassing motivations. The main difference – and it is an important difference – is the recognition of the *intuitive* level which is largely responsible for the inarticulate and active involvement consumers have with advertising.'

What all this leads to, in practice, is sessions reminiscent of psychiatric hospitals. The first step is to recruit consumers off the street – the researcher will know roughly the mix he wants in terms of factors like age and sex and social background and more specific ones such as being users or lapsed users of a certain brand. None of them will be sure what it is about. Those who co-operate will do so because they're curious and in return for some small payment, almost certainly in kind, at the end of the session.

They are taken to a room and placed under the control of a 'moderator' whose job it is to make them 'reveal themselves'. Cooper says, 'We want to get people to drop their rational guard.' The moderator's skills are said to be crucial. One researcher says it is important to get the consumers relaxed but also 'lively at the same time: it's no good if they're too laid back'. If the session is an important one, observers, and video cameras, will be concealed behind a one-way mirror.

Apart from role playing, as in the example of women pretending to be brands or kitchen surfaces, Cooper uses a number of other 'methods for exploring the consumer psyche'. They include individuals being encouraged to come up with fantasy solutions, pretending to be dreaming to come up with a picture of the ideal world; and stimulating conflict between members of the group, making them compete to 'sell' products or advocate ideas.

In one method, psychodrawing, people are asked to draw their feelings about a concept or product, using colours and shapes of their own choosing. In a political research project – on the political party, the SDP – one voter drew a lattice shape with an 'X' outside in one picture and a number of figures with joined hands in another. The first, it was explained by Cooper later, reflected 'a view of politics today. It is portrayed as an inpenetrable hubbub, comprising warring factions. The "X" denotes the respondent, who is outside and remote from the whole process.' The other, it hardly needs adding, showed what the respondent – an SDP voter – thought politics *ought* to be like. This, it should be added, happened before the SDP's own infighting which tore the party apart.

In a similar project more specifically designed to contribute to the advertising strategy, people were given 'masses of paper and crayon' and asked to draw their feelings about Walnut Whip, a cone-shaped, ultra-sweet confection made by Rowntree Mackintosh. Respondents came up with 'cave-like images' that were also 'full of movement'. According to Cooper, 'It was as though they were getting inside the product in a very playful way.' The drawings were reflected in the advertisements that had swirling masses of cloud and surreal architecture. Another session for Maltesers (a Mars-made candy) produced drawings that were delicate and etched like a shell or a leaf – a message that it was the *delicacy* of the sweet that appealed, says Cooper. The fact that Mars, a hard-sell, hard-nose company, utilises such research is an indication of how deep it is entrenched.

In addition to using drawing, Cooper also asks some group members to model their feelings in clay. He himself volunteers this is 'rather extreme', but he adds that he finds it especially useful with men. The male, it seems, fights to hang onto his rational attitudes in front of the researchers. Giving him a piece of clay and letting him play with it is said to be a way of helping him to be 'more open, more intuitive and more prejudiced'. Cooper says that the 'uterus' modelled by the

Mercedes owner was both 'a bit of fun' and also a useful piece of data for the ad-makers. (The modeller, incidentally, placed himself in the middle of his creation – 'surrounded with soft warm protection'.)

A lager drinker fashioned his piece of clay into a depiction of how he felt when he drank traditional English bitter beer. The result was a solid-looking lump: 'He's saying that's how his stomach feels, heavy.' An obviously disgruntled supporter of the SDP produced a model with a number of holes in it. The woman herself described it as a 'sieve with ever-widening holes through which hopes are fast disappearing'. The act of modelling, says Cooper, helped her to express herself more clearly.

Summing up the use of such techniques, Cooper and Judie Lannon say, 'What is important is to enter by whatever method the inner world of imagination, intuition, private language and play which are the meaningful stuff of advertising.' Qualitative methods, they claim, 'allow us to see the world as consumers experience it' and also 'allow us to explore cultural concepts such as beauty, pain, fun, hope and play as they are defined and experienced by real people in their everyday lives'.

Looking at such studies it's easy to see that researchers like them and find them fun. One says, 'Groups are very exciting. People find themselves getting excited even about quite mundane things, because the process itself is exciting.'

The growth of qualitative research in the United States has been fuelled by the demands for more creative advertising. One researcher calls it 'the touchy, feely part of market research', and the research director at the American Advertising Research Foundation describes it as the epitome of 'being close to your customer'. At Leo Burnett, Chicago, the use of 'depth interviews' has grown dramatically since 1972 when Barbara Thomas, a group research director, was asked to develop a group to conduct such interviews. That year she conducted fifty-nine group discussions; by 1987 she and colleagues led over 400 groups and 1,300 individual depth interviews. The smaller, New York agency, Smith Greenland, enthuses that qualitative research is 'the single most important means of understanding the rational and, more importantly, the emotional issues which affect consumer purchase decisions.'

Researchers for one lingerie company found their insight not by listening, but by watching. Flexnit, a high-class women's underwear manufacturer, gathered together women by advertising in local newspapers. It was noted that throughout one session three women 'adopted a defensive posture, their arms folded across their chests'. They also 'persisted in making negative, almost hostile, comments'. And the reason: the women were A-cup bra wearers, apparently a breed neglected by the manufacturers. They thus 'felt neglected and resentful'. Further research found that 18-20 per cent of American women had A-cup bras. The company therefore positioned and targeted its own

A-cup (under the lovely name A-OK) with great success. This story, according to Frederick D. Buggie, the president of Strategic Innovations International, has a moral; 'You have to be very sensitive to signs and signals . . . Consumers are not creative and they are not going to tell you the answers. You can't simply ask them what their needs are. You have to read them.'

Steve Barnett, a cultural anthropologist, has taken this philosophy and turned it into a thriving American business. He once spent three years in villages in the south of India listening to discussions about marriage between cousins. That was in pursuit of his doctorate at the University of Chicago. Today he is still listening to people, but now it is about what people think of products from energy supply to drugs. Like the UK's Cooper, he uses groups and encourages game-playing (like getting people to build a nuclear plant out of wooden blocks). He has also put television cameras into people's homes.

His work, says Barnett, founder of Planmetrics Inc, a New York based research company frequently shows up a great contrast between what people say they do and think and how they really behave. An example was seen when he put TV cameras into 150 homes in a project for a group of electricity supply companies. Many of Barnett's studies are directed towards helping formulate advertising strategies, but in this case the companies were concerned as to why their projections about the amount of fuel people would use were constantly below the real figures. Barnett's finding after studying the video films was that, 'People might say they kept the things at sixty-eight degrees, but it turned out they fiddled with them all day. Older relatives and kids – especially teenagers – tended to turn them up, and so did cleaning ladies. Even visitors did it. In a lot of homes, it was guerilla warfare over the thermostat between the person who paid the bill and everyone else.'

Barnett taught at Princeton, MIT and the University of Chicago, before 'going commercial'. He likens his research to 'hanging about on street corners'. Ten to fifteen people take part in his three to four hour-long group sessions (in return for small payments for their time). Ordinary market research, he believes, is 'highly artificial'. 'You have an interviewer asking very specific questions to a stranger who, chances are, has given almost no previous thought to what he's being questioned about. The subject winds up giving the answers he thinks he's supposed to give.'

The contrast emerged in two projects involving a new health food and a new running shoe. 'Conventional market research told the companies that people were interested in detailed data on the vitamin content of the food and lots of information on how the shoe was engineered. Our panel showed just the opposite; that what potential customers really wanted from both products was a general sense of feeling good.'

Planmetric's clients include Westinghouse and Gulf States Utilities as well as major manufacturers of household products and fragrances. At the centre of the company's claims is a premise that cultural beliefs are a powerful, non-conscious form that shape people's values, attitudes and behaviour. Planmetric claims it can identify those unconscious beliefs by using groups at which people are presented with a hypothetical challenge or situation. The researchers videotape and later pick up key words or actions.

In one project sufferers from a 'certain type of disease' were taped as they discussed the pain which they suffered. Barnett says he later found forty-five facial and body expressions that the people had used when they talked of the pain and its relief. Those gestures were then studied by actors and incorporated into commercials for the painkiller. Other groups gathered together on behalf of Gulf States Utilities were given building blocks and various household items and told to construct nuclear power plants. They used cake covers to enclose the plant. The observers decided this signified that they believed enclosed plants were safer plants. This was then reflected in the ads, all of which included the dome clicking shut on the plant.

A number of agencies in Britain and more recently in the United States have taken group and 'depth' research and made it a central pillar of their approach to creating ads. A new specialisation has been created. The admen call it 'account planning'. To some degree it is now a feature of nearly every major advertising agency in London, including the offices of the US-owned multinationals. It has also spread further afield. British account planners visit other countries, such as Australia, to lecture and spread the new word. One of the hottest of American agencies – Chiat/Day – has embraced the philosophy and made it one of its cornerstones. 'It is now becoming a world movement,' enthuses David Cowan, director of account planning at Boase Massimi Pollitt, London, which is widely regarded as the spiritual home of this new approach. 'It is the difference between research that kills ads and that which creates ads.'

Account planning was pioneered in the mid sixties by one of the founders of BMP, the late Stanley Pollitt, an eccentric, professorial man described by a colleague as 'an unlikely advertising agency chief'. Pollitt later described his new concept as 'incommunicable' which accounts perhaps for the arguments among some of its practitioners over the precise meaning of the term.

Basically what account planners purport to do is stand in for the consumer, just as the account director represents the client. They claim to be able to do this by carrying out and then interpreting the research into how the consumer sees things. They then represent the customer throughout the creation of the advertising. 'What planning does is put the consumer at the centre,' says Cowan. He argues that this shifts the emphasis from the 'traditional' agencies that are client-dominated. In those the admen allegedly are encouraged to produce what the advertiser wants rather than what is needed to satisfy the target consumer. Planning, argues Cowan, 'liberates' the creative men at the agency: 'What it says to them is, "What you have to do is leave people with this sort of feeling; how you do it is up to you." When you get client domination, he imposes rules – for example, "No humour," or "You must mention the brand name X times . . ." The real sufferer is the brand, the shareholder.'

To do all this, planning relies heavily on qualitative research. BMP, unusually, conducts most of its own. 'We always put a lot of store in it and in a way it's the reason for our seat at the table. A planner may do thirty groups a year, eight people in a group. Over a period of time the planner may have talked to thousands of people in the target market.' BMP has a network of about eighty housewives situated throughout the country. These recruit men or women of the right age and make-up to represent the specific target advertising audience. One of BMP's planners then conducts the sessions. Groups are preferred to 'depth' interviews. Denis Robb, one of BMP's planners, says this is because in one-to-one sessions the interviewer has too much influence on the replies. 'In a group, by making people argue you can bring out their own thinking.'

Out of the sessions comes the advertising strategy: 'What do we want people to do or think? What is the target market? What should we be leaving them with? Those are pretty conventional things . . .' The material gathered is then used to brief the creative team who then produce a rough commercial in the form of an animated film. This is then shown to more groups.

'At this stage you've got a £2,000 animation, not an £80,000 production,' says Cowan. 'You then get a response. If it's right, OK, you make it. If it's wrong, you ask a number of questions: is it wrong because the message is wrong, are you saying the wrong thing after all?' This, says Cowan, proved to be the case with a projected commercial for a cough lozenge called Victory V. One of the advertisements was to have shown the commander-in-chief handing out Victory V sweets before the charge of the Light Brigade. 'It fitted in with Victory, British, Old Established . . . You could see the heat building up in their mouths. The order came and all of them shouted "Charge" because the sweet was very hot. Now what it was saying – that they were strong – was wrong. It was wrong because this area is occupied by another brand, Sharps Extra Strong Mints. Victory V sweets are warm and comforting, not unadulterated hot.' The creative team had to come up with a new commercial with a different message.

At other times, says Cowan, the research with groups shows there has been a 'communication failure'. One of BMP's accounts is Quaker Oats' Sugar Puffs, for which it devised an appealing furry 'Honey Monster'. The monster, recalls Cowan, was originally conceived as a small monster, very loud and rude – 'like a sort of angry child'. When the rough advertisement was shown to mothers and their children the response was 'extremely negative'. Children sat embarrassed; mothers felt that it would encourage bad behaviour among children. The planners, however, felt there was nothing wrong with the idea of the monster *per se*, but in the *kind* of monster. 'It was the *execution*. Changes were made – they were easy to do but he became very different. He was made bigger and clumsy and playful.'

Cowan says that originally the system began for reasons that were 'not laudable'. Soon after it was founded, the agency made some commercials for Smash Instant Potato, ones vitally important to the new agency because the client was the giant Cadbury food company. They cost £16,000 and were a failure, says Cowan. Pre-testing came in – 'it quickly became something else and there is now a philosophical justification for it'. Today the agency insists it is mandatory. Cowan says the agency hopes to get commercials right after one reference to groups. 'Sometimes we have two, three or four cracks. Usually after four you have lost control of the situation.' He says it is harder to adopt the system with press advertisements where finished photography is more important. 'On TV the idea is more dependent on dramatic rather than production values. Detractors would say, "It's all in the production values." We would say it is in the core of the idea.'

Some critics query whether groups of six to eight people can be held truly to represent hundreds of thousands or millions of people. Cowan argues, 'If everyone is motivated for different reasons, you don't have a mass market. So if you talk to thirty people in the target market you are tapping into the reason people buy the brand. People can be different in their ages, jobs, education, whatever, but if they buy the brand they are united by their need, desire, attitudes that lead them to buy that brand. That is how brands unify populations. These people who buy are united by what they like about it.'

Planning as an agency philosophy has a major benefit for both the agency and the client quite irrespective of how well it may or may not work. Because the ads are 'tested' by being placed before 'representative consumers', they can both believe that decisions to run them have been made on something like objective grounds. Many agencies urge clients to observe the testing process. 'For the client,' says Cowan, 'it means more effective advertising, advertising more grounded in reality, advertising that's more scientific with a small "s" because it's still an art. It's less risky. He [the client] feels more that it's the right thing for him to do.' Martin Boase, BMP's Chairman, likens the planner to the navigator in an aeroplane (the pilot, he volunteers, is the account man). 'It means a three-discipline team in the centre: a planner who is about objectivity, an account man who is about expediency in the best sense of the word – what can and what cannot be done – and the creative man who is about intuition really.'

Planning's advocates claim it produces work that is both 'creative' and relevant, in other words the best of both worlds. It is that feature that appeals to Jay Chiat, of Chiat/Day, creators of some of the most imaginative and controversial advertising in the US. 'Research – we use a ton of it,' Chiat says. 'We've stolen the British technique of planning so that the research is creative. Clients realise that though it [a commercial idea] may seem outrageous, it has been researched.'

Chiat says that he imported the idea because 'it was the only thing in England which seemed to make some sense. It was research that didn't get in the way of work.' Chiat recruited an ex BMP deputy director of planning, Jane Newman. She says that she met with a great deal of resistance at first from both colleagues and clients. The account managers in particular saw it as a threat. 'Account planning is difficult to describe, it really has to be seen in action; and if you try to describe it to an account man, if sounds as if you're cutting out part of his function.' The breakthrough came, she says, when she stopped talking about planning and began applying it. First colleagues and then clients were won over.

The agency credits planning for the thinking behind its attention-grabbing advertisements for Nike athletic clothes. Nike told Chiat/Day it wanted fun, irreverent advertising. Based on its planning research, the agency said that was the wrong approach. The right one was to emphasise the sweaty reality of athletics and Nike's deep understanding of the athlete. The result was ads that showed athletes in action – Olympic long-jumper Carl Lewis in flight, or a group of exhausted, sweaty runners. Within six months of the campaign Nike sales in Los Angeles reportedly rose by 30 per cent.

If you think the examples given have the ring of researchers having found a hidden truth, then you have both the strength and weakness of all such research, whether you call it 'motivational', 'qualitative' or something else. One of its major appeals is that it does *sound* right. It has the comforting feel of an ancient proverb that has been taken up by the modern scientific researcher, investigated and proved right.

Some are sceptical, arguing that the reason advertising agencies like qualitative research is that it frees them from rigid rules and lets them get on designing ads they like. Others point out that clients like such research because it is both easy to understand and it makes them feel knowledgeable. Raymond Monbiot, the UK chairman of Campbell Soup, has enthused that he believes one of the most instructive occupations for a company chairman is to pass around the tea at a focus group.

One expert, Mary Tuck, a psychologist and ex-advertising agency researcher, thinks that what group discussions really provide is 'a comfort mechanism for decision makers. Its sociological function is to provide hypotheses or confirmations which spread the responsibility of action.'

There are other criticisms: the people interviewed are unrepresentative in that they always consist of men and women willing to be interviewed; in any event researchers are drawn to middle-class people; the sessions, whether one-to-one interviews, or group discussions or play acting, are far divorced from the real world. And then, whatever people do say, someone has to interpret it. 'I have never observed a focus session,' one sceptic told me, 'without everyone going away happy – convinced that what had been said vindicated and confirmed their own beliefs.'

However, a vast part of the research and advertising industry and many huge companies take an opposite view. Invader of the mind? Another way to help the dream merchants manipulate consumer desires? Or a multi-billion-pound equivalent of the Emperor's new clothes? Or, perhaps, a little of each . . . Perhaps the best testimonial qualitative research has is those who have used it – and come back for more. Tough marketing companies like Procter and Gamble and Mars.

Research techniques come in waves and fads. This particular one may last for ever or simply continue to boom for a while and then go into decline. If it does, it will not be too hard to replace. One thing the researchers have is lots of other weapons in their armoury . . .

3

Research and Researchers (2)

'The advertiser and the advertising agency should never forget
that there are two ways of influencing customers and prospective
customers: they are by seducing them or by conditioning them.'
                                Claude Bonnange, co-founder of the agency TBWA

One of Dr Sidney Weinstein's problems when talking about his work is
that not too many clients want to be linked with it publicly. A handful,
like the agency Foote, Cone and Belding, don't mind. The names of
one or two others who have used his services, though not actually
mentioned, become obvious during conversation – British Airways, for
example. But in the main, admits Weinstein, in a slightly hurt voice,
'the others say they don't want it known.' There is, he expands, 'always
the aura of Big Brother. I don't know why. We are not doing this
secretly.'

What Dr Sidney Weinstein, PhD, Adjunct Clinical Professor, Department of Neurology, New York University School of Medicine and Post
Graduate Medical School, and President of Neuro Communication
Research Laboratories Inc, does is clip sensors to people's scalps and
monitor their brain waves while they watch commercials. From this, he
claims, it is possible not only to determine accurately the degree of a
viewer's interest second by second but also whether what he or she is
seeing at any moment is involving his logic or his emotion.

With the information gained, the advertiser can then revise his commercial, thus again – the claim goes – increasing the chance of hitting
just the right spot. Weinstein gave me an example. There was a new
commercial for a breakfast cereal, the main point of which was to
emphasise the product's nutritional value to mothers. The viewer was
supposed to be using the left hemisphere of her brain, that side predominantly involved with analytical thinking. Instead, the researchers noted
a lot of unexpected activity on the right – or emotional – side. The
researchers wrestled with – and finally solved – the problem. The reason
was the presenter – he was far too handsome and watchable. The
mothers were concentrating on him, not on what he was saying. As a
result, the presenter was fired and replaced by a voice-over.

All of this happens several hundred times a year in a small, wood-panelled room in Danbury, Connecticut, one of the New England towns that in recent years have become a magnet for the headquarters of major corporations. There is a single, draped window, a couch and a few chairs, and a TV set. There are no ornaments or pictures on the walls. The overall impression is of a middle-class living room a day or so after new occupants have moved into the building: they've placed the essentials but still haven't unpacked the dozens of other items that make a house a home.

That impression changes when the room is occupied. In the average year, says Weinstein, several thousand people will sit in this room; between them they will watch 'a few hundred' individual commercials. The 'test subjects', usually five at a time, sit facing the TV screen. Sensors, the size of a shirt button, are attached to their scalps. An inquirer once asked Weinstein if an operation was necessary. In fact, the sensors are held in place with a paste which has the consistency of toothpaste. The sensors – which are really electrodes – are connected to a small box behind the viewer. The brain-wave signals are recorded and then processed with a computer.

Apparently, the setting and the equipment have become refined to the point of comparative normality over the years. Dr Herbert Krugman, one of America's foremost advertising research figures who used brain-wave research when he was at General Electric, enthused to me that today subjects sit in a living-room situation, wear sensors so light they cannot even feel them, and that after a while they become 'oblivious' to what is really happening. 'You wait a while, show them a few movies. Then when they look at commercials, it's as though it is their normal behaviour.'

Krugman was an early experimenter in the possible relevance of brain waves to the creation of advertising. At General Electric he had a contract that made such experiments possible. When he joined the giant company in 1967 Krugman made it a condition that he should be allowed to spend one per cent of his department's budget 'fooling around' in the laboratory. General Electric, he recalls, were delighted to agree. From then on, even when his prime task was putting together, say, a $1 million, ten-country survey, he did not neglect his 'fringe' experiments. One day he linked his secretary to a machine that monitored her brain waves. He recalls, 'I put on the TV, and her brain waves changed.' Krugman reported his experiment in an article. He was criticised for publishing after experimenting on only one subject. His reply, he says, was: 'It took Newton only one apple.'

Today Weinstein is *the* man if you want to talk brain waves and advertising. The CV which he gives me leaves no doubt of his credentials. It consists of twelve pages of small, single-spaced print. A psychologist, his research includes work for NASA (on the effects of isolation and sensory deprivation), the US Navy and various foundations (for example, Cortical Evoked Potentials in mentally retarded children, for the Hale Mathews Foundation). Details of his published research cover eight and a half pages. Some are listed as papers written for the US government but classified. He volunteers that, 'I have done work for the government in various areas of intelligence. The Russians are conditioning people not to respond to certain conditions of stress; I suppose we are too. You can beat the lie detector. What you cannot do – and never will be able to do – is suppress your own brain wave.' The brain, he goes on to explain, has to respond in order to try to suppress. 'We ran a chewing gum commercial that had a scantily clad girl. A man walked out mouthing his contempt that she was barely clad. He reacted so much that we checked his reading. We found that when the girl was on screen his interest had been high.'

Weinstein, who first began applying brain-wave analysis for advertising in 1969, explains that he measures two things. The first is the amount of beta-wave activity. Beta waves were discovered more than fifty years ago (and so-named because the discovery came soon after that of alpha waves). Physiological psychologists 'generally agree' that the amount of alpha activity is inversely related to the amount of attention being paid. Alpha waves are characteristic of the normal awake but inattentive adult. As attention to some stimulus increases, the proportion of alpha activity falls and the alpha waves are replaced by the higher frequency beta waves. The inference, thus, is that when beta waves are present the brain is active rather than passive as it is for alpha.

The second measurement, Weinstein went on, is of what is called the Cortical Evoked Potential (jargonised to CEP). This can determine alertness and the degree of attention. Work involving this apparently began with the planting of electrodes into the brains of cats. Click noises were used to stimulate a large CEP in the animals. Then a mouse (in a glass jar) was brought into view. The CEP disappeared. The attention given to the mouse abolished the cat's neural response to the click, Weinstein explained. He applied the system to humans. The first occasion was in the late 1960s in work for the Navy to investigate the brain responses of men who watch the TV screen on a sonar display. Other government work followed, some classified. Studying the literature, one of the pieces of research seemed to involve using the method to test if someone knows a language by his responses to a word.* Weinstein now applies this to watching commercials. He does this by adding imperceptible flashes and clicks roughly every second to what is being watched and heard on the TV screen: 'People say they cannot see or hear them. The brain response says they do.' If the picture being

---

* One can see this as being very useful in interrogation. Generally, there are many overlaps between advertising research and intelligence. Advertising, after all, is a form of propaganda, a major interest of intelligence organisations. Equally, intelligence bodies are interested in how best to persuade selected individuals. Furthermore, they frequently need to know what people really mean when they answer questions.

watched becomes sufficiently involving the brain suppresses the effect of the click.

Weinstein measures for both left and right hemispheres. Evidence that each one has a different task dates back to research on damaged brains. Basically, the claim is that the left hemisphere is the rational one, concerned with reading, analysing, speaking. The right is emotional, involved with seeing and perceiving, receiving and expressing emotion.

Weinstein says he can measure interest left, interest right, arousal left and arousal right, second by second. If a commercial has a logical appeal, the expected pattern would be left hemisphere activity, if emotional, right. However, a commercial that builds up to a strong emotional climax, says Weinstein's research, appears to involve a lot of left (logical) brain activity at the start – the reason, it seems, is that such commercials often start by posing a problem and the viewer worries about the outcome. Once it is resolved (by using the right soap powder or detergent or whatever), activity swings over to the right (emotional) side of the viewer's brain.

In practice, clients can be presented with detail showing the amount of interest for each scene, rating it from zero to 100 per cent. General Electric is a company that has done this, individually analysing commercials by five-second segments. Commercials can thus be altered, most obviously by editing out or cutting down the 'boring' bits.

Also, it is claimed, it helps advertisers to gauge where they should place information in emotional commercials in order to get maximum effectiveness. In one commercial tested the pitch came straight after a father's expression of affection for his daughter. This, the measurements showed, was bad. 'The right hemisphere was still highly activated, and this right dominance might decrease the probability of successful linguistic processing, which most often requires left hemisphere activity to at least an equal degree as right.'

Another use, says Weinstein, lies in determining the degree of interest aroused by celebrities whom advertisers are considering using as presenters or endorsers. On one occasion, the agency for British Airways, concerned about what might happen if celebrity presenter Robert Morley died, began to prepare a contingency list. Clips of other famous British actors and actresses were shown to potential British Airways customers in the United States. The tests produced a list of those who attracted most interest. Weinstein refuses to be drawn in detail, but apparently two who rated low were James Mason and Rex Harrison.

Networks use the tests for a similar purpose. Here Weinstein is not surprised they are not keen to publicise: 'People like Barbara Walters would not be pleased . . .' One network wanted rock stars tested for possible inclusion on its programmes. One was Cher. According to Weinstein, she ranked highest of all in arousing interest in men, third highest among women. The network had duplicated the research with focus interviews. There, apparently, women had said they would not watch Cher: 'They said, "We wouldn't let that tramp in our living room." ' Weinstein claims it was a classic case of people saying one thing and meaning another.

In other work, says Weinstein, more light has been thrown on how much an advertiser needs to advertise. Studies suggest that advertising effectiveness, as measured by EEG arousal, peaks in the second exposure of an ad (thus supporting a theory formulated by Krugman that three exposures to any ad may be enough for it to do its job).*

One agency, Foote, Cone and Belding, has taken left brain/right brain work and created an ad theory – the FCB Grid. 'All over the world, we are having success with the grid,' says David Berger, corporate director of research. The agency's research director in Los Angeles, Richard Vaughn, put together a number of theories concerning brain specialisation, why people buy things, whether products are 'high involvement' or 'low involvement', and the hierarchy of advertising effects. He came up with a chart, or grid, on which purchasing decisions are ranged horizontally from things people *think* they want to things people *feel* they want; and vertically from high risk, high-involvement decisions to low risk, low involvement decisions. Imagine a noughts-and-crosses game with four squares. In the top left, think and high involvement, is '35mm cameras'; a family car is high on the involvement line but right in the centre of rational and emotional; perfume is high feel and high involvement.

Having constructed its grid, FCB found a professor, Brian Ratchford, of the State University of New York in Buffalo, to develop the questions that would get the products located on the grid according to consumers. By 1985 there had been studies in twenty-three countries, 20,000 consumers had been interviewed, and the grid was being used widely in setting advertising strategies. 'Working with the model,' said Berger, 'has led us to pay more attention to whether a brand's advertising should be primarily rational, primarily emotional or a purposeful mixture of the two.'

According to Berger, the agency has found that consumer mental processes in selecting brands tend to be very similar around the world. There are some cultural differences, however. For example, the dog-pampering Swedes regard pet food as a high-involvement decision, not so the Italians.

The enthusiasts of brain-wave research admit that its inroad has not so far been as great as they expected. Weinstein thinks this is because advertisers 'don't feel comfortable with the sophistication of what we're doing'. Some agencies and advertisers told me that the difficulty for them lay in how to interpret any information that emerged. None of

---

* 'Exposure' is not the same as showing; it implies that someone actually pays attention to it. People may be subjected to an ad a dozen times, of course, without being 'exposed' to it in this sense.

the agencies I spoke to, it might be noted, raised any doubts about the morality of making use of brain-wave research, only about its current practicality.

Meanwhile, work to make it more relevant to creating commercials and selling goods goes on. Some of the experiments are in an area referred to as 'brain typing'. It has been found, for example, that younger men tend to be more inclined to a right-hemisphere bias. This, it is suggested, accounts for the greater success of higher sensory ads with them. Work also indicates that product-use can be brain typed. For one particular product category (unnamed), high users were said to be more left-hemisphere biased, low users more right-hemisphere biased.

This raised the possibility of brain typing being enlisted to help create ads. Weinstein and two co-researchers reported, 'Based on the specific target or targets, commercials could be developed with an emotional appeal for a right-hemisphere-biased target segment and with a logical appeal for a left-hemisphere-biased segment. Incorporating both emotional and logical elements may be appropriate for balanced or mixed-bias target segments.'

What brain-wave analysis does do, Weinstein stressed to me several times, is get at what people really believe or feel, as with the women who were asked about Cher. They told the interviewer they did not want to see her on their TV screens, but their brain-wave reactions provided a different answer. It is, of course, the same sort of rationalisation as is used for conducting motivational research or holding focus groups.

In common, one suspects, with those who seek better ways to interrogate defectors and suspected spies, the researchers have experimented with a whole range of devices meant to measure changes in people's autonomic nervous system. A 'psychogalvanometer', similar to a lie detector, has been used to measure involuntary actions of the sweat glands; other machines gauge the dilation of the respondent's eye – a wide dilation is held to indicate a lack of interest in what is being viewed. Advertisements for food have been 'measured' by tests that measure the production of saliva! Most such techniques, in the words of two marketing academics, 'measure involuntary physical response because they are believed to offer a clue to the interest or response to the advertising'. Robert Chestnut, research director of the Advertising Research Foundation, New York, says of tests that involve monitoring whether a person's palms sweat, that they can 'detect general arousal levels in reaction to certain ad messages'. Joseph Plummer, director of research services at Young and Rubicam, New York, says the biggest problem with all such tests is 'validity and interpretation'. Y & R, he adds, uses them selectively because of the cost and because they are 'grey areas' not yet defined, although advances in design and technology have added to their credibility.

Voice-stress analysers are also used. These, too, are a form of lie detector. They are claimed to measure 'sub-audible tremors' or the amount of stress in a person's voice. Unlike machines that measure changes to the sweat glands, heart rate or blood pressure, these do not need connecting to the person being questioned. He or she need not know the device is being used. Either it can be hidden in a pocket or hand (some are no larger than a pocket calculator) or conversations can be recorded and voices 'tested' on playback. The technique was apparently pioneered by the CIA, spread into commercial intelligence and into market research. *Life* magazine's researchers use the device when researching cover ideas. The cover which does best in the test is reportedly invariably selected.

Others have experimented with the use of hypnosis. One American agency called Ruthrauff and Ryan subjected several respondents to hypnosis after they had looked at an advertisement to see how much of the message had penetrated into their subconscious minds, although the experiment was soon terminated. At least one British advertising agency has found it worthwhile using hypnosis. Mrs Jane Lang, a hypnotherapist, conducted an experiment at the Institute of Contemporary Arts in London on behalf of a fashion designer. A number of people tried on and handled clothes, according to an account of the evening by her husband to the magazine *Marketing Week*. Mrs Lang then put volunteers into a light trance in which they revealed their innermost reactions to the garments. 'What was so interesting,' Lang said, 'was that although their conscious reactions varied widely, there was a remarkable degree of agreement about their unconscious reactions. Some had said how they consciously liked a thing, but under hypnosis felt strongly against that item.'

The Langs set up a company, Hypnoscan. One of its first customers was an advertising agency which wanted to make a choice between several pieces of copy. Each version seemed to have merit. But, according to the Langs, 'Hypnoscan techniques revealed one superior candidate by pointing out serious defects in the others, and a successful campaign resulted.' According to Mrs Lang it is not necessary for market-research purposes to put people into a deep trance. She talks people into a state of pleasant relaxation in which the unconscious mind takes over. About 90 per cent of people were suitable for hypnosis, she said.

Other techniques, less sci-fi, aim at getting at the 'truth' by making it possible for people to respond without speaking. Various methods involve viewers of ads punching buttons or turning dials to convey their reactions as they view. During the Reagan-Mondale debates during the 1984 Presidential campaign, the Reagan-Bush research team had people in the audience registering their gut feelings to what was being said via hand-held devices.

Such a device is a feature of an electronic market research laboratory opened in the mid 1980s at Woking, Surrey, as a joint venture between British Direct Television, British Medical Television, and Glen Smith Associates, a research company whose chairman is also managing director of the Children's Research Unit. An electronic handset linked to a computer enables people watching ads to register their feelings. The handset has five buttons, a rating scale ranging from, for example, 'very interested' to 'not at all interested'. Respondents can alter their vote whenever the picture changes on the screen. Observers can thus receive a scene-by-scene picture of how commercials are regarded. 'It allows us instantly – to one-hundredth of a second – to pick up trouble spots in a commercial or to identify its main strengths,' said Smith. 'But there are other, less obvious advantages of the system. In normal group discussions, there are some classic problem areas, especially in the case of children. We have to contend with group pressures and leadership influences. One strong character can sway a whole group. With this system, we control the variables because the voting is private and the system is the same for everybody. In addition, the system appears to encourage respondents to vote as accurately as possible . . .'

Such devices are used in attempts to measure impact, emotional response and credibility of commercials second to second. With some systems, the collected data is then played back in synchronisation with the advertisement in question while respondents are questioned as to why they reacted in the way they did.

American and Canadian systems carry names like Prolog, PERC (Program Evaluation Analysis Computer), ARC (Audience Response Channel) and Perception Analyser. ARC makes play of the fact that it uses a dial and not buttons. The president of the company that developed the system, Tom Westbrook, was quoted as saying, 'An analogy is whether you prefer to drive a car with a steering wheel rather than a push-button pad . . . you can't very well watch an ongoing TV show or political debate and have to decide whether to push one of five buttons to determine what your ongoing response will be.' The dial worked like the dimmer switch on a light, feeding on an electrical impulse into a data-collection device.

Such techniques are not loved by the creators of advertisements. Barry Day, recalling a similar method – ASL (Audience Studies Ltd) – talks of 'its tame test audience twiddling knobs to indicate just how interested they were as the spot progressed. We watched the interest curves with bated breath. Predictably, they tended to droop when the product came on. We drooped along with them.'

The Marschalk Company, New York, devised a system in which consumers are asked to show their reactions by choosing the appropriate picture from a set of drawings. Each drawing has a face with a different expression. The company spurned physiological measuring systems, says Dr Stuart Agres, a psychologist and Director of Strategic Planning, because of the difficulty of interpreting results. It was also dissatisfied with methods that involved asking people to give answers verbally. The problems with such methods, claims Agres, is that they make people 'intellectualise' their feelings and, secondly, 'as a society, we aren't trained to verbalise emotions, and we do so only poorly at best'.

Marschalk found its answer, says Agres, in using the example of very small children who react to facial expressions before they can speak. Fifteen different emotions – including love, joy, tenseness, compassion and mild sadness – were chosen and an illustrator rendered each of them on a face. Consumers look at both rough and finished advertisements and are asked to imagine what it would be like to use the product in the commercial. They answer by choosing the appropriate face. The idea, volunteers Agres, is to 'bypass cognitive response bias'.

Another technique the researchers adopt is to test how *quickly* people respond to questions, something they call 'response latency'. In one such test, computer-controlled slide projectors show photographs of pairs of competing products on a screen, and people equipped with light pens are asked to show which of the two they would be more likely to buy. The computer records the decision and the elapsed time (response latency) for each choice. Two researchers, James MacLachlan, an associate professor in the School of Management at the Rensselaer Polytechnic Institute in Troy, New York, and John G. Myers, director of the PhD programme at the Graduate School of Business Administration, University of California, Berkeley, have argued that their work shows 'powerful justification for using response latency in theater testing of advertising'.

'Psychologists have long known that the speed with which an answer is given can be as informative as the answer itself,' they wrote in the *Journal of Advertising Research*. 'For example, if a person is asked whether they would prefer a Coke or a Pepsi, and they answer quickly "Coke", that indicates a strong strength of preference for Coke over Pepsi; on the other hand, if they were to answer slowly that would indicate a weak strength of preference.' It has been found that when telephone interviewers asked questions regarding preferences between two alternatives, 'faster latencies indicated stronger strength of preference'. The two researchers compared commercials as part of their testing and claimed that 'the response-latency measure is able to identify poor commercials as well as good ones'.

Other devices are meant to 'dehumanise' the questionnaire, removing any bias the interviewer might convey. Computer-assisted telephone interviewing systems not only allow random dialling (in order to give the researchers access to ex-directory numbers) but also ask their own questions. One comparatively cheap system consists of two tape-recorders linked to a small microcomputer as well as an answering machine and printer. It was boasted that it could dial through any list of numbers, no matter how long, and hold conversations with the people at the other end of the line by asking a series of pre-recorded questions.

Pauline Marks, head of a consultancy which had installed the system, explained, 'What happens is that Computel will ring a number that is punched in, introduce itself, as well as the organisation on whose behalf it is making the enquiry, and pause for the reply to be recorded. Once this is done, it will ask the next question on the list and pause again.'

If replacing the interviewer with a machine is regarded as going too far, people can be used more or less as mouthpieces for the computer. The interviewer sits in front of a TV monitor which displays the question he is to ask. He then keys the answer he is given direct into the computer. It is processed immediately, and the computer comes up with the next question for him to read off the TV screen.

Armed with all the data, the interviews, the test results, and the research findings, the researchers strive to find more 'scientific' ways of making advertisements work.

Advertisements can be speeded up by being 'compressed' electronically. With the use of a device called 'the time compressor-expander', both sound and vision are accelerated with such skill and subtlety that viewers and listeners are not aware of what has happened. With the speed-ups used – typically around 15 per cent – voices are *not* distorted. The most obvious advantage is that more can be got into the same amount of time – thirty-eight seconds of commercial can be compressed down to thirty-seconds without any deleting.

However, that is far from being the only advantage or the most important one. More significantly, it is claimed, speeding-up advertisements in such a way increases their power of persuasion and how well they are recalled by both viewers and listeners. Studies published in the United States have indicated that TV commercials that have been time-compressed improved unaided recall by 36 per cent and aided recall by 40 per cent over their normal-paced counterparts.

Time-compression as a method of increasing ad effect seems to follow from a number of psychological experiments and inferences. In the sixties, psychologists Emerson Foulke and Thomas Sticht found that people continue to comprehend messages accelerated by up to 250 per cent. Given control over the rate themselves, people on average preferred a speed 25 per cent greater than the normal pace. Researchers theorised from this that advertisements run at a faster pace hold people's attention better. And with increased attention more information is retained.

Others drew on the evidence from psychologists that people speak faster when they are confident of what they are saying, and of studies that have shown that listeners regard faster speakers as being more knowledgeable, sincere, trustworthy and intelligent. James MacLachlan argues that, 'If we can generalise from psychological research to the world of advertising, then it would be desirable to hire fast spokespersons. However, there is a limitation to the extent to which this is practical.'

It is useless asking the spokesman or woman simply to speak more quickly. Emerson Foulke put what happens into academic language: 'When a speaker attempts to operate his speech machinery at a rate which is much faster than normal, it begins to malfunction. That is, when the muscles involved in the articulation of speech sounds are made to respond too rapidly, the co-ordination of their action begins to deteriorate, with resulting errors in articulation. Furthermore, even below this critical limit, it is doubtful that a speaker can maintain a speaking rate that is faster than his normal rate for a very long time.' The effect of this problem, commented MacLachlan, is that fast speech tends to sound slurred; 'it is usually less resonant and euphonious, and the durations of pauses are greatly shortened'.

However, the problems can be avoided by time-compression. The process works by removing minute intervals – usually of about ten milliseconds – of 'redundant sound' at appropriate places. If the untouched message is compared with the same message time-compressed, the only differences noted are usually in favour of the speeded-up one – it sounds 'slightly crisper and more enthusiastic'. Comments MacLachlan, 'When a speaker is time-compressed he does not sound as hurried as he does if he is asked to talk quickly – this is because pitch, intensity, articulation and the percentage of time devoted to pauses are as they occur in normal speech.'

MacLachlan experimented using radio commercials which he compressed by 25 per cent from sixty to forty-eight seconds using a prototype of the Lexicon Model 1200 Time Compression/Expansion device ('This equipment is widely available in the broadcast industry'). Listeners then heard either the fast or normal commercial and were asked to rate the spokesmen and women on four scales used by researchers to gauge friendliness, knowledgeability, enthusiasm and energy. In three out of four cases, the 'compressed spokesperson' was rated more favourably when it came to knowledge; in the case of enthusiasm the compressed spokesman or woman was regarded more favourably in every case. 'The clearest difference was in the perception of "energetic". In all cases the compressed spokesperson was considered more energetic and in three cases it was significant . . .' Additionally, 'Time-compression did not hinder and, in fact, slightly enhanced listener perceptions in these audio-verbal commercials without music.'

There is also the whole question of *sound* in television commercials. Despite a widespread belief that advertisements are played at a louder volume than the programmes that surround them, television stations deny it. In the US it is against federal law and it is claimed that such a practice would overload the circuits. In the UK the Broadcasting Act makes it clear that advertisements 'must not be excessively noisy or strident'. However, D. J. R. Coulson, the deputy controller of advertising of the Independent Broadcasting Authority, argued in a long letter to me, 'it is extremely difficult operationally to avoid some subjective differences in sound levels, particularly when advertisements are inserted within relatively quiet passages of programme material. I can assure you that the sound level is not deliberately increased during the transmission of advertisements.' The 'loudness' of a sound, he went on to say, depends not upon its peak levels (which can be measured) but on the 'power' represented by the sound. 'This is much more difficult to display accurately on a meter and so provide guidance to the sound engineers. Tests have shown that "loudness" depends very much on various "subjective" or psychological factors outside the control of the broadcasters.' These included, for example, whether viewers were young or old, town dwellers or country dwellers. On average the IBA receives about one complaint a month about 'loud' TV commercials.

However, what the advertiser can do in practice is see that its commercial operates at a noise level equivalent to the highest noise level of the shows around. Whereas that level may last only a brief period during a show, it may remain at or near that point for most of a commercial – thus, in practice, making it louder overall.

The researchers enter the picture in helping to determine the kind of sounds that will best penetrate people's consciousness. It has been found that the human voice has most effect when it is pitched in the frequency range between two and six kilohertz. Engineers can manipulate voice sounds electronically to make them stay within that band. Researchers have also recommended that scripts should make good use of consonants – the human ear is more sensitive to them than to vowels. Background music, of course, is carefully chosen with the help of research to produce the right emotions.

Leonard Matthews, president of the American Association of Advertising Agencies, likens the sound techniques used to a salesman putting his foot in the door. 'People might not like it. But unless the guy gets in, he hasn't got any chance at all.' Al Ries and Jack Trout, of Trout and Ries Advertising, New York, argue that what is said in a television commercial is more important than what is seen. 'We have come to the conclusion that the mind works by ear, not by eye. A picture is *not* worth a thousand words.' To illustrate the lasting power of sound in commercials, they give the example of the classic 'Pepsi-Cola hits the spot' radio commercial which first ran in 1940. 'Nothing, absolutely nothing, went into the mind via the eye. Yet the commercial hit a hot spot. Even today some people can hear the opening bits of Pepsi music and then are able to recite every word of the jingle.'* Quoting authorities on memory, they argue that the ear is faster than the eye in responding. 'Not only do you hear faster than you see, your hearing lasts longer

* The exercise can be repeated with the old Pepsodent jingle – 'You'll wonder where the yellow went . . .' Many people can still sing it though it was current in the *fifties*.

than your seeing. A visual image, picture or words, fades in one second unless your mind does something to file away the essence of the idea. Hearing, on the other hand, lasts four or five times as long.'

There should be a 'complete reorientation from a visual to a verbal point of view' in commercials, they argue. 'We're not saying that the visual doesn't play an important role. Of course it does. What we are saying is that the verbal should be the driver and the pictures should reinforce the words . . . Spoken words should carry the sales message in a television commercial. Most important, you should never let pictures and movement overwhelm the sound. When this happens viewers stop listening and little communication takes place.' They believe that the reason why Procter and Gamble's 'much maligned' slice-of-life type commercials work so well is that the format is verbally driven and rarely contains any visual distraction. 'People don't rave about their commercials; they just remember them.'

It might be argued that at the very least the pictures on the screen keep people transfixed while they listen to the message. What about radio where there is nothing to look at? Most of the time people listening to radio are also doing other things – driving, washing-up, reading the paper. How, in such circumstances, do advertisers ensure that people *listen* to the commercials rather than concentrate totally on what else they're doing? Three researchers, including the manager of communications research at du Pont, came up with an ingenious testing method.

The researchers defined what they called the 'NOLAD' concept – NOLAD being the *no*n *l*istening *a*ttention *d*emand coming from simultaneous activity. In practice, they said 'the actual NOLAD level in almost every activity is constantly fluctuating, often widely. The driver on the superhighway, for example, enjoys a low NOLAD level until he rounds a curve and finds the road in front of him full of wrecked cars, scattered bodies and flashing lights, at which his NOLAD level goes through the ceiling.' No commercial, it might be thought, would stand much of a chance under those circumstances. But the researchers add, 'In similar fashion, most of our daily activities are subject to fluctuating NOLAD demands of unspecified duration.'

To test the ability of ads to register on listeners at different NOLAD levels, the researchers set up an experiment of the sort at which marketing and advertising researchers are so good. They provided a background of 'easy listening' music for people playing television video games of differing difficulty. Interspersed into the programmes of music were six radio commercials. Each commercial, noted the researchers, 'was exposed to a sample of respondents under every set of game conditions – that is, under every NOLAD level'. Afterwards they were questioned about the commercials. From the answers, the researchers rated the ability of the commercials to get over their messages against different NOLAD conditions. Not surprisingly perhaps, some did better than others. However, that didn't mean the ones with low 'total impact' needed to be scrapped. Advertisers simply had to be careful where they were placed: they needed to be sited in programmes such as news, weather, sports where listeners were likely to be concentrating on the message and the NOLAD level low. The researchers recommended that the method they had devised could be employed as a useful method of pretesting radio commercials.

Other researchers have concentrated their efforts on how much effect programmes have on the commercials broadcast alongside them. Leo Bogart, general manager of the American Newspaper Advertising Bureau, argues that surrounding programmes do matter significantly. Common sense and 'sound psychological theory' both 'tell us that an advertising message will be perceived differently if it comes in a natural break than if it interrupts an ongoing drama in which the viewers have become involved. It will be perceived differently if the preceding entertainment has been pleasant or bland in character than if it has been anxiety-arousing or unpleasant,' he told the Advertising Research Foundation. Advertisers, he protested, went on buying by the number of viewers 'without regard for the audience's state of mind'. 'The question of context will become even more important as the nature of communications becomes more complex, as the audience is able to shift back and forth among different modalities – from text to video to audio to stills – as it shifts from the pattern of seeing what's on the tube to seeing what it wants to see.'

One of the problems about research – though reassuring for us targets – is that universal truths are rare. For example, Dr Herbert Krugman believes that while commercials that 'interrupt' programmes may be regarded as 'objectionable' by viewers, 'it is very questionable that this makes them less "effective"'. Using research data concerning all the fifty-six corporate TV programmes sponsored by the General Electric Company during a ten-year period, Krugman claims to have found indications of an opposite effect: 'It is suggested . . . that when an interesting show is interrupted by an interesting commercial the momentum of aroused interest does carry over.'

Many advertisers now believe it is vital that viewers like their commercials – so that they don't zap them. Some researchers have tried to identify the factors that can be built in to produce this effect. Two of them, David A. Aaker and Donald E. Bruzzone, analysed 524 prime-time television commercials in search of the ingredients. It was an important area, they argued, because 'Empirical evidence and psychological theory suggest that well-liked commercials are more effective than commercials that are neither liked nor disliked . . . Knowing viewer reactions to a commercial may become even more critical as the new video technologies provide people with greater opportunities to watch commercial-free television.' They came up with three distinct ways to 'generate positive attitudes' to commercials. The first was to make it entertaining, which generally meant amusing. The second was to make it warm, 'perhaps by focusing on the family, kids or relationships between friends'. The third was 'to make it personally relevant by involving useful information'.

However . . . Yes, there is a 'however'. That does not mean, apparently, that the advertising that people like is necessarily best at selling a product. Jerry Jontry, eastern manager of The Walt Wesley Company, New York, says that the company tests many ads that people *say* they like but 'the word back from the client is always the same – those ads do not sell very much'. The key, it seems, is getting a reaction. 'If there is little or no reaction, you've got a dud, whether they say they like it or not.'

The whole question of using humour in ads has caused controversy for decades. More than sixty years ago the American copywriter Claude Hopkins laid down his rule on using it: don't! In a memorable and much quoted phrase, he declared, 'People do not patronise a clown.' It was a rule observed by most advertisers and creators of advertisements for many years. By his 1963 book *Confessions of an Advertising Man*, David Ogilvy warned against the use of humour, noting that 'good copywriters have always resisted the temptation to entertain'. Throughout the 1970s, noted David Vadehra, president of Video Storyboard Tests, a New York research company, 'advertisers avoided comedy like the plague'. The argument was that although humour might help an advertisement to grab attention, it could also overwhelm the sales message. What people remembered was the joke, not the product.

By the 1980s, however, the climate had changed. Humorous advertisements were widespread in the United States, in Britain, and in other countries, notably Holland. The planning director of Saatchi's, David Stewart-Hunter, monitored all the TV commercials transmitted in the London ITV region one day in 1985 and found more than a third were designed to make viewers laugh or smile. Even David Ogilvy changed his mind. By 1983, in *Ogilvy on Advertising*, he thought Hopkins' views had been true until recently 'but the latest wave of factor-analysis reveals that humour can now sell'.

Research was there, of course, to provide the required statistical backup. A survey of 500 television commercials by the research company McCollum Spielman and Co, found that in a series of tests to measure effectiveness, tongue-in-cheek advertisements substantially outscored two other popular kinds of ads which it called 'celebrities' and 'real people'. The funny commercials were, on average, more memorable and more persuasive than the other two types. Overall, the research concluded, 'humour showed comparative strength on memorability', and humorous commercials were 'reasonably persuasive'.

Agencies and individual advertising men disagree over whether it is possible to formulate meaningful rules for creating advertisements. Many are sceptical. Burton Manning, chairman of J. Walter Thompson USA, knowing that I was to visit Ogilvy and Mather, told me I would be given a lot of paper there containing a lot of rules. An agency's clients, he warned, like to feel that problems are fed in and that there are rules for handling them. But rules, he believed, 'were broken. They [the clients] don't realise it's all a lot of men like me rushing around saying, "Oh God." Clients don't like the uncertainty of the advertising process.'

Manning was right about O & M. Norman Berry, the agency's worldwide creative director, presented me with a book from his shelves with the comment that he believed all advertising men could improve themselves by reading it. The book was *How to Make Your Advertising Make Money*, the latest in a series of such books by John Caples, a veteran copywriter and creator of the classic ad, 'They laughed when I sat down at the piano'. The book's chapter headings are a good indication of its contents and style: '5. 303 words and phrases that sell; 8. How to write headlines that make money; 14. Ways to improve your copy.'

Ogilvy and Mather also has its own rule books. One of them, *How to Create Advertising that Sells*, carries an introduction by David Ogilvy: 'At Ogilvy and Mather we have spent roughly six million dollars measuring the results of our advertising. We have isolated *positive* factors which *increase* the selling power of advertising campaigns, and *negative* factors which *decrease* their selling power.' (His italics.)
Thus, on headlines:

On the average, five times as many people read the headline as read the body copy. If follows that, if you don't sell the product in your headline, you have wasted 80 per cent of your money. That is why most Ogilvy and Mather headlines include the brand name and the promise . . . Headlines that promise a benefit sell more than those that don't . . . Time after time, we have found it pays to inject genuine *news* into headlines . . . Your headline should *telegraph* what you want to say – in simple language.

Few could quarrel, but the guidelines become more specific:

In headline tests conducted with the co-operation of a big department store, it was found that headlines of ten words or longer sold more goods than short headlines.
    In terms of *recall*, headlines between eight and ten words are most effective.
    In *mail-order* advertising, headlines between six and twelve words get the most coupon returns.
    On the average, long headlines sell more merchandise than short ones – headlines like our 'At 60 miles an hour, the loudest noise in this new Rolls Royce comes from the electric clock'.

Or direct-response: 'Tests show that the back page of a publication, or the back of one of its sections, can pull 150 per cent better than inside pages.'

Or on corporate advertising: 'Conquer your fear of long copy. Research shows that readership falls off rapidly up to 50 words, but it drops very little between 50 and 500 words.'

In the *Harvard Business Review*, Ogilvy and Joel Raphaelson, executive creative director of the agency's Chicago office, poured scorn on advertising men who do not 'take the trouble to study the evidence . . . As a rule, advertisers and agencies do not *accumulate* their test scores and analyse them to learn which techniques work best.' About twenty-five years ago, they bemoaned, 'the advertising community lost interest in analysing factors, much to the joy of the lunatic fringe of creative people in agencies who abhor any research that challenges their pretensions to omniscience.' There followed further 'rules'. With television commercials, for example, 'Cartoons and animation are effective with children but below average with grownups . . . Commercials that do not show the package, or that end without the brand name, are below average in changing brand preference . . .' Or with magazine ads: 'Before-and-after illustrations score above average . . . It pays to show the product in use and the end result of having used it . . . Headlines that quote somebody, in quotation marks, score dramatically high – 28 per cent above the average for all headlines recalled, according to one study.'

Ogilvy and Raphaelson face the criticism that some of the most successful campaigns don't follow the 'rules'. This is true, they say, but it leads to a fault in reasoning – 'the doctrine that since *some* people succeed by going against the averages, the best way to succeed is to go against them. A blind pig may sometimes find truffles, but it helps if he forages in an oak forest.'

One of the problems with 'rules' is that even among the believers not everybody's rules are the same. For example, different studies come to different conclusions as to the best place inside a magazine to place an advertisement: the traditional view is that the front is better than the back, the right preferable to the left, but there are a number of studies that disagree completely.

A fundamental problem, in any event, is *how* do you decide whether any 'rules' do work or not? In other words, to widen the question: How do you know whether an advertisement works or not? It's all very well to say short (or long) headlines work best, but how do you *know*?

The point of advertising after all is to *sell*. An advertisement may attract attention, admiration, win awards, be reproduced in glossy coffee-table designer books, and help its creator rise higher and higher. But if it doesn't sell – whether it's an idea or a product or a service – it ought to be judged a failure. Equally, although this might go against the grain, if it is loathed, never wins a prize, is dismissed by fellow admen, and yet sells, then it is a resounding success.

Agencies don't dispute this: all of them argue that their style of advertising is the way it is because it works. One agency, Benton and Bowles, used to run its advertising campaign proclaiming, 'It isn't creative unless it sells.' Agencies enter competitions in which awards are handed out not for creativity but for effectiveness.

There is, however, a problem: how can you tell whether an advertising campaign sells what it is promoting? How can you isolate the effect of the advertising from all the other factors involved? Take, say, a new soft drink. How much of its sales do you attribute to the advertising and how much to other things such as the hot weather, the number of shops that have been persuaded to stock it, its position on supermarket shelves, the shape of the bottle, the price and so on?

Over the years various models have been developed to try to isolate the effects of factors other than advertising in increased sales. Beecham, for example, has what it calls AMTES, its Area Marketing Evaluation System. But some say that you just can't do it. 'No one in advertising seriously believes that the success of a campaign can be truly evaluated in isolation from all the other factors like manufacturing and distribution,' wrote Bernard Barnett, editor of *Campaign*, speaking for cynics.

David Bernstein says that 'in a normal marketing situation' it has been estimated that as many as fifty factors can affect the sale of a product. Helmut Sihler, of the Henkel Corporation, the giant German detergent company, admitted that his company had given up all hope of predicting the results of advertising via mathematical models. 'It is a dream to which we must say not merely *auf wiedersehn* but goodbye.'

What the researchers do in trying to gauge the selling power of an advertisement is measure factors such as whether an ad is remembered or whether it seems to alter people's attitudes. Such factors, it is claimed, offer a measure of an ad's subsequent ability to do its job of selling.

There are many theories of how advertising works. In the 1920s, Dr Daniel Starch, a psychologist, instituted a celebrated technique of rating advertisements. He said that to work, they had to do the following: Be Seen, Read, Believed, Remembered, and be Acted Upon. Another theory, AIDA, says that to be successful ads have to provide this reaction: Attention, Interest, Desire and Action. Yet another, DAG-MAR, specified Awareness, Comprehension, Conviction (to buy) and Action.

For over thirty years there has been a split between researchers who believe that the factor to try to measure is *recall* of an ad and those who believe it is people's *attitude*. Most advertising agency men I saw tended to favour attitude, believing you have to alter it to make people change their buying habits. Researchers measure what people think about the characteristics of a brand (whether, for example, they see a drink as being very strong or very weak or somewhere in between); the extent to which they like or dislike it; and how much they want to buy it. The same tests carried out before and after advertising campaigns show changes in attitude and, thus, it is claimed, the campaign's effectiveness.

The most widely used copy test method in the US, however, even though it is frequently scorned by men in agencies, is a recall one. Burke's Day-After Recall was developed by Burke Marketing Research for Procter and Gamble and it has been described as 'an industry standard for evaluating TV commercial effectiveness'. The company telephones people from its thirty regional offices the day after a commercial has been shown. Researchers call numbers until they have interviewed 200 people who saw the programme in question. This may take up to 5,000 calls. They use a question sequence that begins, 'While watching (name of programme), did you see a commercial for any (product category) or not . . .? . . . for any (brand) or not?' The emphasis is on the percentage who saw the programme and were able to recall at least one substantial element in the particular commercial.

Other companies operate similar systems. SRI Research Center conducts one which provides the information for a regularly featured *Advertising Age* column, Ad Watch. Consumers are asked, 'Of all the advertising for (product category) you have seen, heard or read in the past thirty days, which ad comes first to mind?' The magazine then publishes tables of the best recalled. Thus, in one 1988 table the top two were California Raisins and Budweiser/Bud Light, and Pepsi was fast gaining to challenge Coca-Cola.

At best such research measures only an ad's memorability. Its supporters claim this is vital: to be effective an advertisement must first to intrude into people's consciousness. 'Without recall there is no communication; with recall there may be,' as Robert L. Weiss, of Gallup and Robinson, a research company conducting TV recall tests has argued. To which, many agency men say, 'Rubbish.' 'Nobody has been able to demonstrate a relationship between recall and sales,' says David Ogilvy. Many agencies told me that if a client was known to want high recall scores, it was very easy for the creative men to cheat. 'If you show a girl in a diaphanous gown people will remember, but you'll sell nothing,' says David Bernstein. Many argue that recall tests favour advertisements which are packed with rational information, 'those with simple direct promises made in a very obvious way, such as a presenter telling you things,' says Len Sugerman, of Foote, Cone and Belding. As a result, it underrates advertisements that don't satisfy those criteria.

Accepting these arguments, it might seem that measurements of recall inflate the impact of ads. However, some claim that such measurements actually *under*estimate the effect. One of the most fascinating theories about advertising is the one by Dr Herbert Krugman mentioned earlier, in the introduction. Krugman's belief, in essence, is that the very special power of advertising derives from the fact that the advertisements interest people so little. Watching television, he argues, involves people in 'low involvement learning'. People are not persuaded; nor do their attitudes change. There is, however, a kind of 'sleeper' effect. People *do* alter the structure of their perceptions about a product but nothing happens until they arrive at the store to buy something. Then 'the purchase situation is the catalyst that brings out all the potentials for shifts in salience that have accumulated up to that point. The product or package is then suddenly seen in a new "somehow different" light . . .'

Krugman doesn't believe there is a series of stages such as attention, interest and so on. Mere exposure to advertising can be a sufficient enough stimulus to make a person buy when the consumer sees the brand in the store. 'In my opinion,' Krugman says, 'the public comes closer to forgetting *nothing* it has seen on TV. People just "put it out of their minds" until and unless it has some use. And then one day "Aha!" – the image of the product springs to life again and the response to the commercial continues'. According to Krugman's theory, recall thus *understates* the true, i.e. effective, remembrance of advertising.

In one attempt to measure the direct effect of advertising, British Telecom had three competing agencies conduct different campaigns for its telephone service in different parts of the country. British Telecom then tested the impact of the campaigns through interviews, a tracking study and direct measurement of telephone activity. As a result, J. Walter Thompson was judged clear winner with a campaign featuring animals using telephones and with the catchline, 'For all things great and small, make that call'. BT refused to give exact details of the figures, but said results from quantitative tests showed a response to JWT's work as up to 100 per cent better than the response to the work of their competitors.

Agencies generally were reported to be 'up in arms' about British Telecom's way of choosing a new agency, not least those who lost out. One agency chairman complained, 'It's an extraordinary situation; it seems to be a complete abdication of any sort of judgment. It is an inhuman procedure, which ignores all the beliefs about client/agency relationships being based on chemistry between people.' Adrian Hosford, BT's head of advertising, not unnaturally took a different view. 'OK, so we are criticised by the agencies, but if we hadn't done what we are doing, we would really have deserved the criticism. Given that we have the tools to measure advertising effectiveness, it would be irresponsible for us not to do so.'

Telephone companies, it might be said, are in a special position in their ability to measure extra 'sales'. For all advertisers the attempt to record a *direct* relationship between an advertising campaign and actual action by the customer has always been the Holy Grail. Some weird and wonderful attempts to simulate such a relationship have been devised over the years. In the 1950s an American, Horace Schwerin, brought together people in a New York theatre and showed them films mixed with commercials. Before the show began people were asked to choose an item from a list of brands that they would like to win in a raffle to be held later. After the show, the raffle actually took place.

The winners were then allowed to choose anew from the same list of prizes. The point of the exercise was to see whether the advertising that had been watched had changed people's preferences. It was claimed that change did take place in a significant number of cases.

In the UK in the 1970s, one technique, called Adweight, involved showing cartoons and commercials to two sample groups of housewives. One group saw the test commercial, the other did not. Afterwards, the women were given a sheaf of money-off coupons to redeem in a special shop set up nearby. The researchers claimed it was possible to rate the effectiveness of the test commercial by measuring the difference in sales of the test product between the two groups.

More recently, though, very much more direct and sophisticated systems have begun to emerge. They owe their existence to two electronic developments: first, the scanning devices that register the details of goods at store checkouts, and second the ability to insert into individual television sets single commercials without the viewer knowing what is happening.

Scanning devices, or electronic terminals that read the bar-code labels attached to goods, are designed to identify products as they travel from the warehouse to the checkout. Their most obvious advantage to a manufacturer is that they enable him quickly to replace goods that have been sold. They have become increasingly common. By 1987 over 90 per cent of supermarket products in France, West Germany and the UK carried bar codes.

There are two systems, a twelve-digit one called the Uniform Product code, which is in use in the US and Canada, and a thirteen-digit one, EAN, operational not only in Europe but also in a number of countries outside including Japan and Australia. On the thirteen-digit code, the first two numbers denote the country, the next five the manufacturing or marketing company, the following five the actual product and sizes, and the final one is a check. Detail recorded as the scanner is passed over the bar codes can be fed back to a central computer. There are a number of gimmicky refinements; the scanner can, for example, activate a device that speaks the price aloud.

What scanners show, of course, is what people actually pick up, take to the checkout and buy with their cash. Not what they *say* they will buy or *have* bought. As one US company puts it in its ads, 'Scanners don't lie'. For research companies, the great benefit about scanners is the information they generate. In 1980 a Chicago company, Information Resources Inc, began operating a measuring system, Behaviorscan, in two American towns, Marion, Indiana, and Pittsfield, Massachusetts. What IRI did was recruit 2,500 housewives in each place, and give each household a plastic identification card. Each time the housewives shopped for groceries, they handed the card to the checkout clerk. The ID card was then inserted into the electronic checkout point and thus linked with the scanner. As goods were checked out all the information about them – price, brand, size – was entered on each individual's household file.

Because IRI had already developed classification files on each of its 2,500 households, it was an easy matter for the computer to link up facts about what was being bought with details about the family and its circumstances, such as the number of children, its income and so on. However, IRI went further than that. Each of the households had cable TV, and IRI was able, therefore, to transmit test commercials to some houses and not to others. In addition, meters allowed the company to monitor everything that was watched in each house and for how long. By linking up the information – of who saw a certain commercial and who didn't and who bought X product and who didn't – Behaviorscan could trace a specific link.

By 1987 such was the demand for the service that Behaviorscan was in ten US markets and one German and was taking $75 million a year in revenue. It was also about to enter the UK. However, there were limitations. A major one was that the linkup depended on cable.

In 1985, however, the A. C. Nielsen Company, stung into activity by IRI's enormous success, produced its own version through a new company, ERIM (Electronic Research for Insights into Marketing). Its great breakthrough was that ordinary television sets could be intercepted. ERIM devised a microprocessor device called a telemeter which was attached to target sets. On receiving a broadcast signal the device cut into the normal transmission, showed the test commercial, and then cut back – all without people realising what was happening. Laurence Gold, of ERIM, explained that one of the problems in development was that the test commercials transmitted from the company's own TV station were of higher quality than the normal commercials: 'We had to fuzzy them up a bit to make them look natural.'

As with IRI's system, ERIM's housewives have a plastic ID card so that details of products scanned are recorded on their files. It is possible to play about with a number of combinations. For example, it is a simple exercise to take every household that regularly buys a certain product or even a certain brand of that product and see what happens when you experiment with a series of specific ads. Advertisers can also make use of the information beamed back about people's normal viewing habits related to what specific items they buy. An initial IRI survey, for example, showed that although the people who watch *Dynasty* and *Dallas* in the US are demographically very similar, the *Dynasty* viewers are the ones at whom grocery commercials should be aimed.

A variant of such systems allows the products bought to be computer recorded at home with a hand-held scanner, thus making sure all purchases – not just supermarket ones – are taken into account.

The implications, the possibilities, of such systems verge on the frightening. They scare some of the men who create commercials, too – but for a rather different reason. Having the Holy Grail within sight, it seems, carries its awful dangers. The problem is that systems like Testsight do actually provide a link between advertising message and sales – and almost instantly at that. And some agencies believe that the advertisers will take that *too* seriously. Therefore if an advertisement is transmitted and doesn't shift any extra goods, out!

William D. Wells, director of research services at Needham, Harper and Steers, Chicago, argues, 'The danger . . . is that we may become so fixated in the ups and downs of transient share changes that we will not even think about the possibility that what is being done today may have delayed effects and cumulative effects next week, next month, maybe even next year.' Immediate feedback, he protests, 'puts the panic button into immediately easy reach'. If future advertising is judged in terms of immediate sales response, the ads that will win are likely to be ones consumers complain about – strident, screaming, rush-out-and-buy-now type commercials. 'The question we need to consider now is whether we want to develop a copy-testing system that seems certain to favour junk advertising . . . And we need to consider whether we want to develop a copy-testing system that is virtually certain to work against advertising designed to accumulate favourable impressions gradually over time; to build deep, lasting images; or to enrich the consumer's experience with the product by redefining it in the consumer's mind.' It is, he argues, possible – 'maybe even probable' – that tactics that have immediate impact may be counter-productive in the long run. 'You get a quick fix now, but you pay for it later.'

Researchers routinely explore and evaluate the use of fundamental human motivations in advertisements. Fear is one of the most basic. The advertiser discovered fear many years ago, and it is widely used today in campaigns that range from selling insurance to trying to persuade people not to drink and drive. In what might be considered the ultimate in shock advertising, the father in a Pakistani commercial finishes his dinner, lights a cigarette, suddenly clutches his chest and falls to the floor. In hospital doctors struggle to save his life, but fail. The doctor pulls the sheet over the man's face, turns to the camera and tells the viewers, 'This could be you if you don't give up smoking.' A UK print advertisement for a private health-care company showed a caricature of the Grim Reaper standing over a row of occupied hospital beds with the headline 'When you're old, the last place you want to be is in hospital'. (The Advertising Standards Authority later censured this ad on the grounds that it broke the British Code of Advertising Practice's rules that ban the 'unjustifiable' use of fear tactics.)

The fear does not have to be physical. Fear of social disapproval has been used throughout the century. Recruitment advertising for World War I provides notorious examples. Sir Hedley le Bas, who organised the appeals, later revealed the two which produced the best results. They were:

Five Questions to men who have *not* enlisted.

1. If you are physically fit and between 19 and 38 years of age, are you really satisfied with what you are doing today?

2. Do you feel happy as you walk along the streets and see *other* men wearing the King's uniform?

3. What will you say in years to come when people ask you – 'Where did *you* serve in the Great War?'

4. What will you answer when your children grow up and say, 'Father, why weren't you a soldier too?'

5. What would happen to the Empire if every man stayed at home *like you*?

And

To the YOUNG WOMEN OF LONDON.

Is your 'Best Boy' wearing Khaki? If not, don't YOU THINK he should be?

If he does not think that you and your country are worth fighting for – do you think he is WORTHY of you? Don't pity the girl who is alone – her young man is probably a soldier – fighting for her and her country – and for YOU.

Denys Thompson in his 1944 enquiry into advertising points out that throughout the twenties and thirties these posters were paralleled 'by hundreds of nagging advertisements, insinuating that unless you use a certain soap or wear certain clothes you are an object of contempt to all. Typical is the set of pictures conveying the plight of the girl who couldn't try on a blouse in a shop because "her undies were a sight", and remedied the defect (crime almost) by using X soap.'

Their counterparts today sell a range of goods from coffee to floor cleaners to deodorants. Advertisers aiming at adolescents are frequent users of social fear. Jeans manufacturers are among those who have tried to persuade youngsters that unless they wear the right brand they will be outsiders. Derek Mottershead, the marketing director of Lee Cooper, a jeans company which led the UK market in the 1960s and then lost out to Levi and Wrangler, explained the philosophy behind his company's attempt to regain its position: 'Jeans are sold purely on image. The make of jeans is a cult. If you look round the country certain jeans at certain times are the cult jeans in that area. If the jean of the day is Lee Cooper and the kid goes to school in something else, he might get away with Levis, but if it's something unknown it pushes him out of the social set. At fifteen that's an important factor.'

The researchers have put fear ads under their microscope; conclusions are contradictory. It may, it seems, depend on how much fear the advertisement contains. It has been suggested that fear arousal does work at low levels. However, there comes a threshold beyond which fear triggers a defence mechanism against the message. The Pakistani tobacco industry apparently expected the fear campaign there to have no long-term impact because of its very approach. 'In fact,' reported *Tobacco Reporter* 'many believe that the high emotional level of the appeal may speed the time it takes viewers to "tune out" the message.'

One research team concluded that social fear is a better persuader than promising positive social approval. Their report carried the telling title, 'Fear: The Potential of an Appeal Neglected by Marketing'.

As basic – and more widely used – is sex. Sex has been a favourite weapon in the advertiser's armoury since at least the beginning of the century. Sometimes it has obvious relevance to the product being sold – underwear, a suntan oil, clothing or a perfume. Frequently it has none – cars, building materials, watches and cleansing agents.

It is regarded as an especially dangerous weapon to use, liable to misfire. It is an area in which 'particular caution must be exercised', warns *Behavioural Aspects of Marketing*, a textbook used in the teaching of British marketing and advertising students.

A basic problem is that various groups seem to react to sex in ads in different ways. It is essential to appeal to the ones who might buy your product, alienate only those who do not matter.

Barry Day, of McCann-Erickson, who has lectured and written extensively on sex in advertising, says that because it is the 'most intimate, the most vulnerable expression of the hopes and fears each of us has,' using it is like 'treading a knife edge'. However, the rewards for getting it right are great. 'The advertiser who keeps his balance, when all around are losing their heads and shirt, not only crosses that knife edge. He also finds himself selling like hell. Does Calvin Klein look like he's short of a bob or two?'

The researchers are called into play both to help ensure that the 'right' sex is being used in the 'right' (i.e. effective) way and to try to measure the impact.

The most obvious use of sex in advertisements is to grab attention, a more and more difficult task. Not surprisingly, over the years the sex has been forced into becoming more explicit in order to retain shock impact as social mores change.

A 1915 advertisement for Phoenix silk hose shows a woman standing by a New York traffic cop as she hoists her skirt a few inches to show off her ankles ('A "Hold Up" on the Avenue', reads the caption). Advertisers have worked their way up from there. The use of sex as an advertising ploy became more explicit and common during the 1970s (ironically, as some researchers have pointed out, during the same years when feminists were most active*). By 1980 the *Wall Street Journal* was reporting 'this has become the year of the leer on Madison Avenue'. By the mid 1980s an American marketing director complained publicly that the use of sex had spread to mainstream advertisers such as Diet-Rite and Juicy Fruit. 'Now the women are not only scantily clad but move too! How much more offensive are advertisements going to get? Is everything going to be sold strictly by means of T & A?' A young English creative director, Barry Brooks, defended his colleagues: 'Advertising didn't mix sex up with our daily lives. The great Marketeer in the sky did that.'

At its most basic the sexual approach used depends on whether the audience is men or women, and whether the men are young or old. Not surprisingly, research points to older people and feminists being particularly anti-sex in ads.

Advertisers whose audience is blue-collar male feel that attention grabbing is all – and that the best attention-seekers are bare flesh, large breasts and double meanings. Trade publications are notorious on both sides of the Atlantic. The following examples are taken from British publications:

For bricks – a naked woman perched on a brick, with the caption 'Beautifully made . . . Easily laid.'

For a grinding machine – the machine with a woman wearing only a cap and shirt. Headline, 'Here's a good grinder.'

For a van – a woman sitting in the open rear door, with the words, 'Wide open . . . for exploitation.'

American trade magazines provide similar examples.

For Olympic asphalt – a woman in black stockings crouches legs splayed wide open over a bucket of tar. The copy begins, 'Now that we have your attention.'

For a New York clothing company – the rear of a woman clad in only a skirt, with the words, 'Hot and available.'

For a piece of heavy equipment – a photograph of a woman underneath a headline, 'Trim. Tight. Easy to live with.'

It is woman as sex object: as crude, clumsy and direct as porn mags, justified by those who use them with the claim that the men they're trying to reach stop and look at this kind of ad.

The researchers have tried to throw more 'scientific' light on what kind of sex approach appeals to different audiences. In so doing they have provided at times some heavy doses of the obvious, and at others a wealth of contradictions. Bruce Morrison, a former Miami University

---

* The use of sex in advertisements isn't the same as sexist advertising. In sexist advertisements, woman is treated as an inferior creature, not necessarily a sex object. A classic sexist advertisement is a Canadian commercial for Sucrets throat lozenges that shows a man waking his wife in the middle of the night to complain about his sore throat. She then gets up to fetch him some Sucrets. A sexy ad doesn't have to be sexist, though many are.

professor and now brand research manager with a tobacco firm, examined the relationship between the 'sexiness' of an advertisement and the audience's ability to recall the brand. He found that men related sexiness to the amount of nudity an advertisement contained, whereas women used romantic content in deciding whether it was sexy. However, they could also tolerate an advertisement that produced a high level of sexual arousal and still recall the product, while often the men couldn't even describe the advertisement, much less remember what it was selling.

One study – this time with carefully controlled advertising materials chosen from foreign and industrial catalogues, so the audience had no brand associations – found to the researchers' own surprise that the brand recall of men was significantly increased as the level of nudity of the model in the advertisement increased. The same was true of women, though to less significant levels. The one difference in this test was that the model was male.

Another piece of research concluded that attractive women in magazine advertisements improved ad recognition, but not recognition of what was actually being sold. Two other researchers concluded that men and women rated advertisements carrying models of the opposite sex higher than those portraying a model of the same sex, and that the models produced 'higher behavioural intention' when the advertised product was held to be relevant, like after-shave, rather than irrelevant, like coffee.

With the help of research (and a deal of instinct) advertisers push sex in many guises, from the very specific to ones that leave the audience to finish interpreting the scene themselves – ones where, as one art director put it to me, 'the sex all takes place between your own ears.'

There's foreplay: in the Jordache jeans ad a young woman, bra-less under a lace shirt, reclines on a beach, head thrown back with a look of ecstasy as an intense young man clutches her leg.

There's straight sex: in Pierre Cardin's man's Musk ad a blonde in a blurry grainy photograph seemingly kneels astride a man.

There's a hint of incest: in an ad for Snickers snack food, a mother affectionately ruffles the hair of her teenage son, and says, 'When he comes home from school hungry, there's only one way to satisfy him. And me.'

There's group sex: Obsession perfume ads have three nude men attending one nude woman.

A number of advertisers have made great use of young girls, an approach seemingly thought to be both an attention grabber and to trigger emotions in the target audiences.

Brooke Shields was fifteen when she made the still-arresting Calvin Klein jeans ad: Legs splayed wide apart, she asked, 'You want to know what comes between me and my Calvins? Nothing.'

More recently, in 1987, a commercial for Levi's 501 jeans in Britain showed a young girl tearful at parting from her boyfriend. She opens a parcel he has left for her, and, dressed in T-shirt and knickers, she ecstatically lies back on the bed while she pulls them on. The girl who played the role was fourteen.

In a US print ad for Canon copiers the girl sitting beside the product is dressed like a grown woman in high heels and a suit, but she's a child. The headline says, 'Super features in a super compact body.'

After examining research on their specific target market, some advertisers have decided the right approach is not simply sex, but violent sex.

The UK agency, Zetland, came up with this cinema ad as a result of what their research told them.

A male hand zips up a fly. A punk girl in black leather hurries down a dark alley. Cut to youth, hair grey and wild, skin gleaming, studded jerkin open over naked chest. He strides behind two black dogs straining against their collars. We see a derelict network of dank streets, smouldering fires and a scutter of rats. Menacing male figures lurk in the shadow and the girl is running now in panic. Somewhere behind her the slavering dogs hurtle on. Cut to the girl, surrounded now by faceless, threatening figures, spread-eagled against a wall. Her tormentors move forward – and the grey and glittering owner of the dogs arrives to unleash them on the youths . . . the screen darkens and the sponsor's message comes up. This commercial could be promoting anything from a rape crisis centre to rat-poison, but the message actually reads 'On the streets. Lee Cooper means jeans.'

Zetland described the sinister story-line as a modern fairy story and claimed that the 'post-Holocaust fantasy is common with this age group'. Nick Balmforth, the agency's chairman, said, 'We went for an extremely well-defined sector – the sixteen to twenty-year-old male. He doesn't relate exclusively to violence but aggression, both verbal and emotional, is part of his way of life.'

Other examples of sexual violence abound. What is interesting is their universality. In an American print advertisement two men in evening dress pose with a bejewelled woman in black lace underwear. The copy tells us the men are 'Oliver' and 'the Wizard' while the woman is 'the Mouth'. This trio features in a series in which the men gang up on the woman, teasing her with a mouse, or wrestle with her in holds that provocatively raise her rear: one man holds her arm, the other's hand is on her crotch. The pictures are taken by Richard Avedon, who pioneered what is known as the 'S & M Chic' trend in fashion photography. They are selling perfume – 'The Diors' is the title for this series.

Buffalo, the main French manufacturer specialising in jeans for women, runs a prime time TV spot made by Language agency. A girl, naked but for the product, stands in shallow water, arms bound behind her with skeins of rope. A knife appears in the foreground and in an overtly phallic way cuts the rope. The print version reads 'I've got you under my skin, Bill.' Another French agency, Oscar, created a commercial for the brand C.17, which looks like a scene from Mad Max: a bunch of leather-clad bechained hoodlums are shown attacking a truck; chains are slashed across the driver's face, bodies roll in the desert dust.

A South African print advertisement for Tale Lord jeans shows a denim-clad woman wielding a whip over a shirtless male. In Argentina, television commercials show a woman lying in bed begging for another *pina*, the name of the drink being marketed but a word that in Argentine Spanish also means punch. Feminists threatened to take legal action against the agency which produced this and similar commercials, but Jorge Schussheim, creative director of the campaign, accused critics of being 'sexually repressed'. The black eye was 'obviously painted on' and anyway 'by asking for a *pina* the model undoubtedly means she wants more sex'.

How do you use sex in ads and not alienate women?

Women began publicly protesting against the way they are depicted in such ads with the advent of radical feminism in the late 1960s. One American group, Women Against Pornography, makes annual Plastic Pig awards to advertisements it regards as pornographic. The recipients one year, for example, included: Andrea Carrano shoes which used a barely clad teenage girl; Gillette which showed a policewoman in hot pants; Gray scotch for coupling in a romantic setting a grey-haired man and a girl who could have been his daughter but obviously wasn't; Orelia soft drink for an ad that showed a bottle in juxtaposition to a woman's bikinied bottom; Mattel toys for a scene featuring little girls putting on nail-polish; and Berlei for a commercial (on cable) in which a young woman strokes herself and coos as she puts on her underwear.

Research suggests that it is *innuendo* that women seem to find especially offensive. Nudity does not worry them as long as the image is attractive and bereft of pornographic overtones. A survey by the Advertising Standards Authority in the UK concluded that women *expect* men to like looking at women's bodies, and indeed like looking at them themselves. What they dislike are nasty puns and portions of bodies used to promote unrelated products: crotches to sell video equipment, or a thigh in *Potato Quarterly* beside the headline 'Buy the best bags'. The criterion appears to be whether the body is relevant to what's being promoted. So while nobody objected to a near-nude lying on a beach promoting L'Oréal's Ambre Solaire under a headline 'The only thing a woman should burn is her bra', plenty of women objected strenuously when Harvey Nichols, a prestigious London store, used a naked woman to publicise its fashions. 'What,' demanded one complainant, 'have naked boobs to do with selling clothes?'

One unknown is what the long-term impact of AIDS will be on the sexual content of advertisements. An extreme view is that the public will cease to tolerate such ads. One advertising man recounted the 'tense atmosphere' he noted in a cinema when a Southern Comfort ad in which a boy goes off with a beautiful stranger in a tight dress was followed soon after by the government's AIDS warning. Others think that sex will become more romantic, and, certainly, in 1988 some advertisers, including Klein, swing to a more old-fashioned approach. A third school believes the effect will be nil: that sex will be even more potent an appeal when it has to be confined to fantasy.

There are huge numbers of people who believe in any case that when advertisers *really* use sex to sell a product the viewers are not even consciously aware of the fact. The advertisement they see, in fact, may be no more than a decoy; the ad is doing its real work at another level of consciousness.

The question of subliminal advertising has been with us for a long time. The advertising industry pours scorn on it – 'I was (and remain) convinced that subliminal advertising is, like the unicorn, a mythical beast,' says Barry Day. 'I've been doing this business on the creative side for twenty-five years,' Burt Manning told me. 'I have never met a retoucher or an art director or anybody who ever talked about doing it or who did it.'

The believers would say that all this proves is that there is a massive conspiracy theory. Wilson Bryan Key, who has made a great deal of money exposing 'the secret ways ad men arouse your desires', has written in one of his books: 'Every person reading this book has been victimised and manipulated by the use of subliminal stimuli directed into his unconscious mind by the mass merchandisers of media. The techniques are in widespread use by media, advertising and public relations agencies, industrial and commercial corporations, and by the Federal Government itself. The secret has been well kept . . .'

Subliminal advertising means exposing people to stimuli of which they are not *consciously* aware. The subject has attracted and perplexed researchers for over 100 years. Research has ranged from whether or not subliminal cues can be perceived to whether such stimuli appear to change people's attitudes, behaviour – or buying patterns.

After reading through the literature, it seems fair to summarise that there are few hard conclusions about effectiveness. The textbook *Behavioural Aspects of Marketing* sums up:

Although it has been established for some time that, under controlled laboratory conditions, individuals can perceive stimuli which are presented below their absolute threshold, there is continuing controversy regarding the existence of subliminal perception under normal uncontrolled conditions. Outside the laboratory, the individual is forced to select between numerous stimuli occurring above the absolute sensory threshold. Is it therefore possible that he will attend to a stimulus presented below his sensory threshold?

The actual term 'subliminal advertising' dates back only to the 1950s and was coined by an American market researcher, James Vicary. Vicary claimed that he had discovered a way to reach people subliminally, by flashing advertising messages on a screen so briefly that although they weren't seen consciously they made the viewers do as suggested. The sceptics point out that Vicary, who owned a research business that was not doing well, made himself known throughout the advertising world by his claim. He followed up by revealing a test he had made at a cinema in Fort Lee, New Jersey.

Vicary said he had inserted into a newsreel a single frame that people had noted unconsciously. The audience had been given two advertising messages that way – one to buy Coca-Cola, the other to buy popcorn. He claimed that sales of Coca-Cola went up by 18 per cent, those for popcorn by nearly 58 per cent. The gist of that tale is widely known; it is part of modern mythology. What is not so widely known is what happened next. Walter Weir, an associate professor of journalism at Temple University, has chronicled it. Vicary was challenged to repeat his test under controls and supervision. He accepted and the test was made. 'No change occurred in the purchase of either Coke or popcorn. Under questioning, Mr Vicary admitted he had fabricated the results of his "test" and he had done so because his business was failing and he had hoped to revive it. These facts were all reported in *Ad Age*.'

Vance Packard's *The Hidden Persuaders* brought subliminal perception and its applications to general public notice, although it was not a large part of the book. An outpouring of mass concern about the implications of people being manipulated not just by advertisers but by unscrupulous politicians or even governments led to discussions within the US Congress and the Federal Communications Commission. In Britain the Institute of Practitioners in Advertising set up a committee of enquiry which reported that the dangers of subliminal advertising 'are not justified by any evidence submitted'. Nevertheless, it recommended that subliminal methods should not be employed or experimented with by its members. In July 1958 the IPA Council adopted the report and incorporated a ban on subliminal advertising into its code.

Claims that the Welsh commercial television company had used subliminal messages were raised in the House of Commons that same year. The company denied it, saying that a 'Keep Watching' message shown at the end of programmes had been perfectly visible 'even [by those] with defective eyesight'. Public debate faded during the sixties, probably because nothing emerged in the way of hard evidence. Academic research continued, but the amount declined. Public interest re-emerged in the seventies, probably as a direct result of another book, *Subliminal Seduction* by Wilson Bryan Key. The jacket promised to reveal such things as 'Where the dirty words in an ad for children's dolls can be found' and 'The place in a TV commercial where you can view an obscene act'. An introduction by Marshall McLuhan conferred respectability and its whole premise fitted firmly into the conspiracy theory of history mould. By the mid 1980s the book had sold about a million copies, had been joined by two others (*Media Sexploitation* and *The Clam-Bake Orgy*) and Key was reportedly giving around ninety major lectures a year and able to command $3,000 fees.

What Key claims, in essence, is that advertising agencies as a matter of common practice place subliminal 'embeds' in advertisements. These then manipulate people's buying behaviour via deep-seated psychological motivations. The books are full of examples Key claims to have found. His *cause célèbre* is an advertisement for Gilbey's London Dry Gin published in *Time* on 5 July 1971. The ad shows a frosty bottle next to a tall gin and tonic. Key calls it a 'classic design of subliminal art'. He explains that he asked 1,000 male and female test subjects to look at the advertisement while they were relaxed. Sixty-two per cent described feelings of 'satisfaction', 'sensuousness', 'sexuality', 'romance', 'stimulation', 'arousal' and 'excitement' – and several young women reported they were 'horny'! The reason, he claims, is that artists have deliberately drawn in a number of subliminal cues – among them the letters 'S', 'E' and 'X' in different ice cubes, partially erect male genitals, and a female genital symbol (where the 'vagina is closed, suggesting the owner might be lying down awaiting her turn').

Another example should confirm the flavour of Key's message. In *Media Sexploitation*, Key examines the picture of a girl of about twelve years old. She is standing on a telephone directory and the message (overtly at least!) for Bell Telephone is, 'Are you using your telephone book properly?' Key comments, 'Lightly embedded in the child's leg – to be perceived subliminally – are several SEXes. In the top of her white stocking appears an embedded word FUCK lightly shadowed into the stocking folds. These subliminal stimuli would be most effective in a culture such as North America's where any suggestion of adult child sexuality is instantly repressed.'

It might seem that if you believe that, you'll believe anything. But many people apparently do. Key's books are required reading at advertising classes at some American universities. 'Adfolk laugh, but students listen,' read the headline over a long article by Professor Jack Haberstroh in *Advertising Age*. Haberstroh, a non-believer, pointed out the conventional wisdom was to ignore Key. But 'The problem with this is: He and his notions won't go away . . . Like him, loathe him, he's here to stay.'

Burt Manning argues that belief in subliminal messages, and in Key's books particularly, endures because it confirms what people suspect unconsciously – that their minds are manipulated. 'People tend to have conspiratorial theories, to be attracted to the idea of master manipulators sitting in rooms high above.' He thinks people are both repelled and attracted by the idea: 'There is something attractive about this strong force that is going to bend their minds.' Manning claims to know of only one advertisement in which there was a 'hidden' message. It was in a print ad for watches around Christmas, and it showed a field of Santa Clauses all holding up their wrists. Careful examination showed that one of the Santa Clauses had his fingers raised in an 'Up Yours' gesture. 'That's the only subliminal I ever heard of . . . but now he [Key] has written this book, and I can look into ads of ice cubes and I can see nudes. But you can look into the clouds and create orgies up there, which I'm sure he does . . .'

Dr Stephen Kelly, a teacher on marketing, who turned his mind – and research – to the subject in the *Journal of Advertising*, admitted:

When one is told where to look, it has to be argued that there seem to be images such as the letters S-E-X in ice cubes, phalli in reflections, seductive nude bodies in shadows, and death symbols in the magazine ads he cites. Focus groups run by this author and others have shown that people can find these images, when told how to see them, and in fact, can find such images in other print ads not presented by Key. If they believe they see these images, for them they are there. How can one answer that these images do not exist? Therefore, if the claim is made that advertisers are embedding images in order to stimulate our subconscious, it is difficult to disprove.

Kelly himself set out to see what happened when college students were exposed to dummy magazines, one containing advertisements which Key noted as concealing subliminal messages and the other with advertisements that 'revealed no apparent subliminal embeds'. The students were then asked whether they remembered any of the brand names and any of the illustrations, the point being to see if the ones with 'subliminal inserts' did better. The result: there was no significant difference.

That might seem to be that. But Kelly felt 'it may be premature to judge such ad techniques for having no influence on consumers' because it only measured *recall* and other tests – i.e. for recognition – might be more appropriate.

Six years later a New Zealand government panel came to the conclusion that it could find no evidence that any subliminal symbols in advertisements would have any effect on viewers' attitudes or behaviour. The whole circumstance of the setting up of the panel is noteworthy. It was convened by the Minister for Consumer Affairs, Margaret Shields, after she claimed to see subliminal shapes and messages in a rum advertisement. The ad showed rum being poured into three glasses, and without doubt the liquid splashing into the glass on the right looks distinctly like a penis. The advertisement was discontinued, but the agency denied the claims and said the ad had 'run its course'. The panel, which heard evidence from a number of experts and examined many advertisements, concluded there was no evidence that subliminal messages had deliberately been placed in liquor ads.

It is doubtful that such reports do much to change entrenched beliefs, however. Three researchers interviewed 209 people randomly selected from the Washington DC metropolitan area, found 81 per cent had heard of subliminal advertising and of these over 80 per cent believed it was being used today and another 12 per cent were 'uncertain'. A quite staggering 68 per cent believed subliminal advertising to be successful in selling products, and over half believed it was a technique used by advertisers 'always' or 'often'. At the same time, 'By almost a two to one ratio, those who were aware of the phenomenon believed it to be unacceptable, unethical and harmful.'

The almost mythical belief in the power of subliminal advertising finds its expression in how related phenomena are treated by public and media alike. Thus, in 1986 *The Times* hailed 'a revolutionary and controversial security system poised to make its appearance in the high street this year . . .' Known as 'reinforcement messaging', the new system broadcasts messages like 'Be Honest – do not steal' over a store's loudspeakers at exactly the threshold of hearing so that it is just audible if you stand next to the speaker. A computer monitors background noise or in-store music and maintains output at a pre-set level. Shoppers and staff are said to receive the messages without realising it, and to react accordingly.

The report said a similar 'but reportedly less sophisticated system' had been in use in Portland, Oregon. It used the word 'claim' in reporting that the manufacturers said the system could cut theft by 30 per cent, but beyond that there was an implied acceptance of its efficacy with many quotes from interested bodies as to its morality.

A similar system was reportedly being widely used by department stores. Here, bland music was mixed with messages such as, 'I am honest, I will not steal.' A Toronto estate agent installed such a device in his office to inspire sales staff – it repeated the message, 'I love real estate. I will prospect for new listings for clients each and every day.'

An American company, Stimutech Inc, of East Lansing, Michigan, even set out to persuade people to subject themselves to subliminal messages at a cost of $39.95 a time. For that amount (plus another $89.95 for computer hardware), buyers received a computer programme that then beamed subliminal messages at them as they watched TV. The messages were aimed at such things as helping people to lose weight, control stress, cut down drinking, have better sex – or play better golf. Literature claimed that the system – Expando-Vision – flashed subliminal messages 'at one-thirtieth of a second (faster than the eye can see) while the user watches regular TV programmes'. Wallace LaBenne, a psychotherapist and professor of educational psychology, helped create the tapes, and he explained about the sex tape. 'With sexual confidence we've been using some very positive affirmations and some examples would be: "My body looks good", "My body smells good", "I touch sensually", "My body moves well", "I am a good lover", "My body feels good", "I create excitement". They're all positive affirmations to improve your self-perception.' Because it was self-administered, there was 'no big brother activity here, no manipulation.' It is illegal to broadcast subliminal messages over the air, but the company claimed that it didn't use public airways. How do you know if it works? The company had a ready answer in its literature. 'You know that it works when you start behaving the way you want to. Give it a little time . . . use it consistently . . . then see how your life changes toward the positive.'

The word 'subliminal' has power in itself. The US magazine *New Woman* dreamed up a system it called 'subliminal synergism' which it claimed made more readers look at its ads. It involves placing dominant colours from the four-colour advertisement behind headline blocks on facing editorial pages. The effect of this, it is claimed, is to cause the reader to move her eyes automatically from the editorial to the advertisement. Thus the blue behind the dieting column head 'Reducing' matches up with the blue in the Roche vitamin ad on the right-hand page. Surprise, surprise, outside research (by eye tracking) shows it worked – 'in the case of one cosmetic advertisement which was synergised . . . the *New Woman* ad involvement score jumped to 88 per cent. That is 49 per cent above the 59 per cent norm for all magazines measured to date.'

As a journalist, I am prepared to believe ill of most big organisations, but at the end of the day I remain cynical about subliminal manipulation, in the same way I do about flying saucers, the Bermuda triangle and other such phenomena which obviously satisfy a psychological need in millions of people.

I note with interest that, according to United Press International reports of the time, a subliminal message was used in 1978 by a Midwest television station during newscasts to try to reach a suspected mass murderer. A message – 'Contact the chief' – was sent out at the request of the police after the FCC gave special authorisation. I also note – without surprise – that the suspect did not contact the police.

However, I *have* seen one example of a subliminal symbol.

Making a video recording of a BBC programme on 29 August 1985 I taped by accident the opening minutes of *Sing Country*, a twenty-five-minute extract from a series of country music concerts sponsored on the stage by Silk Cut, a Gallaher cigarette.

The opening seconds of the BBC programme consisted of a montage of scenes from the concert series. The picture then broke into a pattern of colours and shapes before the night's particular performer appeared. There was something vaguely familiar about the pattern though it lasted the briefest of moments. I rewound the tape and froze the scene.

The pattern, blocks of coloured squares intricately interlocked, was the one Silk Cut cigarettes was using as the central feature of its print advertisements.

What I and millions of other viewers had seen (or rather probably not seen consciously because it was so brief) was the visual of a cigarette ad.

I am also bound to report in all honesty that as an ex-smoker it produced in me no noticeable desire to reach for a cigarette . . .

The Rules and Referees

'There are quite a few votes to be won by saying we will tax advertising or stop it.'
Barry Day, Vice-Chairman, McCann-Erickson Worldwide

The couple in the commercial are newly-weds, at last alone on their wedding night. The viewers can't see what they are doing, but there are sounds of grunting and moaning. The bride murmurs, 'Almost.' The word is followed by a sigh of disappointment, and the bridegroom says, 'Let's try again.' At that moment the point of the ad – and the reason for the noises and words – become clear. The couple have been playing with one of their wedding gifts, an Atari videogame.

Or take this print ad. It is dominated by a close-up of the worldly face of a married middle-aged man. 'Every man should leave home at least once a year,' says the headline. Adultery is being enlisted to help sell a sea cruise. Or in another TV commercial two girlfriends talk about how people think they are lesbians (the hint being that, yes, they are) in a campaign that sells soap and deodorant . . .

This is Brazil, Latin America's biggest consumer market, and a country where as far as advertising is concerned almost anything still goes. Most countries, though, have their own – often idiosyncratic – ideas of what readers and viewers can and cannot see in ads. In Malaya, advertisements cannot show armpits. In Turkey, a commercial could not include a man crossing the street against a red light. In Portugal, no one can use slang words. In Ireland, sanitary products are acceptable – provided no diagrams are used. Children can dance in a Smarties commercial in France but adult voices have to sing the words (for the children to sing would mean they recommend the product and in France children can't endorse goods). In the UK, advertisers can advertise some drinks on TV but only at certain times – and must never (to give an actual, true, example) show a man drinking on roller skates.

Cigarette advertising on TV is banned in many countries – but in Spain cigarettes can be advertised provided it is during a launch period, it is after 9.30 at night, and the advertiser is prepared to pay twice as much as anyone else for the same spot. In Sweden, a print ad that shows

a young man and woman in full frontal detail excites little attention.*
In the same country, restrictions on drink advertising are so rigid that
international alcohol companies pay restaurant and club owners to give
table space to the ashtrays carrying their brand names.

For the advertiser – and his agency – the world is not just a land of
opportunity, but also one of rules and restrictions. Some of them are
no more than a nuisance, others may even be welcomed (in that they
protect the advertiser from new competitors more than they protect the
customer from him). Others, though, are seen as a barrier to his
advancement, an infringement (though lawful) to his basic rights, a
restriction on his freedom. All too often, he confides, sinister forces lie
behind the restrictions; he is being attacked not because of what he is
but because of what he represents; he is the public face of Western
capitalism and it is that which is under fire.

What is more, he will tell you he is more under fire in more places
all the time. 'The advertising industry faces a proliferation of regulations
and restrictions on a global basis,' began a paper placed before the
Global Media Commission of the International Advertising Association
in 1984. Even in Brazil, regulations of sorts have begun to emerge. The
advertising and media industries there have been forced to set up a
self-regulating board, which has already ruled that commercials for
cigarettes and alcohol must not be shown before 9 p.m. However,
advertising industry lobbying in 1987 removed a ban on advertising for
tobacco, health treatments, pesticides and alcohol from a draft version
of the country's new constitution.

Restrictions on advertising are worldwide, variable, take into account
factors from deception to taste, and increasingly involve bureaucrats at
all levels from the UN and EEC down to tiny local organisations.

The individual consequences of advertising restrictions are frequently
ludicrous, and become even more so during their telling and retelling
among admen. Nevertheless, to advertisers they can be the dominating
factor in the whole process of advertising. The central point of all
advertising, after all, is for a message to be seen and heard. All
restrictions impede that process. They are imposed on several tiers:
internationally, regionally, and by national governments. The United
Nations' impact is especially strong in countries which have had no legal
restrictions, notably developing nations. There, UN codes may become
the basis for local law. Thus, by 1986 a set of guidelines for the marketing
of baby food adopted by the World Health Organisation in 1981 had
become legally binding to some degree in thirty-nine different countries.

At a regional level, the European Community has several programmes for consumer protection. After nearly six years of debate, in

---

* The male/female nudes were advertising a student newspaper whose message was
that students are consumers!

1984 the Community approved new rules for dealing with 'misleading' advertising throughout Europe. At a national level, in developed countries such as the US and the UK, restrictions again exist at different tiers – from nationwide laws to industry self-policing systems to individual self-regulation either by the advertiser or the media company.

The number of laws relating to advertising is extensive. In Britain, they range from the Cancer Act of 1939 (prohibiting the general advertising of cancer remedies) to the Passenger Car Fuel Consumption Order 1977 (requiring advertisements for new cars which mention fuel consumption to include official Department of Energy figures). The most widely applied one is the Trades Description Act 1968, which prohibits misleading statements about goods and services. Advertisers can be, and are, taken to court. In one case the supermarket grocery chain Sainsbury's was ordered by the High Court to discontinue an advertising campaign for its Saumur wine in which references were made to champagne. The action was brought about by Moët et Chandon on behalf of the entire champagne industry which objected to a suggestion in the advertising copy that the wine could be passed off as champagne. In another, at the other end of the legal and marketing scale, a Sussex plumber successfully sued a sex shop on the grounds that its videos were not as pornographic as claimed in promotional material. ('There's no way they're hard porn, they're not even soft porn. They wouldn't offend anyone,' he told his local newspaper.)

In the United States, a number of federal and state laws concern advertising – from the Fur Products Labelling Act of 1951 (protecting consumers from, among other things, the false advertising of furs and fur products) to the Truth in Lending Act 1968 (requiring details of finance in advertisements of credit plans). The most important, though, is the 1914 act which established the Federal Trade Commission, the federal agency which regulates the greatest number of marketing practices. The Federal Trade Commission Act was an amendment to the Sherman Act, passed by Congress in 1890 because of public clamour over the way consumers and small businesses were treated by huge monopolies. The commission consists of five commissioners appointed by the President. They are normally attorneys and are appointed for seven-year terms. The staff advises them of advertisements which are considered 'deceptive' after outside complaints or their own investigations. The commissioners, if they agree the advertising is unlawful, have formidable powers. The FTC can impose fines and other penalties, including forcing the advertisers to run 'corrective' advertising. However, as John O'Toole has pointed out, although the FTC's sword can be sharp, it can take a long time to cut. 'Formal FTC proceedings may take several years. At least one has gone on for twenty. By the time the matter is settled, the aggrieved consumer has lost faith not only in advertising but in his government. And he's paid dearly, as a taxpayer, in the process. Government is unsurpassed in its ability to turn the simple into the complex – and costly.'

How the FTC interprets its brief may be determined by the political climate even though not more than three of the five commissioners can be from the same party. After President Reagan came to power it stopped being what had been dubbed a 'National Nanny' and decided to reserve its power for what it regarded as outright fraud. Stanley E. Cohen, *Advertising Age*'s Washington columnist, summed up in 1984: 'As the FTC majority sees it, most forms of misleading advertising simply aren't a serious economic or moral danger. It's better to have some cheating, they feel, than to endure a meddlesome bureaucracy. FTC will clobber outright fraud. But half truths and motivational manipulations? The remedy is in *caveat emptor*. Competitors suing each other, and consumers learning to match their wits against the advertisers.' In one twelve-month period, the FTC decided to prosecute only fifteen advertising cases, just one of them against a major campaign by the advertiser, Brown Williamson. That year, the industry's own self-regulation body found four times that many major campaigns unacceptable. A new FTC Commissioner, Daniel Oliver, later said, 'I think rule-making is not a useful way to regulate advertising.' As *Advertising Age* pointed out, the Reagan era left the FTC 'so wary of "overregulating" it has practically vanished as a force in the marketplace'. A new president warranted considering a new role for the FTC.

Advertisers may not want a too-active FTC but that does not mean they necessarily want the commission to stand too aloof. Along that way lies the danger of individual states involving themselves, the so-called Balkanisation of advertising regulation. Thus, in New York a federal district court judge was deciding whether Chesbrough-Pond's Vaseline Intensive Care was superior to Procter and Gamble's improved Wondra in relieving dry skin, while in California a state court was deciding whether it was unfair and deceptive for breakfast cereal marketers to conduct long-term ad campaigns directed at children. At another, attorney generals in New York, Texas and California, were demanding that McDonald's stop 'misleading' ads referring to the nutrition of their meals.

Bruce Silverglade, director of legal affairs at the consumer pressure group, the Center for Science in the Public Interest, warned 'The end result may be that advertisers will be confronted by inconsistent and relatively unpredictable requirements that will pose more nightmares than an active FTC ever did.' In one case, the Center turned to the New York state attorney general's office and the National Advertising Division of the Council of Better Business Bureaus when the FTC failed to act on a complaint against nutrition claims being made in Campbell's soup advertisements. NAD, the industry's self-regulatory body, recommended certain nutrition claims be dropped. New York state required that the company include in future ads the fact that Campbell produces a line of low-sodium soups. Campbell then implemented the terms of the New York agreement throughout the country because it was impractical to produce different campaigns in different regions.

In all countries, whatever the law or the lack of it, what advertisers can say is obviously governed by what the media will allow them to say. In the US until recently, the television industry restricted the amount of advertising – no more than nine and a half minutes an hour in prime time for the networks, fourteen minutes for independent stations. In 1979, the Department of Justice filed suit against the industry trade group, the National Association of Broadcasters, charging that the code had driven up advertising costs by restrictive supply. Three years later, a US district court judge signed a consent decree under which NAB and Justice agreed to eliminate the restraints.

Theoretically, at least, stations can now broadcast as many commercials as they wish. In practice, stations are governed by what their advertisers will accept – big advertisers especially have strong views about too many ads and the resultant 'clutter' effect diluting the message of their own commercials. The media, nevertheless, does have a great deal of power over what is broadcast and in the United States the three television networks can cause whole campaigns to be scrapped. Each major network has a department of broadcast standards which can decide not to screen a commercial for a variety of reasons ranging from the belief that it is patronising to a specific group to (a major reason) that it is 'in bad taste'. Advertisers sometimes complain that in attempting to displease no one the networks necessarily err on the side of excess caution. Len Sugerman, of Foote, Cone and Belding, objects that the standards the networks set are 'totally unrealistic': 'What they promote is a sanitised advertising.' C. Richard Williams, a New York copywriter, has complained, 'The point is, an acceptable commercial is what the network says it is. And that's a lot of power in the hands of a small group of people.'

It is a mammoth task. ABC, for example, previews about 45,000–50,000 commercials every year, accepting only about 60 per cent of them. About 3 per cent are rejected totally, the other 37 per cent are judged acceptable with modifications. Much of the judging is necessarily subjective, although ABC says editors assume long-term responsibility for various product categories so they develop specialised knowledge. 'What we are basically looking for,' says Alan Wurtzel, the man in charge of overseeing the Standards and Practices process at ABC, 'are standard things about taste and appropriateness.' They are areas open to a great deal of interpretation although, in practice, both agencies and their 'censors' develop understandings of what is and what isn't permissible. To complicate matters this sometimes varies from network to network. In 1983, CBS would allow people in beer commercials to be shown actually drinking, but the other two networks would not.

In the UK, the two commercial television channels as well as commercial radio are policed by the same body, the Independent Broadcasting Authority. (In January 1988 the government announced proposals for commercial radio, including new national and 'community' stations. The decision was seen as heralding the phasing-out of the IBA's role in radio.) Under an Act of Parliament, the Authority has the duty and power to ban any advertisement that could reasonably be said to be misleading, and to decide which classes and descriptions of advertisements and methods of advertising should be excluded.

It is allowed to set the maximum amount of advertising that can be transmitted (seven and a half minutes an hour). It also publishes a Code of Advertising Standards and Practices. The code runs to twenty pages, and the index refers to its attitude on subjects ranging from bank advertising through the use of doctors in commercials (out!) to the requirement that children in advertisements should be 'reasonably well-mannered and well-behaved'. The code covers both the general and the very specific. Hence: 'Preamble 1. The general principle which will govern all broadcast advertising is that it should be legal, decent, honest and truthful.' As to the specific: '6 (b) The expression "News Flash" must not be used as an introduction to an advertisement, even if preceded by an advertiser's name.' Or: '33 (j) Advertisements must not suggest that regular solitary drinking is acceptable.'

The IBA receives about 20,000 scripts a year for pre-clearance and asks for changes in 20 per cent of them. Peter Rennie, chairman of the copy-clearing committee, finds it 'fascinating to observe the creative energy which is devoted [by the 20 per cent] not to the pursuit of excellence but to the formulation of the undeniable half-truth, to the apparently supportable claim of efficacy, the implied superiority of one product over another – or, put simply, to the weasel.' Once the commercials are made they are previewed by specialist staff and the programme companies to ensure that they conform with the agreed script and that there is nothing unacceptable about the tone and style of presentation or other aspects of the film treatment of the subject. Between 2 and 3 per cent of these finished films are sent away for further revision. As to what is acceptable, IBA staff claim they are more in touch with realities than the advertising agencies who make the commercials. The IBA, they say, constantly carries out surveys into public taste and trends. 'Taste and decency' emerges as the most difficult area, according to Harry Theobalds, the IBA's head of advertising control.

Perhaps inevitably the enforcement of rules in such areas produces strange 'case law'. Advertisers cannot have a hangover in commercials, only a 'headache with upset stomach'. You cannot show a mirror over a fireplace (for safety reasons easily imagined). It is when they are applied to specific commercials that the rules take on an air of surrealism. One script began with a salesman walking into a pub. It was ruled that the ad would only be acceptable if the man was shown to be carrying a raincoat. The reason: a salesman without a raincoat obviously had a car parked nearby. You cannot imply drinking and driving. A raincoat would show he was on foot. In another, for a lager, an animated can was shown with a face. The can had to be redrawn. The face on it did not *look* twenty-five years old.

Another, for Heineken lager, which in Britain specialises in zany commercials, portrayed a situation in which Punch and Judy's marriage was in trouble. Judy had gained control of the truncheon and was beating Punch; only after drinking Heineken would Punch be restored to his rightful, traditional place as the aggressor. The vetters said 'No': the scenario was too violent.

A few more: a script for a commercial for Polo mints was turned down because it featured a dangerous weapon, a Smith and Wesson, shooting a bullet through the hole in the centre of the sweet. The word 'lefty' was ordered out of another script. In this, a Blimpish character was seen writing to his daughter abroad about the London magazine, *City Limits*. The character was derogatory about the magazine, saying it included 'a lot of lefty news about London'. Stewart Routledge, the IBA's head of copy clearance, explained, 'The Broadcasting Act forbids us to accept any advertising directed at any political end, whether serious or unserious. And frankly, I don't know where you draw the line between the two.' An ad that would have featured John Bull, a Union Jack, the door of Number 10 Downing Street, and a voice-over urging, 'Buy a Hermann's chicken and create a British job' was banned completely. The copy clearers decided that the ad clearly implied government support for Hermann's chickens!

Such meticulous care in pre-screening does not satisfy every viewer. The complaints, though sometimes serious, provide a guide to English looniness. One viewer complained that the British Airways commercial in which Manhattan flies into Britain is 'insensitive to those living under noisy flight paths'. Another protested that having a Scottish character say 'hoots', 'makes fun of Scots'. One other argued that a Kentucky Fried Chicken ad was 'degrading women' because it showed a young man 'buying chicken for a young lady'. An ad for Cockburn's port was accused of being offensive to Russians, while one for Hamlet cigars – in which a man's wig is knocked off in a restaurant – was criticised for being likely to offend wig wearers. Channel 4, the upmarket commercial channel, was not only criticised for running a come-on for a rock music programme with the advice, 'Warn your neighbours they could need ear plugs', but was actually censored. The authority agreed that the advertisement was likely to encourage viewers to be a nuisance to their neighbours by playing their televisions loudly.

However, a complaint from a viewer who objected that in a Quavers snack food advertisement a parachutist dropped a wrapper while falling ('an unacceptable encouragement to cause litter') was rejected. So, too, was one from a viewer who claimed to have heard in a commercial for Walkers French Fries the words, 'The Holy Ghost is taking a bashing'. (The phrase, he was told, was in fact, 'The old ego's taking a bashing.') One ad attracted 'stacks' of letters of complaint, and is probably an excellent pointer to the kind of issue that most concerns some Britons in the late twentieth century. In an ad created by Saatchi and Saatchi, a frog hopped off a Servis washing machine. One viewer complained because 'a frog has clearly been given an electric shock to make it jump'. The frog was, in fact, a very expensively-made mechanical one.

The system is not a totally statutory one. Although ultimately it gains its authority from statute, there are also elements of self-regulation in that advertising men sit on the Advertising Advisory Committee, the consultant body for the IBA's Code of Advertising Standards and Practice. More importantly, it is the programme companies – usually in the form of their top sales executives – who pre-vet the advertisements with IBA staff. Peter Rennie, when chairman of the Independent Television Companies' Association copy committee, the clearing group, was sales director of Granada Television, one of the five major networks. The committee's responsibility, he told a seminar, 'is not formally to the IBA – it is to the television companies, not simply because they pay them but because the television companies see, through the effective application of a number of codes of practice, a very important means to protect their revenues base.'

Given the British system of broadcasting, the advertisers have probably got in the ITCA/IBA control apparatus the best (in their terms) for which they can hope. 'We are not against regulations,' several advertisers and agency executives rushed to volunteer. That may be true. But even if it is, the regulations that most admen want are those which they frame and police themselves. There is nothing especially unusual – or sinister – in this. Many other groups prefer self-regulation to legal or other outside control, including (in Britain) the press, the police and lawyers. All of them advance the same justification: the public, they argue, gets a better deal under such a system because the admen (or pressmen or lawyers or whatever) know the business best and have a committed interest in seeing that the system works. Thus the Advertising Association in a joint statement with the Confederation of British Industries has argued, 'Self-regulatory codes are very flexible and they can quickly be adjusted to meet changing conditions. Codes elicit a high degree of industry commitment. Practitioners adhere both to the spirit as well as the letter of the codes. Consumers have easy access to the complaints procedure. Sanctions can be swiftly enforced.' Others are frequently more sceptical.

By the early 1980s, industry, trade and advertising associations had developed self-regulatory codes in at least thirty-five countries. Many of them subscribed to the codes of practice formulated by the International

Chamber of Commerce. Those codes, started in 1937, are general, stressing principles rather than giving detailed guidelines. Even when there is self-regulation it does not exist alone. The usual pattern is a complex mixture of self-regulation, law and the rules and practices of the broadcasting organisations. The actual mix varies from country to country. Not surprisingly, much of the advertising industry's own propaganda is concentrated on persuading the public and the legislators that a system in which self-regulation features large is the best one.

The American Association of Advertising Agencies has a film, *The Advertising Industry: The Case for Self-Regulation*, which shows the route a commercial has to travel before being broadcast. Leonard Matthews, president of the AAAA, said, 'The self-regulation story is one that needs to be told time and time again through all types of media to a wide range of audiences. Ultimately, it is a crucial key in our industry's efforts to improve the public's attitudes towards advertising.' Britain's Advertising Standards Authority also has a film – available on free loan – which illustrates how (to use its own words) the ASA 'operates in the public interest to ensure that advertising is "legal, decent, honest and truthful" '. In addition, the ASA advertises itself directly to the public: in one recent year, it spent nearly £400,000 on advertising and promotion in addition to the free space it was given by media owners equally keen that self-regulation should continue supreme.

While not denying that self-regulation may have some very real advantages, it remains for the advertising industry a state of affairs not unlike old age: it may not be ideal, but it is immeasurably better than the only other alternative. The history of self-regulation, in fact, is one of actions taken by the industry in order to head off outside control. The British system is a good example. Although the IBA governs television and radio advertising, all print, poster and cinema advertising is policed by the Advertising Standards Authority (ASA), a body set up by and financed by the advertising industry. It is probably true to say that the majority of advertising men in other countries, faced with increasing controls, look at what the British admen have achieved with envy.

The ASA is a 'watchdog' organisation devoted to seeing that print, poster and cinema advertisers operate within the restrictions of the British Code of Advertising Practice, which is an adaptation of the International Chamber of Commerce's international code of advertising practice.* The ASA's literature lays great stress on its 'independence'. Thus, in one of its leaflets – 'The Advertising Standards Authority:

---

* With the growth of financial advertising, the Takeover Panel was given the task of controlling advertising during takeover bids, and the Securities and Investment Board unit trust and investment promotion.

What it does and how it works' – it says: 'Although it is financed by the advertising industry (who are, incidentally, as interested as is the consumer in banning unacceptable advertising), it works independently of the industry. It has to be independent to be fair and unbiased about consumers' complaints. For this reason, the Chairman is independent and so are the majority of the Council members.'

What, not unnaturally, the ASA does not say is that it came into being in the first place because of the growth of commercial television and the fact that the government had decided it should be subject to controls. This immediately showed up the incongruity of a situation in which the rest of the media – the vehicle for the majority of advertisements – was *not* regulated. The advertising industry thus got together to create a self-regulatory system to head off any government action. It established its Code of Advertising Practice and in 1962 set up the ASA to monitor and adjudicate complaints based on it.

To quote from ASA literature designed for the public:

Here's briefly how the system works. You write in with a complaint. If we think your complaint is well founded we contact the advertiser. We instruct him either to amend it before the advertisement runs again. Or if it is not a simple matter of correction, we ask the advertiser to remove it totally. Because advertisers know we have teeth the system works very quickly and effectively. It also has the blessing of the owners of the vast majority of the country's newspapers, magazines, poster sites and cinemas, who don't hesitate to withdraw an advertisement which contravenes the Code and who would not run advertisements which we have banned.

In 1986, for example, the ASA received 7,820 complaints, of which it pursued 1,941 which referred to advertising copy (others were considered outside the ASA's scope – they referred, for example, to television ads – or were to do with mail order delays). Of these, 787 complaints were upheld either wholly or in part. 'The great majority of advertisers assured the Authority that they would not repeat the offence and adhered to that promise.'

There are obvious limitations of the system. There are a lot of ads to monitor. In 1978, a review carried out by the Director General of Fair Trading found 13 per cent of ads in *national* newspapers and magazines did not conform to the code. That percentage is not high – but it does represent a considerable number of *individual* ads. Even if they are 'caught', advertisers don't *have* to pay heed to the ASA's judgements. For example, of eight advertisers of slimming products and services judged in one month to have made misleading claims, more than half of them had received other ASA condemnations in the previous year. Nor does all the media commit itself to the self-regulatory system. Some of the slimming ads appeared in *Girl About Town*, a widely read free magazine oblivious to the code.

Since June 1988 there has been a theoretical backup legal power: the Director-General of Fair Trading can seek injunctions to prevent misleading ads appearing. However, his intervention was regarded as very much a last resort after existing channels were exhausted. Therefore, the ASA's role was not diminished. There remains the code itself. It is hardly objectively constructed in that it always reflects how far the industry has been forced to go at any time in order to head off more severe restraint. Then enforcement itself frequently concerns minutiae. The ASA's adjudications often seem to have less relevance to deceptive practices than to English silliness. Fourteen people complained about ITT using the loss of Van Gogh's ear in an advertisement for stereo equipment. 'The one person who wouldn't appreciate what we're selling,' said the headline. The ASA refused to uphold the complaints (though it thought the copy was 'in bad taste'). Another advertisement urging people to drink Guiness was judged unacceptable. The ad, a spoof of announcements to save water, said, 'There is no shortage of Guinness at the moment . . . remember – drink as much Guiness as you like.' The ASA said this would generally be understood to be humorous, but also that it encouraged excessive drinking.

Winston Fletcher, a well-known advertising man, has written of the ASA investigating 'an endless stream of bellyaches, most of which are amiably dotty, and then castigating mercilessly such infamous perpetrators of wickedness as the George Cinema, Glasgow, which once deviously advertised itself as showing *Jungle Book* when the repellent truth was that it was showing *Planet of the Apes*.' Fletcher mentioned complaints from two women named Joy who found the headline 'We've made a contraceptive sheath for Joy' embarrassing (this complaint was upheld) and others that contraceptives called 'Black Shadow' were degrading to the coloured community (not upheld). This did not prevent him joining its council years later. It often seems that the ASA is like a motor mechanic who, given a car full of major faults to repair, spends his time tuning the radio and adjusting the seats.

Not infrequently the difference between what is considered 'right' or 'wrong' or allowable or not allowable seems no more than semantics. A French manufacturer was prevented from advertising a claim that Helancyl, a herbal soap, would make people slimmer. However, the ads *were* allowed to say that the product 'has helped over one million French women to keep their svelte look'. The Oxford dictionary, pointed out Philip Kleinman, the advertising and media commentator, defines 'svelte' as 'slim'. Beecham was prevented from advertising its pheromone-based perfume, Andron, as a 'sexual attractant'. The claims were changed to say that the scent 'transmits attractant signals to any male (female) within sensory range with a message so powerful, so exciting, there can only be one response'. The MFI furniture chain ran an ad comparing kitchen equipment, headlined, 'For £600 you can buy this Siematic kitchen from Heals. Or, for £600, swallow your pride and buy this kitchen from MFI.' The only problem was that MFI's kitchen in the ad featured a number of items – like the oven, working surfaces and sink top and taps – not included in the price. The amendment insisted on by the ASA was a sentence noting this fact which a trade commentator later described as 'very hard to find, and it is in type so small that it is difficult to read . . .'

Flora, a high-polyunsaturate margarine, has built a whole campaign on hinting as blatantly as it can that it helps protect men against heart attacks – something the ASA will not allow it to say directly. Thus the copy refers to 'the margarine for men', to the product being high in polyunsaturates (though it can't say what that means) and urges 'make it part of a healthier way of living'. This way the *letter* of the regulations is satisfied.

The system has another limitation. What happens when the ASA does decide against an advertisement and then goes on to enforce its view? The answer, to an outsider at least, is, 'Surprisingly little.' What the advertiser does is to assure the authority that he will not repeat his 'guilty' act. The majority, the authority says, then adhere to that promise. Along with that goes the (adverse) publicity of being listed in the authority's monthly case list with the possibility of wider notoriety if the case is reported in a national or local newspaper. It is not necessary to be very cynical, however, to feel that by that time the advertising has done its work.

For example, British Rail, as part of a campaign to highlight a number of claimed improvements, produced a highly persuasive poster that appeared to show that its record for punctuality was better than most people imagined. A poster was covered with red dots and black dots; the red dots represented trains that had run late the previous year, the black ones which had run on time. The predominant colour was black. It emerged later, however, that one important reason for the great disparity between the area that was black and the area that was red was that the red dots had been printed more closely together than the black ones in order to give a false impression. British Rail was asked by the ASA to withdraw the poster: the case received a single column mention in *The Times* ('BR asked to drop misleading poster'). It would be interesting to know how many of the false impressions were, therefore, corrected. Given that there is an ASA and that such a piece of dishonesty fell within its terms, the action it took might seem remarkably ineffectual, not to say fairly pointless. There is surely something Monty Pythonesque about a body that puts an organisation on trial, finds it guilty, and whose power is then limited to telling it – no, *asking* it – not to commit the same crime again. It might be argued that the specific British Rail case, though obviously a clear one of deceit, is only minor. But the same system – trial, decision, then toothlessness – applies to all the cases in which the ASA is involved.

A solution might be 'corrective advertising' where the advertiser is forced to confess his deception publicly. Advertisers and agencies, not surprisingly, do not like the idea. The concept of such advertising was spawned in the United States where the FTC has the power to order corrective advertising, as it did, for example, in the case of Continental Baking Company. The company claimed that consumers would lose weight eating its Profile bread. The bread's main characteristic was not that it contained fewer calories than other bread – but was cut in thinner slices. Profile was required to run 25 per cent of its advertising containing corrective statements, such as one featuring Julia Meade, the actress, which went: 'I'd like to clear up any misunderstanding you may have had about Profile bread from its advertising or even its name. Does Profile have fewer calories than other breads? No, Profile has about the same per ounce as other breads. To be exact, Profile has seven fewer calories per slice. That's because it's sliced thinner. But eating Profile will not cause you to lose weight. A reduction of seven calories is insignificant . . .'

Opponents claim that the weapon has not proved a very effective one. They point to the FTC's order that Warner Lambert correct the impression that its Listerine mouthwash helped to prevent colds and sore throats or to 'lessen their severity'. The corrective ads, which ran over a fifteen-month period, cost the company $10 million. However, surveys conducted for the FTC before and after the corrective campaign showed very limited impact. The number of people who believed Listerine was capable of preventing colds and sore throats had dropped, but only from 31 per cent to 25 per cent.

Self-regulation came later to the United States than to Britain, but, as in Britain, it arose out of fear of the alternative. For decades the US industry spurned controls. Albert Lasker said allowing regulations would be like burning down a barn to get rid of the rats. Its attitude did not change until it found itself faced by a powerful consumer movement which, it became obvious, was not going to go away. Faced with growing public concern, in 1971 the American Advertising Federation, the American Association of Advertising Agencies, the Association of National Advertisers and the Council of Better Business Bureaus set up a self-regulatory organisation, the National Advertising Review Board (NARB). Under the system, a National Advertising Division (NAD) of the Council of Better Business Bureaus receives complaints about false or misleading ads. Most frequently decisions are made at this level. If not, the case moves on to NARB which sets up a panel comprising three people from advertising companies, one from an agency and one from the public. Unlike Britain's ASA it covers all forms of media, including television.

The system does have failings. One is that, like the ASA, NARB cannot impose fines or other penalties and advertisements are frequently stopped only after campaigns have already finished. During one random year, for example, over a third of the cases were still unresolved more than six months after complaints were first made. Another is that advertisers do not *have* to co-operate. The Buckingham Company was asked in 1987 to substantiate its advertising claims that its Scotch, Cutty Sark, was preferred over Dewar's in a taste test. The company simply refused – on the grounds that 'no one other than NAD had questioned the advertising'. Furthermore, it is not concerned with local advertising – a big limitation in a country where nearly 90 per cent of newspaper advertising is local.

On the credit side, because there is government regulation it is an *extra* level of protection. Because of this the system in the United States seems less faulted than the one in Britain – provided the American government level remains active, and not just a token.

Although the National Advertising Division theoretically encourages and solicits complaints direct from consumers, most come from aggrieved competitors. A glance through any NAD monthly case report shows the range. In Vol 13, No 4, a 'competitor' challenges AT & T/ American Bell Consumer Products over a claim about 'genuine Bell' phones, arguing some Bell phones are made for them by other companies and are thus no different from models obtainable elsewhere; another 'competitor' queries the claim that 'nothing cleans like' Windex glass cleaner; Mercedes Benz disputes Chrysler's claim that fifty automotive engineers prefer the Dodge 600ES to the Mercedes 300D; Tampax challenges Playtex Tampons for a claim that it 'protects better' than other major brands . . .

The advertisers who are challenged are thus forced to substantiate their claims (provided, of course, they co-operate). All the companies given in the example above did so to NAD's satisfaction; Playtex, for example, supplying detailed information of tests in which women wearing different brands of tampons were monitored.

One reason for the dominance of advertisers v advertiser complaints in the US is the huge incidence of comparative advertising. By 1983 it was estimated that almost a quarter of all American advertising campaigns involved comparing the advertised product (favourably, of course) with that of a rival. Comparative advertising is a form of advertising liked more by consumer bodies and free marketeers than by advertisers and agencies. In the US, both the networks and the ad industry were lukewarm to the idea until the FTC exerted pressure for comparative advertising. Even now, some argue that the substantiation for claims insisted upon by the self-regulators is *too* stringent and thus discourages smaller advertisers from taking on major ones, in a comparisons battle.

The supporters of comparative advertising argue that it encourages competition and the flow of 'real' information. Its opponents retaliate that it leads easily to misleading advertising and, in any event, is all too liable to bring advertising generally into disrepute. They point out that in Sweden, a country much admired by consumer lobbyists for its laws and 'market court', comparative ads must be 'significantly complete'. They must list all major differences between the products being compared, including the shortcomings of the one being advertised. Leonard Matthews, president of the American Association of Advertising Agencies, though describing comparative advertising as a 'perfectly valid and effective technique in many cases', has said, 'When competitors slug it out in their advertising, there's a chance that the consumer will wind up believing neither of them. And they'll grow tired of the argument. I've seen some early research that seems to indicate that people react negatively to what they regard as "name calling", and it just confirms for them an already negative attitude about advertising.'

The trend, though, is clear. When, in the mid sixties, Avis began hitting out at Hertz with its 'We try harder' campaign, the car rental company was trail-blazing. Now comparative advertising is a commonplace approach for car companies, airlines, banks, insurance organisations, credit card companies – even producers of spaghetti sauces. Among those who boast they're better than their competitor or competitors are major advertisers such as Pepsi Cola (the taste test), Volvo, Sony and General Motors.

The advertiser v advertiser battles have become less gentlemanly as they have become more frequent. The Drackett Co urged customers to use its Vanish toilet cleaner because rival brands could wreck their plumbing; the Pillsbury Co claimed that rival pizzas tasted 'like cardboard'. *Penthouse*, challenging *Playboy*'s readership claims, showed the *Playboy* rabbit with his nose grown long with the line 'Who's been stretching the truth?' Airwick, in an ad for its rug and room deodoriser, Carpet Fresh, illustrated a man smiling as he smelled its product, another holding his nose as he sniffed rival Arm and Hammer. Federal Express in a swipe at the US Postal Service showed a customer being driven to using its service by two postal clerks who sat around taking no notice of him until they pulled down a shade in his face. Some companies have rushed to court to protect themselves. Alberto Culver took $4.3 million off Gillette and its agency JWT after ads said that its shampoo left hair oily.

In Britain, Volkswagen led the way in comparative advertising by promoting its Polo at the expense of Ford's Fiesta – 'Underneath it's still a Ford'. Other car companies followed. The longest and roughest battle was one involving the unlikely figures of two competing lawn mower companies. One, Qualcast, realising it had to do something to fight off the rival Flymo machine, which works on the hover principle, decided to attack its weak point – its (then) inability to collect cut grass. Qualcast's campaign – 'It's a lot less bovver than a hover' – led to protests to the IBA, front page news stories, and questions in the European Parliament. Flymo retaliated. In one ad it advertised for 'old

Qualcast Concordes' that were 'falling to pieces' offering to take them in part exchange for its own model. At the height of the war, executives at Flymo would refer to their rivals only as 'them'. Robin Wight, of Wight Collins Rutherford Scott, Qualcast's agency, said, 'I regard comparative advertising as a specialist tool. It needs greater skill because things can explode in your face.' Qualcast is convinced the campaign halted Flymo's rising sales. Others believe that the controversy and resultant publicity helped the whole market.

Comparative advertising is still banned or edged with restrictions in many parts of the world, but its use has been spreading steadily. In Europe, it is becoming increasingly widespread. Even in Asia, where brand comparisons have been widely banned, inroads began in 1984 when Thailand decided to allow the practice.

Companies at the receiving end of competitor claims rush protesting to networks' regulatory bodies or the courts with increasing frequency. Often the adjudicators are forced to wade through masses of technical data and 'expert evidence' from both sides. Richard Glitter, vice-president of broadcast standards at NBC, recalled, 'We had one case that turned into a fight between scientists over the validity of using an electron microscope to support a claim in a commercial. It took us weeks to get to the bottom of that one.'

One argument against comparative ads is that it is not difficult for companies to rig the research that lies behind its claims of superiority. One of the bloodiest and most expensive battles has been between Burger King and its rivals McDonald's, the market leader, and Wendy's. Burger King derided competing burgers on grounds of taste, size and the method of cooking (it broils, rivals fry). As an attention grabber and a way of selling more of Burger King's product, the battle was successful – newspapers conducted man-in-the-street interviews, TV stations reported charges and counter charges, and radio talk shows organised their own taste competitions. The battles ended when McDonald's filed for an injunction and, as part of the settlement, Burger King dropped three of its spots. In one, a girl was shown complaining that McDonald's burgers were 20 per cent smaller than Burger King's. What they neglected to say was that their own cost 20 per cent more.

It was left to a columnist in Burger King's home city, Miami, to reveal the 'evidence' that the company had for its central claim that its own burgers were preferred over McDonald's and Wendy's. This, he said, was based on a 'carefully worded' survey that was never released publicly. One question that was asked was whether consumers liked their burgers garnished to individual specifications or already prepared. When, not surprisingly, the majority said they liked to order their own extras, Burger King said that consumers preferred having burgers fixed 'their way' by a three to one margin and implied that only at Burger King could consumers get burgers 'their way'.

That pales, though, beside the comparative advertising of a US company called Jartran which attacked a rival, U-Haul International. Jartran admitted during a lengthy federal court case that it photographically reduced a U-Haul truck so that it would be the same size in an ad as a Jartran truck. U-Haul was awarded $40 million, a record judgment.*

For big advertisers and agencies what is happening at home is not the only concern. Wherever they look they are likely to see advertising regulation (or self-regulation) growing. Consumerism as a movement in both the US and the UK declined in importance in the eighties compared with a decade before, but as a world movement it has continued to grow in assertiveness. Consumers are not the only people exerting pressure, however. Others include civil rights groups, the print media worried about the growth of broadcast ads, and governments and groups concerned about the cultural impact of advertising that emanates from other countries. Nor, by any means, are all the pressures from opponents of capitalism. There are operators of smaller businesses worried about the advertising power of large companies. Professor J. J. Boddewyn, professor of International Business at Baruch College, New York, has pointed out that businessmen themselves are critical of some aspects of advertising, 'particularly in Europe where they resent ads that insult their intelligence, are untruthful or grossly exaggerated, and those directed at children . . .'

Even advertisers who are not directly affected by restrictions abroad are increasingly likely to feel some impact from those controls. 'Business will have to pay greater and better attention to what is happening abroad – at least in some pilot countries such as Canada, Sweden, the United Kingdom and the United States,' believes Professor Boddewyn. 'Nowadays, "problems" and "solutions" travel quite well because of the spread of communications and the existence of international organisations designed to share experiences. When the FTC speaks up about comparison advertising or children ads, other countries listen; and when EEC countries strengthen and standardise their foodstuff labelling requirements (which impact on their advertising), the United States is likely to follow their example sooner or later. In that respect, "global" advertising is more of a reality than we may think – at least as far as its regulation is concerned.'

The Third World is a special battleground for multinational advertisers and their critics. For advertisers the developing nations represent great opportunities. They also offer people real benefits – goods are often better than local products; brand-name protection is real. They bring variety. Despite the often justified criticisms of their actions, the international pharmaceutical companies do introduce life-saving drugs.

* It was a case full of ironies. One was that the ad had been awarded a 'Golden Effie' by the American Marketing Association for effective campaigns. The second was that the case cost U-Haul $2.5 million in costs but as Jartran went into liquidation it was expecting to recover only $2.4 million in total.

Critics, however, find no shortage of charges, many concerning advertising and promotion. Advertising, argued a United Nations technical paper, 'may facilitate the transfer of consumption patterns of developed countries to developing ones, by introducing needs which may not be appropriate, given the income and demand structure in developing countries.' Furthermore, its effect seemed to be strongest on the very poorest 'as exemplified by the Latin American peasant who carries with him a stone painted to look like a transistor radio, because he cannot afford to buy one.'

Wealth is used to advertise 'largely light consumer goods such as tobacco, cosmetics and soft drinks, while basic human needs have not been met', argue other critics who describe the process as 'questionable'. Not only does advertising help sell the wrong things to people who can't afford them, it often does so at prices that are inappropriately high. The UN report referred to Kenya where 'breakfast cereals (from multinationals) can cost one hundred times more than locally available staple foods'. Yet more – the advertisers often use selling techniques that would never be allowed in the developed world. The picture is of some international confidence trickster who as one country polices itself moves on to the next, and then the next and so on . . .

For both sides – the transnational advertisers and their agencies, and their critics – the battle over the sale of baby milk in the Third World has a very special significance. Sylvan M. Barnet Jr, chairman of the advisory council of the International Advertising Association, believes that the World Health Organisation's decision in 1980 to place its weight behind consumer groups' disquiet about the marketing of breast milk substitutes was a watershed. 'Afterwards,' Barnet says, 'it was fair game for soups or for anything reconstituted from water. Now it is pharmaceuticals. The consumer groups are organising. These people are the most rabid of consumers. Now they're talking about "junk" food. Who is going to say what is "junk" food? But they want to write codes. They are crazy.' Advertisers at the American Advertising Federation annual meeting in 1986 were told by a Swedish consultant that they had a 'growing responsibility' to defend the industry against the WHO and others who regarded advertising as a weapon 'to force people to buy things they don't need and don't want.'

No one who looks objectively at the events that led up to the formulation of the WHO Code in 1981 can feel anything but anger and disquiet about the advertising and marketing practices of the multinational companies involved. The companies began concentrating their attention on the Third World as the Western market for baby milk formula reached saturation. Aggressive marketing soon began to have its impact: breast feeding declined, the use of formula increased.

Warnings began to be sounded as far back as the 1950s. They became louder and more frequent throughout the 1960s and 1970s and in 1977 resulted in a consumer boycott of Nestlé, the largest of the thirty or so international companies involved. The charges against the companies – and especially Nestlé which held 50 per cent of the market – was that because of their tactics in areas of illiteracy and great poverty babies were being harmed or even killed. Mothers were spending money they could not afford and were then overdiluting to save cost and thus causing malnutrition. (According to Unicef, Third World bottle-fed babies are two to three times more likely to suffer malnutrition than breast-fed ones). Even worse, unsanitary conditions – bad water, unsterilised bottles, no refrigeration – were causing formula-fed babies to get sick, sometimes die. Dr Derrick B. Jelliffe, of the UCLA School of Public Health, coined a name for it, 'commerciagenic disease', due to indiscriminate advertising and promotion.

Given what was at stake, advertisements were appalling in their appeals. One, in India, showed a mother and baby close up, their noses pressed together. 'Easy to digest Angel baby milk food is as gentle as your love,' said the message. 'Give your baby the benefit of modern research,' urged a Pakistani ad. Pictures in advertisements showed beautiful babies in the arms of upper-class women. Formulas were presented as scientific and upmarket. Fears were planted: 'Mother's milk is sometimes deficient in providing the complete nutritional need,' said the ad for the product S26. Breast feeding was denigrated as dated, inferior, unchic. A woman was shown with her child at her breast. 'For a woman to feed her baby like this every four hours just isn't convenient,' read the text. Nor was it only advertising. Samples of formula were handed out in hospitals by 'mothercraft nurses' who were really saleswomen in costume. Companies bought the co-operation of doctors with gifts, travel and equipment.

In facing criticisms, the companies showed what now seems to have been an amazing insensitivity, not just in moral terms but in knowing how much they could get away with. When they reacted in concert, it was with public-relations responses, not with any acceptance that something might be wrong after all.

In 1981, the WHO Code was adopted (over US objections). It recommended that direct advertising of infant formulas be prohibited and that consumers be informed that breast feeding is best. The following year Nestlé bowed to pressure and announced it would stop advertising and sales promotion practices which discourage breast feeding.

Skirmishes continue (there are accusations that the code is broken) but there can be no doubt who lost and who won. Both sides see wider lessons. The consumer activists say that the message for international marketers should be clear: they should not use the absence of sophisticated regulations in the Third World to try to get away with practices they would not dare attempt in the developed world. One consultant has suggested international marketers should adopt a simple rule of thumb: 'If you can't get away with it at home, it's better not to try it elsewhere.'

Many international advertisers, though, see a different message. Whatever the rights and wrongs of the baby-milk campaign (and some argue that for Third World women it's a pyrrhic victory in that activists would have done much better ensuring accurate and helpful advertising rather than bringing about a situation in which it is withdrawn) the result is that consumer organisations have tasted a glorious victory – and they like it. In consequence consumer groups are looking around for more work, anxious to engage in new battles. Health Action International, a Brussels-based consumer lobbying organisation, for example, is pushing for a code for the pharmaceutical industry similar to the infant formula one.

Multinational advertisers and their agencies believe this could have disastrous and devastating effects. The industry has fought back with increasing force and sophistication everywhere, both in developed and in developing countries.

The UK advertising industry was instrumental along with, notably, the European Association of Advertising Agencies and the International Chamber of Commerce, in pulling the teeth of EEC rules for dealing with misleading advertising throughout Europe. The rules, approved in 1984, had been under discussion for nearly ten years. The advertising industry's opposition forced the commission to drop many of its initial proposals. Originally, proposed rules covered both 'misleading' and 'unfair' advertisements and insisted on legal remedies against offenders. By the time the rules were finalised, 'unfair' had been dropped altogether, the issues of comparative advertising and corrective advertising had been left to individual countries, and complaints could be dealt with by either a court or by a body like the UK's self-regulatory ASA. Philip J. Circus, legal adviser to the Institute of Practitioners in Advertising in London, referred to the final directive as a 'pale imitation of the first draft' and pointed out that it was a 'tribute to the tenacious fight of the ad industry associations across Europe'.

In the United States, the ad industry began being more aggressive from 1978. The 'trigger' was FTC proposals to ban TV advertisements directed at children under eight and of sugared food products to those under twelve, and to prescribe the words that could be used in advertising over-the-counter medications. The industry carried the fight to Washington, the courts and the public.

The International Advertising Association's regular 'Intelligence Summary', sent out to members in eighty countries, provides a running guide to the battlegrounds. Issue Number 32, for example, lists more than thirty items concerning legislation/regulation either of a general nature or relating specifically to tobacco, alcohol, children or sexism. More than twenty different countries were involved, from the Philippines ('Bill calls for creation of Consumers Board of Advertising with powers to pre-clear all ads . . .') to Israel ('New law will ban cigarette advertising on radio and TV, in cinemas and on public transport . . .').

The IAA, originally formed in New York in 1938 as the New York Export Advertising Association, expanded into Europe with the multinationals and their agencies in the fifties and sixties, then into Latin America and in the 1980s began 'exploding' into Asia, the Pacific, the Middle East and Africa. Its mission, says Barnet, 'is to keep track of these restrictions and to fight them in Strasbourg and Brussels and for the rest of the world in the UN system.'

The advertising industry frequently sees dangerous, sometimes sinister, types with dubious motives behind the movement for increased restrictions. Barnet voiced a popular view. Like a number of other Americans I spoke with, he saw the battles over advertising restrictions as part of a wider struggle between the free market and Marxist economies. Advertising, he argued, 'is the visible part of the private sector.' At the same time, he added, the irony was that communist countries were themselves using advertising more and more. 'It is very exciting,' Barnet said, 'I know who is going to win. It is going to be the market economy.'

Some admen referred me to the example of Greece where the administration of the Socialist prime minister, Andreas Papandreou, blamed advertising for the country's high inflation. The government was said to have harassed the industry at every opportunity.

Robert Goldstein, of Procter and Gamble, also sees this as 'one of the common threads at least in countries in the West – that it is an anti-capitalist movement'. In the Third World he thinks advertising is attacked as 'the most visible symbol of Western products and Western culture'. It provides a focal point for the 'several grievances' the Third World has against the West. Goldstein sees a number of other common threads, including 'so-called consumer protection'. That, he says, attacks 'real or imagined grievances against its particular standards or its particular preferences . . . The bottom line is, "We the unelected feel we have a right to substitute our view for the public's either because the public is stupid or incompetent." ' Goldstein gave the example of a 'leading person' at the FTC. 'I had lunch with him once. What he said was "I cannot believe that if all the money spent on candy bars was spent on peas, beans, carrots . . ."' Goldstein waved his arms in disbelief. 'Catering to *his* wishes was more important than catering for the wishes of the public . . .' Goldstein adds two others: advertising *is* 'an intrusive kind of practice' subject to scrutiny and criticism because it is there, and sometimes it *is* misleading – 'Just as there are some shoddy products, there are some shoddy ads.'

Some admen argue that the politicians who promise restrictions are no more than cynical vote-getters. Others point to the bureaucrat and his desire to produce both paper and legislation. Peter Rennie, chairman of the ITCA copy committee, has attacked 'the bureaucracy of the EEC where law-making has become a sport – a bureaucracy which is staffed in large measure by people in search of a cause with which to justify their existence.' Philip Circus claims that every official employed by the European Commission manages to account for 233 sheets of paper each working day. 'If all the paper produced by the commission in a year were laid end to end it would go round the world forty times.'

Still others see a new and especially dangerous kind of opponent, those who, they say, focus their campaigning on one issue and really do appear to believe that it is the single most important issue in the world. Mike Waterson, of Britain's Advertising Association, instances animal rights campaigners and those opposing smoking and drinking as examples. 'We are now getting press releases by the RSPCA about animals in advertising,' he said. 'Advertising always gets it in the neck. You don't see the animals in the laboratory. You do see the hairspray ads. You don't see people getting drunk. You do see the advertisements.'

Waterson, a trim, neatly-bearded economist, is a familiar fighter for ad freedom on several continents. In Washington, he has testified for the US ad industry before a senate commerce committee, assuring it that there was no reason for the United States to further restrict cigarette advertisements in an attempt to reduce smoking because this had already been tried in Western Europe and had been unsuccessful. In Australia, he has argued advertising's case with two state premiers and taken the battle direct to the public on TV and radio in the wake of a Labour government's election victory.

Like many people, advertisers and advertising agencies often say things privately that it would be 'bad PR' to exclaim publicly. This is one of the values of trade associations and of men like Waterson: they can say these things for them. Thus Waterson wrote on one occasion, 'The Advertising Association does not offer its views on the treatment of cancer to either the British population or Government. Yet the BMA is not only happy to comment on advertising matters, but does so in language of an extreme and intemperate nature. The BMA has urged a complete ban on tobacco advertising without a shred of evidence to back the wildly exaggerated claims it has made.'

Sitting across the desk from Waterson in his small office overlooking the main entrance to London's Victoria Station, it is easy to see why he is in such demand as the industry's freedom fighter. He manages to sound both intense and reasonable. The words pour out so fast that there's a fascination in wondering how and when he will draw breath. He *wants* to convince. The setting – small, cluttered with no signs of the luxury and self-cosseting of ad agency offices – adds to the conviction that he's doing this because he believes, not for the money. It's a persuasive combination.

Waterson was previously a consultant economist with Urwick Orr and Partners, the well-known management consultants. Much of his work was abroad. He then joined Guinness, 'largely because I married a French girl and I wanted a setdown job.' There, he said, he found himself as part of a team looking at whether advertising was working. After six years he joined the AA as director of research.

There is a memento of the Guinness days on his walls – two ads that were meant for use in the Cameroons but were banned by the company as being too erotic. In them a young light brown woman holds a glass of Guinness. Her nipples show through her clothes. She licks her lips sexily; the expression is one of open invitation. Waterson explains their history; he has obviously done so many times before – the ads are a good talking point. There is another picture, of a cycle race in which the contestants are nude women; he doesn't volunteer information about this and I don't ask.

Many of Waterson's public pronouncements have been specifically about the advertising of tobacco and of alcohol – drink advertising, particularly, is a special interest. But his arguments – basically that advertising has no impact on *total consumption* of products and that, therefore, bans don't achieve anything – are used to fight restrictions over a wider area. The argument advanced has been called 'the domino theory of advertising control'. In essence it says: today, control over products like tobacco and alcohol; tomorrow, a whole range of others from confectionery to cars. Those who argue for controls are seen as Dracula-like: let them taste blood, the argument goes, and there just won't be enough necks in the world. It is an argument believed by many admen. It is also, it should be added, one that the beleaguered drink and tobacco industries especially happily encourage in their search for allies.

Waterson sees Britain as being the centre of the fight against the restrictionist lobby. He says this is so for a simple reason: 'We had the attacks first. In America the attacks on drink have not been very fierce despite the example of Prohibition. Here it has been active for the last five years.' There has also, he adds, been a 'great avalanche' of attacks in Britain on the advertising of other products. Much of it, he believes, is a reflection of the British attitude to selling: 'Here there is a much deeper ingrained feeling that trade is bad. The word "salesman" is still a dirty word here. We call them "representatives" . . .' Because of these attacks, the advertising industry in Britain has long been gathering together all the research arguments to rebut the restrictionists. Therefore, when advertisers in other countries found themselves under attack, the British industry was able to help. That very morning, Waterson volunteered, he had sent 300 copies of his monograph 'Advertising and Alcohol Abuse' to the US Senate.

Waterson talks about the anti-advertising lobby in curiously detached tones, not unlike a military man giving a briefing on the enemy. He, too, sees a 'common thread – the anti-capitalist thing'. 'The lobby against advertising has always been there,' he explains. 'It is completely multinational.' The 'fundamental reason', he continues, is 'advertising must visibly express our free market system, so anyone who is against the free market is against advertising.' Recently, though, he says, there has been a change of approach. 'The general attacks on advertising have to some extent dried up. This is because the Galbraith view that advertising is wasted is discredited.' Jimmy Carter, it emerged, was much responsible for this. President Carter – 'he will go down as one of advertising's greatest friends' – had started deregulating from 1977. As a consequence, opticians in America had begun advertising. 'The FTC sent out people with bad eyes. They found a 34 per cent difference between the lowest prices in states where opticians could advertise and ones where they could not. That single finding destroyed everyone's feelings about how advertising worked. The reason in retrospect is that without free information you can charge what you like.'

However, that proof of the positive nature of advertising, claimed Waterson, hasn't stopped the attacks, only changed their nature. 'In its place has come a whole string of (attacks on) specifics – tobacco, alcohol, confectionery, prescription medicine . . . It is much more difficult to refute because it is based around the product rather than the advertising. Although everyone thinks of cigarettes as being evil and drink as only evil when taken to excess, the arguments about advertising them are identical. They are that increases in consumption are bad and that, as advertising increases consumption, advertising is bad.' Waterson doesn't believe that more or less consumption does necessarily mean a larger or smaller problem when it comes to drink. A growth in a country's wine consumption, for example, he says, could mean that 'people who drink bitter have become wealthy and drink half a bottle of wine. Therefore, it could mean that people who drink modestly are drinking a little bit more.'

Waterson's major argument, however, is that advertising *doesn't* increase the total consumption of items like tobacco or alcohol which are 'mature' products in marketing terms. This means they have been on the market for a considerable time as distinct from new ones which are still finding their customers. 'We have gone to very considerable lengths to look at the research. We believe that of all the studies done in this world – we have fifty or sixty on file – only one or two suggest advertising has an effect on mature markets. We say that the evidence suggests that advertising doesn't have effect on mature markets.' All it does, he claims, is work at the brand level – in other words the users of product 'X' are persuaded to switch to product 'Y'.

He makes a rare pause, either for impact or to rest his voice which is hoarse ('I was giving a talk last night'), and then delivers what is obviously meant to be the knockout punch. 'If it were true that advertising increases the sales of drinks and tobacco it would increase the sales of motor cars too, and thus increase the GNP. The argument carried to its logical conclusions is fatuous.'

Others dispute this point (as do some the claim that the example of the American opticians proves that advertising necessarily must mean cheaper products or services). Waterson himself volunteers that a lot of people in the advertising business don't particularly like the argument 'because they say advertising sells.' The anti-lobby, he adds, gets 'a tremendous amount of publicity', but he does not regard this as the significant point. Their views do not hold sway in 'places where it matters'. In Parliament, he says, there is 'well over 60 per cent not anti-tobacco advertising and over 80 per cent not anti-drinking advertising. We know these totals have been increasing in our favour over the last four years. The fact that you see endless articles about some issues doesn't mean the legislators feel that way.'

He doesn't spell it out but the inference is that the Advertising Association, whose function is mainly lobbying, is largely responsible for that. Generally, he adds, the AA is not unhappy about regulations in Britain. 'I think in general terms the UK control system is believed by the individual, consumers and government to be a very advanced system that is better than any other system in the world.' The AA, he adds, is a 'very low profile outfit'. However, things could change. 'If it comes to the worst, if it looks as though drink advertising will be banned, we will go public in a way we never have before.'

In its struggle against restrictions, the advertising industry has begun to argue that the ability to advertise is a fundamental human right. What is at stake is not the sale of frozen peas but FREEDOM. 'It is *not* the case that advertising exists by courtesy of the state or of tolerance,' said Peter Thomson, director general of the Advertising Standards Authority. ' "Commercial speech" is no less free speech than journalistic speech or political speech.' 'Only as a last resort should a category of advertising be banned,' argues the AA's *Speaking up for Advertising*. 'Not only is a ban a restriction on free speech, but carefully regulated advertising can both promote acceptable use of product and warn of any inherent dangers.'

In pursuit of that argument admen quote from Article 19 of the United Nations Universal Declaration of Human Rights ('Everyone has the right to freedom of opinion and expression: this right includes freedom to hold opinions without interference and to seek, receive and impart information and ideas through any media and regardless of frontiers') and from Article 10 of the European Convention for the Protection of Human Rights and Fundamental Freedoms. The question, says the IAA's chairman, Sylvan M. Barnet, is 'whether we can find a legal base to protect advertising'. In the United States advertising has been described as having second-class protection under the First Amendment of the constitution which guarantees freedom of speech. Guidelines were established by the US Supreme Court in 1980 which said that the government could restrict advertising but that government interest must be substantial (e.g. the health of its citizens must be at risk), that regulations must directly advance public interest, and regulations must not be more restrictive than necessary. However, six years later on a five-four vote the Supreme Court sent shudders throughout the advertising industry when it ruled Puerto Rico could ban certain advertising for casino gambling. It marked the first time that the Supreme Court had upheld a ban on truthful, accurate advertising. The counsel for the American Association of Advertising Agencies, David Versfelt, commented, 'It's a dark day for Madison Avenue.' However, the right to advertise was still widely seen as a basic freedom. The chairman of the Congressional subcommittee that oversees the FTC, Rep. Thomas Luken, commented on calls for a ban on tobacco advertising, 'Advertising is a form of speech and freedom of speech is guaranteed by the Constitution . . . I see no basis for imposing restrictions which abridge that right.'

As to the European Convention, advertisers grew much excited by an opinion written by two lawyers for the International Chamber of Commerce. The ASA's annual report for 1984-5 summed up, 'Although the right is qualified by reference to the interests of national security, the protection of health and morals and the like, it is the view of Lester and Pannick [the two lawyers] that "arbitrary or unnecessary restrictions on advertising are likely to constitute a breach of Community law . . ."' Philip Circus enthused, 'The message now is that advertising can claim its due right to free speech. It is up to those bureaucrats and pressure groups who wish to see it [i.e. advertising] restricted to justify their case. The ad industry has been given a very big drum, and it must bang it with all its might.'

Others, including many advertising men, were less optimistic. However, none could deny that the *idea* of advertising as information (and thus entitled to protection) was an attractive one. The authors of a paper on restrictions presented to the IAA said:

> Describing advertising as 'information' is entirely accurate and 'rings true'. Indeed, based on the notion of advertising as information, arguments against restrictions could be successful in a number of Third World countries influenced by Anglo-American traditions. There is solid support in international, regional, and domestic law for protecting advertising as information. At the same time, the unconventionality of arguing that restrictions violate international human rights might catch the proponents of such restrictions 'off guard' . . . Elevating a discussion of restrictions on advertising to that of international information flow and human rights could shift the terms of the debate and place the burden of justifying restrictions on those seeking to erect barriers to advertising.

To such claims some consumers at least have argued that far from having limited freedom advertisers already have more than most people in that they can *buy* time on TV.

The fight is not all one way. A major reason for specific restrictions has always been that some ads – or the products they promote – contravene 'good taste'. As times change, so does what is acceptable.

In 1984, a woman appeared on TV screens in St Louis, Missouri, and talked about how she had learned to trust disposable enemas when she was having her first baby. 'I still trust it to give me fast relief from constipation,' she said in that particularly convincing tone of sincerity associated with TV commercials. Enemas were one of those 'unmentionables' of advertising. The company waited for the viewer response. The world did not collapse. The all-powerful three TV networks were convinced; they, too, would take enema ads. The CB Fleet Co, of Lynchburg, Virginia, the company which had already pioneered television advertising for disposable douches, had broken another advertising barrier.

What society regards as acceptable has altered out of all recognition in the last two or three decades. It is hard, for example, to credit that it was only just over twenty years ago that court battles were fought over the publication in the UK of *Lady Chatterley's Lover* by people who really did seem to believe a nation's morals were at stake. It is, perhaps, even harder to believe that once not only were advertisements for toilet paper banned, but so too were displays.

Even today in Britain toilet paper is advertised in a cloying way. Bowater-Scott's Andrex toilet tissue – £100 million worth of loo paper a year and the seventh largest grocery brand in the country – uses a soft and cuddly puppy in its ads. The puppy plays with the roll to illustrate that it's soft, strong and value for money. A Martian placed in front of a TV screen would never guess what it is actually *used* for. It is interesting to compare the approach with Germany. There Hakle Feucht, in ads for its moist toilet tissue, urges, 'Do something for your better half.' One ad shows rows of line-drawings of different bottom shapes. Another sketch shows bottoms on a lavatory seat with the line, 'What the dermatologist recommends to his family.'

Taste, subjective though it is, is an important ingredient in advertising regulation. The IBA's code includes a blanket exclusion under clause twelve which says, 'No advertisement should offend against good taste or decency or be offensive to public feeling.' In the mid eighties some forbidden areas in European TV were matrimonial agencies (the Italian state station RAI, the IBA and the Irish RTE), loans (RAI), employment agencies (France, RAI, RTE, IBA), war toys (the second German channel 2DF), margarine (France), and betting (IBA, RTE). Under the banner of good taste, newspapers and magazines have refused to publish ads for products ranging from KY jelly – a lubricant used for intercourse and tampon insertion – to incontinence aids. *Modern Maturity* banned the latter on the specific grounds that they showed the downside of ageing.

To show how subjective it all is, it is perhaps worth noting that publication *was* found for an ad for a California mortuary which capital-ised on the 1985 Mexican earthquake disaster with the proclamation, 'If, God forbid, LA is next our commitment will remain unshaken.' And for another, in South Africa, which showed a woman, dress torn open, collapsed across a sofa, apparently dead or dying, a knife shown nearby. The ad was for a sofa padding – the thief had been searching for it!

'Unmentionables' may be more unmentionable or unshowable in some countries than in others. An ad showing a small child's bare bottom was withdrawn in Italy after it was ruled 'licentious', but ones showing women's bare breasts are common there and acceptable. Aubry Wilson and Christopher West in an article on the marketing of 'unmen-tionables' in the *Harvard Business Review* defined them as 'products, services or concepts that for reasons of delicacy, decency, morality, or even fear tend to elicit reactions of distaste, disgust, offence, or outrage when mentioned or when openly presented.' They include a wide range including personal hygiene products, burial arrangements and other death-related services, and certain types of medical treatment (such as for haemorrhoids). Advertisers have special problems. They also need, wrote Wilson and West, to be 'hyperactive to overcome the resistance threshold and, in addition, must develop specialised techniques to circumvent the problems caused by unmentionability'.

In the Depression years, the 'technique' adopted in American print ads for personal hygiene was a mixture of vulgarity and an attempt to shame. Thus, 'His heart quickened at the soft fragrance of her cheeks, BUT HER SHOES HID A SORRY CASE OF ATHLETE'S FOOT.' In ads for indigestion remedies, sufferers burped into the reader's face. Close-ups of women's hairless armpits dominated magazine pages: 'His quick eye saw that the soft white beauty of her underarm . . .' Bad breath wrecked romance – a Listerine ad showed a lovely woman in distress and the words, 'HER Honeymoon – and It Should Have Been MINE!'

Fifty years later they seem tasteless, not so much in subject as in approach. Today's ads for unmentionables, in the US and the UK at least, are mostly discreet, anxious not to offend. Nevertheless, the list of taboo products that make the giant step over to advertising acceptability continues to grow yearly. Britain relaxed its TV ban on advertisements for haemorrhoid treatment at the end of 1986, allowed advertising for a cystitis-relief product the same year, and gave per-mission for commercials for incontinence aids the following year – although not between 4.30 p.m. and 9 p.m., viewing time for children and families.

The classic 'unmentionable' has long been the condom, AIDS and the pressure to allow its promotion notwithstanding. The *Harvard Business Review* authors noted:

. . . its use during the most intimate of human activities has led to high unmentionability. The Victorian era alone produced a strong and lingering association between the sheath and other unmention-ables such as illicit premarital sex, surrounding it with an aura of sin and guilt. Its very prophylactic properties of preventing venereal infection added to its unmentionability, since venereal disease was not a risk in marital sex, and reinforced the sheath's connotation of clandestine sex.* On top of this, the distribution channels of back-street shops and surreptitious sales to men in dirty raincoats produced total unmentionability.

Contraceptive advertising over the last two decades provides a mirror view of public attitudes, complete with the appropriate doses of hypoc-risy. In the UK, the ads for Durex condoms in the mid 1960s were couched in terms that were so coy that it is a wonder readers even knew what was being advertised. The word 'contraception' did not begin to appear until the late sixties, and then the ads were low key. One, published in the *Sunday People*, said, 'A young couple join hands. He puts a ring on her finger. And the conspiracy of silence begins . . .' There was a breakthrough when Durex's manufacturers, the London Rubber Company, felt able to refer to the product as a 'protective' and later still when it could be called a 'sheath'.

In the early 1970s, the Pharmaceutical Society decided chemist shops could allow contraceptives to be displayed openly although it was three years before the nationwide chain, Boots, decided it was safe to do so. The word 'Durex' was still not a polite word to speak aloud. Its makers set out to 'normalise' it. The company sponsored a racing car with the idea of emblazoning the Durex name across Britain. The BBC decided to protect public morals. First it refused to show the main race at Silverstone unless Durex signs were covered; later it pulled out of the Race of Champions at Brands Hatch because of the 'generally unacceptable volume of advertising on cars'. Nothing had been said previously about the names of cigarette brands.

In the late seventies, as fears about the pill – the condom's major rival – increased, advertising was directed to women. By the 1980s, the ads, in terms of what had gone before, edged out of the closet. One headline argued, 'You don't make love twenty-four hours a day, so why use twenty-four hours a day contraceptive?' It was, however, only a step. In 1984, a rival, Warner Lambert, launched its own brand of condom with ads that carried the headline, 'Ultrasure. The only sheath with an effective spermicide where it really counts.' Several newspapers refused to carry them, including the *Daily* and *Sunday Telegraphs*, the *Sunday Times*, *The Times*, the *Sunday Express* and the *Daily Mail*. The

* In France, it is still not acceptable to call the sheath a *contraceptif*; the term is *preservatif*, thus suggesting the use should be for hygiene reasons, an attitude, of course, which accords with that of many other countries since the AIDS epidemic began.

Daily Mail had previously refused Durex ads on the grounds it was a 'family newspaper'. Perhaps that was not as ironic as Rupert Murdoch's *Sun*, objecting to using the word 'sheath'. Or *Playboy* which turned down an ad for Durex's then new black condom, Black Shadow.

The London Rubber Company's commercial general manager, Janice Morgan, told me that she was 'heartened' by how far things had progressed. 'I believe prejudices are breaking down. I think the days of objections to words like spermicidal are gone. Let's face it, it's still a personal, intimate thing. You accept the climate in which you work.'

In the United States as in the UK, condoms only emerged from under the drugstore counter at the beginning of the seventies. Five years later Trojans, the leading brand, went on TV, appearing on KNTV, ABC's affiliate in San José. After a flood of complaints, the commercial was taken off the air by the station. Press coverage of the ban produced a backlash and the ads were allowed back on the air.* The experiment was not repeated, however.

In the mid 1980s, contraceptives remained one of the last remaining personal products banned by all three US networks and by most local TV and radio stations. Donald Wear Jr, vice-president of policy at CBS, explained his network's reasoning in a letter to a pressure group: 'On the CBS television network we strive to entertain and inform but not offend. While some believe that . . . contraceptive advertising on a national level is needed, a great many others would find this kind of advertising an intrusion on their moral and religious beliefs and take offence.'

The AIDS epidemic – and more specifically the fact that condoms provided one of the only defences against its spread – forced changes in policy. AIDS campaigns throughout the world promoted their use. 'Trust is good, condoms are better', proclaimed the German government's campaign. A Norwegian commercial showed the letter 'A' rejecting a sexual advance until the letter 'I' put on a condom. A Swedish advertisement could not have been more direct: it had a girl holding out a condom to a man removing his trousers and saying, 'If you don't use a condom, there's nothing doing.'

In the United States beginning in 1987, a number of television stations began taking ads, as did many magazines. The radio and TV ban was lifted in Britain. One company president was quoted in *Time* as saying that AIDS was 'a condom marketer's dream', a statement he later claimed had been taken out of context but not, let it be noted, before his advertising agency (Della Femina, Travisano and Partners) resigned the account. His language might have been intemperate, but what he said was true. An article in a trade magazine began, 'No one doubts that the AIDS crisis is an enormous marketing opportunity for the

---

* One newspaper reputedly produced the memorable headline: 'First Rubber Commercial Snaps.'

condom industry . . .' Sales battles developed. LRC Products launched a 'glamour' product, Durex Gold, aimed at the sixteen to twenty-five-year-old market, with the advertising line, 'When a man loves a woman.' A small company producing a line called Jiffi sheaths used the memorable slogan, 'Real men come in a Jiffi.'

However, the change was less than it might have seemed. British TV might have decided to allow ads, but the rules were strict enough (no giving offence, no showing unwrapped condoms and so on), to cause one commentator to write that no one would be able instantly to recognise what the advertiser was selling. American stations insisted the message should be disease prevention, not birth control. Time Inc's decision to take condom ads in its seven magazines including *People* and *Sports Illustrated* carried with it the proviso that they should 'address health and prevention of disease'.

Before all this happened Spain was having a mini-revolution as far as condom advertising was concerned. An ad for US-made Prime condoms was allowed on the state run national TV, RTVE. Viewers saw twenty seconds of a series of stills showing two-, three- and four-child families and finally a couple with no children. A voice announced, 'They are thinking about it'. The director general of the advertising agency, RSCG, exclaimed, 'It's a landmark in the history of Spanish advertising.'

The fact that the ad appeared in Spain, a Catholic country with a long history of sexual puritanism, illustrates that societies do not always take the expected attitude to advertising sensitive products.

To the English at least – who see the Germans as humourless, regimented people – there is surprise in seeing a German ad in which a man rides a moped with an enormous pack of contraceptives under his arm. But France and Italy provide, perhaps, the two most startling examples. France, with its reputation for sexuality, has a very liberal attitude to contraceptive advertising. Right? In fact, completely wrong. Until the AIDS crisis the French did not allow condom advertising of any kind (and now it is aimed at preventing disease). Italy, although Catholic, allows lightly clad couples to roam happily on screen beaches as voices proclaim, 'Good loving is good for love.' A poster ad for a condom has only two words, albeit highly significant ones, 'Travel Safely.' In a print ad, for a brand called Sensipan, a prince kneels over a Sleeping Beauty, and the message is that he will need help in order to wake her!

Not far behind contraception as a taboo is what the trade in Britain calls the Sanpro market. Feminine hygiene products are an enormous business: over £100 million a year in the UK, nearly $900 million in the US. They are an essential repeat purchase with an intense brand loyalty, making them prime subjects for advertising – where it is allowed.

What the manufacturers all want are young first-time users. They know that once young women find a product with which they are happy they are likely to continue buying it. In the UK, until late 1985 the most attractive media to them, television, was barred. The IBA allowed a test period in 1980 to gauge audience reaction. It attracted 1,200 letters of complaint. Five years later the Authority tried again, allowing a two-year test period – but only on Channel 4. Harry Theobalds, IBA's controller of advertising, said, 'By nature of its programming, Channel 4 tends to attract the sort of mature audience that won't be shocked or embarrassed by this sort of commercial.' There were, however, stringent conditions. No unwrapped towels or tampons could be shown on screen, there was to be no suggestion of social insecurity, and no use of potentially offensive words such as 'odour'.

America had taken this path ten years earlier, allowing feminine hygiene products onto network TV from 1975. Before the decision was taken, test ads were screened and viewers were polled for their reactions. Over the years the words of US commercials have become increasingly graphic. By the mid 1980s the networks were still receiving a 'fair amount' of anti mail although one, NBC, said it was decreasing. Taboos still exist, however. One was broken in 1985 when Tambrands were allowed to use the word 'periods' in an ad for its Tampax brand on ABC and NBC. It was preceded by tests in six cities. Viewers were asked to respond to the ad in which the scene shifted from a woman standing by a locker to a ballet rehearsal room. 'Do you change your life for one week because of your period?' asked the ad. However, the initial reaction of one network, CBS, was to reject it – 'period' was too slangy; the network would show the ad if the words 'menstrual cycle' were substituted.

In the UK, print ads have reflected changing acceptability. The advertisements for feminine hygiene products have generally fallen into two groups: those illustrating the product and those showing women (often dressed in white) enjoying a glamorous life style, riding horses, playing tennis or about to go on stage. In 1985, the agency Bartle Bogle Hegarty produced a new campaign for Lilia-White, the market leaders, which included an ad showing a young man clad in frilly pink lingerie, his hand clasped to his head in anguish. The headline read, 'Have you ever wondered how men would carry on if they had periods?' Arrows pointed to parts of the man's body with comments such as, 'How can I go to the Cup Final when my head's throbbing?' . . . 'Don't expect me to shave with these spots all over my chin' . . . 'I can't possibly clean the car with this nagging backache.' The copy concluded, 'After 104 years in the business, we aren't naïve enough to imagine we could make your period a lot of laughs, exactly. But we're certain we can make it less of a (dare we say it?) bl**dy nuisance.'

'Unmentionable' products may represent huge markets or comparatively small ones. The market for incontinence products in the United States, for example, is already worth $250 million a year but according to industry analysts will grow to a staggering $6 billion. That, say, for graveyards may be tiny in comparison. Nevertheless, they all share the need to advertise to protect their market. Fred C. Hill, the owner of three cemeteries in south-eastern Pennsylvania, is suffering like the rest of his business from the fact that his customers are living longer, that when they die they're more likely to be cremated, and that his expenses are rising. He sees advertising and marketing as crucial because there is no impulse buying. 'Dad never gets up in the morning and says to Mom, "It's a sunny day, let's go buy some cemetery lots,"' he told the *Wall Street Journal*. Funeral ads are often folksy. One from Restland Inc, Dallas, shows a widower with his mongrel dog on a porch, talking about how his wife had persuaded him to buy a plot. Then she'd died. He would have found it hard to cope by himself, he tells viewers.

The fact that a product or service is considered 'unmentionable', though, means ads for them *are* distasteful to some of those who see them. These people may number millions. This, in itself, presents a special problem to the whole advertising industry. It is one that intrigues Burton Manning of J. Walter Thompson. In the US, he points out, the market is so enormous that even a relatively tiny number of customers responding to an ad's blandishments can constitute good business.

'The implications of that are interesting to me. It's the paradox, the pinchers we are all in. There's a list of things people don't want to see. People fought to kick haemorrhoids off the air . . . Feminine hygiene shouldn't be allowed on – they find the very product offensive . . . Laxatives . . . In certain parts of the country, brassieres.' The 'pinchers', says Manning, is that those who don't want to see some products are often the majority. However, the people *not* turned off by haemorrhoids advertising are those with haemorrhoids . . . 'A woman having menstrual cramps is not going to be offended by an advertisement that tells her it can help. We know the sales refute that they [the people who directly want the product] think it is so terrible. However, the majority are disgusted, infuriated, angry – so it's another thing that goes into their total judgment of advertising.'

Because America is so big, concludes Manning, an advertiser can risk offending the majority of people to reach the minority that he is after. 'I always ask myself what I would do if I was that entrepreneur, what I would do if what I had was offensive to 95 per cent but without advertising to them I wouldn't get the 5 per cent. I think if my life, my future was tied up in my product I would do what others do. I would say, "It is legal, it is a fine product. I am going to advertise." '

'Unmentionable' advertising, as magazines and networks know, is likely to offend precisely the people who are most vocal. Manning says advertisers have become 'more realistic' about such letters now. '[In the past] if the advertiser got a couple of negative letters he would pull [his ad] off the air. Now he will assess whether it really is damaging . . .'

The other plus for the industry in its battle for the freedom to advertise is the entry – as advertisers – of groups previously barred from promoting themselves. The American opticians mentioned earlier have been joined by other groups to whom the very idea of self-advertisement was once an 'unmentionable' in itself.

In 1978, a fifty-four-year-old, 300-pound Madison, Wisconsin, lawyer rose bare-chested from a lake in a TV commercial, spoke one line, and proved the world as it applied to the professions and advertising had changed. The line was, 'If you're in over your head because of bad debt, we'll put you through bankruptcy for $250.' The lawyer, Ken Hur, went on to even more tasteless commercials: he even dreamed up one in which a convict died in the electric chair but only after telling viewers, 'I should have called a legal clinic.' Lights on his chest then lit up with Hur's number.

Hur's on-screen antics might make most of his fellow professionals squirm with embarrassment, but he is a symbol of sorts. Starting with the US, and increasingly throughout the rest of the world, the professionals are now being allowed to advertise. A *Focus* magazine round-up in October 1984 showed accountants were allowed to advertise with no restrictions in Belgium and Switzerland and with some restrictions in Finland, Greece, Italy, Sweden and the UK. Architects could advertise with restrictions in Finland, Greece, Italy, the Netherlands, Sweden, Switzerland and the UK, doctors in Finland, Greece, Italy, Spain and Sweden, and lawyers in Finland, Italy, Sweden and the UK. An *Advertising Age* survey the previous month showed three countries where all four professional groups are allowed to advertise: Australia, (Sydney), the United States and Brazil (the only one with no restrictions attached). Two others, Canada and the UK, allowed accountants, architects and lawyers, but no doctors.

Although the total amount of money involved is small compared with the advertising of products, it is a significant and important development. First, it enrols in the advertising process many of those who have often been most contemptuous of it. Second, it brings in consumer lobbyists on the side of advertising. Before the UK's solicitors were allowed to advertise, the Consumers' Association's legal adviser, David Tench, was arguing that it would give better information to the public and open the profession to healthy competition: 'The only thing worse than misleading advertising is a prohibition of advertising.'

The change is so recent and at such an early stage that it is easy to underrate how radical it really is. The Bar Council in 1970 expressed what could have been the feeling of all the professions at the time: 'Advertising,' it told the Monopolies Commission, 'is generally regarded as inconsistent with the whole conception of a professional man as one who joins his professional colleagues in the performance of a service to the community, who is bound by strict rules of conduct in his relations with his colleagues and his clients and who recognises a higher duty than that of a mere compliance with his client's wishes whatever they may be.' Many professional men in both the US and the UK are still uneasy about the changes, still seeing advertising with all its implications of selling and competition, as alien to their 'place in society'. Chief Justice Warren Burger made it clear he regards it as huckstering, diminishing the role of the lawyer. Nevertheless, ads *have* become more and more common. Lawyers spent an estimated $60 million on TV alone in the US in 1987. One attorney pointed out that advertising is now 'a must' for anyone just beginning.

Professional bodies in the UK imposed their own restrictions on their members' advertising, but even here further liberalisation soon became apparent. Solicitors, for example, were initially banned from TV advertising, but the ban was later lifted. Some professionals were accused of going 'over the top' in the early heady days of being allowed to advertise. In Australia, the firm Price Waterhouse came out with an ad that showed Tarzan beating his chest and yelling 'Aah ee Aaaah!', with the balloon, 'Price Waterhouse has more clients in the top 500 companies than any other firm of chartered accountants.'

The United States provided the most striking examples of the quandary in which professionals suddenly found themselves – how to strike the balance between modern marketing methods and professional decorum. This was most marked within the medical profession where the FTC ruled in 1982 that the American Medical Association, and by extension other medical societies, cannot stop their members from advertising. Plastic surgeons adopted stances right across the spectrum. At one end, a former president of the American Society of Plastic and Reconstructive Surgery protested, 'Plastic surgery should be sought out, not sold.' At the other, was the instigator of this ad:

The screen shows a sculpture of a woman's face; she is middle-aged, and the skin is wrinkled and creased. There is soft music, and a voice asks, 'How do you feel inside? Youthful, vibrant, up to date? But the ageing face often leaves a different impression on others or affects the good feelings we have about ourselves.' The scene moves to a doctor in white. 'I'm Doctor Donald Levy. Your face is your billboard to friends, co-workers and loved ones.' And onto the screen comes the line: 'The Clinic of Cosmetic Surgery, Milwaukee, Wis.'

But, as in so many areas of life, the extreme clears the way for others to follow. By 1987 the 'acceptable' face of medical advertising was well on its way. Nearly 60,000 physicians in family practice across the United States launched the profession's first national advertising campaign. Magazines like the *Ladies' Home Journal*, *Family Circle* and *People* carried ads asking, 'Ever wish you had a doctor who specialised in you?' An invitation followed to send for a list of local physicians. Advertising had taken another big step.

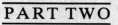

PART TWO

THE
TARGETS

5

Consumers

'The novice at advertising frequently gives the public credit for too much intelligence.'

Printers' Ink, 2 September 1903

'. . . children, like everyone else, must learn the market-place . . .'

Seymour Banks, vice-president Leo Burnett, USA

During the desert campaign of World War II, General Montgomery hung a picture of his ultimate rival, Field-Marshal Rommel, in his caravan. Montgomery believed that he had to understand the mind of the German commander in order to defeat him. The picture was an aid to that understanding.

Today advertisers regard their potential customers in much the same way as Montgomery regarded Rommel. Consumers are a target. Admen talk of 'hitting them with a rifle, not a shotgun'. Instead of portraits on the wall they use psychological and other profiles. Depending on the system of attack being used, the target can be seen as a 'C1C2', a 'belonger', a 'light grazer' or a 'G23'.

The four terms are neither exhaustive, nor interchangeable: the first comes from the UK's system of dividing people by social class, the second and third from US systems that group consumers on their lifestyles, and the fourth is a way of classifying people by the streets in which they live. What they, and other systems, all have in common is the belief that people in the same group have a number of inbuilt characteristics on which the advertiser can capitalise to sell his product. The fourth system, called ACORN, divides Britain into thirty-eight groups of people (in the US it is forty-four) according to their neighbourhoods. From this it is possible, it is claimed, to specify, for example, which group is most likely to drink a specific brand of coffee or to most want to borrow money. What it does, said one marketing man, is to quantify much more scientifically something burglars have always known – that where people live is related to what they buy and own.

It only works, however, in a world where the amount of material collected on people is vast to an almost unimaginable degree and where computers enable it to be sorted and used in countless different ways and combinations. The National Information Systems, Maryland, USA, offers details on 100 million people 'linked to your office'. 'The Information Age,' it says, 'has arrived,' and urges, 'Marketers should take full advantage of the information explosion to target specific individuals by economic, demographic and life-style characteristics.' Its consumer database offers detail on 80 million individuals, under the headings: name, address, city, state, zip, sex, date of birth, phone number, car make, model and year, wealth rating, length of residence, driver's licence renewal date, head of household, youngest member's year of birth, oldest member's date of birth and sex, household wealth indicator, households with people sixty-five and over . . . and so on.

The survey for the trendy American lifestyle classification system VALS – since spread to other parts of the world – involved asking 1,635 people eighty-five pages of questions ranging from their sexual habits to what brands of margarine they ate. From such material SRI International, California, discovered a group they called 'sustainers' who drink more instant breakfast products than any other group, and another known as 'achievers' who like cocktails before dinner.

Armed with such details about their target customers, companies site stores, decide where to advertise (including where to put their billboards) and frequently just *how* to advertise. Thus, Midway Airlines, of Chicago, analysed its frequent business travellers, found most could be classified as 'achievers', and its ad agency put together a campaign for its Metrolink service using the specific promises and exact words judged likely most to attract that group. Print ads promised 'That first-class feeling at less than coach fares', TV commercials sang of 'You're on your way up, make it the best, on your way up, put yourself first' and showed young achievers at work and aboard the airline.

Some agencies take all the classification research data and use it to write a biography of the target customer. Smith Greenland, a New York agency, whose clients include Givenchy perfumes, Johnnie Walker, and Brut/Fabergé Menswear, aims to put together 'a person, a living, breathing person, to whom we address our advertising'. Norman Goluskin, the agency president, told me, 'We will give him or her a name, an age, a birthplace, a family background, an educational background, a whole lifestyle as well as a set of attitudes about his life and the world he lives in.' He likens it to an actor in the theatre playing to one member of the audience. Thus the target for their Johnnie Walker Black Label Scotch ads is 'Tony Giordano – an achiever, a man who's on his way up, a man who wants his Scotch to be a Trophy of Success'. Goluskin elaborated further: 'He's thirty-four, a lawyer. Tony is a guy business is important to. He wants to show his success. He's got a big house, drives a Mercedes. He's a hard driving guy. The kind of guy who has to go to Minneapolis and his son is in a play. He'd go (to Minneapolis) though he'd call his son and talk to him after the play.'

Goluskin showed me some print ads that had resulted from targeting 'Tony'. A number played on straight success. One, created to run around the time of the Oscar and Emmy awards, showed the Johnnie Walker bottle on a plinth with lights, and the words, 'For those of you whose success cannot be measured by an Oscar, Emmy or Tony'. A second group of ads, explained Goluskin, incorporated a subtle change in approach – to take account of the fact that even people like 'Tony Giordano' had started to think about the premium price of the brand. Thus these ads anticipated the customer's thoughts and – playing on his self-image – threw them back at him. One, showing a Fabergé gold egg, carried the headline, 'Did Czar Nicholas quibble with Carl Fabergé over the price of eggs?' In another, the page was dominated by a photograph of the Taj Mahal reflected in its ornamental lake, and the caption, 'When Shah Jehan saw the contractor's bid, did he say, "Make the pool a little smaller"?' 'They're always a little tongue in cheek,' said Goluskin. 'We're saying that some things are just expensive and worth the price.'

Classification systems are not new. At their simplest they can divide the world into men and women, young and old, married or unmarried. All that is necessary is a characteristic which can be identified and measured and which is not shared by the whole population. Their significance to the advertising business, in the words of one market researcher, stems from the fact that until 'the millennium dawns on earth . . . some animals will continue to be more equal than others. We will find it useful to separate the sheep from the goats, the geese from the swans and the pigs from the men.' All, of course, in pursuit of separating the sheep and the swans from their money.

The best-known system divides people by social grade. Given the complexity and pervasiveness of the British class structure, it is not surprising that it is still widely used and regarded. It divides people into six groups, and is based totally on occupation – factors like income, lifestyle and education play no direct part although they are there by inference. Top of the list are the A's – 3 per cent of the population and comprising the higher managerial, administrative and professional people. In practice, this means lawyers, doctors, clergymen, architects, chartered accountants, university professors, directors of large companies, MPs and policemen of the rank of chief superintendent and above. Other groups are: B – 12½ per cent, intermediate managerial, administrative and professional; C1 – 22½ per cent, supervisory or clerical and junior managerial, administrative and professional; C2 – 32½ per cent, skilled manual; D – 21 per cent, semi- and unskilled manual; and E – 8½ per cent, those at the lowest levels of subsistence: casual labourers, pensioners, widows and the unemployed.

The mass market is the group labelled C2D. In the United States its equivalent would be the 'middle majority', a group comprised of the 'lower middle' and 'upper lower' classes. For marketing purposes at least, America does have a structured class system despite its reputation as the land of equality. They are classified to a system devised by W. Lloyd Warner during the 1940s. America's class system again takes occupation, but also uses the source of income (though not the amount), education, family background and dwelling area. The top division is the upper-upper: locally prominent families, third or fourth generation wealth; merchants, financiers or higher professionals; wealth is inherited. Next come the 'lower-upper: newly arrived in upper class, *nouveau riche*; not accepted by upper class; executive élite, founders of large businesses, doctors, lawyers. At the bottom are the lower-lower: unskilled, unemployed, and unassimiliated ethnic groups; fatalistic; apathetic.

Although the class system still has its fierce adherents, its problem is that it has less and less to do with how much – and how – people spend in a changing world. Richard Webber, the young statistician who invented ACORN, points out that in Britain clergymen rank AB as a social class, but are now down among the E's in terms of income. At the same time, the low status C2D's, make up some of the biggest spenders in the market. In terms of money, 'middle class' has had to be redefined. *Time* in an ad aimed at company advertisers has urged them to go for people with income, not the classification of 'middle class':

> Just a few years back, a comfortable middle-class income might have been $20,000 a year. Today, that same income barely covers essentials. This is the meaning of downward mobility. After spending $5,800 for food, $5,500 for shelter, and $1,300 for clothing, the average middle income family of four is left virtually empty handed. They will have less than $2,000 a year left over in discretionary income: *less* than $2,000 to spend on things like stereos, cable TV, and the family vacation – let alone education . . . More than half of *Time* subscribers earn incomes of over $30,000, and a lot of them make a lot more.

It is a truism that the world is changing fast, but for advertisers and admen it means that they now have a target which seemingly just won't keep still. Take, for example, the 'average' American household. A generation ago the typical household was a family – Mom, Dad and one or two children. Other kinds of household were statistically rare.* Today, more than half of America's 85 million households contain only one or two people. What was a 'typical' American household now

---

* In marketing and advertising, a 'household' is a dwelling place; the number of occupants is immaterial.

represents less than a third of the total. Advances in birth control, more women working, increasing divorce and other factors have changed the face of America – and other developed countries – for ever. Other things have happened – some without obvious reason. For example, the famous baby boomers not only delayed getting married but very large numbers of the men continued to live at home, with mother and father, instead of setting up their own homes.

Trends cover continents. Consuming has become more important. There is more leisure. Real wealth is increasing – the two-career baby-boom couples with their two salaries are swelling the upper income group. Attitudes have changed. The 'us' society of the sixties turned into the 'me' generation.

It is not just the changes, but the speed of them. 'It has never moved this fast before,' said J. Walter Thompson's Burton Manning. For advertisers it sometimes presents the problem of just what to target – a market that exists now or one that will be there next year. It may be impossible to do both. Manning gave a hypothetical example. 'There is a project – let's say it's a TV set. There's a segment in the market-place that wants a Victorian approach to design. The advertiser knows that if he makes them, he can sell a certain number and make a good margin. He also knows that the group of people who represent the future will look at the product and its design and come to a negative conclusion: they'll say, "I don't want these products in my home." Do you make the decision to make this TV set and sell it? Or do you bite on the bullet and build on what is going to sell in the future?' Ten years ago, says Manning, the risk would not have been great. It would have taken two to three years before the 'future' market began to decide the company's products were not for them. Today the effects of advertising have their impact on that group in nine or ten months.

As the speed of change increases so more classification systems spring up. One marketing research man, Brian Allt, has divided them into six 'indirect' categories, ones that he calls – *physical*, which is sex, age etc; *circumstantive*, marital status, have children, working/not working etc; *consumptive*, including income, social class, household size; *related ownership/usage*, e.g. gardeners for the shed market; *locative*, i.e. where people live; and *personality, tests, and social attitude*. (The 'direct' ones are those specifically relating to the product – i.e. users, recent buyers, intending buyers, non-users . . .).

A simpler way is to group them by the three 'ics' – demographics, psychographics and geographics. Demographics embraces the *facts* about a person and his life – his sex, age, income, car ownership, education etc. In principle at least, all the details included here are verifiable (though in practice it's obvious they are not – if someone says he's nineteen how can you be sure he is not eighteen or twenty; more practically, how honest are people about what they earn?). Geographics are self-explanatory. Psychographics means personality types: lifestyles, values, attitudes.

The three systems co-exist, although as in everything related to advertising there are fashions. Geography featured large in the fifties, demography in the sixties, psychographics rose in the seventies and is much in vogue today.

In the seventies, a number of advertising agencies and researchers undertook detailed surveys to classify consumers into psychological types. Although such surveys involve questioning a large number of people, they are said to employ one of the 'simpler methodologies' in consumer research. They also result in easily absorbed findings that are interesting in the same way as horoscopes and capsulated pieces of advice in *Reader's Digest*. Usually people are given a number of statements and are asked to indicate whether they strongly agree, agree, are neutral, disagree or strongly disagree. Areas covered include a person's activities such as work and hobbies, and interests such as food, and opinions. The agency Benton and Bowles thus divided housewives into six categories; Needham, Harper and Steers identified five male and five female types.

A good example of the material that emerges is shown in a study that divided American men into eight groups after a survey involving 4,000 people who answered about 300 psychographic questions. Two of the groups are sufficient to convey the flavour: *Group 2*, 'the traditionalist' (16 per cent of total males) – a man who feels secure, has self-esteem, follows conventional rules. He is proper and respectable, regards himself as altruistic and interested in the welfare of others. As a shopper he is conservative, likes popular brands and well-known manufacturers. Low education and low or middle socio-economic status, the oldest age group. *Group 5*, 'the pleasure-oriented man' (9 per cent of total males) – tends to emphasise his masculinity and rejects whatever seems to be soft or feminine. He views himself a leader among men. Self-centred, dislikes his work or job. Seeks immediate gratification for his needs. He is an impulsive buyer, likely to buy products with a masculine image. Low education, lower socio-economic class, middle-aged or younger.

Questrel, the qualitative research subsidiary of AGB, Europe's largest research company, has divided the famous yuppies into seven groupings in Britain. Among them were 'the traditional striver', said to be cautious and conservative, with ambitions geared to a comfortable home life with lots of dinner parties, and 'flash Harry', who is shaking off working-class origins, spending heavily on prestige brands and status symbols. (Yuppies can become dinks, it should be noted. Or, in other words, double income no kids couples, a tempting target for advertisers because of their large incomes. One marketing professional has even subdivided them into U-dinks and L-dinks, upper- and lower-class ones.)

Yankelovich, Clancy and Schulman, a well-known American research organisation, has taken all the baby-boom generation (the 76 million Americans aged twenty to thirty-nine) and split them into just three groups. These are the 'self-starters' said to be independent-minded and best influenced by ads stressing tangible features; the 'materialists', most likely to be influenced by ads full of user imagery, portraying eager, active shoppers. And the 'nesters', concerned with family and traditional values and looking for product satisfaction and value.

Yet another grouping of people comes from the giant McCann-Erickson agency whose London office claims to be able to identify eight groups each for men and for women. The men include those it calls 'sleep walkers' and 'pontificators', and women 'lady righteous' and 'lack a daisy'. Its 'lively lady' group, for example, is 'self-assured, ambitious, competitive, materialistic, sociable, go-getting, sensual, instinctive, emotional, likes men and is a working woman with an active career'. She buys brands that are 'glamorous, exotic, exclusive, clever, fun, lively, sensual, enjoyable'.

The best known of such systems, however, is VALS.

The giant Timex Corporation, its watch business struggling, decided in the eighties to move into the home healthcare market with a selection of new products including digital thermometers and blood pressure monitors. Timex, entering a market already estimated at $3 million and thought likely to double or even treble within four years, decided to put all its marketing and advertising faith in a psychographic system that its Madison Avenue supporters have hailed as 'the best thing since sliced bread'.

The system is VALS, a typology that divides Americans into nine lifestyle groups ranging from the 'survivors' struggling to exist at one end of the scale to the 'integrated' ('These rare people have put it all together') at the other end. Timex was by no means the first company to use VALS (it stands for Values and Lifestyles) but what was especially interesting was how *much* the corporation relied on it for every aspect of selling its new products, from lining up its target market to the detailed composition of the ads.

As a first step, Timex used existing research data to decide which of the VALS groups it should aim at. It decided there were two, the ones known as 'societally conscious' and as 'achievers'. That decided, it devised packaging that would appeal to those two groups. Clothing of models was carefully chosen so as to look both natural and full of status. There was stress on 'human interaction' – one package showed an older couple, their hands brushing lightly together. When it came to advertising, Timex's agency, J. Walter Thompson, worked and re-worked the ads until each detail was judged to fit the two types. Models were made to look self-satisfied; settings were upscale but mature and comfortable; when homes were shown they had lots of plants and books. Several taglines were tried before Timex found the one that it felt best hit the targets – 'Technology where it does the most good.' 'This,' said

Jim Dean, marketing director at Timex Medical Products, was 'relevant to achievers by virtue of the benefit derived from the use of technology.' When ads were shown on TV they were placed in news programmes, the only ones that the two groups generally bother to switch on, according to VALS data. Within months, each of the three Timex products had become the biggest seller in its market-place, a success story that did not convince VALS critics and sceptics but which, once again, did confirm the beliefs of VALS followers and explains why it had become the trendiest segmentation system of the decade.

VALS was devised by social scientists at SRI International at Menlo Park, California, while monitoring social, economic and political trends during the 1960s and 1970s. SRI, formed in 1946 as Stanford Research Institute, describes itself as a 'self-supporting, problem-solving organisation that provides research and consulting services to business and government throughout the world'. It is a non-profit corporation with a research and consultancy income of about $200 million a year. Its seventy-acre headquarters site adjoins 'Silicon Valley'. VALS' creator was a marketing analyst named Arnold Mitchell who joined SRI in 1948 and who in 1960 with two colleagues published *Consumer Values and Demands*. The report suggested that a neglected area of market research lay in how people's values influenced their spending patterns. Over twenty years later, in his book *The Nine American Lifestyles*, Mitchell referred to the report as a 'first groping effort'. The system in its present form emerged in 1978 in a report, *Consumer Values: A Typology*. It uses a mix of demographic information (such as age, education and income) and attitudes as shown by answers to a number of questions to arrive at its categories.

In its extensive literature, VALS says, 'In its formulation heavy reliance was placed on the works of personality theorists working in the area of developmental psychology. Abraham Maslow in particular was important, although a wide range of psychological and sociological theorists were consulted along with demographic and market research data. So the sources contributing to the typology were diverse and often empirical although the system framework itself was conceptual.'

VALS gives its users four major categories and nine groups. 'It should be understood from the start,' says SRI, 'that these lifestyle categories are not fixed and immutable. Many people grow from one level to another as children, as adolescents and as adults. Some very few may start at the bottom and reach the top within a lifetime, but far more common is movement of a level or two.'

The first major category is what VALS calls the NEED-DRIVENS which is divided into two lifestyle groups. The first is the *Survivors* (4 per cent of the population) – the most disadvantaged group in society: extreme poverty, poor education, old age, many now infirm. The second is the *Sustainers* (7 per cent) – 'a group struggling at the edge of poverty'. Better off and younger than survivors; many have not given up hope.

Next come the OUTER-DIRECTEDS who 'conduct their lives in response to signals – real or fancied – from others. Consumption, activities, attitudes – all are guided by what the outer-directed individual thinks others will think.' There are three types. *Belongers* (38 per cent) – who constitute the large, solid, comfortable middle classes. Key drive is to fit in, not stand out. Family, church, tradition loom large. *Emulators* (10 per cent) – ambitious, upwardly mobile, status conscious, macho, competitive. They want to be *achievers*, though many will not make it. *Achievers* (20 per cent) – they include many leaders in business, professions and government. Competent, self-reliant, efficient. Tend to be hard working, oriented to family and success. 'These are the affluent people who have created the economic system in response to the American dream.' And thirdly, there are the INNER-DIRECTEDS. In contrast with the outer-directeds, 'they conduct their lives primarily in accord with inner values – the needs and desires private to the individual – rather than in accord with values oriented to externals. Concern with inner growth thus is a cardinal characteristic'. Again there are three types. *I-Am-Mes* (3 per cent) – a short-lived stage of transition from outer- to inner-directed. Typical person is young and fiercely individualistic. *Experientials* (5 per cent) – the previous type as they 'mature psychologically'. People who want direct experience and vigorous involvement. *Societally conscious* (11 per cent) – they've extended their inner-direction to society as a whole and they support causes such as conservation, the environment and consumerism. Many are attached to simple living and nature.

Lastly, there is the COMBINED OUTER- AND INNER-DIRECTEDS – the *Integrated* (a mere 2 per cent). 'They meld the power of Outer-Direction with the sensitivity of Inner-Direction. They are fully mature in a psychological sense.'

It is, of course, possible to regard VALS with its categories, types and jargon as mumbo jumbo, a great hoax, a piece of pseudo-science. One critic told *Ad Forum*, 'If you look at the societally conscious and achievers, almost anyone who's breathing fits in.' Dr Herbert Krugman told me, 'When [SRI] made a presentation to the Market Research Council they were laughed out of the room. But they made headway in the agencies because they need gimmicks to show they understand the consumers . . . VALS is very popular. All the professionals snigger, but agencies have used it to interest clients.'

By the mid 1980s, however, SRI had 130 VALS users, including the major TV networks, advertising agencies such as McCann-Erickson, Young and Rubicam and Doyle Dane Bernbach, publishers such as *Time*, and major consumer companies including AT & T, Avon, Coca-Cola, General Motors, Procter and Gamble, R. J. Reynolds and Tupperware. Among banking clients were Citicorp-Diners Club. The gospel had also spread around: in Britain, it was enlisted on behalf of the Conservative Party in the run-up to the 1987 general election.

Among the research heads at advertising agencies, Joseph T. Plummer is one of VALS' most fervent believers. Plummer, an executive vice-president and director of research services at Y & R in New York, has enthused, 'It feels we've emerged from the Dark Ages. Before VALS, we had 100 different abstract images of the consumer. Now we see real people and get a sense of how they live and why they buy. It's a new dimension. VALS places a premium on understanding a consumer's attitude towards life in general; it gets marketers closer to the people they are trying to reach. VALS has helped all of us, it has become part of our vocabulary.'

One of Y & R's clearest uses of VALS was in the putting together of a new advertising campaign for the brokerage house of Merrill Lynch. That company shifted its account to Y & R after twelve years at Ogilvy and Mather. O & M had introduced a campaign, featuring a herd of bulls galloping across a plain, under the slogan, 'Bullish on America'. A year after Y & R took over, both the herd and the slogan had gone. In their place was a lone bull (seen wandering through the canyons of Wall Street or huddled in a cave) and the words, 'A Breed Apart'. It was all due to VALS. According to Plummer, Y & R decided that the 'Bullish on America' campaign was appealing to the wrong VALS' group – the theme was pure belonger and appealed to traditionalists. And that, said Plummer, was not what was wanted. 'We all love to see America grow, but the heavy investor wants an investment firm that's going to help *him* get a big share of that growth.' The group the campaign needed to reach was the achievers.

Out went the herd and the 'warm, round, comfortable, reassuring' belonger words of the original campaign. Instead, Y & R set out to communicate the feeling of being individualistic, unique and self-confident. The slogan – 'A Breed Apart' – was meant to say, 'Like you, Mr Achiever, we are a breed apart.' The single bull acted as 'resourceful as an individualist'. Individual words were chosen carefully – ones like 'innovative, resourceful, brute strength, finesse'. As the campaign developed the lone bull was shown in a number of symbolic situations, meant to reflect different financial predicaments. It pawed through the snow for grass in hard times, crossed a babbling river in good times to reach rich pastures on the other side, stalked through a china shop, uncovered a needle in a haystack . . . 'These themes,' said SRI, 'aligned the corporate image with the rugged individualism and "can do" spirit of Achievers.' According to Merrill Lynch, it worked. Within eighteen months, surveys showed that the percentage of people who noticed and remembered a company ad had increased from eight to fifty-five; furthermore, its share of the market on the New York Stock Exchange was up two points.

It does not, of course, require any special knowledge of research or marketing or advertising to know that when advertisers consider the VALS groups they're rather more interested in the 'belongers', the 'emulators' and the 'achievers' than they are in the 'survivors'.

It is highly likely that our young 'achiever' is also, to mix the classification system, an even stranger-sounding animal, a 'heavy grazer'. The 'heavy grazer' is a creature born of what Leo Shapiro, a Chicago consultant, has dubbed 'the grazing society'. This classification, too, its followers claim, has a practical application in that if the advertiser finds himself a 'heavy grazer' he also finds a man or woman likely to be interested in buying a whole number of other (specific) products.

Shapiro claims to have first spotted the evolving 'grazing society' in 1978. Grazers are described as people, often young, who less and less sit down for traditional meals; instead they munch something here, something there, eating on impulse rather than three times a day. They are more common in New York than in London, though the English secretary who picks up a pastry on the way to the office, has a stand-up sandwich for lunch and a hamburger on the way to meet her boyfriend and another meal with him later, is a grazer.

There are a number of reasons why 'grazing' should have come about: more single people, smaller households, varying family schedules, female careerism and even the increased availability of fast food (encouraged by the other factors but also one in its own right). Shapiro and Dwight Bombach have contrasted today's situation with that existing as recently as 1940. Then, 'the average American family ate at least two meals a day as a group, around the same table. Mother spent four to six hours a day getting ready to feed them . . . Just one generation later . . . we have as many as twenty "food contacts" a day – and spend as little as twenty minutes eating together.'

Shapiro claims the 'grazing society' has a number of characteristics of its own: it is 'one where people expect to live autonomously. They eat when and where they get hungry; sleep where they happen to be; get money, information, services, medical care when and where they need them. As a result, in the grazing society, home is no longer a place with special meaning. Stated extremely, home is a place you visit. Managing and manipulating time is a major preoccupation of the grazing society. People are obsessed with fitting time to their needs, rather than fitting themselves to the demands of time.'

To Shapiro, it represents a 'cultural revolution' with profound reverberations in marketing and advertising. One can be seen in the advertising for fast food. Twenty years ago fast-food restaurants sold themselves in their ads as just that. Now they and their agencies know that as people eat away from the family more and more, the desire for 'togetherness' becomes more intense – hence ads that sell the idea of families getting together to eat at their local hamburger or pizza restaurants. Shapiro believes, though, that the implications go way beyond such things. People, he and his co-worker Dwight Bombach claim, can be divided on how much they graze. And 'Those who are heavy grazers are the most active consumers going.' Shapiro's consultancy conducted a survey of a national sample of households in which consumers were given a 'grazer score' reflecting the number of meals eaten at home with the rest of the household, versus those eaten away from home or at home without the rest of the house present. The scores ranged from nine ('for the consumer that grazes most actively') down to one. Those scoring seven, eight, nine were called 'heavy grazers', those in the middle 'medium grazers' and the three, two, one scorers 'light grazers'.

Shapiro claims that how much or how little people 'graze' was shown to be directly related to spending on clothing, travel, the utilisation of computers and interest in signing up for money-management services. Thus, the Shapiro figures showed that 'heavy grazers' estimated it would cost them $3,080 to replace their wardrobe compared with $1,757 for 'light grazers'. Over half the 'heavy grazers' had flown in the previous year compared with less than a quarter of the 'light grazers', and 28 per cent of the heavies felt they could operate computers 'very well' compared with 10 per cent of the lights. Other figures purport to show 'heavy grazers' drive more, buy more houses, and – perhaps understandably – use more credit. In all, 'Among all the more or less mobile members of our energised American society, heavy grazers are your prime prospects for sales of practically everything.'

Lifestyle systems are easy, fun to read, and the best also seem to make sense. These key attributes, say critics, are what have helped to make them so successful.

Systems that tell advertisers *where* their targets are located are equally vital if admen are to satisfy their 'rifle shot' boast. Another system, a geographic one, allows advertisers to identify specific areas – down to as small as 150 households – where the inhabitants drink most vodka, eat brown sauce, read the *Sun*, play tennis, post off their films to be processed, or any one of a number of combinations. 'Almost frightening, isn't it?' one consultant in direct marketing commented to me. It operates in both Britain and the United States, and at the time of writing had also spread to France, Germany and Sweden. Its uses include advertising but extend beyond it. In the UK, it is used to decide which particular drinks individual pubs should stock, where new stores should be sited, and to 'personalise' mailing shots with text senders believe will fit the personality and circumstances of the recipient.

Ironically, the system that does all this was first devised by a young economist and town planner, Richard Webber, when he was looking at the problems of urban deprivation in Liverpool. Webber's admirers say that the work, which began in 1973, even identified Toxteth as a potential trouble spot; eight years later the area's frustrations erupted in riot and flames. Be that as it may, Webber's work at that time ended up in filing cabinets and specialist libraries. The irony was that when it re-emerged, it did so because of the potential for selling goods to the far-from-deprived – the major relevance of deprived urban areas was knowing where they were in order to avoid them.

Webber's system came to be called ACORN. It has a problem: it is *not* easy to understand. Its spread, it is said, has taken place *despite* that. Webber himself has wrestled with a definition. The simplest he has managed is that 'it is a method of defining and reading target audiences on a geographic basis'. ACORN itself stands for 'A Classification of Residential Neighbourhoods'. Webber explains that, working for the government-funded Centre for Environmental Studies, he found that when he applied a system called 'cluster analysis' to the official census statistics for small areas within Liverpool it was possible to define a number of distinct kinds of neighbourhood. These varied considerably in the types of 'disadvantage groups' they contained.

Webber went on to apply the same technique throughout the country. He found he could define thirty-eight distinct neighbourhood types, each different in terms of population, housing and their socio-economic characteristics. Webber did not envisage it as a commercial tool. That was left to a man called Ken Baker who heard about it at a seminar and promptly saw its value. Baker's company, the British Market Research Bureau, is responsible for a survey service called Target Group Index. This provides data on product and brand usage over a large variety of products and analyses this against readership of magazines and newspapers. Makers of, say, a brand of coffee, can judge from it where best to advertise. Baker decided to categorise all the 24,000 items in that survey geographically according to Webber's system. The result, he found, seemed to show conclusively that the respondents in one neighbourhood actually did favour different products and services from those in another. Furthermore, they did so even when they were apparently the same people in demographic terms. The AB man living in Hampstead, London, was very different – in what he bought – from, say, the AB man in Esher, Surrey.

The commercial possibilities had been noticed by CACI, a company founded on the US West Coast in 1962 by two computer-science specialists. Webber joined them in 1979 and ACORN was refined. By 1985, it was claimed by CACI that it had supplied ACORN services to over 70 per cent of the market leaders in Britain, including retailers, banks, building societies, TV rental companies, brewers, car firms, and direct mail companies. It was also established in the US and was rolling into Europe. In the US, it bills itself as 'Geo-demographic' system – one that combines the best of geographics and demographics to predict lifestyle: 'People who share similar demographic, housing and socio-economic characteristics tend to live in similar neighbourhoods and share similar lifestyles . . . and thus present similar potential for products and services and similar preferences towards media, direct mail, and other promotions.'

In the US, ACORN breaks down the country into forty-four distinct neighbourhood types of market segments, in the UK thirty-eight. A comparatively small geographic area, particularly in cities, can include widely contrasting ACORN neighbourhoods. For example, in one voting ward in Camden, London, the two most common ACORN groups are one whose characteristics are immigrants and single-parent families, and another with expensive self-contained flats populated by AB's who are big credit-card users and air travellers.

I asked CACI what they could tell me about the people who live in a small area chosen at random. The area we picked was a half-mile radius of 104–110 Gregories Road, Beaconsfield, Bucks, a very wealthy area near London. Simon Hay, one of the analysts, then produced twenty-two sheets of computer print out, each eleven by fourteen inches. Among the information it contained was:

A breakdown of the number of people in the area by age-group and country of birth, how many were employed (a high 95.9 per cent), the number of houses owner-occupied, by size (number of rooms) and how many households owned cars (13 per cent owned three or more). The number in different social classes and socio-economic groups and the number with educational qualifications, the industries people worked in – and how they got to work. Detailed information on car ownership from age to size to cost. Income levels in the area, credit cards held, mortgages and overdrafts. The amount of travel last year – where people went, how and what it cost. What inhabitants have at home from TVs to hi-fi to central heating. What they eat and drink – they're heavy on vegetables and ice cream, ground coffee and pasta, for example, and – not surprisingly – low on fish fingers, tea-bags and sausages. What they drink (high on sherry and port, table wine and even higher on the gin). How often the people there eat out. What they like to buy – records, tapes, books (and what kind), typewriters, watches and a host of other things, what newspapers they read (the *Financial Times much* higher than average, the *Daily Star very much* lower), and their TV viewing habits.

ACORN was the first in the UK but has been joined by a host of rivals: Pinpoint's PIN, CCN's Systems' Mosaic, McIntyre Marketing's Super Profiles, Sales Performance Analysis' Marketing Machine. By 1987, there were nearly twenty in all. In the US, the Claritas Corporation has PRIZM, started in 1974, which divides the country into forty cluster groups using material from the census. Claritas gives the groups memorable – and trademarked – nicknames as well as numbers. For example, Number 31 is 'Sun belt singles', 13 is 'Norma Rae-ville' and 39 is 'Marlboro country'. Descriptives are equally snappy. Number 5 is 'Furs and station wagons' – 'typified by "new money" living in expensive new neighbourhoods. These are well-educated, mobile professionals and managers with the nation's highest incidence of school-age children. They are winners – big producers, and big spenders.' They are a long way away from Number 6, 'Hard scrabble' – which 'represents many of our least fortunate areas from Appalachia to the Ozarks to the South Texas Border country and the Dakota Bad Lands . . .'

Another, ClusterPlus, from two companies Donnelley Marketing Information Services (part of Dun and Bradstreet) and Simmons Market Research Bureau, claims to be able to rank users of products right down to individual homes. It says it can do this because Donnelley has a mailing list of 73 million individual households – almost 90 per cent of the entire United States. In its trade ads, Donnelley italicises the fact to make sure the vastness of its capability is not missed. Each of these households, says Donnelley, contains individual lifestyle characteristics and each has been coded with the clusters of the forty-seven neighbourhood types which the company has devised to divide the US (again, using the census). That, it seems, is only the first major stage. That data is then linked with material collected annually by Simmons in which 19,000 American households reveal demographic, psychographic and media information as well as 'consumption patterns' for 750 categories of product and 3,500 individual brands. 'Now,' says Donnelley, 'you can actually measure differences *within neighbourhoods*, right down to the individual household making the purchase decisions.'

As to what detail is revealed by the fact that someone is a resident of one particular neighbourhood type, Donnelley gives this example for 'Cluster S 01':

Demographics – established members of the community. Very affluent, high disposable income, well educated, professionally employed, homeowners, prime real estate areas, children in private schools, highest socio-economic status. Psychographics – sophisticated, intelligent, well informed, style conscious. Preferences – news and business magazines, luxury products, mail order purchases, gourmet foods, imported wines, golf, tennis.

The more one learns, the more it has the feel of Big Brother about it all, even though the end application may be no more than attempting to sell a specific brand of car or make of storm-window. It is interesting to contemplate the outcry if any government intelligence agency was known to have such computer data on all its individual citizens.

However, the belief in the myriad of classification systems as an aid to advertising is not universal. Even those who are convinced that, say, psychographics does help produce effective advertising sometimes recognise other difficulties. One is that people often do not want to be seen as they are, but as they would prefer to be. The last thing the admen should do, therefore, having found out about someone is feed that information back to him in an ad. Even if the adman does use the information, he should take care not to let the customer know what he knows! Malcolm Fishwicke, director of creative research at Foote, Cone and Belding, London, believes that those who disregarded this rule were responsible for one of Britain's best-known brand failures, Strand cigarettes. The ads, still widely remembered, were devised in 1960 by the agency S. H. Benson for the Wills tobacco company to launch a new, cheap filter cigarette. They featured a Sinatra-lookalike wandering sadly through lonely locations with only his cigarette to keep him company. The ads became talked about, the theme music a hit. The cigarettes did not sell! The potential customers obviously did not like the way the advertiser saw them – as lost, lonely people.

There are many who claim that the most important single factor in targeting people is their *age*. The stage of life people have reached determines not only what they want but what they can afford. The young and the over fifty-fives have more disposable income – that is income they can spend on what *they* like – than the middle-aged couples bringing up children. And, as one insider puts it, it may be attitudes that attract people into department stores but it is income that determines 'whether you go to the top floor for the designer clothes or the bargain basement'.

'Phases of life' is a fashionable concept in West Germany. One system classifies men into six groups, from the 'Innovative market newcomers' at one end ('young, single . . . high freely disposable income . . . always willing to try something new, full of plans . . .') to 'Steady home oriented types' (older, single men age forty and over . . . highly conservative, few contacts, undemanding, watch a lot of television . . .). Everywhere the baby boomers excite special interest from advertisers, because acquisitiveness is regarded as one of the group's dominant characteristics. *People* magazine boasts that two-thirds of its 21 million readers are boomers. 'Whether it's a break dance or a gelato break, if baby boomers think something's cool it becomes hot. They've caused cookie shops to proliferate. Personal stereos to come in countless variations. And aerobics books and tapes to be found in stores all over town. As children of prosperity, they're accustomed to indulgence. And as prosperous adults, they can well afford them.'

There are a lot of them (75 million in the US in the mid eighties) which makes them worthwhile for mass market targeting if there are common characteristics. Thus Ted Bates Advertising, New York, decided that striving was one key common factor, and made it the centre of a campaign for Michelob beer – 'Where you're going, it's Michelob'. The boomers' sub-group, the yuppies, are beloved of advertisers not least for what quickly became regarded as their main characteristic – the desire to acquire to the point of product worship. But one research company, Market Facts of Chicago, has attempted to create a bigger pool of yuppies by claiming that in addition to those who satisfy the demographic conditions (an estimated 1.2 million in the US) there are also 'psychographic yuppies' – people who '*think* and act like yuppies'. According to Market Facts, 'psychographic yuppies' are people with these (among other) characteristics in common: they make fresh coffee from beans; drink imported beer and wine; own a personal computer; use automatic bank machines; watch *Cheers*. Non-yuppies, however, eat pre-sweetened cereal and instant potatoes; shop at K-Mart; listen to 'blaster' portable stereo radios; live in small towns; and watch the 'A Team'.

Whether they are yuppies or not, there is one inescapable fact about the young: they are growing fewer while the old are becoming more plentiful. For advertisers, the elderly become more important. Researchers have already coined a number of names for them. One of the most unappealing is 'the geromarket'. They have also begun to subdivide; thus there are 'young old' (fifty-five to seventy-five) and 'old old' (over seventy five). With both birth rates and death rates falling, one in every three adults in Europe was over sixty by the early 1980s. Furthermore, they were responsible for a lot of buying power. Over a third of all the income in the US was in the hands of those aged fifty and older. Some observers concluded that the only reason advertisers were not concentrating more of their efforts on the elderly was because it did not suit their own image. Harold Lind, a British economist specialising in media and advertising, complained, 'The general belief in creative departments (of advertising agencies) appears to be that if you can avoid thinking about advertising to the old, you may be able to remain a superannuated teenager for the rest of your life.'

Others dubbed it 'the marketer's last frontier'. But ultimately advertising money tends to end up where the opportunities are, and by the eighties the trend was unmistakable. Infatuation for the young remained undimmed, but a number of commercials for general mass products began to have a slightly less youth-oriented quality about them. Models began to reflect the fact that as we age we put on the odd extra pound; the couple in the Freedent commercial were wearing dentures but could still enjoy dancing together. Furthermore, the negative images of a few years before had largely disappeared. Today it is hard to imagine an advertiser coming up with a commercial like the 1979 one for Country Times lemonade which used an old man's deafness as an excuse to repeat the name of the product.

It was a trend that crossed countries. In France, Michel Suquet of SOFRES, a marketing consultancy, noted a much greater use of older models in ads. 'Senior citizens in advertising are meant to convey an image, a feeling of experience, advice, affection. But mid-lifers are also starting to come into their own as a market in their own right.' A survey there showed why: the over fifties accounted for over 34 per cent of coffee sales, 40 per cent of the mineral water market, and more than 42 per cent of the port buyers. They also ate more beef and lamb, pasta, cheese and marmalade and drank more wine than younger French men and women.

It is not just that more people are getting older but how people act and are seen is also changing. Carbonated soft drinks are associated with youngsters, but a piece of 1987 research showed a third of Americans over fifty down them regularly. Over fifty can now be sexy – Joan Collins baring her cleavage, not grandma knitting by the fire. Adland has reflected the change. Ms Collins – admitting to being in her fifties – was hired as advertising spokeswoman for Revlon's Scoundrel. Catherine Deneuve, appearing for American Home Products' Youth Garde moisturiser, revealed to the camera she is in her forties, and added 'Come closer, I have nothing to hide.' A forty-five-year-old Nashville mother of three was featured in an ad for Germaine Monteil's Supplegen Instant Action Firmer, a skin-care product. The company's president, Stewart Rohr, said, 'We and others in the cosmetics business had long been guilty of using twenty-two-year-old models for products bought primarily by older people.' Johnson and Johnson, in the UK, advertised Empathy, a shampoo 'for hair over forty' with the line, 'Now there's no age limit to looking good.'

Admen and marketers began to devote more attention on how best to feature older people in their ads. Mo Drake, a creative consultant, referring to the over fifties, warned against 'Those smug faces with the inevitable pipe stuck in them . . . the blue rinses tottering off to a ticky-tacky bungalow in some seaside paradise . . . out of touch in-laws . . . grey-haired dummies being knocked down by arrogant teenagers – if they are portrayed at all, older people are treated with much less than the respect they deserve.' And he advised fellow admen, 'Never forget their lives have been spent in the second quarter of the twentieth century. They are part of our world – of modern communications. Don't speak down to them or treat them as if you're talking to somebody in the last stages of senility. Remember, they have time on their hands and a surprising amount of disposable income. But having been around longer than other people, they are by no means push-overs for flippant advertising.'

However, there was no doubt that the over fifties, no less than anyone else, need their ads to be packaged as dreams. Like the young, older people like to see themselves portrayed in the way they would *wish* to be or perhaps as they see themselves (research shows that most elderly people regard themselves as thinking and feeling ten years younger than they actually are). Thus it was a forty-five-year-old woman who was chosen to feature in the Germaine Monteil ads, not a sixty-five-year-old. And though her hair was grey it was long and flowing. One company, Ramada Inns Inc, found that whatever the reality of their own lives, older customers wanted to see people in promotion pictures jogging and gardening, not baking and knitting. And advertisers find romance sells: an Enterprise Holidays ad in the UK, modelled on a fifties film poster, has an elderly couple entwined against a backcloth of sea and palms; the couple in the ad for *Seniority* magazine both have grey hair but their hands are linked and they toast each other across the dinner table.

However, advertisers do approach the elderly with mixed feelings. They want to sell to them, but at the same time many do not want their products identified with them. By association, products enjoyed by the old are thought to be seen as unexciting, dated, not sexy.

There is another group of consumers, also important as buyers, to whom advertisers have an even more ambivalent feeling, even though here the customers are trend setters. The gay market is a 'minority' market, but it is not a small one and it has a number of features to lure advertisers. The Kinsey Institute for Sex Research in the United States estimates 5–6 per cent of the adult population is predominantly homosexual, and roughly two out of three homosexuals are men, a total of over 11 million people. Many researchers, however, regard this figure as too conservative, and a figure of about 24 million men, or 10 per cent of the adult male population is widely accepted.

There is little argument about the attraction of the homosexual as a buyer – his affluence. *The Economist* began an article on the subject, 'If the novelists Ernest Hemingway and Scott Fitzgerald were alive today, they might rephrase their legendary exchange thus: Scott, "Homosexuals are different from us." Ernest, "Yes, they have more money."' Avanti Marketing Services of San Mateo, California, surveyed gay males in 1982 to obtain what was claimed to be the first national demographic study. It showed, for example, that while the percentage of all American households making $20,000 a year or more was 53 per cent, for gay male households it was 66 per cent. For households earning $50,000 or more, the national figure was 6.7 per cent, the gay figure was 15 per cent. The typical gay had an upper income and few financial obligations. He was college educated, a professional or middle-level white-collar worker, and often shared a home with another working male. The latter, of course, meant a home with two large disposable incomes. And no wife or children.

Other survey material since indicates gays are spending a lot on entertainment and vacationing, on drinking expensive liquor and driving status cars. Gays are also claimed to be trend setters in a variety of areas from discos to white wine. Peter Frisch, publisher of the *Advocate*, an American gay magazine, claims, 'They were the first people to drink Perrier in this country, the first to worry about health and exercise and to change from drinking hard liquor to white wine.'

Perrier is one of the companies that advertise specifically to gays. Another is Seagram which offered a bar mirror in its ad for Boodle's British Gin. The mirror featured six 'famous men of history' all purportedly gay though that fact was not mentioned in the ad.* The gay market

* The six: Oscar Wilde, Lawrence of Arabia, Walt Whitman, Edgar Allan Poe, Beethoven and Edgar Dégas.

was targeted, with some success, as a group likely to experiment with what was a small, expensive and little-known brand. Film makers have discovered the gay market for ads. Paramount first experimented with *Saturday Night Fever* and nervously waited for a backlash that did not come. 'The Statue of Liberty did not fall down,' said Gordon Weaver of Paramount. 'State frontiers did not close. When politicians who are notoriously conservative seek gay support, well, you know things are changing!' Another company, Twentieth Century Fox, promoted *Making Love*, a film about a man who left his wife for another man, with different campaigns directed at heterosexuals and homosexuals. The husband, the wife and the 'other man' featured in both. However, in the heterosexual ad the 'other man' wore a shirt; in the gay ad his chest was bare.

The ad agency for the French cigarette, Gitane, decided the US gay market was a good target for a low-budget campaign because its product seemed to make a 'statement about style' of the kind liked by homosexuals. Sales, it is said, went up 30 per cent. Even the notoriously conservative drug companies have begun to target gays. Pfizer market Rid, a treatment for crablice, apparently highly prevalent among gays. 'Do your friend, and yourself, a favor, and introduce him to RID,' says the headline. The *Advocate* includes ads from Bombay gin, Dewar's scotch, Miller beer, Columbia, Universal and Paramount pictures, CBS records, BMW and Volvo and Honda dealers, as well as from banks.

In campaigns outside the gay press, homosexuals may be seen as an important secondary market. Even if they cannot be wooed directly, the wise advertiser is careful not to alienate them. One gay advertising executive has suggested that advertisers should make certain that all references in ads designed to interest homosexuals as well as heterosexuals should be firmly 'male oriented'. That meant no reference to a wife, or a married couple, and that the models should all be men.

Homosexuals in the UK are believed to be equally affluent. A survey among readers of the magazine *Gay News* showed they were ten times more likely to visit the theatre or own a video machine than the 'average' man, spent three times the male average on alcohol, twice the average on clothes and nine times the average on toiletries. They might appear a desirable target. However, British advertisers seem reluctant to have their products openly associated with homosexuals, a prejudice that has doubtless been reinforced by the existence of AIDS. Nor - even if homosexuals in Britain constituted 10 per cent of the adult male population - would the market be so enormous as to provide irresistible temptation. The pages of *Gay Times* (which had incorporated *Gay News*) are not starved of ads, but they are not from big-name national companies. Ads for products like clothes, toiletries and alcohol are conspicuously absent. A cigarette advertiser, another obvious group, told me he could see no way in which his company would want to be associated with 'such people'.

In neither Britain nor the United States are female homosexuals singled out by companies for advertising or even for research. The reason is twofold: first, as women they are presumed to earn less than male gays; second, they are thought more likely to adopt the circumstances of traditional marriages, including bringing up children. This in turn would mean two things: less disposable income than their male equivalents, and also that many of the ads routinely targeted at housewives would be just as relevant to lesbians.

With increased competition and growing fragmentation of society, marketing to all minorities has become more important. Advertisers have been forced to seek out smaller and smaller markets with money to spend. Nowhere is this more marked than in advertising to ethnic groups, which reflects not just a change in status but their (cash) value to the advertiser. One pre-World War II ad for National Beer depicts the black-as-servant phase – it has a white-coated black carrying the drink on a silver tray. 'Lawsee, Lawsee!' reads another old ad, 'folks sho' whoops with joy over Aunt Jemima Pancakes.' Yet another, for toothpaste, pictures a black boy eating a watermelon and says, 'Go right ahead, Sambo! Sink those ivories in that luscious watermelon.' In another ad, this time calculated to inflame Hispanics, a stereotype Mexican *bandito*, complete with sombrero, ear-to-ear tooth-filled grin and moustache, is the centre of an ad disguised as a reward poster: 'WANTED for theft of Fritos Corn Chips.'

It would be a foolhardy advertiser who would present such ads today. Ethnic political power apart, vast markets are at stake. America's 25 million blacks have an annual disposable income estimated at more than $200 billion. As a percentage of what all Americans spend it is small, but is also more than the gross national products of Denmark, Norway or Indonesia. The Hispanic market, though smaller in the first half of the eighties, was growing faster than any other segment of the population.

Stereotypes do live on. Blacks complain of token non-white faces tucked away in the background of advertisements; others talk of an 'obsession' with showing blacks dancing, singing and playing basketball. The fault, say many insiders, lies with the fact that there are so few black people holding power at advertising agencies.

A number of big advertisers have turned to black-owned agencies. Coca-Cola handed over all its black consumer advertising worldwide to Burrell Advertising of Chicago, the country's largest black-owned agency. Burrell's other clients included McDonald's and Procter and Gamble. Thomas Burrell started his agency in 1971 at the age of thirty-two after working as a copy supervisor at another Chicago agency, Needham Harper and Steers. The following year he persuaded McDonald's that his agency could help the company increase its share of the black market. It remains its biggest client. Blacks have to be approached as blacks, believes Burrell. 'Black people are not dark-skinned white people. There are cultural values which cause us to be subtly different from the majority population.' He also believes that as an audience they are 'much more complex and sensitive' than white consumers: 'If I can sell to black consumers I can sell to anybody.' Burrell's ads frequently incorporate black food preferences and slang; commercials aimed at children have had black children jumping rope 'double dutch' style. Like all ads, though, they are the stuff of dreams, even if the dreams are sometimes peculiarly black. Several present idealised and sentimental black family situations: in a McDonald's spot, a black mother picks up her son at a day care centre and off they go to meet Dad who is waiting at McDonald's. In a Coca-Cola commercial, a young black girl sits in front of the TV and watches a gymnast perform; the scene moves to the girl practising in front of her beaming parents in the front yard; finally she makes a perfect score in competition. The emotions depicted are universal, but the way they are presented has a special potency for black audiences. The families in Burrell commercials share great love and joy. It is an ideal that often contrasts with the real world of the American black. 'In many black households,' Burrell has said, 'there is no real close-knit family situation.'

Perhaps for the most obvious reasons, advertisements aimed at blacks portray an even more-than-usual idealised world. The models are all young, beautiful and wear designer clothes; fathers and sons groom their hair together; brandy is sniffed from enormous balloon glasses; the settings include casinos and exotic beaches. A number are obviously aimed at a group that Earl G. Graves, publisher of *Black Enterprise* magazine, has dubbed the 'buppies' – black urban professionals with ambition to improve themselves. 'I assume you drink Martell,' says the beautiful woman in one glossy print ad as she pours a glass of brandy.

The Hispanic market in the United States is not only a minority market, but is in itself a mix of three smaller minority markets: Mexican, Puerto Rican and Cuban. Most speak Spanish, almost half of them only that. America's Hispanics have their own TV, about 100 full-time radio stations, and their own newspapers and magazines. Not least among their attractions for advertisers is that Hispanics are said to favour big-name brands and are more likely than other Americans to stay with a brand if they like it.

An evening watching commercials on Hispanic TV produces great feelings of nostalgia. Watching, you suddenly realise that this was the way it was on all TV once upon a time. Against a background of palm trees, a doting Hispanic housewife serves her husband dinner. In another, a girl impresses her date with her cooking – all thanks, it emerges, to Mum's good advice about which product to buy. It is not surprising that an official of Goya Foods Inc, producers of Hispanic speciality foods, told the *Wall Street Journal* that if the company transmitted some of its Spanish-language ads on English-language TV 'every woman's group in the country would be after us'.

Of all the target groups, however, there is one that holds a very special place. One of the most repulsive print advertisements of 1985 showed a young American teenager, eyes hidden by dark glasses but mouth curled in a gentle, knowing sneer. He wore a blue/black patterned tuxedo with black lapels and a black and white spotted bow tie. His arms were folded aggressively like a bouncer who wants to convey the fact that whatever you do you don't mess with him.

He speaks: 'In our Yuppie Puppie household, I've got a VHS, my sister's got a Beta and my architect mother can't set the time on either of 'em.' To reinforce it, further text reads: 'Yuppie Puppies are worldly. Yuppie Puppies are with-it. Yuppie Puppies are 25,000,000 strong and growing!' What's more – and this is the point of it all – 'Yuppie Puppies watch Nickelodeon' – the children's cable – 'that's as sharp and smart as they are.'

It so happens that Nickelodeon is far from being a bad television channel – its programmes are a refreshing alternative to the networks' diets of cartoons and super heroes. But the advertisement is a telling illustration of how the advertising world views young people. Nickelodeon (born in spring 1979) originally ad-free, found by 1983 that it needed additional revenue – and that meant commercials. Nickelodeon's general manager, Cy Schneider, promised the Advertising Club of New York it intended to become 'a major contender for the millions of dollars invested in advertising to reach children' by TV. The precocious young man in the ad is a target – his sheer 'worldliness' (translation, desire to buy and own) makes him an ideal one. This, the ad is saying, is someone ripe for the plucking . . . and we can deliver him.

The millions add up enough to matter a very great deal. A 1985 survey of spending by seven- to seventeen-year-olds in Britain showed £320 million spent on clothes, £198 million on confectionery, £179 million on records and tapes, £110 million on crisps and a similar sum on soft drinks. Teenagers in the US were estimated to have spent $48 billion on a range of goods from clothing to videogames, snacks, cosmetics and records.

But that is only the beginning of their importance to advertisers. Children are targeted not just for what they buy themselves but for what they can persuade others to buy. They are, for example, the ultimate target for the $13 billion worth of toys bought in the US every year, much of it by parents and other relatives. And there's a further power still. To twist the old saying about getting children young enough, advertisers believe that if you persuade an eight-year-old to open a bank account (in return for a lot of giveaways like piggy banks and school sets and membership of a club) the odds are that bank may have him or her for a lifetime. Such thinking runs across a gamut of products and services. Yankelovich studies for the magazine *Seventeen* in the US say 29 per cent of adult women still choose the coffee they preferred as a teenager and 37 per cent use the same brand of cheese. When it comes to cosmetics, 41 per cent go on to use the same mascara, 29 per cent wear the same fragrance and 33 per cent use the same nail polish. 'If you miss her,' *Seventeen* warns advertisers it is trying to lure into its pages, 'then you may miss her for ever. She's at that receptive age when her looks, tastes and brand loyalties are being established . . . Reach a girl in her *Seventeen* years and she may be yours for life.' Clairol, launching a new range of hair colorants called Glints in the UK, aimed its ads at teenage girls. Heather Auton, the company's group product manager for hair care products, said, 'If you get them when they're young, then, even if they lapse after a few years, they will come back when they are in their thirties.'

The child of the eighties is seen as an especially good target. Selina S. Guber, president of Children's Market Research, New York, refers to 'significant differences' between the children of the eighties and even those of the seventies which 'cannot and should not be overlooked by marketers and advertisers'. Today's young consumers, she says, 'are aware of brands and status items even before they can read'. A 1987 study by McCann-Erickson, London, claimed young people in the UK were obsessed by consumption and bought more because they saw brands as an expression of who they are. *Campaign* commented, 'That message is good news for advertisers.'

Not surprisingly, the attacks on young people are as carefully researched, planned and created as on any other group of consumers. In the toy market, for instance, where seasoned multinationals now see the developed world as one vast opportunity, the targeting becomes more sophisticated, the approaches more aggressive. Budgets are big: in the UK, Rainbow Toys planned to spend £6.4 million on advertising and promotion during 1985, Palitoy £10 million and Mattel £6 million on TV advertising alone.

The sheer size of the advertising and promotion aimed at children can be breathtaking. Kool-Aid soft drinks is one of General Foods' most important brands in the US. In 1985 it was said to be behind only Coca-Cola and Pepsi brands in terms of the amount drunk, but, very importantly, the first choice among children. Ads featuring the Kool-Aid man (a giant animated pitcher that rescues thirsty children) occupy $25 million of airtime a year. However, that is not all. A Kool-Aid comic book, put together by the Marvel Comic Group, is distributed free – 3 million copies, in fact, making it the largest single comic book in the US. The Kool-Aid man makes personal appearances across the country; the trademark appears on 100 items including clothes and toys; and Kool-Aid sponsors events ranging from games, free swimming and safety programmes, The drink's senior product manager, Mark S. Kapsky, told the *New York Post*, 'We now want kids' involvement with Kool-Aid to be wherever they are, at home, at play, at school.' Heinz in 1986 added about $2.5 million to its advertising budget to target specifically the under thirteens with animated hamburgers and french fries that giggled when squirted with a ketchup laser. The same year

Pepsi began promoting its drink to a younger audience by giving away Crayola markers with two-litre bottles.

Advertising to children is – or should be – more than just an opportunity to sell products. Because the target is children, a sector which by its nature is a vulnerable group, there are strong issues. In part, these are reflected in the rules that govern advertising to children. These vary in their degree of restriction both from country to country (England is less controlled than the rest of Europe) and from year to year (the United States relaxed its controls under Reagan's presidency). Their very existence, however, proves that universally there is some acceptance that children are special as a target group. It would be naïve, though, to believe that there is not a huge gulf between, say, the concerned parent and the marketer who is trying to line up children in his sights.

The one central point that must not be forgotten – no matter how it is fudged or ringed with restrictions – is that the object of it all is to sell a product or a service to a child, either directly or indirectly. Don Blundell, UK marketing director of Milton Bradley, a large US toy company, explained to *Marketing* magazine that it was necessary to 'advertise to children to create the desire within them to own the product. We almost have to ask the kids to go to their parents and ask: "Can we afford it?"'

The importance of children as a market is comparatively new. It was not until the sixties that advertisers recognised the potential profitability of the youth market and developed television advertising aimed specifically at them. A few far-sighted admen had seen the day coming and had anticipated it with relish. Thus, this extract in 1951 from the American magazine *The Sound Track*, reproduced in *The Shocking History of Advertising*:

Speaking of surveys, we tried an experiment the other evening . . . To a curly headed four year old being tucked under the covers we posed this question: 'Susie, which brushes teeth whiter?' 'Colgate's, of course, Gramp.' We couldn't resist another. 'Which product washes clothes cleaner?' Without a moment's hesitation, 'Tide.' We tried once more. 'Which coffee gives the best value?' When she replied 'A & P, and now goodnight, Gramp,' we hurried out of the room with our questions beating at our brain.

Where else is brand consciousness firmly fixed in the minds of four year old tots? How many pre-school age Americans are presold on how many different products? How can we get reliable data? What is it worth to a manufacturer who can close in on this juvenile audience and continue to sell to it under controlled conditions, year after year, right up to its attainment of adulthood and full-fledged buyer status? It *can* be done. Interested?

That, of course, as admen will probably rush to point out, was over thirty years ago. In advertising, as in so many areas, all the 'bad' things happened yesterday and today's practitioners have long seen the light. Yet the following remark, about television advertising, by Raymond McDonald, vice-president of marketing for the Tonka Corporation, is circa mid 1980s: 'You have to figure out how to capture a child's mind. They have to know just how to think about the product.' Advertising people will argue that they haven't created the situation; they're just accepting the world as it is. Thus Selina Guber, the New York children's research specialist, can say, 'Whether we approve or disapprove of the materialistic and money-oriented youth culture of the 1980s, it is a fact of life and marketing.'

Television is, without doubt, the most powerful deliverer of advertising messages: nowhere is this more marked than with children. It is not surprising that much of the disquiet that has been voiced about advertising to children is linked with worries about the influence of television more generally. Action for Children's Television, an influential American pressure group, lists seven facts under the heading 'Believe it or Not!' in its literature. Two of them refer specifically to advertising, but all are related:

The average American family watches more than six and a half hours of television a day.
Children watch an average of twenty-seven hours of TV each week or almost four hours each day.
By the time they are eighteen, most children will have spent more time watching TV than in school.
Advertisers spend over $600 million a year selling to children on television.
Children see about 20,000 thirty-second commercials each year or about three hours of TV advertising each week.
Most of the programmes children watch were made for adults.
Over a million young children are still watching TV at midnight.

As Professor Donald Roberts of the Institute for Communication Research at Stanford University has pointed out:

From the perspective of those advocating abolition or regulation of child-orientated advertising, commercials represent a particular threatening kind of content. First, children are viewed as a 'special' audience, one that is particularly vulnerable to television's messages. Indeed, a primary concern of television research has long been that young children, because they lack cognitive skills and the life experiences necessary to evaluate messages as adequately as might an adult, are likely to learn from and be influenced by TV content, even though it is essentially intended only to entertain them . . . Not surprisingly, when a highly sophisticated industry takes aim at a particularly vulnerable target in order to sell a product, the threat is 'obvious' to most observers.

Companies that advertise to children aim to trigger those particular emotions that will make children want and demand whatever is being showed. Nowhere, perhaps, is this more obvious than with the selling of 'fashion' or 'concept' dolls like Sindy and Barbie. It is an enormous business: £50 million worth of them are bought in the UK alone each year. It is instructive to study the face of a small girl as she watches a commercial for Sindy or Barbie; emotional yearnings are writ large. 'Role playing,' David Brown, Pedigree's managing director told *Marketing* magazine, 'is very important, and here the fashion doll comes, quite literally, into play. With their dolls, girls can act out social situations, fantasies they are not yet capable of – like winning the gymkhana – or roles they have not yet grown into.'

What emerges in terms of actual ads may prove disquieting even to advertising professionals. Collett Dickenson Pearce created an ad for Sindy in which the doll lies stretched out and alluring on a beach, with the headlines 'Miss August: Playmate of the Month'. Among the critics was Peter White, creative director of the agency Butler Dennis Garland, who wrote that it made him 'uneasy'. 'I don't have a daughter, but if I did, I wonder if I would like to think of her playing with dolls advertised in this manner. Of course, it's a clever play on words. Of course, it's well produced. Of course, it's attention getting. Of course, everyone knows that children like to emulate adults. But in the end, there's a world of difference between little girls and girlie magazines.'

The ads, of course, are meant not only to trigger fantasies but to convince the young audience that it is the particular doll or toy being shown that will satisfy that need, fill that void. With millions at stake, it is not a job that the advertisers and their agencies can take lightly. Specialised research services abound. 'Children don't think or react like adults,' says McCollum Spielman Research of Great Neck, NY, and Chicago in the messages it directs to the advertising trade. 'We know it takes a lot more than a "Smiley Face" scale to get meaningful actionable data from children and teens. It requires a thorough understanding of how kids of different ages and genders think and act.'

'K.I.D.S. Ages six–eighteen. We research them qualitatively and quantitatively,' boasts Primary Research; 'Youth Research is all we do . . . Children should be seen and not heard. We've interviewed over 27,000 children.'

Glen Smith, managing director of Children's Research Unit, a specialist UK company, has explained methods he uses. The primary technique, he told a gathering organised by the Institute of Practitioners in Advertising, was the 'matched pair' interview. The company had developed this technique specifically for interviewing children. It was used in addition to group discussions and individual interviews in order to 'refine' and 'extend' the information collected. Two children are matched in terms of age, sex, educational level, social class and locality, and the interview is then conducted by one of the company's child psychologists.

There is a period of 'initial familiarisation', followed by a 'game', albeit one with a very commercial point. One child – called the 'secondary' child – is asked to leave the interviewing room, while the other – the 'primary' child – is shown the advertising under test. The child outside returns, and the 'primary' child describes to him what he has seen; the situation is then reversed and the process repeated. 'The technique,' said Smith, 'enables the child psychologist to identify those aspects of a commercial which have registered with the children, to ascertain how effectively the advertising messages have been communicated, and to identify any distortions which have occurred. It is also revealing to note the type of questions which are put to one child by the other, by way of enhancing comprehension: these questions often reflect the child's information priorities where advertising is concerned.'

It is this information that enables the adman to refine his advertising, altering emphasis, changing ingredients if need be, to be more certain of hitting the target. Research material rarely surfaces in public. First, it is guarded because advertisers recognise the area as a 'sensitive' one; second, to the cereal companies, toy makers, computer firms, and snack producers who commission it, it represents valuable weaponry against competitors. By reading the trade literature and talking to admen, however, it is possible to identify some of the rough rules of the trade:

Animation is the most effective technique of all, perhaps because it allows the child's fantasies to be most excited.

Visual action is what counts. (The Children's Research Unit suggests switching off the sound, and noting the reaction.)

It's all right to show adults being made fun of – but children must not be derided.

Children envy children slightly older than themselves – so if you want to get a seven-year-old to buy a product, show him a ten-year-old enjoying it.

In selling a doll, the advertisement should communicate that the doll baby is *asking* for the love of a good home. Toys for boys, on the other hand, must trigger toughness and aggression.

If there is only one character in an advertisement, make him a boy – girls won't be accepted by boys but boys will be by both sexes.

In many cases the child is only the first target, a weapon to be primed and fired at the real target, the parent. Scholastic Inc, of New York, in one survey came up with the finding that advertisers wanting to sell home computers should concentrate on reaching teenagers, notably, the twelve–fourteen-year-olds, because they were the people who held the real influence in brand decision making. Another survey, conducted for Warner Amex Satellite Entertainment Co, concluded that the cable TV industry would sell more subscriptions if it aimed some of its marketing efforts at children instead of parents. The study showed that a significant number of teenagers asked their parents to buy cable TV, but it added that the total was not nearly as high as it could be if cable operators advertised to them. 'A significant marketing opportunity is being ignored,' said Marshall Cohen, vice-president for research.

Teenagers influence the choice of brands bought in supermarkets: a Beta Research Corporation survey found that six out of ten supermarket teenage shoppers had a hand in making up the family grocery list; four out of ten actually selected the brands. Other survey material claimed 20 per cent of American teenage girls have a large say in what luggage the family buys, 32 per cent influence typewriter sales, and 26 per cent are a deciding factor when it comes to buying bed linen. The rise in the number of single-parent and two-parent working has had an impact. Kevin Reilly, a Darien, Connecticut, researcher who specialises in information on children, says that a lot of them report they do the family shopping. 'They choose between Kellogg's and Post Raisin Bran, between Pepsi and Coke.' Perhaps most stunning, one company, M/E Marketing and Research, a specialist in helping companies reach children, says that children start making brand decisions around the age of four.

Fast-food operators concentrate on children, aiming to activate them into exerting the pressure that will get the family down to McDonald's or Burger King or Wimpy. Burger King, announcing a new campaign, talked of the 'buying and decision-making power of children nine through twelve'. General Foods Ice Magic is a topping for ice-cream, generally served up by mothers. General Foods, however, knows who makes Mum buy – a UK campaign ran in fourteen children's comics and in cartoon inserts in adult publications with the aim of reaching a target seven–eleven-year-old group. The cereal manufacturers are experts. Ads sometimes provide the initial lead-in to giveaway offers which involve coupon-collecting and, thus, repeat buying. One for Kellogg's Rice Krispies, offering stickers in return for tokens, ran in children's comics. The ad represented the first token – 'Add this token to three of the order forms which can be found on special packs of Rice Krispies . . .'

None of these ways of approaching the parents, it must be confessed, compares with the notorious post-war campaign by the American Television Manufacturers' Association to spread the use of television. Advertisements were inserted in more than 1,000 newspapers, all designed to shame parents into buying sets for their children. A tearful little girl and a sulky older brother were shown in a large illustration, with the text, 'There are some things a son or daughter won't tell you.' The children, it emerged, were ashamed to be with their friends because they had not seen the same TV shows. The children, too proud to tell their parents, had borne the 'bruise deep inside'. There was an outcry and some newspapers refused to carry the ad. Later, it was replaced with a 'positive' advertisement. In this one the children were happy and the text said, 'You'd give them the world if you could – this Christmas you can.'

Again, that was long ago. However, Americans in 1984 were given a commercial for Apple Computers that was also addressed to children. This told them how to persuade their parents to get them a home computer, with the hint that without one they would suffer indignities. Sid Bernstein, the advertising columnist, commented, 'Apple will deny that its commercial makes this appeal, and it will insist that its coaching kids in how to influence their parents is all good-natured fun. But the basic appeal is undoubtedly there.'

Palitoy, a division of General Mills, adopted a similar approach albeit on a smaller scale in Britain. Parents buying toys were asked the name, age and address of the child for whom it was being bought. As Christmas neared, the children received their own letter enclosing leaflets urging them to buy Action Force military vehicles. The children were told that if they bought four from the local toyshop, they would receive two free figures and a set of battle gear 'all in time for Christmas'. Trading Standards officers received complaints from parents who believed that the leaflets encouraged children to pressure parents. They were told there was nothing the officers could do; the advertisers were not breaking the law.

There are rules. They change, but an international round-up showed the following picture. In Australia ads to children were restricted to 9 a.m. to 10.20 a.m. In Canada, they were only allowed on weekday mornings. In New Zealand, they were restricted to 3 p.m. to 4 p.m. Australia, Germany, Holland, New Zealand, South Africa and Switzerland banned ads to children on Sunday and some national holidays. Quebec Province, Canada, allowed no TV or radio advertising aimed at children under thirteen. Belgium, Denmark, Norway and Sweden allowed no 'children's' advertisements on TV or radio. Finland, France, Holland and Turkey restricted the use of children in food advertisements. Austria, Canada, Holland, the Philippines, Singapore, South Africa, and Switzerland limited the use of cartoon characters to endorse products. In Australia, Singapore and the US, cartoon characters could not *recommend* products though they could present them.

There are a number of special rules regarding confectionery. Health warnings have to be included in Chile, Malaysia, Mexico and New Zealand. Sweet ads in Japan and Holland have to remind children to brush their teeth. Holland bans the use of children under fourteen in confectionery ads and in any event bans all such ads before 7.55 p.m. The Netherlands Advertising Council said that it believed on the basis of expert advice that there is a 'causal connection' between brand advertising on radio and TV and the extent of consumption: 'The council is of the opinion that advertising for these sweets may constitute a menace to public health.'

In the US and the UK the rules are such that admen seem to regard them more as a minor nuisance than a real constraint. There is an air that it is the powers-that-be doing its Mommy-knows-best act, and, thus they are not to be taken too seriously. Of the US, David Ogilvy in *Ogilvy on Advertising* writes, 'Gentle reader and fellow parent, if you think it unseemly for researchers to enrol children as guinea pigs, it will comfort you to know that they are now protected from us admen by ferocious regulations. For example, we are no longer allowed to tell children to importune their mothers to buy our products.' He lists a number of US regulations in force:

Appeals shall not be used which directly or by implication contend that if children have a product they are better than their peers, or lacking it, will not be accepted by their peers . . . Material shall not be used which can reasonably be expected to frighten children or provoke anxiety, nor shall material be used which contains a portrayal of or appeal to violent, dangerous or otherwise anti-social behaviour . . . Each commercial for breakfast-type products shall include at least one audio reference to and one video depiction of the role of the product within the framework of a balanced regimen.

Ogilvy comments, 'Just try writing a commercial which obeys *thirty-four* regulations like these.' (His italics.)

Britain, too, has rules. The Independent Broadcasting Authority Code says, 'No product or service may be advertised, and no method of advertising may be used, in association with a programme intended for children, or which large numbers of children are likely to see or hear, which might result in harm to them, physically, mentally or morally, and no method of advertising may be employed which takes advantage of the natural credulity and senses of loyalty of children.' The Code of Advertising Practice, which covers print ads, bans 'direct appeals or exhortations to buy' unless the product concerned is one that the child himself should reasonably be expected to buy, ads that 'encourage children to make themselves a nuisance to their parent', and insists that the results shown as obtained by a product should not exaggerate what a child might obtain, as well as others. Rules, however, are obviously open to a wide range of interpretation. The *Guardian* pointed out that despite the rule that children should not be exhorted to buy unless the product is affordable by them, Matchbox were advertising car race sets to them that were priced at over £60. Generally, in any event, rules in the UK are much less stringent than in the rest of Europe. For example, children can be freely used in ads. Children, thus, sell to children.

In both the US and the UK there have been attempts to tighten the restrictions. In Britain, the Annan Committee on Broadcasting recommended that advertisements be banned from within or between children's programmes. No advertisements are, in fact, allowed in children's programmes lasting thirty minutes or less. In the US, the Federal Trade Commission in 1978 set up a project involving banning or limiting ads to children. It considered, but never formally proposed, a ban on all commercials during shows aimed at very young children; a ban on ads for highly sugared foods, including candy and some breakfast cereals, during shows seen by older children; and a requirement that advertisers devote money to public-service messages promoting good dental and nutritional habits. Not surprisingly, it attracted massive opposition. In 1981, it was killed off after the FTC staff recommended the proceedings should be scrapped. The staff, in a ninety-five-page final report, refused to 'clear' ads to children, however, and said they remained a 'legitimate cause of concern'. The staff said that evidence 'supports the conclusion' that children aged six and younger are essentially defenceless against advertising designed for children but that an advertising ban – 'the only effective remedy' – was impractical.

Action for Children's Television later attempted its own – novel – remedy. It attempted to force advertisers to begin and end every ad directed at children with an inaudible signal that could be blacked out by an electronic device parents would attach to their TV sets.

Under President Reagan, the FTC rescinded some of the restrictions on toy advertising. It decided to allow companies to resume using in their children's toy ads such camera techniques as slow motion, freeze frame and tracking and stroboscopic lights. The commission had barred those techniques in 1971 in response to complaints that two toy manufacturers deceived children into thinking that their toys, Hot Wheels and Johnny Lightning cars, were capable of drag strip speeds and other impossible feats. *Advertising Age*'s reporter commented that the FTC decision 'chipped away at the notion that children's advertising should be bounded by special, stricter standards of conduct than advertising in general'. Earlier, the Federal Communications Commission had essentially begun a hands-off policy on children's television, including advertisements. In 1988 Congress restored limits on the amount of advertising in children's programmes—ten and a half minutes per hour at weekends, twelve on weekdays—only to have it vetoed by President Reagan as one of his last acts as president. Supporters vowed legislation would be reintroduced in 1989.

In Europe, toy marketers could draw comfort from the effects of satellite television and the moves towards commercialised broadcasting. They looked forward to an ease in restrictions, a reversal of the trend of recent years. Satellite stations like the UK's Children's Channel were beaming their messages into countries where advertisements were banned.

In both Britain and the US there has been surprising reluctance to act against one masterstroke of marketing devised by the toy companies. In 1983, American television began airing programmes that were based around toys. The first, *He Man and the Masters of the Universe*, was followed by a flood of others all seeking to enjoy the same media and merchandising mix. By 1986, there were said to be over sixty shows where the editorial control lay with the toy companies. A *GI Joe* series, for example, included ninety half-hour shows featuring all the characters, vehicles and weapons in Hasbro's GI Joe line. The list of shows included Kenner's *Care Bears* and *Strawberry Shortcake*, Wallace Berrie's *Snorks*, Hasbro-Bradley's *Transformer* and *GI Joe*, Tonka's *Gobots*, Mattel's *Rainbow Brite* and American Greetings' *Get Along Gang*. All were names that rapidly became well known to kids on both sides of the Atlantic.

In Britain Mattel's agency, Saatchi and Saatchi, described *Masters of the Universe* in a trade ad as a weekly half-hour commercial for its client. A competitor objected; the series was suspended. By December 1984 the show was back on the air. What was new about the toymakers' masterstroke (which in marketing terms it surely was) was that it had taken the old idea of basing toys on characters in books or programmes and turned it inside out. Now the toys came first. Then the programmes. At a commercial level it made great sense to both the toymen and the television companies. The toy firms received a literally priceless amount of exposure for their products; the broadcasters got a pre-sold audience for their new programmes.

With the help of the *He Man* series, Mattel sold more than 70 million plastic figures in the US in three years. In both the UK and the US Mattel was so pleased by results that it gave *He Man* a companion series, *She-Ra, Princess of Power*. Hasbro-Bradley's Transformers toy line (toys that can change from vehicles to robots) attracted more than $100 million of sales in their first year with the help of the show *The Transformers*, making it the most successful toy introduction ever.

Thundercats, another toymaker/television tie-up is worthy of a special mention. It began as a six-minute tape by Lorimar-Telepictures based on the successful elements in other successful series. It was shown to focus groups, tested on cable television (with viewers being surveyed by telephone) and then, and only then, made into a programme. By the winter of 1986, it was showing on 132 stations in the United States, and the shops were full of Thundercat characters. Furthermore, Lorimar had a system whereby they offered broadcasting stations a percentage of the toy profit in their area in return for screening the show.

It is not only that television is being used to sell the toys; it is the TV series that makes the products desirable. The toys don't *do* anything. They have to be moved about by hand. The action comes when they are animated on screen and that's what makes the toys more than they actually are. Chris Wicks of Zodiac Stores, a large UK toy chain, said,

'Still a lot of ads make it look like the product can sing and dance and fly, when it can't.'

The manufacturers say they need television. Peter Brown, UK managing director of Tomy, Japan, said, 'We use TV to drive our business. In the UK, TV has become the toy catalogue. If it's not on TV, it won't get on the kids' shopping list.'

The whole practice has brought a series of protests. 'This is the worst kind of exploitation,' said Frank Worme, president of the National Association for Better Broadcasting in the US. 'It's deceptive and cynical because kids can't tell when they are being pitched.' A British toy retailer, Peter Kreiger, complained that the public and children are being 'brainwashed'. 'Parents come in and demand plastic rubbish. When I point this out to them, they say, "Yes, I know. But it's the one he wants," when another would do just as well. Or they come in and say, "Have you got 'X'?" and I ask them if they know what it is. They say, "No, but he says he wants it."'

Robert Krock, of Action for Children's Television, complained, 'The subtle, more insidious problem with programme-length commercials is that they are displacing other kinds of children's programme in the name of vested-interest commercial speech. Newspaper editors would never dream of turning over their editorial pages to advertisers; yet that's exactly what broadcasters are doing with children's television.' Critics recalled that in 1969 the Federal Communications Commission had rules against such programmes. One toy company had argued then that Mattel's *Hot Wheels* was a thirty-minute commercial. The FCC agreed, and said, 'We find this pattern disturbing; more disturbing than the question of whether the commercial time logged is adequate. For this pattern subordinates programming in the interest of the public to programming in the interest of its saleability.'

Advertising trade magazines in both Britain and the US have voiced disquiet. 'It's surely time the ground rules were reviewed,' said *Marketing* in an editorial under the headline, 'Not playing the game'. *Advertising Age* headed its editorial 'A TV licence to steal from kids' and said, 'You can hardly tell the commercials from the programmes, especially if you're too little to comprehend what advertising is and, certainly, to be sophisticated enough about it to know a licensing deal when you see (watch) it.' And it warned, 'Although it takes the American public a while to react to excesses, reaction is sure to come, and many more voices will be heard.' The toymakers and the broadcasters, on the other hand, could not see what the disquiet was all about – or, at least, they purported not to see. Douglas Thomson, president of the Toy Manufacturers of America, wrote to *Ad Age*, 'I frankly do not understand your reference to "stealing". As in all businesses, the TV show and product is presented with the producer and manufacturer risking reputation and financial resources. If the consumers perceive value in the entertainment, they respond by watching and buying. If not, they turn off and don't buy. The measure is always value, and there is no theft involved that I can see.' George F. Schweitzer, a CBS broadcast group vice-president told *Business Week*, 'Why should it be wrong if the toy inspired the programme and not the other way around? We evaluate programming on entertainment value and not on its merchandising ability.'

In the UK, there are some minor restrictions – a commercial for a toy cannot be shown on the same day as the series that features it. In 1987, the IBA and toy trade bodies settled down to what were described as 'low key discussions' on the overuse of fantasy and emotion in toy ads. One station, the TV-AM breakfast network, decided after discussions with the IBA to cut its percentage of toy advertising from 20 per cent in 1986 to 17.5 per cent the following year and 15 per cent in 1988.

The programmes have their counterparts in the print world – magazines like *Barbie*, a 'fashion and lifestyle' magazine built around the doll, and with a readership said to have an average age of eight. Peggy Charren, the director of Action for Children's Television, said, 'It's incredible that magazine publishers are finding more ways to turn a kid's world into a commercial.'

In 1987, the emergence of 'interactive' toys provided a further complication. Mattel's *Captain Power and the Soldiers of the Future* is linked to a half-hour programme. Child viewers use a special hand-held weapon to take part in the battles being shown on screen. TV programmes are programmed with light patterns that can be received and decoded by the child's weapon. Children can fire at the screen and record – and receive – hits. Many observers were cheered by a decline in the ratings of toy-based programmes in 1988. But most reserved their applause, noting that the main reason was that with success the companies had become complacent—storylines, for example, were almost non-existent. However, without a change of heart or regulation, it remained in their power to turn that around.

Arguments between advertisers to children and their critics often take place on specific points like the ones raised above. In reality, however, what is usually implicit is a clash between two different basic beliefs – whether or not it is 'fair' to target children in the selling process. A staff report of the Federal Trade Commission in 1978 gave a good summary of the critic's stance: 'Many believe it is unfair to advertise any product on television to children who are so young . . . that they cannot understand the selling purpose of, or otherwise comprehend or evaluate, commercials and thus discount them, if they so choose, as adults or older children can.'

It is not just academics and consumerists who feel disquiet about toy company activities. Euromonitor is a UK organisation which prepares business reports on trading trends for industry insiders. Its report on toys described marketing strategies in the industry by companies like Mattel and Hasbro-Bradley as questionable in both business and moral terms. 'Advertising to children infringes on parents' desire to influence their children in ways they think proper. It is difficult to see why the advertisers should gain access to the upbringing of children. The negative aspects of a marketing-orientated industry are clearly visible in toyshops where copycat ranges jostle each other as evidence that the industry's innovative thinking and energy are now predominantly directed into marketing rather than the production of attractive toys.' And the National Association of Toy Retailers in Britain carried out a survey of members which showed that 70 per cent of them were hostile to the hard-sell approach of the leading US and Japanese toy companies. Retailers believed that a curb on ads would force manufacturers to make better toys. (It must be noted that retailers are worried about high volatility brought by massive ad campaigns; they fear being left with stocks once the advertising stops.)

Donald F. Roberts, of Stanford University, in a survey of the debate, has listed a number of arguments against the advertiser. One is that child-orientated commercials are bound to engender parent-child conflict if the parent refuses when the child asks for the object of the commercial: 'To the extent parents resist, family harmony is at risk.' Another is that commercials for young children 'may create a kind of materialistic or consumption-orientated value system that is at odds with what the world needs in a time when we are all encouraged to believe that conservation of resources is one of the more worthy goals to which we can strive.' The other concern of those who would regulate is the products themselves. 'Over 80 per cent of children's advertising deals with four categories: toys, cereals (primarily sugar-coated cereals), candies, and fast-food restaurants. This is not a product array designed to allay the fears of parents or other groups concerned with children's welfare.'

The Australian Consumers' Association has concerned itself with this last point. In its 'consumer's view of Australia's food industry', *Processed Food: A pain in the belly*, it complains of the 'offensive picture' which emerges from analysing television between 3 p.m. and 6 p.m. when children constituted the largest audience. 'In this time slot the proportion of food advertisements to total advertising rose to 44 per cent on Channel 10. Fewer than 10 per cent of foods or drinks advertised could be appraised as making a nutritional contribution which was not marred by the addition of fat, salt or sugar. Considering that sound nutritional practice ought to be established in childhood, and that television is a key source of education for most children, it deserves the greatest censure that children are getting the most and the worst kind of food messages from Australian television.'

As a detailed example, it said that a child watching one of the channels (Channel 10) each day of a week the association studied during the

3–6 p.m. period could have seen: a thirty-second commercial for Peters Super Hero icecreams (screened five times), Cadbury's Dairy Milk Chocolate (twice), MacDonald's (fourteen times), Pepsi-Cola (twice) and Lifesavers (five times). It commented 'The role of jingles in enhancing the product's appeal to the child also deserves attention in this time slot. Seventy-six per cent of advertisements for ice-cream, ice-blocks, sweets and snacks used a jingle to get their message across, compared to 53 per cent of total food advertising for the week studied.' The association was particularly scathing about 'hidden sugar' and the products that contained it – fruit-flavoured powdered drinks like Tang, Zest and Robinson's Lemon Barley which contained as much as 12.8 per cent sugar, and a number of breakfast cereals, one of which (Kellogg's Honey Snacks) contained a breathtaking (or tooth-rotting) 52.2 per cent sugar.

As to the claims of the commercials, the report was equally critical. Milky Way chocolate bars sold themselves (as they do in the UK) as 'the sweet you can eat between meals'. The comment: 'with 73 per cent sugar and 17 per cent fat, this claim is promoting a product which has a negative nutritional value and is entirely likely to ruin the appetites of the children, for whom it is promoted, for their normal meals.' Or of a Mars bar with its claim that its good things help your day, 'Glucose, caramel and chocolate are not "good" in the nutritional sense.'

A further argument, heard more strongly in the US than in the UK, is that ads to children present and reinforce stereotype people. Thus, Action for Children's Television argues:

> In the world of commercials, boys play with toy trucks and racing cars. Girls play with makeup, dolls, and miniature household appliances. Moms offer snacks to the gang; dads get out and toss the football around. If women have careers at all, they're mere diversions from their kitchens and their men: 'I can bring home the bacon, fry it up in a pan, and never let you forget you're a man . . . 'cause I'm a woman.'
>   How constructive are these advertising stereotypes?
>   Sexism, racism and ageism emerge in more subtle ways as well. Women may be on camera, displaying the product, but the voice of authority convincing consumers to buy is usually male – 90.6 per cent of the time, according to one Screen Actors Guild study. Blacks are given fewer speaking roles than whites, and they are usually the ones being instructed – more often than not by a white man – in the right product to buy.

Those who defend advertising to children – not just the specific advertisers concerned – have their own arguments. The first is one that is applied to all attempts to curb the right to advertise: if a product can be manufactured and distributed legally, it should then also be legal to advertise it. The second is that advertising on television is necessary in order to finance and maintain children's programming. A third is that given this is a commercial world, being exposed to advertising is actually a part of a child's growing-up process: in an (artificial) ad-less world, children would not learn to cope with commercial messages.

A fourth is that children are more capable of handling advertisements than the Nanny-figures give them credit for. The international sales and marketing director for Mettoy toys, R. M. Hall, told a Marketing Society conference that the child consumer is a 'self-opinionated individual. He or she is an expert fully capable of seeing through marketing chicanery.' Glen Smith, managing director of the Children's Research Unit, says:

> There is a school of thought which holds to the view that children are like little sponges, absorbing the advertiser's messages, programmed to acquire the product at all costs. Our own research experience shows that this is emphatically not the case. We find that children are aware of the purpose of advertising at a very early age, and that they apply their own quite stringent criteria when evaluating advertisements. Although wide individual differences occur between children of the same age, children demonstrate a quite sophisticated knowledge and comprehension of advertising claims and techniques, often rejecting particular commercials, with a well developed scepticism towards product claims.

And:

> Children . . . are consumers in their own right – despite their limited spending power, they are assiduously courted by advertisers, in the hope that, once snared, they will be for ever hooked. This is to reckon without the child's own self-protection instincts: children are highly adaptive, and quickly develop a shrewd resistance to the various temptations on offer. They may seem to be hypnotised by a television commercial, never losing eye contact with the set, as adults do; in reality however, they retain only what they consider relevant in terms of information and entertainment value, operating a highly effective screening system to block out what they do not consider to be of value to them.

Is that true? There is a vast amount of research that can be called on by both sides. In reviewing it in 1983, one academic, Donald F. Roberts, isolated a number of conclusions he believed emerged from it:

> 1. The typical American child views approximately fifty-five commercials a day. It is 'relatively well documented' that children are particularly apt to attend to and learn from child-orientated commer-

cials. Given these two factors, 'it would be surprising if there was not a good deal of evidence that children are affected by such exposure.'

2. Research, in fact, 'has consistently indicated that children learn from commercials and that they attempt to use what they learn to influence parental purchase decisions.'

3. Several surveys have found a positive relationship between heavy exposure to commercials and acceptance of commercial claims, belief in ads and the desire for advertised products.

Roberts cites one 'convincing demonstration of the persuasive power of child-oriented advertising'. In this, two researchers obtained a list of boys' Christmas gift requests in both early November and late December, a period spanning the peak toy commercial season. They measured the amount of exposure to commercials and 'children's cognitive and attitudinal defences against commercials'.

The researchers, J. R. Rossiter and T. S. Robertson, found that children with the strongest defences selected fewer television-promoted toys in November than did those with the weaker defences. 'However, by late December, strong anti-commercial defences made no difference. Apparently a heavy advertising campaign was adequate to overcome even the most resistant children's initial defences against commercial appeals.'

In arguing for fewer restrictions, the advertisers would probably dispute such findings. But privately they are more likely to nod in agreement and hope their own advertising has such potency. It is, after all, what it's all about.

6

The Sick

'Promoting drugs to doctors these days is much like selling soap
to consumers. It's all in the marketing.'

Wall Street Journal

In a narrow, converted town house, just north of Trafalgar Square,
opposite one of the three theatres that occupy the street, a number of
doctors are taking part in a different kind of theatricals. Each one has
been given paints and paper and has been told to paint what comes into
his mind. The finished pictures are striking in their subject matter and
in the abandon of their execution. One has depicted a sunset over a
sea, another the gate of a nuclear plant with a 'Danger' sign, a third a
prison . . .

'Astonishing material,' says Peter Cooper, a psychologist, as he shows
them to me later. They are what psychologists know as psychodrawings;
each of them presents what a doctor feels about different brands of
anti-diarrhoeal drugs. The nuclear plant, for example, is one doctor's
representation of Searle Pharmaceuticals' drug, Lomotil. The paintings,
Cooper explains, reveal 'how human General Practitioners are in their
prescribing behaviour'. The psychodrawings are one of the ways
Cooper's company gets doctors to relax, to reveal themselves. Others
involve getting the doctors to act out roles, to brainstorm, to complete
partly-drawn pictures, and to say what comes into their heads when
words are thrown at them.

Cooper's client on this project is one of the major pharmaceutical
companies, wanting to know how best to target a drug at its doctor
customers. What these doctors – chosen to represent the doctor population at large – reveal will be discussed, analysed, presented to marketing and advertising men, and used in the increasingly competitive battle
to get drug brand names on the prescription pads. The gatherings are
known in the jargon as ECGs – 'Extended Creative Groups'. They are
used because doctors are believed to be especially bad at revealing the
truth in response to direct questions. 'If they are interviewed, they will
treat you like patients,' says Cooper. 'The doctor has feelings associated
with brands like ordinary consumers, but you have got to get him to
relax.'

Doctors are subject to the most intensive sales pressures of any group in the community. As much as 20–25 per cent of sales may be spent on promotion. Drug marketers are among the world's biggest advertisers. Even in the UK, where the amount spent is restricted by government, each doctor is the target for over £5,000 worth of promotion a year.

It is not the doctor as ultimate consumer that is the target, of course. It is the doctor as giver of drug-based relief. The figure of £5,000-plus falls better into place when another is added – the £58,000 worth of drugs that the average British GP prescribes each year.

The drug industry is a vast, complex, secretive, international business. But the rationale of heavy advertising is simple to state and to understand. The range of drugs available for prescribing is huge – about 6,000 in the UK, 2,000 of which are listed in MIMS, the drug reference guide that doctors keep on or in their desks. No doctor can keep track of all those individual drugs, and, in any event, many are what are known among marketing men as 'me too' medications – drugs that are near-identical to perhaps scores of others. In practice, therefore, a doctor's prescribing is generally limited to about 400 drugs and only 200 of those on a regular basis. The aim of a drug company is to get its drugs on that short list. 'What you want,' said one executive of an advertising agency specialising in drugs, 'is that when the doctor diagnoses a certain condition, his first thought is for your brand.' Another explained: 'Your drug *has* to get a place. If you get it wrong at the beginning (when the drug is introduced) you have had it. You don't get two bites at the cherry. If a doctor starts to think of your drug as a reserve product, there is no way you are going to remedy that later.'

The answer, then, for drug companies would seem to be relatively simple. Doctors are trained, scientific men, specialist handlers of drugs. Therefore, you give them the facts and they make up their minds – and their lists – on a purely rational basis. The truth, according to professionals who market to doctors, is not like that at all. Doctors, they say, are vulnerable to the same kind of techniques and pressures as any other group of individuals. Perhaps the major difference, they add, is the degree of pretence that is necessary: doctors resent being thought of as irrational and open to emotional persuasion as other people. It is instructive that when the UK trade publication *Marketing Week* asked eleven drug companies for their co-operation on a proposed feature on the industry, only one agreed and then, according to the magazine, in such a bland way as to be of little real help. The pharmaceutical admen I saw, however, (and they all wished to remain anonymous) were in no doubt about the nature of their task. 'They [doctors] think they decide on scientific grounds,' said a man from one of the major American agencies. 'They don't. They choose drugs the same way consumers choose goods.'

This may mean deliberately choosing one branded drug in preference to a non-brand equivalent. The effect of this can be striking. At the beginning of 1985, for example, Valium in Britain cost seventeen times as much as diazepan, the same drug under another (non-proprietary) name. Routinely, 1,000 tablets of a drug could vary in price between £1.50 and £13.60 depending on whether the doctor prescribed the generic or the (chemically identical) branded version.

The pharmaceutical industry as we know it today is less than forty years old. Until the 1940s most drugs were naturally occurring substances (such as digitalis and opium). Aspirin was one of the very few synthetic pharmaceutical substances. Penicillin was discovered in the 1940s. However, it was not until the following decade that specific pharmaceutical chemicals started to be developed and synthesised in significant quantities.

The industry has a number of important characteristics. One is that it is predominantly international. There are about one hundred large and medium-sized companies. A major reason for the internationalism is said to be the huge research and development costs – a company must have worldwide sales to realise its investment. Research is a subject that constantly recurs in discussions about pharmaceutical advertising. Research and development cost the industry in the UK £650 million in 1987, ten times that worldwide. The big promotion budgets, it is argued, are in part necessary to help companies recoup these big research costs. Bayer, the huge German pharmaceutical company, said in one of its corporate ads, 'We start off by examining as many as 8,000 substances; this is followed by intensive research, an extensive series of tests and investments totalling up to DM 90 million before a new Bayer drug can go into production. The whole process takes around ten years.'

A number of countries, such as Austria, Belgium, Holland and Sweden, have found it more difficult to compete internationally. Only five countries remain in the big league of innovators: Britain, Germany, Japan (a recent entry), Switzerland and the United States. A small group of American, German and Swiss multinationals, however, dominate the business. In 1986, *Chemical Insight*'s list of the top ten companies consisted of four American (including the first, Merck and Co.), two German, two Swiss, one Japanese and one British (Glaxo at number seven). The multinationals that dominate are those which discovered many of the most-used drugs and learned to sell them worldwide. Globally, the industry is worth about $80 billion, about a quarter of that accounted for by prescription drug sales by US companies.

One key feature of the industry is that, in the words of George Teeling-Smith of the Office of Health Economics in London, 'It is based on the production of new knowledge rather than mere chemicals. It produces treatments rather than tablets. The chemical substances themselves have little intrinsic value and are cheap to produce.' The value of the right knowledge translated into the right pill marketed in the right way can be quite staggering. Thanks to astute promotion, one drug, Pfizer's Procardia (of which, more later) achieved sales of $17 million in its first twelve weeks despite its similarity to existing products from two other companies.

Promotion has been a feature of the industry since early days. In 1944, one writer, Denys Thompson, in *Voice of Civilisation, An Enquiry into Advertising*, noted: 'It is . . . surprising to find that doctors – members of a profession which one might have thought proof against patent medicine advertisements – can be influenced by pressure of publicity just as much as any other section of the community. This is proved by the steady increase in the amount of drugs prescribed under proprietary names.'

As far as selling drugs, however, there has been one enormous change. Today the marketing of a drug may be *the* most important thing about it. The drug itself may have little to justify it other than the niche that the marketers – with the help of advertising – have carved for it in the market-place. In the early days of the industry, there was little call for advertising. New drugs that were developed fulfilled a need; furthermore they usually generated publicity for the role they satisfied. However, that situation lasted for only a brief period. Fuelled by huge investment, new products began to pour forth. They could still claim to be unique in that they actually did things existing products could not do, but the sheer number of them necessitated an increasingly active marketing machine.

The next stage, the present one, saw the same outpouring of new products – except that now most of them are not unique at all. They are what marketers call 'me too' products – no better, no worse, not fundamentally different, from those other products with which they compete. By 1984 there were said to be about sixteen 'me too' pain-killers that had been developed to relieve arthritis. Hans-Peter Hauser, head of international marketing at Ciba-Geigy, noting that the innovation rate got slower and slower after the early seventies, has said, 'It used to be that R & D came up with products and said "You sell them". Now, as competition gets fiercer and the industry approaches maturity, the marketing end becomes more important.'

Pharmaceutical companies will claim benefits for all their new drugs, of course, but even insiders, in private, concede they are often of no more real significance than, say, the different fragrance given to one of several competing floor cleaners or the bottle shapes of rival orange flavour soft drinks. One adman, speaking on the eve of the launch of a new drug, confided to me, 'Between these four walls, a doctor could offer you any one of four or five others and it would do the same thing. The point is that once you have the machine you have to fuel it. Most big companies are built on one significant breakthrough product. Then they have a lean period before they come up with another. In the lean period, when there is no breakthrough, they've still got to come up with the goodies.'

One reason for so many 'me too' products is that the area within which the companies concentrate most of their energies is to a large extent a self-limited one. Those illnesses that most interest the drugs companies are those most common in the developed world that need constant medication. Two doctors from the DHSS Medicine Division in Britain, when reviewing innovation in the 1970s, noted that during the period thirty remarkably similar products for the treatment of heart disease were launched, but only one was an NCE (new chemical entity – i.e. a product that's new or has significant advances). The new product was oxamniquine, used in the treatment of the world's most common disease, schistosomiasis (bilharziasis), a parasite infection. Innovation, they argued, is 'directed towards commercial returns rather than therapeutic need.' 'Most R & D is now going into chronic diseases,' said one insider. 'They're drugs for a maintenance kind of therapy.' In other words drugs that keep on being prescribed perhaps for years and years.

Over 8 per cent of the advertising money that was being spent in American journals in 1987 was for anti-hypertensive drugs. In total cardiovascular drugs took over 25 per cent. Some other major areas were beta blockers (nearly 8 per cent), antibiotics (nearly 7 per cent), anti-ulcer preparations (5.21), antiarthritics (5.05), and non-narcotic analgesics (3.52).

It seems to be generally accepted that in the near future at least the situation will not change. Clifford Jellett, of Louis Harris International Medical Surveys, told a conference in Zurich, '*Real* therapeutic advance will be a rare event. It will become increasingly difficult to differentiate new products from existing agents.' He also said, 'Marketing has become more and more concerned with brands, less so with products – more concerned with brand imagery and personality, with positioning and targeting certain sectors of the market, and less in aiming haphazardly at the total market – with lifestyle influences on purchase behaviour as a predictor of likely purchase. This situation has become more and more true of pharmaceutical marketing, as more and more products emerge with little therapeutic difference between them, and competition increases.'

The *Wall Street Journal* considered the example of Isordil, a nitrate drug prescribed to heart patients to prevent severe chest pains. At that time it held 46 per cent of the US market. The newspaper noted that the producers, Ives Laboratories division of American Home Products Corp, claimed it was longer acting and in some ways more effective than competitors although some doctors thought, 'Isordil differs little from competing drugs.' However, the newspaper noted, Ives had 'promoted its nitrates so aggressively for so long that many doctors think only of Isordil when they think of nitrates.' And it commented, 'If the success of Isordil illustrates anything, it's that promoting drugs to doctors these days is much like selling soap to consumers: it's all in the marketing.'

Wyeth Laboratories is another of American Home Products units. It sells Ativan, which was introduced into the US in 1977. Ativan had one problem: as an anti-anxiety drug, it emerged in the shadow of Hoffmann-La Roche's tranquilliser, Valium. The two drugs could perhaps be described as being 'very similar'. Wyeth needed a marketing edge if Ativan was to take off. It found it in tests (which it had promoted) that showed its drug was expelled from the body more quickly than Valium. The medical significance of this is regarded as arguable. Nevertheless, it provided a focus for a marketing drive. By 1981 Ativan was outselling Valium in a number of countries, including the other drug's homeland, Switzerland.

The growth of the 'me too' product is not the only reason for the move from the product to the marketing. Drugs introduced in the period of innovation – like Valium – are coming off patent. That means competition from generic copies. The generics are helped by pressures (from government and health insurers) for cheaper prescriptions and by the fact that doctors now appear to trust generic drugs more than they once did. In America companies have deluged doctors with prescription pads that contain the printed words NO SUBSTITUTION. Some companies have also given their pills *shapes* that generic rivals cannot copy. Thus Valium was produced with a hole in the middle of the pill, and American Home's Inderal tablet was made in the shape of the letter 'I'. Some advertisements have very skilfully managed to draw distinctions between their subject product (good) and the generic rival (bad) when they don't really exist. In its ads for Melleril, an antipsychotic drug, Sandoz used the brand name when discussing 'good' qualities of the drug, the generic name when discussing the 'bad' ones. The US Food and Drug Administration, which protested the ad, said that it had seen similar approaches before, but this one had merited a letter because it was so obvious. The ad showed a worried elderly woman holding a prescription bottle with the headline, 'It may be Thioridazine [the generic name] but is it Melleril?'

Privately, drug companies and advertising men justify their defence of the brand on medical grounds by claiming that although their drug may be no different chemically from its generic rival, it does actually do the patient more good. Judie Lannon, of J. Walter Thompson, London, and Peter Cooper, confronted this point directly in a paper. They wrote:

An important question is whether taking a branded analgesic as opposed to unbranded can actually increase pain relief. The hypothesis is that there would be increased confidence and added values in a brand from its marketing and advertising, and if this is so it would provide proof of the efficacy of branding actually influencing the mind's control over bodily processes. Indeed this proved to be the case.

Double-blind trials demonstrated that branding accounts for a quarter to a third of the pain relief. That is to say, branding works like an ingredient of its own interacting with the pharmacological active ingredients to produce something more powerful than the unbranded tablet.

Or as *Which?* put it in a slightly different way in its discussion on the analgesic Pharmacin. 'You might *expect* the blue and white Pharmacin capsules to do you more good than the ordinary white aspirin BP tablets, and this may affect how well you think they have worked . . .'

Although there is even more marketing, more aggressive marketing, and more 'scientific' marketing, most pharmaceutical companies are reluctant to publicise or discuss the fact. Whatever the truth, it is better to be seen as businesslike but altruistic, more like healers than hucksters. Marketing, commented the *Financial Times* 'has a somewhat nasty ring to it within the drug industry'.

Not every company is taciturn, however. Pfizer of New York is the world's sixth largest drug company. Its president, Dr Gerald Leubach, likes the label 'a hot marketing company'. He says, 'I came into this industry when marketing consisted of giving away golf balls. It's almost unbelievable how marketing has changed; it's now almost as scientific as anything we do.'

Drug companies not infrequently see themselves as misunderstood, maligned and mistreated. The high cost of research coupled with the (to them) shortness of patent protection makes it necessary for companies to recoup investments quickly. The average cost of developing a new drug in 1987 was said to be £60–£100 million. The patent period in the UK is twenty years (in the US it is seventeen). Research and testing, argues the industry, can eat up as many as twelve years of that. Furthermore, the claim continues, it can be another two years before the doctors begin prescribing the drug in significant quantity. In the UK, that leaves only six years before rivals can begin producing a cheap copy. 'It is not long to make a profit,' said one spokesman.

There is increasing pressure from governments. New Zealand, for example, has limited the *quantities* of drugs that can be prescribed. In the UK, there is a ceiling on the amount that may be spent on promotion (in 1987 about 9 per cent of turnover) and since 1985 doctors have not been able to prescribe some branded drugs, claimed to have cheaper equivalents, on the National Health Service. Consumer groups also regard drug companies increasingly as a target.

It would be a short-sighted young drug adman, however, who saw this as a time to seek new horizons. Stephen King, the creative director of Medicus Intercon, New York, in an article extolling the business, enthused:

Healthcare advertising is a great place to stay and a great place to grow. The fact is that healthcare advertisers today are the communicators for an industry that's on the brink of some very dramatic growth and some very basic change. For one thing, the drug industry itself is becoming much more competitive . . . Industry sources tell us that more than 1,000 new drugs are awaiting approval by the FDA – drugs that will need to be advertised to physicians and healthcare providers. The larger and more competitive market is being widened still more by the advent of generic drugs. As these lower-cost substitutes become more readily available, pharmaceutical companies are finding that their older, established drugs, now off patent, are facing intense price competition, and they are mounting brand-name-orientated promotional programmes to meet that threat.

Today, [continued Mr King's rallying call] pharmaceutical companies spend considerably more than $2 billion a year on advertising to healthcare professionals. Our segment of the industry offers comparable salaries and unparalleled creative and account management opportunities for the talented professional. Healthcare advertising may be narrower than our consumer alter ego – but it's just as tall.

The marketing effort to imprint company and brand names on doctors' minds begins the day students enter medical school. The Public Citizen Health Research Group has listed some of the attempts made to keep the company names fixed in the minds of budding American doctors:

Thus, a student may first listen to a patient's heart with a stethoscope provided by Eli Lilly and Company. He or she may learn to recognise the different heart sounds by listening to tape recordings from the school library, featuring the various sounds made by the healthy and diseased human heart, interspersed with the words 'Merck Sharp and Dohme' at frequent intervals. He or she may study with the aid of a series of well-illustrated handbooks on various medical subjects, a gift from the Upjohn company, or look up strange new words in a medical dictionary from Sandoz Inc. When the young doctor is in the last years of medical school and begins practical training, he or she may enjoy anything from pocket notebooks from CIBA Pharmaceutical company to doughnuts and pizza parties provided by other drug companies. All of this helps to create a favourable image of the drug company in the mind of the young doctor.

For junior doctors in Britain's hospitals, there are regular expense-account type drug company lunches to relieve the monotony of canteen food, together with gifts of 'goodies' ranging from soaps and (logo embroidered) towels to drug samples. In 1987 a promotion budget of £1.5 million to £2 million was said to be the amount for a drug launch in a major UK market. An executive at one of the agencies specialising in drug company ads broke this down as £500,000 on ads in the major medical press, £400,000 on producing material including films and videos, £150,000 on public relations directed at medical journalists, and the rest on the additional cost of medical reps (known as detailmen in the US) who would concentrate on 'selling' doctors on one product instead of the usual two or three. The mass of the promotion is directed at the country's 30,000 general practitioners – for the simple and practical reason that they prescribe 80 per cent of the pharmaceutical business's £2 billion worth of NHS drugs. Hospitality in various guises plays a not inconsiderable part. Commonly there have been free meals for doctors and their wives at local restaurants, free fishing expeditions, the use of photocopying machines on permanent 'loan', and a host of giveaways including erasable video tapes. Professor Michael Rawlings of the department of pharmaceutical science at Newcastle University says consultants get the same treatment 'only laid on with a trowel'. The reason, he says, is not because they prescribe drugs in significant amounts but because they are opinion formers 'whose endorsement of a product influences its use among local GPs'.

Professor Rawlings, a member of the Committee on Safety of Medicines, argued in *The Lancet* that doctors were in grave danger of losing public confidence because of allegations of corrupt dealings with the drug industry:

> The charge against us is that in many of our dealings with the industry we have become corrupt; that in return for needlessly and sometimes recklessly prescribing their expensive products we accept or even demand rewards on a breathtaking scale. Most doctors believe that they are quite untouched by the seductive ways of the industry's marketing men, that they are uninfluenced by the promotional propaganda they receive; that they can enjoy a company's 'generosity' in the form of gifts and hospitality without prescribing its products. The degree to which the profession, mainly composed of honourable and decent people, can practise such self-deceit is quite extraordinary. No drug company gives away its shareholders' money in an act of disinterested generosity. The harsh truth is that not one of us is impervious to the promotional activities and that the industry uses its various sales techniques because they are effective.

The two main avenues of promotion are the sales rep (or detailman) and advertising, including direct mailing. Visits take the largest share of the available money, roughly 55 per cent in the UK. Advertising and direct mail take about 30 per cent – about £55 million in 1987. There is a limit to the amount that can be spent on calls – the limit is obviously determined by the time doctors are prepared to make available. This has been declining; the average rep in Britain was said to be seeing only three or four doctors a day, each of them for only ten minutes.

As competition and promotional spending grew, advertising outlets also grew. By 1984 the average British GP was receiving twenty-three different medical publications through his door every month. In many of these, advertising often constituted over half of the pages. In the wake of increased government restrictions (including the promotion ceiling) some have vanished, but still doctors were hardly starved of their ad-filled reading matter. BRAD (British Rate and Data) lists over 250 medical publications.

In the US there are now estimated to be about 500 medical journals a month. By 1985, physicians were receiving as many as seventy journals a month. The number of publications was still growing – at the rate of about fifteen a year – fuelled by growing ad dollars and one of them asked rhetorically whether the pharmaceutical industry should bring new journals to a halt. With commendable disinterest, it added that it thought not. 'It is probably best to avoid trying to judge what is or is not good for the physician, who alone can take that choice.'

Even given the vast range of such journals, some marketers were reported to be widening their target audiences to embrace other groups who could have influence on drug buying – nurses, and hospital and nursing home administrators. Pharmaceutical companies have also moved into other media more adventurously than their consumer counterparts. There are several medical television networks, physicians band radio (it works on a fixed band receiver given out free to doctors), a computer network ('Physicians call PHYCOM, because PHYCOM is always on call. They call to keep updated on medical news. To get the very latest product prescribing information in minutes . . . Even to request product samples right from their own computer screen . . .').

Lloyd Millstein, director of the Division of Drug Advertising and Labelling with the Food and Drug Administration's Center for Drugs and Biologics, in a signed article, voiced a concern that the public can tune in to the programme (and the ads). The best known, Lifetime Medical Television, was available to any of the 21 million US households with access to cable TV. Other programmes went out on conventional TV in the early hours of the morning. The reason why the public communication networks had to be used, said Millstein, was so that doctors could be reached and so that they would get 'live action, stylised computer graphics, music, colour, and all the pizzazz that may be lost with other forms of communication.' Millstein noted that surveys indicated high viewership by physicians and other health professionals of programmes and commercials. He showed that he was in no doubt what the programmes were all about: 'the bottom line in all this is whether these marketing efforts not only will play a role in informing physicians and other health professionals, but also influence prescribing behaviour enough to compensate for their cost.'

With so much competition for the drug companies' ads, advertising to the advertisers is a mini-industry in its own right. Its publishers know that *American Family Physician* is 'The Magazine Doctors Study' because they offer rewards for readers who complete a quiz based on contents. *Annals of Internal Medicine* is 'the journal with standards so high that only 17 per cent of all articles submitted are accepted for publication' – a sign of the quality that makes for 'highly effective exposure for your advertising'. *Monthly Prescribing Reference* provides 'an opportunity to advertise to physicians while they're actually prescribing'. And if the advertiser wants to reach doctors who are catching up 'with the one clinical subject that medical school overlooked' the choice must be *Medical Aspects of Human Sexuality* (as it is for the ruggedly handsome, not too youthful physician deep in reading in the illustration). If, on the other hand, he opts for TV, *Lifetime*'s target market package is now 'guaranteed to deliver *your* message to *your* selected speciality audience . . .'

In all of this, television may have the most impact, but experts say that today's doctors still prefer print. 'Part of the bias of physicians is that they grew up reading, not watching television,' said Bill Bologna, president of the US agency, Bologna International. 'Volumes of written material aren't frightening to them.' This must be just as well when a journal can run to 400 pages, perhaps 200 of them ads. Print is said to have another edge: the doctor can choose when he reads it. On the other hand, time has to be set aside for viewing or radio listening. Television programmes have been trying to overcome that by concentrating their programming on Sundays. 'They're labelling it "Physicians Day",' said Bologna's creative director, Frank Hughes.

All advertising has the problem of trying to be heard above the surrounding clutter. Given the mass of information directed at the doctor (as much as 180 pages a day according to one estimate) drug advertising has to work hard. Research by the Eyescan organisation showed that doctors may give only three seconds to a previously exposed advertisement campaign. 'This,' commented Paul Vine, media director of the UK agency, Publitek, 'is just about enough time to glimpse the visual and read the headline.' Drug ad professionals, therefore, need to attract attention no less than their consumer colleagues – and they need to do so while working within a framework of rules. 'The reason for specialist agencies like ours,' said John Kallir of Kallir Phillips Ross, one of America's top medical-pharmaceutical agencies, 'is that we've learned to live with the restrictions.'

The drug companies do have a number of factors working in their favour; not least is the pressure on doctors to prescribe *something*. Sir William Ostler, one of the great names of medicine in the nineteenth century, said, 'A desire to take medicine is, perhaps, the great feature which distinguishes man from other animals.' Today, the desire is intense. Society suffers from what has been called the 'pill/ill' syndrome: for every ache and ailment it expects a remedy. The average British GP has six minutes for each patient. One estimate is that two out of three people he sees have illnesses that are self-curing, but the majority of patients expect – and get – a prescription. A British Medical Association report, *Is your medicine really necessary?*, argued that patients should realise that many complaints are self-limiting and will disappear without treatment and others cannot be cured with drugs. Many patients, said the report's author, Dr John Lewis, felt they had not been properly treated if they left a consultation with their doctor without a prescription. Twenty million prescriptions for tranquillisers were issued every year. Many patients complained of 'nerves' and felt tranquillisers were a simple remedy. 'They cannot accept that the cause for the "nerves" must be faced up to.'

Advertising, however, appears to have encouraged doctors to adopt the same attitude as patients. Advertisements for minor tranquillisers have provided many examples throughout the years. A 1969 ad for Wyeth's Serax showed a woman in a headscarf slumped behind bars made up of brooms and brushes, with the headline, 'You can't set her free. But you can help her feel less anxious.' One, for Roche's Valium, illustrated a man working on his PhD. He was, said the caption, suffering from 'persistent indigestion'; the copy urged, 'For this kind of patient with no demonstrable pathology – consider the usefulness of Valium (diazepan).' In 1979, another US ad showed pictures of old people in various pursuits; in persuasively written copy the ad argued that increased longevity could mean more stress ('Retirement for example brings on problems . . .') which in turn was more taxing because people were older, but if help was needed . . . Then came the pitch.

Valium has also been suggested to American doctors as a remedy for what critics dubbed 'non-ills'. The drug was suggested, for example, for people experiencing symptoms of illness such as heart disease when tests suggested that there was no such condition present. The logic would seem to be that the symptoms must have been caused by anxiety and therefore a tranquilliser was in order.

The putting together of ads directed at doctors follows the same general path as creating ads for any other group, from housewives to sports enthusiasts. The average time from first discussions to first publications is four to six months. Potential customers, in this case doctors, are brought in early to find out what they are looking for in any new product in the field. This is then compared with what features the drug offers, and a decision is made on how to target it. An ad agency comes up with a number of approaches (probably three or four) and these are shown to doctors by market researchers. Eyescan machines may be used to register how long a doctor gives the ads in mock-up of a trade journal. From all this comes the finalised campaign.

Because doctors have to be wooed at least as hard as any other consumers, multi-page ads – to give a blockbuster effect that conveys the importance of the new drug – and teaser ads are sometimes used. 'Few,' wrote Jenny Bryan in *GP*, 'will forget the Lowry like figures of the advert for Moducren earlier this year racing across page after page towards a giant Moducren tablet at the end of it all.' One thing to avoid, apparently, is ads that look clinical. Martin Page, of Deltakos, which is the specialist medical agency belonging to J. Walter Thompson, told *Hot Shoe*: 'GPs are normal human beings. In ethical advertising you use the same principles as in consumer advertising. The ad must still be appealing. I try to avoid blood and guts shots: they're seldom necessary. The biggest thing is getting the idea across – aiding understanding of what a product can do.' Because the ad information had to sell a product 'we need beautiful images as attention grabbers'.

Thus, Deltakos' ad for Spiroprop, an anti-hypertensive from Searle, was a beautifully photographed, atmospheric, full-colour shot of a pearl in an oyster. The point of the exercise was to convey the feeling that the two drugs that had been put together to form the new one added up to 'something out of the ordinary'. Page explained that to do this, 'We had to have out of season shells flown in from a private oyster farm on the Isle of Wight. Then we borrowed some cultured pearls from Ciros in Regent Street. The plant and fish came from a tropical fish shop. Even the bits of wood had to be right; we found those in an antique shop.'

To an outsider, a roam through medical ads is a revelation. Moduretic, another anti-hypertensive, this time from Merck Sharp Dohme, is the star of an ad dominated by an ice floe. The word 'Hypertension', carved in huge letters in the ice, is melting under a beam of sunlight that has broken through clouds. Bernard Burridge of the agency Paling Ellis explained that the ad used the sun as the hero – 'product if you like – penetrating the ice, melting it'. The idea was 'that the product gets rid of hypertension by dispersing the problem.' In another, from the agency McCormick Intermarco Farner, a beautiful young girl sits near the window in a room that could have come from the pages of *Town and Country*. She has flowing black hair and her robe is open exposing one bare and shapely leg. A careful look shows she is injecting herself. The ad is for Humulin – an insulin. Intal Inhaler (from Fisons) has a large photograph of Nick Gale, a young judo champion, kneeling on the mat looking ready to fight. 'When Nick Gale told us he was asthmatic, we weren't going to argue,' goes the catchy caption. Almost the whole page is filled with a naked back in an ad for Parke, Davis' Ponstan. The message is not subtle but it is striking – a corkscrew has been twisted deep into the flesh.

'Research has shown that doctors prefer to see an *idea* rather than the product itself,' one agency art director told *Hot Shoe*. 'Showing doctors pills is not on.' What admen do have to do is give the prescribing information, although by 1986 the FDA was hinting it might allow some latitude. In any event, the information is very much dominated by the central visual image and its message. Sometimes it almost vanishes, rather like government health warnings in cigarette ads. Martin Page told *Hot Shoe*, 'In medical advertising you're bound by law to give all the prescribing information. When you make a claim, it must be backed up by facts. As an art director you try to hide all this away. It has to be legible, that's all.'

Drug advertising, like all other advertising, has vogues. In recent years, many drug advertisers in the US have concentrated on multi-page ads. Bernard Burridge of Paling Ellis believes the reason might be the difference between private practice (US) and National Health Service (UK) where the doctor has no financial interest in what drugs are prescribed. 'So maybe that's why the drug companies feel they need to give him [the American doctor] everything in the ad. Whereas in the UK the doctor doesn't dispense the drugs himself, and doesn't have an interest financially. If a doctor's going to make more money finding out about your product, then maybe you'll attract him to read a four-page ad.' Kallir, though, thinks it's pure fashion. 'I think it started under pressure. There were some companies – Roche was one – that really believed in print ads so they had some spectacular ads. Then one company saw that Roche had had four pages and said, "I'm going to have six." So Roche came back and said they'd have an insert on heavy paper . . . It just escalated.'

One reason may be the much greater importance of direct mail in the US. In the UK it has suffered as a medium both because of the rising costs of postage and because, more simply, 'doctors don't like it much' according to one ad agency. (Even so doctors can receive up to about twenty pieces of direct mail a week.) The key ingredient of direct mail is a mass of information which, sorted with the help of the computer, can be used to attack precise targets in the right way. Over its whole spectrum, pharmaceuticals are the most researched and documented of all industries. One company alone, IMS International, boasts that it has drug-store surveys in over forty countries, physician-usage studies in twenty-seven countries, and hospital and promotional surveys in ten countries.

John Kallir entered the drug advertising business in the US in the 1950s and remembers that he saw about ten mailings a day. It fell into disrepute. 'A lot of physicians were irritated by it; it was junk and made the cost of the drugs higher than they need be.' Today there is less mail but because of computerised lists it is pinpointed. 'There is not one list any more,' says Kallir. 'We build lists for different clients and different products.' In both the US and the UK, reps return information on doctors which drug companies file on computer. It will include non-medical as well as medical interests. Much is gathered from the doctor in what Kallir calls 'the few minutes relaxation before he sees the next patient'.

American drug companies are able to utilise a system not possible in England. American banks routinely return used cheques, not something which is generally done in Europe. In the seventies, researchers had the brilliant idea of sending cheques made out for small sums to doctors.

On the back, the company, Medical Audits, listed a few carefully worded questions. If the doctor accepts the cheque – and it's usually for only one or two dollars – it goes into his bank and then back to Medical Audits. Most doctors complete the questions. In the early days the returns were around 70 per cent and even now they exceed 40 per cent. A drug company can thus, for example, buy a list of cardiologists known to use a specific drug if that's their target. 'It's good for copy-writing,' says Kallir. 'It gives you an idea of the audience.'

Direct mail *can* work in the UK. A Direct Marketing Award went to a campaign for Janssen Pharmaceutical. Thirty-two thousand GPs were offered a free cassette of Beethoven's Pastoral Symphony via a four-page mailing shot promoting Motilium, an anti-emetic/anti-nauseant. The company hoped a fifth of the doctors approached would respond, thus leading the way to further contact. The actual response was a staggering 44 per cent. In the promotional month, monthly sales grew from 55,000 to 90,000 and reached 110,000 three months later.

As in the US the key element is that direct mail is increasingly better targeted with the help of vast files of detail collected about doctors, their views, and prescribing habits. There are two groups of doctors that especially interest drug companies. In marketing jargon they are the 'innovators' and the 'early adopters'. The subject's guru is a man called E. M. Rogers whose work is to be found in text books on marketing behaviour. Rogers identifies five groups who begin using products. The first are the 'innovators' (2.5 per cent of a market, he says), the next the 'early adopters' (13.5 per cent), and after these come 'the early majority' (34 per cent), 'the late majority' (34 per cent) and finally, the 'laggards' (16 per cent).

The innovators are the trail-blazers, the people eager to experiment with the new ideas. The early adopters are the people who adopt the innovation when it seems to be successful. As a group they're respected by others, and thus have an impact on what happens next. The whole process is known as 'diffusion'. In selling products, its uses are obvious. As each group is believed to influence the next group down, extra effort can be expended on the innovators and the early adopters when a product is first launched. This is obviously important with new drugs when doctors may be naturally cautious and nervous. Innovators among doctors, one insider explained to me, are those who do not see the perceived risks; they see the *advantages* of the new drug. If they can be persuaded to adopt the drug from the start, this will bring it to the attention of the much bigger group of early adopters – and so on . . .

One of the major pieces of information that drug reps report back is a doctor's attitude to prescribing, thus allowing him to be classified on computer files. It does not end with that, however. There are companies that specialise in bringing together such information. Scriptrac in the US claims to be able to identify 'innovators through traditionalists' product by product category. 'YOU,' it boasts to drug companies in its own promotional literature, 'can target promotions to the most receptive audience.' It claims its service is used by thirty-one companies.

In the UK, a new service offering similar breakdowns was begun by Haigh, Walsh and Associates. Known as DOC.P.A.L. – Doctor Priority Action List – the system boasted it used 'sociological methods' to profile GPs in terms of their behaviour. With visions of what anti-drug industry MPs would think of such a service, DOC.P.A.L. was marketed with some discretion. In essence, however, the service brought together the results of a year's questioning of GPs who were asked, for example, to tick which new drugs they would prescribe from a given list, and whether they listened to comments from fellow doctors about drug prescribing. Other information recorded included interest in drug therapy classes, and their medical activities outside general practice. This information, together with details already on file, was then computerised and became available for use by drug companies for priority targeting, mailing or for invitations. The men behind the service, Jeremy Walsh and Barry Haigh, were obviously torn between their desires to extol the scheme and not to bring it to the attention of people outside the industry who might 'misinterpret it'. It was, they said proudly, as far as they knew the first service of its kind in the world at that time. It was also, one told me, 'a bit sensitive'. DOC.P.A.L. now comes from Walsh Mander. Current literature boasts that 24,000 doctors' details are on file. As for effectiveness, 'An independent validation demonstrated that improvement in product uptake can be over 30 per cent higher when the promotion uses a researched profile in conjunction with DOC.P.A.L. rather than simply promoting to a random group.'

The question would seem to be not whether doctors are influenced in their prescribing by the ads, but by how much. Some insiders argue that the persuasion which does take place is necessary and commendable. George Teeling-Smith, of the Office of Health Economics, says: 'Even the most important and useful innovations must be vigorously promoted if society is to benefit from them and if their innovator is to gather funds to continue his innovative activities. In this respect doctors are human beings, not scientific paragons, and they too have to be persuaded to adopt a new medicine into their practice.'

It can also be argued – again persuasively – that drug advertising is highly regulated. There are both voluntary and statutory sanctions, though one of the great skills in this as in a number of other areas of advertising is getting across the pitch without – if possible – breaking the letter of the law. In the US, the FDA has been charged with monitoring drug promotion since 1962. It is claimed that the fact the FDA takes relatively few actions against drug ads is evidence of how well the industry regulates itself (in 1987 the FDA monitored over 29,000 items of drug promotions; no remedial ads were ordered, no legal sanctions were taken, and only four regulatory letters were sent).

John J. Fisher, president of the advertising agency Frank J. Corbett Inc, Chicago, has likened FDA requirements that ads include 'all the bad things' as well as the selling points to ads for toasters having to state, 'You've got to be careful when you plug it in because it can cause an electric shock.' In the UK, a code laid down by the Association of the British Pharmaceutical Industry is meant to ensure that advertising is both responsible and accurate. Data sheets outlining all relevant information on products, including warnings and side-effects, have to be presented to doctors. The Consumers' Association publishes a review of developments in medicine (*Drug and Therapeutics Bulletin*) and the BMA and the Pharmaceutical Society produce the *British National Formulary* which provides an account of available treatments. The arguments, therefore, are that the ads (and other promotion) are carefully controlled so that true and fair information only is conveyed, and that in any event doctors have many other sources for the information they need on drugs.

Both these arguments appear to be true, but only up to a point. In the UK, there is a way round the limit that companies are allowed to spend on promotion (by 1987 it was down to 9 per cent of the value of the NHS sales). This is to produce 'educational material' such as sponsored publications dealing with specific areas of treatment or to organise workshops or seminars. Such methods are not included in the rules. As far as advertisements themselves are concerned, it must never be forgotten that their purpose is to sell products.

Because companies *need* marketing and advertising that works, rule bending and breaking is not that rare. It may happen with official connivance. In the US, drug ads must include contra-indications, warnings and other cautionary information. That might seem to make television advertising difficult if not impossible. However, under President Reagan, the Food and Drug Administration decided it would allow advertisers to meet the *spirit* of the law and forget the *letter* of it. The sixty-second ads, the FDA decided, could be balanced by providing audio or visual statements about specific cautions for the products. Brief summary scrolls for products ran at the end of a programme. John Kallir, the veteran pharmaceutical adman, instanced it to me as one of the examples of the FDA being more lenient under Reagan – 'though they would deny it'. The information ran, he said, at such speed 'you have to be a champion speed reader. People laugh. Even when it's one of your own products where you have the detail half memorised you can't read it. It's ridiculous, but the FDA says it's full disclosure. The law is satisfied.'

Sometimes the excesses are in promotion. Rheumatologists were taken to Venice on the Orient Express for the launch for an arthritic drug, an event that was shown in a BBC programme. The televised scene, said Dr Brian Lewis, a member of the General Medical Council, the profession's ruling body, had been greeted with disgust. In another case, family doctors were offered equipment worth £20 from Servier Laboratories to set up an age-sex register, provided they prescribed only that company's influenza vaccine. In a third, doctors and their families were invited to a day out at a private club with a special bar extension and rides on a lifeboat to help promote an Astra Pharmaceuticals drug.

Many are in advertising itself. In the US, drugs have been advertised before being approved by the FDA, comparative ads have detailed the deficiencies of competing brands without revealing the advertised drug's own problems, and there has been a growing tendency, in the words of one FDA executive, to make claims that fall 'outside the limits of good advertising'. One example was Procardia, a heart drug from Pfizer Inc, mentioned earlier as achieving $17 million worth of sales in twelve weeks. The campaign, said the FDA later in the year in a ten-page letter to Pfizer, was 'false and misleading in its overall messages'. It had misrepresented important warnings (thus it 'increases the risk of serious adverse reactions to patients'). Procardia was a valuable treatment for angina caused by coronary artery spasms, but according to the FDA it was being promoted as a 'first line' treatment for all types of angina, despite the fact that Pfizer's own research indicated other drugs were as good if not more useful in most cases. If that was not enough, the FDA also objected to claims in brochures that the drug was better than a rival 'by making carefully worded positive statements' about itself and 'remaining silent' regarding any 'similar actions' of the competing drug.

In Britain the Department of Health complained of a 'worrying increase' in complaints about drug firms going too far in their advertisements. A letter to companies concluded 'You have been warned.' Some drugs were being promoted to treat conditions for which they had not been licensed; others had been advertised before being approved by the Committee on Safety of Medicines. The following year an experiment was conducted by the *Sunday Times* into the readability of vital information on side-effects. This has to be included in advertisements by law which says the information should be printed in a 'clear and legible' manner. Eighteen doctors were asked to look at a 'typical small print advertisement', one for Xanax, a tranquilliser from Upjohn. The newspaper reported, 'Two GPs and a radiologist found it almost impossible to read. Three other doctors, a young houseman and two consultants, needed to use a magnifying glass. One GP had to use a ruler to follow the line of print. Eight doctors struggled through the words but made comments such as "difficult", "can hardly read it", "no wish to read on".' The print was even smaller in another advertisement, for Bolvidon, an anti-depressant from Organon.

The same year Pfizer's UK managing director said he would write to doctors admitting that an advertisement for the company's asthma inhaler may have caused 'some misunderstanding'. Ads had claimed that the drug might 'ultimately help to break the destructive progression' of asthma and chronic bronchitis to heart failure. It was withdrawn after the company was censured by the industry code of drug practice committee.

The *Sunday Times* again that year listed a number of 'misleading advertisements' that claimed 'that drugs are safer than they really are and patients have been put at risk or where dubious or non-existent advantages were claimed'. They included:

Persantin: the health service spends £5m a year on this drug, which is said to prevent strokes and heart attacks. This claim is at best dubious and at worst useless. According to the scientific evidence, treatment with aspirin (which delays blood clotting) is more effective.

Cordarone X: a useful drug for controlling abnormal heart rhythms, it was advertised in 1983 with the claims that it '. . . enjoys a wide margin of safety . . . the side-effects and contra-indications seem minimal . . .' In fact, as an editorial in *The Lancet* pointed out, the skin of some patients taking the drug went grey, and it causes gastric and nervous disturbances. At least eight deaths have been associated with the drug. The manufacturers, Sanofi, withdrew the claim from its advertisements voluntarily, saying that it referred to the drug's short-term use only.

The authors claimed that many infringements of the law go uncorrected because the Department of Health has no comprehensive monitoring system for drug ads. Many complaints were passed on to the Association of the British Pharmaceutical Industry (ABPI). 'However, the penalty for breaking its code of practice is merely the withdrawal of the offending advertisement . . . A misleading advertisement may run for months before being corrected – and then it has had an impact on doctors.'

The DHSS does, in fact, have a section, the Medicines' Division, responsible for monitoring drug promotion. With, in 1987, a staff of only four, it had only once acted against a large company, Roussell, for its claims that the drug Surgam offered gastric protection and thus reduced the chances of internal bleeding (a constant problem with anti-arthritic drugs). The company was convicted of publishing a misleading claim when it was pointed out that it conflicted with a warning required by the Committee on Safety of Medicines that Surgam should not be given to people with gastro-intestinal upsets.

The ABPI can suspend companies from membership, a step which it had taken only once up to 1987 although it had been in existence for twenty-nine years. Then Bayer, the UK end of the giant German company, was suspended indefinitely after salesmen used bogus trial cards to persuade doctors to prescribe drugs. The doctors thought they were taking part in scientific trials and completed cards given to them. In fact, data never went beyond the salesmen. In return for their work, doctors received money (£15 per patient to whom they gave the drugs in question), and in specific cases store shopping vouchers, photographic equipment, a television and a sponsored US visit. Bayer claimed that the actions were a purely local initiative. The ABPI, however, decided Bayer had brought the industry into disrepute.

The promotional excesses pale when compared with some that have emerged in the Third World. Consumer activists and doctors claim, often with chilling detail, that drugs are promoted that in many cases have been withdrawn or are unapproved in their own countries. Doctors are persuaded to prescribe some potent ones without being given adequate warnings as to side-effects.

The Third World spends about $12 billion a year on drugs, and most countries have no choice but to buy from the Western companies that dominate the international trade.

The companies are accused of only developing and promoting drugs that are best suited to the West. Only a third of research funding throughout the world is directed at Third World diseases. Between 1977 and 1980, fourteen European drug companies were estimated to have spent $126 million on finding new drugs for tropical diseases. *The Economist* pointed out this was 'little more than the R & D costs of getting a single drug to market in the developed world'.

Third World countries, it is alleged, are persuaded to take vast quantities of vitamins and tonics that are largely unnecessary. They are then promoted with ridiculous claims. Vitamins are advocated to offset senility, for example. An Indian campaign, by Roche Vitaminets Forte, sowed this seed of worry: 'Your child is intelligent, but is he alert?' The advertisement then listed symptoms said to be associated with 'vitamin starvation', including the child being unwilling to go to school or leaving his pencils or books behind or complaining about other children. All 'symptoms' that would doubtless show that at least 95 per cent of well-nourished Western children were also suffering from the 'deficiency'.

At a more dangerous level, potent drugs are marketed in a reprehensible way. Oxfam found that anabolic steroids (that carry universally recognised dangers) produced by Organon of Holland and intended to treat rare bone diseases, were being sold as appetite stimulants for children in Peru and other countries. In Bangladesh, a 1981 advertisement for the drug, Orabolin, showed children playing with the headline, 'Help the child to grow with Orabolin.'

In East Africa, the West German company Schering has been attacked for marketing drugs described as 'useless' to treat men worried about their potency. One advertisement, for Proviron, shows an African couple on a bed; he is sitting on the edge, head down in a pose that speaks of disappointment and failure. 'Infertility and potency disorders can be a distressing problem,' says the heading. Another, for Tonovan, from the same company, shows a rich young black man standing by a car with the words, 'Tonovan gives a man that something extra.' Both drugs are essentially derivatives of the male hormone testosterone. Dr Andrew Herxheimer, of Charing Cross Hospital, London, and editor of the *Therapeutics Bulletin* told the magazine *Africa Now*, 'The companies are exporting outdated nostrums to the developing countries. There have been patent medicines playing on men's fears of impotence for many years, but doctors in the West now know it's all magic and useless. The companies know that perfectly well too.' He added, 'The main cause of impotence is psychological and these drugs only work if people believe they will. But if doctors want this placebo effect they should use inert substances, not ones which are pharmacologically active.' A member of the British Committee on the Safety of Medicines pointed out the 'Prolonged use of testosterone can cause liver damage . . .'

An eight-year study published in the US listed scores of examples. They included the selling by roadside vendors in Indonesia of the drug clioquinol (brand name, Entero-Vioform). This anti-diarrhoeal was banned in Japan and withdrawn from the US market ten years before, after being linked to cases of acute abdominal pain and, in some cases, brain damage and blindness. In the Philippines, the antibiotic chloramphenicol was being prescribed for infections ranging from influenza to acne, and the drug guide used by doctors carried no mention of the possible side-effect, a deadly form of anaemia.

Consumer activists have been pressing for a code to regulate international pharmaceutical marketing, to be policed by the World Health Organization. The industry in turn points to its own code of behaviour, claiming that the only effective control is a voluntary one. Companies, it is argued, have taken steps to improve matters in terms of training and information. Marketing practices have been changed; steroids, for example, are no longer promoted as growth stimulants for children. The battle has signs of being a continuing one.

Contrary to what might seem self-evident to the layman, doctors are not specialists in drugs when they qualify. Pharmacology courses in training schools are described as 'rather brief'. In any event, medicine has changed so fast in recent years that doctors have come to many drug developments after training. 'It's an alarming thought,' wrote Dr Vernon Coleman in 1982, 'that most of the doctors in practice today qualified before the contraceptive pill was generally available and completed their training in pre-Valium times.' A forty-five-year-old doctor, he pointed out, would have qualified before oral contraceptives, tranquillising drugs like Valium, Ativan, Mogadon and Librium, Aldomet (methyldopa) for high blood pressure, the widely used anti-infective drug Penbritin, Intal for asthma prevention, the more effective control of unwanted blood-clotting mechanisms with drugs, and before the hazards of drugs like thalidomide were recognised.

But it is part of doctoring, of course, to keep up to date. Coleman, for one, believes that a disproportionate amount of this updating comes from ads and promotions. 'Unfortunately the majority of doctors still gain much of their information about new drugs and techniques from films and literature paid for by the drug industry – hardly the most objective source.' Doctors would probably deny this – certainly those I spoke with did so. However, the work of Professor Jerry Avorn, director of the drug information programme at Harvard Medical School, provides interesting information. Avorn set out to find what eighty-five doctors in the Boston area believed to be the key factors when they prescribed a drug. Sixty-eight per cent of them said that ads had minimal importance. The greatest influence on what they prescribed, said 88 per cent, was their clinical experience and academic training. Sixty-two per cent said scientific studies published in journals were important.

On face value, the conclusion might be that the drug industry was wasting a great deal of money. However, Avorn had included trick questions in his survey. The answers to these, he says, proved that, whatever they said, doctors *were* being influenced by the ads. The survey asked doctors about two types of prescription drugs that were being promoted as having benefits that Avorn says were not supported by evidence. The first drug was propoxyphene painkillers. According to Avorn, the scientific evidence is that they are at best only equivalent to aspirin. Half the doctors surveyed, however, said the drug was *more* effective than aspirin. The second drug was vasodilators, promoted as being capable of enlarging blood vessels to improve blood flow to the brain and legs. Avorn says that the drugs have been promoted as aiding thinking processes in senile patients and being able to improve bad circulation caused by hardening of the arteries. Medical literature, he claims, overwhelmingly indicates that, contrary to the promotion material, the drugs are not useful. Seventy-one per cent of the surveyed doctors, however, believed impaired blood was a major cause of senility and 32 per cent said they found cerebral vasodilators useful in managing confused geriatric patients.

Professor Avorn has no doubt what his material means: 'Drug advertisements are simply more visually arresting and conceptually accessible than are papers in the medical literature.'

In any event, if doctors are only human when it comes to prescribing, aren't there hidden motivations that advertising can attack? According to some evidence, there certainly are.

Two British researchers – Peter Cooper, the psychologist mentioned earlier, and Giles Lenton – believe as a result of their work with doctors that when it comes to prescribing, GPs sometimes have 'intuitive, private and sometimes emotional reasons for prescribing particular drugs'. 'Our starting point,' they said in a paper they presented to the British Pharmaceutical Market Research Group, 'is 'that GPs are human and therefore subject to the same stresses and fallibilities which affect all of us.' GPs, they continued, '*seem* to write prescriptions as a result of objective, detached examinations and diagnoses under some circumstances, but as likely as not they will be making choices of treatment and prescribing brands on the grounds of psychological factors.' They identified four factors:

1. Routine coping – prescribing without conscious thinking ('I find myself prescribing X, it just pops into my head at the time').
2. Stress – under pressures of time and uncertainty about just what to do.
3. Game playing ('Treatments can be given and brands prescribed as a way of "punishing" patients, "toying" with them . . . (or) to comfort and befriend patients').
4. Self-gratification – 'Thus we find GPs playing out the roles of Dr Magic, Dr Wise, Dr Science, Dr Kind etc. Particular brands can fuel these self-images.'

Cooper and Lenton suggested that their findings might be used in marketing and advertising. Seemingly, what the ads would have to get across was 'how brands *help* GPs to cope, *relieve* his or her frustrations with patients and symptoms, or which *satisfy* desires for good (or sometimes ego-involved) styles of doctoring.'

There is another way that drug manufacturers can exert influences on doctors: by advertising direct to the ultimate consumer, the patient, so that he or she can then ask for a drug by name. This has already happened on a small scale and though the practice goes in and out of favour many believe it is only a matter of time before it becomes commonplace. Dr Philip Brown, former managing director of Deltakos and now a medical publisher, told a British Pharmaceutical Marketing Club annual workshop that in the future he envisaged, say, half-page ads for prescription drugs in the mass circulation *Radio Times*. 'I know it is expensive, but all your chronic arthritics are sitting there watching television.' A number of factors, according to Brown, pointed to such promotion: the swing to self-medication, greater understanding of medical matters; and the fact that chronically ill patients knew more about the effect of their medicines than their doctors would ever know. Experience had shown that patients seemed to be able to generate prescriptions by asking for them. 'It can take a lot of time and a lot of promotional effort to persuade a doctor to change his prescribing habits for, say, his hypertensive patients, but if the patients ask for the latest beta blocker they read about in yesterday's newspaper, results can be achieved in weeks that advertising in medical journals and surgery detailing cannot achieve in years.'

In 1983, Boots Pharmaceuticals began advertising its anti-arthritis drug Rufen on US TV – the first time viewers had received a direct pitch for a prescription drug. The commercials urged arthritic sufferers to ask their doctors to prescribe the drug if they were not already taking a similar drug manufactured by Upjohn under the brand name Motrin. The ads stressed that Rufen was less expensive than Motrin. The first ads ran for four and a half days in the Tampa-St Petersburg area before the FDA stopped them on the grounds that because there were claims about efficacy there should also have been full disclosure of all other information. Boots reacted by producing a simplified version that left out any mention of arthritis and only stated Rufen was cheaper than Motrin. That ran for six weeks before the company halted the ads for evaluation. Print ads had hard-hitting copy. 'If you have arthritis,' began the copy, 'and your doctor has prescribed ibuprofen, you should know that he can now prescribe it under two brand names: Motrin and Rufen. And while Motrin-400mg and Rufen-400mg are interchangeable, there is an important difference: Rufen can cost you considerably less.' (Ironically Motrin was Boots' own drug, licensed from 1974 to Upjohn. The licence, however, was a non-exclusive one, hence Boots' own entry into the market later.)

Advertising prescription drugs to the public began to be discussed seriously once Reagan supporters took control of the FDA in 1981. The FDA experimented with ads for fictitious products in print and on cable to see whether it was possible to transmit risk information as required by law. By 1986 it was encouraging drug companies to experiment more with consumer-oriented ads. At least one of the possible beneficiaries of a potentially large advertising category, the CBS network, did its own studies. These showed (surprise) that consumers 'want more information about prescription drugs'.

Pro and anti groups have formed. Consumer bodies are anti, though not it seems individual consumers (a 1987 study by Scott-Levin Associates showed 70 per cent would like to see more direct advertising of prescription drugs). Doctors are non-committal or anti. Advertising agencies, diplomatically, have perched on the fence in public at least, but said they agreed the question merited discussion. A congressional sub-committee spent two years examining the subject. Thirty-seven drug companies gave their views. Only two – Sandoz Inc and Kalipharma Inc – favoured the idea. Two others – Marion Laboratories and Merrell Dow Pharmaceuticals – supported it with conditions that included not using brand names in ads. The sub-committee chairman, Representative John D. Dingell, had no reservations as to where he stood. 'It is my view that the mass promotion of prescription drug products is not in the public interest,' he said in a letter to the FDA that accompanied the report. But was the door really closed? The significant phrase in the staff report was that mass promotion of prescription was an idea 'whose time had not *yet* come'. And perhaps it was equally significant that those drug companies that opposed the idea also gave the indication that their attitude would be different if advertising to the consumer ever really began. Merck, for example, made it clear that if a competitor mounted a major ad campaign, 'we could not rule out that we might find it necessary to respond with some new market initiative of our own'. CBS developed a list of guidelines ready for the potential new category.

In any event, the door opened a few inches. Even while frowning on consumer advertising, the FDA has showed no qualms about "health information" advertisements. Nicorette, made by Merrell Dow, is a nicotine-containing chewing gum that doctors can prescribe to smokers who are trying to quit the habit. Full-page ads by Merrell Dow ran in 1985 in such widely read general magazines as *Time*, *Newsweek*, *People*, *Sports Illustrated*, and *TV Guide*. There was, it said, a medication doctors could prescribe to help. The key feature was that nowhere in the ads was the product ever mentioned by name.

Another company, Burroughs Wellcome, ran an estimated $4 million worth of advertisements in 1986 for the drug Zovirax which is used to treat genital herpes. The advertisements appeared in magazines like *Cosmopolitan* and *TV Guide*. One showed a couple on the beach, she snuggling lovingly into his shoulder. The copy ran, 'The hardest thing she ever had to do was tell Roger she had herpes. But thanks to her doctor, she could also tell him it's controllable.' The ads did not mention the drug by name – but as it was the only prescription one on the market, that hardly mattered.

In 1988 TV commercials urged viewers with stomach problems to go to their physicians and ask about 'available treatment programs, sponsored by Smith Kline, the ulcer experts'. Smith Kline happens to manufacture Tagamet, an ulcer drug, which was the second largest selling drug in the world in 1987. A major step came in 1987. Sandoz produced ads for its antihistamine Tavist-1 which appeared in twenty-five major market newspapers. These broke tradition by naming the drug. The FDA attacked the development, got Sandoz to stop – but, nevertheless, promised to re-examine the subject. Other chinks were easily discernible in any event. There was the prescription advertising on cable and early a.m. special programmes for doctors, but there for anyone who tuned in. Hoffman-La Roche sponsored thirty-minute 'public education programmes' aired on about 100 commercial stations throughout the country. These had titles like 'The Fat or Fit Test', 'The Sex IQ Test' and 'The Medical IQ Test'. Celebrities such as actress Hope Lange gave the shows mass appeal – the company has claimed as many as 10 million viewers. Roche delivered two minutes of commercial time and received opening credit on each show. A Roche spokesman told the magazine *Medical Advertising News* that, when possible, commercials related to the subject matter of each programme.

The development of consumer medical publications is a likely future possibility. Here the drug companies could approach the people not through ads as such but with information in editorial form. This, in fact, would be much in keeping with a development that has been growing since the late 1970s. Since that time, drug companies have shown a growing tendency to try to place information about new drugs in the mass media, thus building demand that way. One analyst, Dr John T. Curran, of L. F. Rothschild, Unterberg and Towbin, New York, traces the trend back to an anti-arthritic drug called Clinoril, launched by Merck in 1978. 'Sales exploded and drug companies realised that you can create tremendous consumer demand for a new product if the patient population is as aware of it as the professional community.' Clinoril was not, in fact, markedly better than other anti-arthritics around. But Merck's PR resulted in its being hailed as a major advance. It was even mentioned by Walter Cronkite on the CBS-TV evening news.

The most striking single example, though, was Eli Lilly and Co's launch of Oraflex in 1982. Reporters were lobbied with information for weeks before a Waldorf-Astoria Press Conference at which Lilly officials talked of the drug's possible role in reversing the effects of arthritis ('leaving many reporters with the mistaken impression that it was the only compound with such possible benefits,' reported the *Wall Street Journal*). Lilly scientists toured smaller newspapers and broadcast outlets. More than 150 newspapers and several hundred radio and TV stations carried stories following the press conference. Prescriptions soared from 2,000 to 55,000 a week, bringing Lilly near $1 million a week in new revenue. In Britain, where the drug was called Opren, press releases claimed it was the 'single most exciting development in the field of arthritis treatment since the discovery of aspirin', a television personality hosted a touring road show for GPs, and specialists were invited to attend a conference – on a Rhine cruise boat.

The massive publicity for Opren/Oraflex backfired. When reports of side-effects began to emerge, the high profile achieved by the publicists ensured these were widely reported. As the scale of the disaster emerged (by November 1982 the drug was alleged to have caused sixty-five deaths in Britain), Lilly's overpromotion was seen as a setback for the whole industry. Dr Robert Temple, director of drug review for the FDA, commented, 'Well, it came back to bite them, it came back to bite everybody, to bite the whole industry.' Certainly it made the industry much more cautious, but it did not diminish the need for promotion. 'I think you'll find,' one pragmatic adman told me, 'that they won't so much be good as more careful.'

In their pursuit of the consumer many pharmaceuticals companies have been turning more of their attention to those drugs that *are* sold direct to the patient, the over-the-counter medicines. For some multinationals it has provided a way of diversifying from the increasingly crowded and competitive prescription market. May and Baker of the UK and G. D. Searle and Co of the US are among those who strengthened their international role in the non-prescription area. Ciba-

Geigy of Switzerland created a non-prescription unit in the UK and stepped up its activities in other countries. Its officials said that the company wanted its fastest growth to come from non-prescription products. In Britain, in one twelve-month period, at least sixteen companies which previously marketed drugs only to doctors formed non-prescription divisions and produced consumer launches.

Two other factors have played a major role: as part of the health boom, consumers have been seeking more self-medication; at the same time, governments have been allowing a number of drugs previously available only on prescription to be sold over the counter. All this means more advertising.

Self-medication – and the rush to cash in on it – is nothing new. Nor is its relationship with advertising. In the period 1870–1900 in the US there was hardly an ailment without its patent remedy. For indigestion, Hostetter's Celebrated Stomach Bitters; for fatigue, Ayer's Sarsaparilla; for aching muscles, Barker's Linament; for women with flat chests, Egyptian Regulator Tea that would give them 'graceful plumpness'. Laxative Bromo Quinine would 'cure a cold in a day'. Even if it did not, the customer was probably happy with life – the tonic had a 21 per cent alcohol content, which was, however, as nothing compared with the 44 per cent in Hostetter's Bitters.

There were fortunes to be made. Lydia E. Pinkham's Vegetable Compound had sales of $300,000 in 1883. In Britain, Thomas Holloway, producer of Holloway's Pills, died that same year, sending the Stock Exchange into nervous tremors – the bulk of his self-made wealth of a reputed £5 million was in stocks and shares. The business was a fraud and sometimes a dangerous one. Holloway's Pills, which were actually aloes, powdered ginger and soap, were sold for over fifty complaints including tumours. In the United States, Dr King's New Discovery for Consumption contained chloroform (which quietened the cough) and opium that made sufferers *feel* better temporarily, but did nothing to fight the bacillus.

The vast sales were a tribute not only to greed and public gullibility and fear (and not least to the cost of doctors) but also to the power of advertising. The most clever medicine pushers ploughed money into newspaper advertising. The Ideal Sight Restorer promised 'the inestimable blessing of sight'. The proprietors of Dr Sage's Catarrh Remedy offered a $500 reward 'for a case of catarrh he cannot cure'. Kickapoo Indian Salve proclaimed itself the 'perfect cure all' for all skin problems from barber's itch to piles. Holloway claimed he had 'A key to Health' and poured more and more into advertising – £5,000 in 1842, ten times that the year he died. 'Take Holloway's Pills' was found posted in major cities throughout the world – as well as on the Great Pyramid. Posters in the US during the Civil War showed wounded Union soldiers reaching out for his ointment!

Well into this century, just prior to World War II, it was still almost anything goes with patent medicine ads. 'Rushed to hospital with GASTRIC ULCER,' said one, '. . . as soon as I was able to take any medicine after the operation the hospital doctor prescribed Maclean Brand Stomach Powder.' Another for Phaylex catarrh tablets, asked, 'Do you suffer from weakening night sweats? Is there a tendency to vomit in the morning to remove the catarrh slime from your throat?' Sometimes the tone was reasonable and pseudo-medical:

Your doctor will confirm these health facts. 1. In normal health the blood and tissues are slightly more alkaline than acid. 2. The maintenance of the correct ratio of alkali to acid is essential to good health. 3. Much ill health nowadays is associated with a prolonged disturbance of this alkali-acid balance. 4. Modern conditions make it extremely difficult to regulate the balance by diet and mode of life alone. Fortunately an ideal balancing factor is available to all in ENO's 'Fruit Salt' . . .

Today's business works within prescribed limits, both in what it can dispense direct to its customers and in what powers it can claim for its products. It is still a source of huge returns – $8.5 billion worth of US sales in 1986. It still retains its faith in the power of advertising. And it still, say its critics, uses such advertising as skilfully as it is able to persuade people they need some products that are useless (such as vitamins and laxatives) and even potentially harmful (such as cold cocktails). The BMA's booklet *Is your medicine really necessary?* argued, 'What you almost certainly do not need as a patient are those proprietary preparations that are so heavily advertised in the press and on television. These include cold cocktails, slimming pills, vitamins, tonics, laxatives and health salts.'

Vitamins is one of the growth areas. In the UK, the number of advertised brands has soared and now totals well over fifty. New brands are said to be emerging 'almost daily'. Vitamins, of course, have one enormous advantage for their sellers over most other non-prescribed drugs: people take them when they are feeling fit as well as when they are feeling ill. The sales of cough medicines, analgesics, laxatives and indigestion tablets are limited to when people do not feel well and want to *cure* something. One adman enthused over vitamins' near miraculous qualities – for the marketing man. People bought them for reasons ranging from believing they would improve their skin texture to the length of their lives, the strength of their nails or the potency of their sex. If the users felt good, it was because of the vitamins. If they felt less well, they would have felt even worse but for the vitamins. It was like the old joke about the man in a railway carriage who tears up copies of *The Times* and throws them out of the window. Asked why, he replies, 'To keep away the elephants.' 'But there are no elephants,' exclaims a bemused travelling companion. 'There, you see how well it works . . .'

The consensus of medical opinion on vitamins seems to be that they are the most un-needed of self-treatments. *Which?* asked itself which was the best value of 'hundreds of pills in the shops', and concluded, 'None of them. Don't waste your money. You should get all the vitamins you need from the food you eat.' *Marketing* magazine spoke to a 'leading manufacturer' who told them, 'The national press tried to make a story, but found that most manufacturers did not dispute what *Which?* said.'

The over-the-counter drugs market is huge. In the United States, the largest segment – analgesics – is worth over $2.1 billion, the second – cold remedies – around $1.8 billion. In the UK, the order is reversed – Britons seem to have fewer headaches and more colds (or, alternatively, to worry more about the latter). In fact, about a third of all non-prescribed medication in the UK is treatment for coughs, sore throats and blocked noses. Analgesics have a little over a quarter of the market, and remedies for stomachs and guts (including indigestion tablets and laxatives) about 14 per cent. There are about 1,500 individual products, about 300 of which receive sizeable support.

It is a hard-fought market-place with tough talk and hard campaigning. A Sterling Health manager greeted the launch of a rival with the words, 'We won't stand back and let anyone threaten our position. Historically, Hedex has been the country's fastest growing brand and we intend to keep it that way.' When Sterling's Panadol, already sold in seventy countries, was introduced in the US market $15 million was spent on a TV campaign. Furthermore, in one month 2 million coupons were redeemed for free samples, and – because the company hoped for drug referrals from doctors – 100,000 samples went to physicians. So did endorsement letters – written and signed by computer – from Sterling's own 12,000 US employees to their own doctors.

The tough marketing and heavy advertising is essential, of course, because most of the time the patent medicine business is another 'me too' marketing-led world. Pharmacin, from Optrex, Hoechst's UK over-the-counter subsidiary, was launched as the pain-reliever 'for people with no time for aches and pains'. Its active analgesic, like many pain-relievers, is ordinary aspirin (most of the non-aspirin are based on paracetamol). Its makers decided it should be in capsule form – research showed capsules have a more modern image than pills. Its colour was also determined by research – blue and white. The research revealed people felt single-colour pills looked too much like sweets, pastel colours were seen as 'weak'. Two-colour, on the other hand, was seen as a combination of strength and achievement. The dark blue was regarded as indicating safety, calmness and gentleness.

Advertising has to imbue these products with what Optrex marketing manager, Annette Bradshaw, called 'a certain magic' in order to give them brand loyalty. *If* consumers are going to pay three times as much for aspirin in a blue and white capsule as in a white tablet they have to *believe*. Women are the heaviest users of analgesics, the reason they are widely featured in commercials. A US ad for the paracetamol-based Panadol, for example, had a middle-aged woman saying, 'My Julie's wedding day – was I nervous. What a headache!' American Home Products ran a campaign for aspirin-based Anacin portraying authentic-looking people in terrible pain. In one, for example, a miner's sooty face filled the screen. 'Tell you what,' he said, 'you go down half-mile shaft, it's dark it's . . . damp.' He rubs his eyes, he's sweating, you can tell he's in pain. ''Bout 12 million ton of rock on you, and, uh, you get a headache, buddy . . .' The agency, William Esty, conceded that the portrayal of the various occupations shown might not be fully accurate. Sam Alfstad, a creative director, told the *Wall Street Journal* the ads were like a stage play where 'you create an illusion of reality'. The actor playing the miner did press-ups between takes to produce the sweat.

Cold and cough cures have to work even harder – after all, analgesics do work most of the time but the only treatment for a cold remains bed and aspirin. Ad approaches vary – Contac (from Smith Kline Beckman) has people singing and dancing, an unstated promise of what you'll feel like. Actifed (Burroughs Wellcome) has a pitch from a former astronaut who explains that in space sinuses don't drain and noses don't run 'so cold tablets really have to work'. Like Actifed does for him.

Richardson-Vicks, makers in the US of twenty different cough and cold treatments, conducts weekly telephone surveys of the public to find where colds are most prevalent – then it increases its marketing in those areas. Ronald A. Ahrens, president of the health care division, acknowledged the role of the message in the company's strong presence in the market – 'we know the cold remedy consumer and we gear our message to get a response. Frankly our products are no better or worse than anyone else's.'

Even according to the company that makes them, some well-known 'remedies' are in fact useless. The *Observer*, London, obtained an internal memo from the London Rubber Company, Britain's biggest producer of non-prescription cough medicine. The document, from the research and development director to the managing director, written in September 1980, said, 'None of the existing products has any significant active ingredients.'

Makers of drugs that come off prescription can promote the fact that they *do* work. Ibrufen is a pain-reliever that was discovered in 1962 and used only in prescription drugs until over twenty years later. Bristol-Myers' ibuprofen product Nuprin entered the US market with ads that said, 'This is the pain-relieving medicine for which doctors have written a hundred million prescriptions.' In Britain, ads for Nurofen combined the back view of an attractive nude woman, her body dotted with targets with the headline, 'A breakthrough in the relief of locked-in pain' with details of how the active ingredient had been prescribed by doctors throughout the world for more than fourteen years.

Makers of drugs coming off prescription have a special problem in the UK. There are three divisions of drugs: those that can only be prescribed by doctors (POM); those that can be bought direct by consumers but only from pharmacists (P); and those that can be bought and sold in other outlets, such as supermarkets. The system is meant to be a safeguard for consumers in that 'P' drugs are only bought when a qualified person is present. Some pharmacists in America have asked for a similar situation to be introduced there.

To complicate matters, though, the drug maker whose product is moved from 'POM' (doctors only) to 'P' (direct via a pharmacist) has to make a choice. 'P' products can be advertised or prescribed by doctors – but not both.

There is a way round this. Imodium is a prescription-only anti-diarrhoea drug in the UK. Not just 'a drug' in the sector, but the brand leader. Then it was deregulated. The problem was that if the makers, Janssen Pharmaceuticals, advertised it and created a new market, they would lose £2.5 million worth of prescription sales.

The answer was not to advertise Imodium, but to bring on to the market a new drug for sale in pharmacies, named Arret. A drug which, in fact, was essentially the same as Imodium. Having done that, the way was clear for a full-blooded mass-market campaign. A target was chosen (young people – less entrenched in their ideas) and so was an approach – humorous. Ads appeared with headlines like 'Montezuma's Revenge', showing a cartoon of a man rushing from the beach, his face contorted, his hand clutching his stomach. It proved easy to sell the drug into the pharmacies – they already knew it under another name.

Thus, Janssen gained the best of both worlds: managing to attack the doctors and their patients direct at one and the same time – without breaking any rules, without alienating anyone. Even their rivals were moved to reluctant praise. 'A lovely piece of marketing,' enthused one. And that, as the whole industry knows, is what selling drugs is all about.

Smokers

'We are the number-one brand in the world. What we wanted
was to promote a particular image of adventure, of courage, of
virility . . .'
        Aleardo Buzzi, European president of Marlboro cigarettes

William Bernbach, one of the few truly great figures of the advertising
business and founder of the agency Doyle Dane Bernbach, died on 2
October 1982. For thirty-three years Bernbach had refused to let his
agency handle a cigarette account.

On 17 December 1982 – eleven weeks later – DDB announced it had
a new client and a new product to handle – Philip Morris, the giant US
tobacco company, and its Parliament cigarette brand. The agency felt
forced to comment on the coincidence of the two events. Bernbach,
explained Cary Bayer, the company's PR director, had already indicated
before he died that he would accept a tobacco client belonging to
another agency if a DDB merger with that agency took place; in any
event, Bernbach had also told the chief executive officer of DDB
International that since he (the CEO) was in charge of day-to-day
operations he should decide which accounts to take (or not to take).*

Less than two years later, in October 1984, the agency was far enough
removed from the Bernbach era to be able to announce another (and
much larger) new account - an estimated $50 million assignment from
Brown and Williamson Tobacco, involving the brands Kool, Viceroy
and Lucky Strike. Agency executives were said to be 'euphoric'.

Cigarettes are a very special product. Not to put too fine a point on
it, they can kill people. To help sell them, to imbue them with images
and make them glamorous and desirable, might seem to call for a degree
of pragmatism. Fortunately for the tobacco companies, such pragmatism
is not hard to find in the advertising industry: the Bernbachs are notable
for their rarity.

The link between advertising and the cigarette business is a close and
vital one. The industry *needs* advertising in a way few, if any, other

---

* The talks, which came to nothing, were with Foote Cone and Belding, who had
Lorillard, the US's fifth largest cigarette maker, as client.

industries do. It has the money to buy what it needs – in the US alone, smokers in 1986 spent over $30 billion buying 600 billion cigarettes. Its only limitations are the constraints placed upon it by governments.

For their part, the advertising agencies see rich pickings. Cigarette advertising is one of the world's biggest product categories: companies spend $2 billion a year on conventional advertising and millions more on activities such as sponsoring sporting and arts events to side-step restrictions. Fifteen per cent commission on $2 billion is a lot of money. But more than that, the major cigarette companies have been diversifying in an attempt to shift some of their dependence away from what might be seen literally as a dying business. This means that an agency that stands aloof from a multinational tobacco company's cigarette business also cuts itself off from several other chunks of prime prospects. British-American Tobacco, the British multinational, had diversified by the 1980s into stores (Gimbels and Saks in America and International and Argos in Britain), paper (Wiggins Teape) and beauty products (Yardley, Lentheric, Mornay and Cyclax).* And tobacco-owning conglomerates can be touchy clients. In 1988 Saatchi and Saatchi lost $80 million worth of cookies and candies business from RJR Nabisco, parent of RJ Reynolds. It was fired because it made a TV commercial for Northwest Airlines in which passengers cheered a smoking ban.

To an outsider, Doyle Dane Bernbach's change of heart might have seemed especially cynical, but it certainly was not unique. Ogilvy and Mather used to have a 'no cigarettes' policy. In England, Saatchi and Saatchi was not only an agency without a cigarette account until 1983 but it also handled the anti-smoking Health Education Council. In fact, thirteen years before, in 1970, Charles Saatchi and his partner Ross Cramer in the creative consultancy Cramer Saatchi had created the HEC's first full-scale anti-smoking campaign. Five separate ads, published in the national press, used a hard, factual approach: 'Why do some people wish they had lung cancer?' ran the headline on one. The answer: those who had emphysema because 'lung cancer kills you relatively quickly'. Another described what happens to nicotine particles in a smoker's lungs. 'These particles gradually build up into an oily tar, that irritates your lungs until they become infected and clogged with pus and phlegm. Then, as more of this septic discharge forms, the mixture of tar, pus and phlegm sometimes rises up into the throat and is swallowed. But the rest of it slithers deep into the lungs, where it

* Six multinational companies dominate world cigarette production outside the monopolies of the communist countries and those state monopolies of France, Japan and Italy. Together they produce about 40 per cent of the world's cigarettes. They are: from Britain, British-American Tobacco Industries and the Imperial Group; from the US, Philip Morris Inc, R. J. Reynolds Industries Inc and American Brands Inc, and from South Africa, the Rembrandt Group (Rothmans International).

congeals and festers. It's not surprising that smokers cough, are short of wind, have bad breath, and are more susceptible to crippling incurable diseases.'

The trade magazine *Campaign*, reviewing the campaign, wrote, 'Nauseating? Without a doubt. It is not surprising that two Cramer Saatchi employees have stopped smoking since they started work on the campaign, and Charles Saatchi himself has cut down to one or two cigarettes a day.'

Cramer Saatchi went; Charles Saatchi and his brother Maurice became Saatchi and Saatchi. In September 1983, the agency took its first cigarette account – the Silk Cut brand from Gallaher (the UK arm of American Brands). Trade observers in Britain drew attention to the fact that eradication of this major product gap must have been welcome to Saatchi and Saatchi in the same week that the agency announced its launch on the American Stock Exchange. Others pointed to a similar 'coincidence'. Boase Massimi Pollitt took on *its* first cigarette account – the Dunhill brand overseas – just a month before it went public in the UK. The magazine *Marketing Week* noted that 'the sheer size of most cigarette accounts must set many an adman's eyes wandering'.

The third side of the advertising pyramid, the media, also has an enormous interest in cigarette advertising. Philip Morris Cos and RJR Nabisco (which embraces R.J. Reynolds) were the first and fifth largest advertisers in the United States in 1987. In the UK in 1987 Gallagher was the eighth largest advertiser (to put this into perspective, companies like Mars, Heinz, Vauxhall Motors and Bass Breweries were all well below it). However, these figures tell only part of the story. Because cigarette advertising in both these countries is banned from TV, cigarette advertisers dominate print and posters. Philip Morris in 1987 was the biggest magazine advertiser in the US, the second largest outdoor and the fifth biggest newspaper-space buyer. RJR Nabisco was first in outdoor, fourth in magazines and nineteenth in newspapers. Many magazines would find it hard if not impossible to survive without cigarette advertising. A publication may carry 150–200 pages of cigarette ads a year. Almost half of *Soap Opera Digest*'s ads are for cigarettes.

The tobacco trade sees itself as a beleaguered industry. Increasingly, since the early 1960s, it has been cast as one of the world's great villains. In the UK in 1962 (with the publication of the Royal College of Physicians' first report) and in the US in 1964 (the Surgeon General's report) public attitudes to smoking began to change dramatically. Since then other reports constantly produce new and damning accusations. A World Health Organization publication in 1984 blamed cigarette smoking for a million premature deaths a year.

Compulsory health warnings, a variety of curbs ranging from those on advertising to ones indicating *where* people may and may not smoke, rising taxes, an increasingly sophisticated and vocal anti-cigarette lobby have all combined severely to restrict (or even stop) growth of consumption in Western developed countries.

Those tobacco company executives I met gave the impression of feeling (genuinely) that they were much maligned. People do smoke (still 40 per cent of the adult population of Britain) and the companies supply a (completely legal) need, they argue. Think, too, of the taxes they pour into the economy (£5,737 million in the UK alone in 1986–7), or the jobs the industry represents, often in areas where unemployment is high. In the Third World, where their activities are often most under attack, they might well argue that tobacco is a cash crop not subject to the fluctuations of world commodity prices; as a product it represents employment, exports, education, training and prosperity.

One does not have to be in favour of smoking nor of their activities to have some sympathy for the position in which the cigarette companies now find themselves. They see the battle as being one of survival. They may be hell bent on diversifying but cigarettes are still the centre of their economies. BAT, for example, still draws 65 per cent of its profits from the $10 billion worth of cigarettes which it sells in seventy-eight countries. (I concede in advance all the arguments that might be advanced about the survival of its customers.)

That said, the cigarette companies *have* fought back. Advertising has been a major weapon and professional admen their willing sword bearers. If you happen to believe that the advertising of cigarettes is reprehensible (as I came to believe while researching this chapter), it is nevertheless easier to feel some understanding towards the tobacco men than towards the admen. In private, the admen do *not* (with very rare exceptions) appear to believe the arguments they advance or allow to be advanced in public as to advertising not encouraging smoking or delaying its demise. They are, quite simply, at this level, not concerned. Their job is a pragmatic one. Their problem is not whether they should do it, but *how* best to do it. Some, when pressed, will argue that they are like advocates – the client has the right to have his case presented in the best way. But even here, mostly, you have the feeling that it is an argument repeated rather than genuinely believed. The cigarette companies can at least feel that it's their own survival that is at stake. The ad agencies are not talking about their own life or death, but about larger or smaller profits.

From their beleaguered foxhole the cigarette companies have switched targets and approaches. The young have become more important as middle-aged smokers have kicked the habit. So have women. And so, too, has the developing world – a ripe opportunity not only because cigarette consumption per head is low compared with the developed world, but also because curbs there are still relatively light.

Equally, as some areas of advertising have closed (TV, for example) or become more hedged with rules and conditions, new styles of advertising have been developed (ones where, for example, a symbol or colour is all that is needed to provide a brand reminder) and new avenues have been opened in linking cigarettes with prestigious activities or sporting events.

Advertising has been an integral part of the cigarette business from the moment mass production began. Today's multinationals are largely descendants of an empire created by one American, James Buchanan Duke, over 100 years ago. Until the 1880s cigarettes were rolled by hand for a small market. Duke, who took over his father's tobacco farm in North Carolina in 1880, transformed the industry. First, he acquired the rights to the newly developed Bonsack cigarette rolling machine which could turn out 120,000 cigarettes a day compared to a hand roller's 250. Second, he set out to market aggressively. Soon he was spending about $800,000 on advertising out of sales of $4,500,000. Within a few years he had bought out his rivals. His 'Tobacco Trust' sold nine out of ten of America's cigarettes. Despite that, it maintained a heavy advertising programme ploughing back up to 20 per cent of sales revenue into advertising in newspapers, magazines, on billboards and on cigarette cards which he introduced. His aims were to build loyalty to his own brands and to persuade more people to smoke cigarettes. George Washington Hill followed the Duke tradition. As president of American Tobacco, he teamed with the adman Albert Lasker. By using the new medium of radio and memorable slogans (like 'Reach for a Lucky instead of a sweet'), they trebled the sales of Lucky Strike in five years.

Branding and advertising was firmly established in Britain before the end of the nineteenth century. A number of ads associated women with smoking (without actually showing them doing so), a foretaste of approaches to come. Player's cigarettes adopted its famous bearded-sailor figure in 1898 – a real sailor who sold the use of his likeness in return for 'a bit of baccy for myself and the boys on board'.

Until the 1960s cigarette companies were largely free to advertise in whatever way they wished. It was possible to overstep boundaries, but not easy. In 1930, for example, the *New York Times* reported that an unnamed cigarette firm had promised the Federal Trade Commission it would cease claiming that smoking cigarettes enabled women to 'retain slender figures'. Nevertheless, as E. S. Turner points out in his *The Shocking History of Advertising*, cigarette firms went on to 'prove' that cigarettes aided digestion, increased alkalinity, and saved people from neurotic dissipations such as doodling, pencil-chewing and key juggling! Turner reports that one company asked, 'How are your nerves?' and suggested male readers should try a simple test. This consisted of unbuttoning the waistcoat with one hand, starting at the top, and then rebuttoning with the same hand. Anyone who could not do this in under twelve seconds had bad nerves and needed to start smoking!

Far from doing you harm, cigarettes were good for you in many ways. 'More doctors smoke Camels', boasted one advertisement. A classic fifties television commercial for Kool called the cigarette 'As cool and as clean as a breath of fresh air.' A man puffed, smiled and told viewers, 'Your mouth feels cleaner, your throat refreshed.' To reinforce the message, his face on the screen gave way to pictures of sparkling snow and a rivulet of water.

Cigarettes were *fun*. Animated Lucky Strikes danced on the TV screen. You did things *better* with a cigarette. In a Marlboro commercial, a man worked on his car with total absorption. 'You forget to eat,' he said. 'I don't forget to smoke though.' Advertisers of other products included cigarettes in their own commercials – a Mum deodorant ad had a man smoking, no doubt to show he was a *real* man and not some wimp.

None of this is to say that there were no voices raised against cigarettes or cigarette advertising. In 1904, a young woman was put in jail in New York for smoking a cigarette in public. Organisations including temperance bodies and Boy Scout associations as well as individual senators attacked smoking and advertising, especially to women and young people.

But it was not until the 1960s that cigarette advertising came under real attack, thus producing advertising that endures today – advertising that needs to circumvent increasingly strict restrictions. It is clear that a firm correlation exists between the controls governing cigarette advertising in a country and the 'creative' content of the advertising that appears. What the advertiser is trying to convey is relatively constant; it is the *how* that is forced to adapt. In this respect it is not unlike the photographs in skin magazines. In some countries a suggestive pose may be all that is allowed, in others a bare breast, in some pubic close-ups. What the publisher is 'selling', however, is constant.

Constraints on advertising vary from country to country and from time to time, but in general they are becoming more weighted against the cigarette companies who are fighting an aggressive but essentially rearguard action. This fight includes such things as setting up lobbying organisations, persuading other advertisers that bans on tobacco advertising will be followed by ones on other products, and in general using the industry's considerable political and economic clout.

The Tobacco Advisory Council, representing Britain's cigarette manufacturers, has run campaigns with headlines like '9 out of 10 people wish to be free to decide whether they will smoke or not'. In the US the Tobacco Institute produced nine ads offering a booklet entitled 'Answers to the most asked questions about cigarettes'. Philip H. Dougherty, the advertising columnist of the *New York Times* noted that the booklets on offer were not actually printed at the time the advertising campaign began. He commented, 'But as far as the advertiser goes, the wonderful psychological benefit to a book offer is that many people who do not bother to send for one are inwardly assured that the advertiser does indeed have answers.'

In Australia, such advertising boomeranged on cigarette companies when the Tobacco Institute ran a page ad in the *Sydney Morning Herald* and the *West Australian* headlined, 'Smoking. Let's be sensible about it.' The ad observed that the evidence against smoking was statistical, and included headings such as 'No convincing argument against smoking' and 'Addiction label unwarranted'. There was an enormous reaction against the ad. A number of advertising agencies also resented it – but not because of what it tried to do, but because they thought the conception was unworthy of the subject. John Doorley, creative director of one Sydney agency, attacked the 'poorly conceived and executed nonevent' and said that if ever the Australian cigarette industry 'needed some ads with real guts it's now, when only the best will do'.

In one unusual move, an individual cigarette company, R. J. Reynolds, produced its own pro-smoking ads. The campaign, created by Leber Katz and Partners of New York, included the line 'Some of you might question our motives'. The ads tackled public smoking, fire safety and youth smoking. The message of the ads was that there were two sides to the smoking argument. The tone was frequently conciliatory and reasonable. One was headed 'Some surprising advice to young people from R. J. Reynolds Tobacco'. It began:

Don't smoke.
For one thing smoking has always been an adult custom. And even for adults, smoking has become very controversial.
So even though we're a tobacco company, we don't think it's a good idea for young people to smoke.
Now we know giving this kind of advice to young people can sometimes backfire.
But if you take up smoking just to prove you're an adult, you're really proving just the opposite.
Because deciding to smoke or not to smoke is something you should do when you don't have anything to prove . . .

The industry has also commissioned much research, the results of which have confirmed its stance. This is not, of course, either surprising or in the slightest way unethical. A 'new independent examination' by Metra Consulting, commissioned by Imperial Tobacco and Gallaher, concluded in 1979 that 'in a comprehensive statistical analysis of the UK situation covering the last twenty years, no evidence has been found of a significant association between the total level of media advertising and total cigarette sales'. The report obviously pleased the industry. The Tobacco Advisory Council gave me a copy, as no doubt they had given them to many other people over the years. Several researchers, not all from the anti-smoking lobby, pointed out that research not infrequently turns up the answer people want and is usually then open to some dispute. In this case, there was a great deal of dispute. Nevertheless the Metra research *looks* impressive, and in that alone no doubt does the job that is asked of it . . .

However, in reality the industry's battle is not so much to prevent more restrictions, but to delay their imposition – to buy time. With daily world sales of around 5,000 billion cigarettes, time is a commodity well worth buying.

By the mid-1980s, cigarette advertising was totally banned on television in most European countries, though allowed with constraints in Spain and Portugal. In 1987 the Spanish cabinet approved a bill to ban tobacco and liquor ads. The noose tightens bit by bit, even in countries with relaxed attitudes. In the Argentine, TV advertising is allowed and it is possible to use heroic figures engaged in macho activities, but smoking can no longer be *directly* linked with physical exercise. For Camel, this meant changing ads so that the Camel man no longer crossed dangling rope bridges but was confined to calmly filling his canteen as he sat on a rock and lit up.

In Britain, the tobacco industry's agreement with the government includes: advertisements should not claim or imply that smoking is a sign of manliness, courage or daring, or that it enhances feminine charm. Advertisements should not feature heroes of the young or appear in publications aimed at young people. From 1986 they were banned from magazines with a female readership of over 200,000 and where a third of the readers are fifteen to twenty-four. As a result of the 1986 agreement, cinema advertising – long a way of attacking the youth market – was prohibited. (Cigarette ads on TV were banned in 1965.)

The United States has fewer controls over cigarette advertising than most other Western countries. There are just four specific restraints: cigarettes cannot be advertised on radio or television; warnings must be displayed on packages and in advertisements; advertisements have to include levels of tar and nicotine; and advertisements are not to appear in youth media or to use illustrations or themes attractive to young people.

Many countries insist on health warnings being included in ads. In the UK they run at the bottom. David Abbott of the London agency Abbott Mead Vickers, a rare one that will *not* handle cigarette accounts, told me, 'You learn skills. One of the things you learn as a designer of a forty-eight-sheet poster is that you put a headline at the top. That is where the eye goes. In the end the health warning has become wallpaper. I am sure the companies and the agencies would rather it wasn't there, but they have found ways of minimising it.' An art director at another agency explained that it was an elementary part of designing a cigarette ad to do it in such a way that the eye was attracted away from the warning.

It is striking how often the warning is now used by advertising men as a spoof in ads and illustrations in their own trade press. The US magazine *Adweek* introduced a feature 'Does Design Sell?' using a full page imitation ad with a note boxed at the bottom right corner: 'Warning: The Surgeon General has Determined that Design in Ads is Dangerous to Your Wealth'.

Restrictions are one side of the triangle. The other is what the industry wants to convey. The third is how it manages to do that in the circumstances that apply in the specific country concerned.

Over twenty years ago, shortly before advertising was banned on British television, a copywriter gave the authors Pearson and Turner his personal check-list when working on a cigarette ad:

1. It's an initiation symbol – a proof that you are on your own in the tribe and have achieved independent manhood.

2. A nipple substitute – something you still feel the urge to suck in times of stress.

3. A proof of sociability, to show that you are liked and people like you in return.

4. A virility symbol – a symbolic penis advertising the fact that in your estimation you can always have a woman anywhere and at any time you want one.

The authors added 'Not everybody was prepared to go so far, but there had been frequent appeals to manliness . . . Equally, there had been a strong strain of snob appeal . . .'

An examination of today's print ads in the US, the UK and in international media such as *Time* magazine, makes it very clear that the cigarette companies heavily utilise three approaches.

The first involves featuring the cigarette brand as an elegant and status-giving object in its own right. The message is: carry *this* pack, smoke *this* cigarette – and you, too, take on something extra, something special, become someone more desirable or exciting. Such ads are found in all countries, though more widely in countries such as the UK, where the restrictions curtail the sex and fun type advertisements.

Sterling cigarettes uses Bang and Olufsen stereos, Steinway pianos and a Porsche automobile in its ads to project an upscale image. Stride packets are portrayed against a background of lush, racehorse-rearing country. Rothmans shows the coach and footmen used to deliver its cigarettes to clubs and embassies in central London. Mild Seven, Japan's biggest selling cigarette, pictures an impossibly blue private pool with a decanter of white wine and lounging chairs waiting for the bathers once they've finished swimming. Dunhill and Cartier packets stand beside gold lighters. Names and packaging are important: Cartier is a case in point, so is Harrods (in ads the pack is depicted against a brightly lit store). Packs have coats of arms – like Raffles with its gold emblem against black pack.

The success and status approach is particularly prevalent in the Third World. Here, smoking the right brand is the secret of attracting the pretty girl or attaining the right to drive the big, shiny car. In Nigeria, Player's Gold Leaf brand is 'The cigarette for the VIP' and features sharp, business-suited blacks. In Kenya, Embassy uses the image of a dynamic black businessman against a montage of planes and distant places. 'The smooth way to go places', says the message.

The image and the reality could not be further apart – the status-sold smokers can often afford to buy their image-filled cigarettes only as single sticks. But never mind that they can't afford the whole packet – they represent the market of the future. While Western smokers average 2,500 cigarettes a year each, counterparts in the Third World average only 300, a statistic cigarette marketers see as a major opportunity.

The second approach is one of linking smoking with health and well-being, surprising as this might seem. Over the years this has had to be done more and more subtly, mainly because of regulations but also because of greater public sophistication. The cigarette industry has a long history of such advertising. To counter reports linking smoking with cancer in the fifties, cigarette companies had actors dressed as doctors smoking vigorously in commercials. One actor endorsed L & M Filter with the words, 'Just what the doctor ordered.' His doctor, he said, had advised him to try L & M and he had found 'more flavour' coming through.

When pressure brought a crackdown on such blatant approaches, manufacturers turned to health-by-association by using virile, well-known people. John Wayne proclaimed himself a Camel fan (an endorsement whose irony was not to be apparent for many years). Mildness and 'lack of irritation' or absence of 'worrying' featured in many ads. Eva Gabor said, 'I don't worry about my throat since I changed to Camels.' Opera star Marguerite Piazza went further. She 'made the three-day Camel test under the supervision of a noted throat specialist'. Wonder of wonders, 'She found that there was no throat irritation due to smoking Camels.' Sports stars were linked with cigarettes, an obvious way of associating health and fitness with the habit and a brand. Thus baseball star Mickey Mantle and tennis player Pancho Gonzales smoked Viceroy.

Today's ads necessarily have to be more obtuse, but therein, of course, lies the skill. Newport cigarettes makes great play with the word 'alive' – 'Alive with pleasure' is the headline above a picture of two young people very full of joy and life. Sportsmen (no longer big names) still feature – a bare-chested tennis player, racket still in hand, clasps a freshly lighted Kent between his lips. His female counterpart, racket in hand, cardigan open over tennis whites, hair blowing in the breeze, clutches her (freshly lit) Salem. The Bright man skis and surfs. In the UK, the approach has to be more indirect, using association through other activities, notably sponsorship, and through ads for holiday companies with the same name as the cigarette brand (of which more later).

The third approach involves associating the cigarette with glamorous and exciting people and their lifestyles. The Lucky Strike man wears shades, a black leather jacket and rides – alone and free – on his motorcycle across empty countryside. The Vantage man drives racing cars – 'Vantage performance Counts. Performance so good you can taste it.'

These men are not just macho, they're men who know what they're doing. The Winston man, climbing rope and gear slung over his shoulder, strikes purposely away from his helicopter across the rugged terrain. He's on his way to rescue someone. You feel if anyone can save that someone, this is the man. The other inference is more subtle – this man *knows* what life's about *and* he smokes; it must be all right . . . Merit's seamen, sweeping out to the open sea or navigating giant tankers through narrow straits, belong to the same category. Rothmans' man conveys the message in shorthand. The ad shows a hand holding a Rothmans' pack. The only other part of him that is visible is the cuff of his sleeve. In international magazine ads (not subject to government restrictions even though they circulate in countries where restrictions normally apply) the sleeve has rings – the man is a pilot, someone else responsible for lives, someone else who knows the score. In England, such imagery is no longer acceptable under the voluntary code. The sleeve has to be bare, but it is very dark so that it resembles a uniform. I was told (by a Rothmans' competitor) that the ad continued because research had shown that readers still 'saw' a pilot's sleeve when they looked at the ad.

If you don't aspire to macho, there are other smoker-heroes with whom you can identify. The Kool man, eyes closed, caresses his saxophone through a solo ('There's only one way to play it'). The Barclay man is cool, worldly; he pauses from lighting a cigarette to glance knowingly at the woman who has rested her hand on his shoulder ('The pleasure is back').

The men have their female equivalents. More's woman, tall and elegant in a long black strapless dress, pauses from playing pool watched by an admiring man. Vantage's woman relaxes (but only briefly, you feel) with a cigarette beside a dress-maker's dummy. Her own dress is expensive, her jewellery gold and chunky; the surroundings – from the little that can be seen – reinforce the image of a successful designer. Satin's lady wears silk and reclines among deep cushions – 'Go ahead. You deserve this Satin moment.'

The cigarette as shared sex object survives in some ads. A tousle-headed blond male, naked to the waist, crouched legs wide apart, says 'Light my Lucky.' You feel he has been carefully chosen to appeal to both men and women. Cigarettes go with couples being together. Salem couples hug each other delightedly – without letting go of their lighted cigarettes ('Share the spirit. Share the refreshment'). Kent couples walk barefoot on white sands. In Austria, Milde Sorte smokers lean against palm trees and gaze adoringly at each other, freshly lighted cigarettes in hand. Frequently the smokers come in groups. The one thing all the groups have in common is that they are having fun. Cigarettes enhance that togetherness, add to that fun. The Newport group sings along to an accordion. The Player's people are laughing and joking in a bar.

One of the most famous associations of cigarettes with glamour and excitement is the Marlboro cowboy. He rides high in the saddle on enormous outdoor advertising boards that tower over the sidewalks in the Dominican Republic; his weathered, experienced face gazes out from the pages of the *International Herald Tribune*; in Hong Kong he's young and wears a white hat and rides a white horse. Wherever he is, the Marlboro cowboy is one of the world's most pervasive and potent advertising symbols. Because of him, Marlboro changed from being a woman's cigarette and a minor brand to *the* macho brand and not just the world's biggest selling cigarette, but the world's largest selling packaged goods product. It is a brand leader in countries that include Germany, Italy and the US itself – where one in every five cigarettes smoked is a Marlboro. World sales in 1985 were estimated at about $6 billion.

The Marlboro man is almost a cliché of the power of advertising. What is not so immediately apparent is the brilliance of the idea as a way of overcoming differing advertising restrictions. Barry Day, worldwide creative director of McCann-Erickson, has written:

> Emotionally Marlboro owns the West. Whether it's a grizzled cowboy shading his eyes from the burning ember as he lights his cigarette from the campfire, a roundup of wild horses or simply a loving close-up of saddle and spur, there are few places in the world where the identifying brand name wouldn't immediately spring to mind. So potent is the symbolism that it allows the advertiser to 'tailor' his message according to the ever-increasing degree of restriction prevalent in a particular country. You can't show someone smoking? You don't need to. The symbols say it all.

And the image that comes across? Two researchers, asked school-children to act out the smoking of named brands. The Marlboro smoking style, they found, was 'full of determination, facial grimacing and suggests that a drag from a Marlboro is not child's play. One definitely knows a "decent" cigarette is being smoked. In short, it is a tough smoke for tough men.' As to its mythical appeal for adults, they cited Australia and pointed out that it is one of the most urbanised nations in the world and most people who smoke Marlboro are, therefore, urban dwellers (as must be true in most other countries). 'The advertisements are not designed for people who are like the Marlboro man but for those who would like to be like him. Marlboro advertising is perhaps the most blatantly escapist of all cigarette advertising. It offers transformation of the harried, rushed and crowded urban man to the open spaces, freshness, and the elemental toughness and simplicity of Marlboro country.'

The man who began all this, over thirty years ago, was a squat single-minded adman, a 'genius' according to many advertising professionals. The agency he founded in 1935 operates out of Chicago, a reason it is said, for Burnett's great strength – that of being able to operate closer to the 'real' people. Burnett, like the best advertising he produced, was folksy – and tough. Among its literature is a large poster with Leo Burnett's quote: 'When you reach for the stars you may not quite get one, but you won't come up with a handful of mud either.'

In 1954, Burnett was reaching not so much for a star but for an idea to transform the filter tip Philip Morris brand called Marlboro. The problem thrown at the agency was how to change it from a woman's brand to a man's cigarette. The agency was told everything about the cigarette could be discarded but the name. Burnett called a brainstorming session at his farm outside Chicago. During discussion on masculine images, Burnett himself remembered a *Life* magazine cover of a cowboy. That picture, it was said later, 'symbolised everything they wanted to represent the new Marlboro cigarette'.

In fact, only one of the first new Marlboro men was a cowboy. Others included deep-sea fishermen, policemen, and car mechanics. They had tattoos (meant to hint at a romantic past) and were older than models in other ads. These were tough, *mature* men with tough jobs and interesting backgrounds. The full-blooded Marlboro Country campaign came in the sixties as a specific response to the first smoking and health report by the Surgeon General. Philip Morris wanted a change in the campaign, something that would lift the brand in the wake of the report.

In 1971, cigarette advertising ceased on American radio and TV. Until then, over 80 per cent of Marlboro's budget had gone into TV. Marlboro country's great strength as an advertising campaign was that it translated easily from TV into print and to outdoor boards, just as it has translated internationally as a concept in the 180 countries where the brand is now promoted.

The Marlboro man's success has been responsible for a whole breed of other macho heroes, all chasing the same stage coach full of gold. Perhaps the one who got closest was the Camel man, a rugged individualist depicted by American actor Bob Beck, until a decision in 1986 to begin to phase him out for a younger, smoother successor. Like the Marlboro man, he is mature. He has a shock of hair, a moustache and – usually – a cigarette between his lips. Ads show him trail-blazing in exotic locations. In one, he rafts a Landrover across a jungle river. In another, he perches atop a propeller-driven aircraft surrounded by forest. It is real male fantasy material.

The original ads were created by Batten, Barton, Durstine and Osborn, better known as BBDO. The agency's internal house journal was instructive about the reasoning behind the campaign. 'Because cigarettes, like only a few other product categories, are consumed so visibly, they make personal statements about their user that are closely connected with the imagery associated with the brand. But if advertising fails to provide the imagery, it may never attract large groups of smokers who might otherwise choose the brand.' The advertising created for Camel Lights, the journal explained, was 'a recognition of these market forces'.

The strategy is straightforward: attract younger adult male smokers by identifying the brand with a lifestyle so that it is more pleasure-oriented than work-oriented. A lifestyle that may be idealised but is still within their reach. That lifestyle is personified by the Camel man – a single, rugged individual who appears in every ad. He's always seen in a striking outdoor setting. Often he's involved in an activity that presents a challenge, some adventure and sometimes an element of risk. The single line of copy – 'Where a Man Belongs' – says as much about his environment as it does about his cigarette.

The campaign imagery is reflected in advertising throughout the entire Camel Brand Family . . . and, in addition, two new promotional ventures, Camel Expeditions (travel tours) and The Camel Collection (men's clothing). This unified approach, including the use of the classic Camel packaging for all cigarette brands, complements Camel's long heritage of product quality with authentic user imagery that target prospects can readily identify with.

The Camel man, like the Marlboro campaign, is adaptable depending on local restrictions and culture. In Brazil, for example, Camel's global agency, McCann-Erickson, modified TV commercials to make Beck resemble a rich tourist on vacation. It did this after Brazilians reacted unenthusiastically to ads showing the actor performing survival tasks in the jungle. Brazilians, it seemed, could not understand why anyone would want to do such things – they themselves avoid jungle! In Hong Kong the Marlboro man has to be younger and look as though he *owns* the ranch and because the Chinese are social he is not shown alone.

In Britain, however, restrictions are such that the macho-smoker marketers have experienced difficulties. Neither the Camel man nor the Marlboro man are now allowed in ads. 'The Marlboro cowboy,' said David Williamson, deputy director of the Advertising Standards Authority, 'is regarded as a young hero and any association between cigarettes and healthy outdoor living is not allowed under the current code.' 'It's a problem,' Philip Morris' director of business development was quoted as saying. The company changed agencies in an attempt to find a solution. New approaches were tried. Saddles, spurs and chuck wagons gave way to ads that utilised the familiar white pyramid of the pack in inventive ways. In one, for example, it became the searchlight beam of an advancing locomotive forging through mountainous country. At the time of writing it was not a problem they had solved.

Another major cigarette manufacturer, however, had long before anticipated the UK's tougher stance on cigarette advertising and had formulated its own unique solution.

If Marlboro dominates the world cigarette market, another filter-tip cigarette – Benson and Hedges – occupies that position in Great Britain. It, too, has risen from being a minor brand to being the market leader, also changing its image along the way. By the foresight of its manufacturer and its ad agency, it has done so with an advertising campaign that – short of a total advertising ban – should continue to be immune to tightening restrictions because it doesn't actually *say* anything. In the words of McCann-Erickson's Barry Day, 'a wealth of hints, but little for the legislators to get hold of . . .'

Benson and Hedges in the UK is a brand produced by Gallaher which since 1975 has been owned by American Brands, the direct descendant of Buck Duke's cigarette empire. It is *not* the same brand as the Benson and Hedges cigarette sold in the United States where Benson and Hedges is a Philip Morris brand. Gallaher is not Britain's largest cigarette operation, but it is its most successful one. Much of that success is due to a decision it took in 1976–77 to change the way it promoted and advertised Benson and Hedges Special Filter.

Until that time Benson and Hedges Special Filter had been carefully positioned as an 'upmarket' cigarette. For more than a decade Collett Dickenson Pearce, then the most creative of the English agencies, had produced advertisements showing the pack beautifully photographed in various settings. Each ad also included a pun utilising the word 'gold', the colour of the pack. Thus in one the pack was shown on a Caribbean beach next to a treasure map, a compass and a space with the words, 'In the main gold is easier to find nowadays.'

In 1974, an ex-Gallaher secretary who had worked her way up through the company became marketing manager of Special Filter, an appointment which, she recalled later, 'caused quite a few ripples. It was the company's hottest property.' Maggie Green, then forty-three, is a sensible-looking woman with an elfin haircut. She wears a shirt and skirt, and works in a partitioned-off section of an open-plan floor. The only pictures on the wall are framed cigarette advertisements. Her handshake is soft, and her manner gentle but firm. She's the highest ranking woman in a tough company in a male-dominated industry. ('It always disappoints me that I've now been in Gallaher fifteen years and how few [women] are coming up behind me. But if they [the women] want it to happen, it will. I don't think anyone should lay down a red carpet and ease them in.')

Benson and Hedges Special Filter at that time was an important brand not so much because of what it was but what it *could* be. It was far and away the market leader in its sector, king size filter, but the whole sector was only 10 per cent of the market. Two things, however, were on the horizon, one (for the company) good, the other not so good. The first, the good, was that the whole market was going to change. Because of the new European Community rules, king size cigarettes were no longer going to be more heavily taxed than short cigarettes. With the price differential eroded, a boom in king size filter sales could be expected from 1976 (the year of the tax change). In anticipation, Gallaher's competitors were busily introducing new brands. But in B & H Special Filter, Gallaher's already had a potential mass-market winner if only it could be projected in the right way.

The second, the not so good, was that further restrictions on cigarette advertising were abroad. One of them, recalls Green, was 'a nasty little clause that said you cannot show the pack in luxury surroundings'. Exactly the approach that had been taken in the brand's advertising until then.

'We knew we had to change things,' says Green. CDP, the agency, were given three criteria for a new advertisement approach:

The pack had to be the hero of the ad.

If we could do away with words we would be grateful. (This because of present and possible future restrictions on what actually could be said.)

And we wanted to get younger people. It had always been a cigarette for a night out. It was a cigarette mum and dad smoked. Young people didn't, because they did. Obviously we would like to appeal to the young.

Green recalls: 'We used to go over to the agency and burn the midnight oil. There was fifteen–eighteen months of work. We went out to new photographers. I would send the photographs back. New ideas came back looking like old ads. We really wanted to jump the barrier.'

What finally emerged was an approach that the head of one international agency described later as 'changing the whole face of advertising' in Britain. The conception was a surrealistic one. Art photographs showed the cigarette pack in fantastic situations. Over the years the pack has become a tube of paint oozing colour, a beam of light through an open door, a lightbulb surrounded by moths . . .

The idea made many people at Gallaher nervous. Some suggested a different approach, others wanted to research the idea first, something that had not been done on the brand before. 'Everyone was scared stiff that the campaign would ruin what was a rock solid brand,' says Green. On the other hand, if Benson and Hedges Special Filter was to become the major brand on the about-to-boom market it *had* to make a break through. To do that Gallaher had to get the cigarette smoked by the mass market C2D2s.

The decision was made to go ahead with three ads – ones showing the pack as part of Stonehenge, in a bird cage, and in a mouse-hole. 'We *felt* we were right,' says Green, 'but we knew we would get a lot of flak.' In the event, Gallaher started getting 'fan mail' almost immediately. 'One man wrote that he was driving his car in Chelsea, saw an ad and had to stop and go back to look at it more carefully.' The ads also 'picked up every award in sight'. Most importantly for Gallaher, they worked. The cigarette sold in greater and greater numbers, and research showed that the smokers were precisely the ones the company wanted – young men.

By March 1978 Benson and Hedges Special Filter was the biggest selling cigarette in the country. Today it accounts for about 15 per cent of the total market. What is more, says Green, because of the advertising it has also managed to retain a status image. 'People still regard it as being very special although it is number one. When it was made number one we had to restrain ourselves (from publicising the fact) – that's the last thing our customers want to know.'

Within the ad industry, the campaign – still running strong – has taken on legendary proportions. Others have tried to emulate it but without making the impact. In the best of the competing campaigns John Player produced a series of pun illustrations on the theme of black. One showed a magazine page divided into two halves with a half cigarette pack on one side and the other side coloured black, and the line 'Half Black'.

Green also believes that the campaign has changed the status of working on cigarette ads inside agencies. Many people, she says, did not previously want to work on them because they felt there was little they could do creatively. The Benson and Hedges surrealistic ads proved that 'you could be creative'.

Green concedes that the ultra creativity of Benson and Hedges' approach is due to the restrictions on advertising. 'You have either got to be just straight and have a line which cannot offer any kind of promises or you have to develop a campaign such as ours which is totally different.' Speaking about restrictions, she chose her words with care. At one stage she began, 'So because we had seen a way round the code . . .' She stopped immediately and amended her words: 'Because the code was there it had triggered us into being more creative.'

There is no doubt about the admiration the campaign attracts, even from those who are personally opposed to cigarette advertising. David Abbott, the noted English copywriter, told me, 'I can look at a Benson and Hedges campaign and admire the technical skill and ingenuity. I can feel nothing but admiration for the craftsmanship, but regret the fact that it is there.'

Green did not smoke while we were together. She admits to being an 'occasional smoker' but says she has to be 'offered one first'. How does she view the opposition to cigarette advertising? She thinks that Gallaher has a special problem because of its high advertising profile. 'I always say our advertising does a lot of good but also a lot of harm because it is so noticeable that the anti-lobby can pin an attack on us.' More generally, she believes, 'As long as we abide by the code we have a right to sell and while we have that right we have a right to advertise.'

In Britain, it would appear, the admen have taken the restrictions and risen above them. In Italy, where advertising is banned completely, the admen have to be even more inventive.

Italy is a country often cited by the tobacco lobby as 'proof' that banning advertising has no effect on cigarette smoking. Advertising has been totally banned there since 1962 to protect the national industry from imports. Nevertheless, argues the Advertising Association, cigarette consumption in that country grew by 76 per cent between the ban and 1980. This, it comments, 'certainly does not suggest the ban was successful'. The Tobacco Advisory Council in 'Advertising Controls and Their Effects on Total Cigarette Consumption', makes Italy the first of the detailed examples in its appendix of illustrations, and again after giving consumption figures year by year says there is 'no evidence to be deduced from the . . . data that the advertising ban has had any restricting effect on total consumption'.

The most popular mild cigarette in Italy is Kim, a British-American Tobacco brand, aimed specifically at women. Women and smoking were linked in advertisements before the end of the last century. Women held cigarettes but did not actually put them between their lips. However, as E. S. Turner pointed out, 'If people chose to assume that these girls were smokers, well and good.' The 1920s was the first time cigarette advertising was *directed* specifically towards women. Good advertisers are swift at sensing and reacting to social change. A mood of liberation was abroad and cigarettes were to become a symbol of rebellion against the past. The first notable advertisement was one for Chesterfield – a woman sitting on a couch next to a male smoker was saying, 'Blow some my way.'

The next major attempt to target women came in the late 1960s as tobacco companies sensed the potential of the new liberated woman. Philip Morris led the way, in 1968, with Virginia Slims, and its image of the striving, independent woman, together with the famous slogan 'You've come a long way, baby.' In the wake of its success other women-targeted brands poured into the market.

By the 1980s research apparently showed that women were ready to indulge themselves as well as trying to strive ever onward. The result, from Lorillard, was Satin, a cigarette with a satin-paper filter. Ads emphasised, 'that special moment of time that women want for themselves'. 'Spoil yourself with Satin', read the headline in one. Beneath, a woman – smoking – reclined on a couch with a white Persian cat. 'Go ahead,' read the caption. 'You deserve this Satin moment. So enjoy the smooth, silky taste of new Satin with the luxurious Satin tip.'

In 1987, Philip Morris launched a brand called Star in Switzerland, a key cigarette marketing country because regulations are relatively lax and because of the proximity of France, Germany and Italy. This was positioned unashamedly as a fashion accessory, with five different candy-coloured packs.

The cigarette companies have no doubts about the growing importance of the female market. All the research has pointed to women being prime customers of the future, provided they can be hooked skilfully. One significant set of statistics from the Health and Human Services Department in the US, showed that in the second half of the seventies the number of male teenage smokers fell, but the number of female teenagers taking up the habit soared by a staggering 40 per cent. Edward A. Horrigan, chairman of R. J. Reynolds, attributed the rise to changing lifestyles, with women copying an old-fashioned image of men. He told *Business Week*, 'In the old days, a guy would go into an airport bar and order a Scotch; now that same guy will order a Perrier. But the woman who is an account executive or creative director emulates the man she knew about ten years ago who smoked and drank. So she'll have a Scotch or maybe a glass of white wine and light up a cigarette.'

By 1982 cigarette companies had decided that Europe was ripe for a fresh assault. Peter Parsons, sales manager for BAT (UK and Export), told a conference of tobacco retailers in Majorca early that year, 'the number of women smokers is likely to increase in the future, and the effect for our business is that they will be of greater importance to cigarette marketing than they have been in the past. That could mean more overtly feminine brands as yet another market segment is developed.'

The BAT executive was obviously preparing the ground for a specific company offensive because in May 1982 Kim was brought to Britain as 'a cigarette aimed specifically at women smokers'. However, BAT faced a problem: since 1977 UK advertisers have not been allowed to suggest female smokers are 'more glamorous and independent than non-smokers' or that 'smoking enhances feminine charm'.

Kim was going to have to find a way around that troublesome code, but the company had already handled a much bigger problem in Italy where there is no legal advertising at all.

Sometimes the ad industry finds itself in quandary. There are things that its practitioners do from time to time that they are reluctant to publicise abroad. At the same time, the way they cope with a particular problem may be instructive to other admen – quite apart from the fact that they are proud of their achievement.

Thus did *Grey View*, the international in-house magazine of Grey advertising, find itself devoting two pages to such a success. One page was dominated by a pair of glossy female lips holding a cigarette with the Kim name, and a headline, 'How to Make a Product Successful when you can't even run an ad for it.'

The author was Ugo Gatti, founder, president and managing director of Milano and Grey. He began, 'Advertising is a field in which you must apply creativity in every possible way if you want to achieve success. For example, let me tell you how, with a little creativity, even a restrictive law could not prevent the successful launch of a new product.'

Milano and Grey was assigned the Kim brand in 1974, the year after it was introduced on the Italian market. 'The crucial problem,' recalled Gatti in his article, 'was how to advertise the brand without getting into trouble with the law.' For six months the agency 'got articles into major women's and news magazines explaining to Italian consumers that in France and Germany there was a cigarette called Kim.' At the same time the agency was 'trying to create a concept that could build up the image of Kim permanently without any risk of violating the law'. It did this by making an agreement with 'top fashion stylists' who produced creations in the same colours as the packaging of Kim cigarettes. These ads were lawful. 'The background was always the silhouette of our cigarette pack.'

Next the agency devised an even more devious way of reaching young people. It sponsored a radio programme featuring the latest hit records. Each song linked the singer who was about to appear with Kim cigarettes. Thus – and the example is from Gatti himself – 'And now the latest hit by Barbra Streisand. It is easy to imagine how smart she would look in a beautiful dress created by Pancaldi in Kim colours.'

Gatti does not say whether the permission of any of the singers was sought (which seems unlikely) or whether there was any reaction to the use of their names. However, this was only the first technique devised to get the Kim message over to young listeners. The second was even more cunning. Again in Gatti's own words:

'For two years we have always tried to include, among the selected songs, one that had a mention of smoking in the lyrics: "I'm alone and I light my cigarette"; "the flavour of my first cigarette". At this point, immediately after the word "cigarette" or "smoking" a musical jingle echoed "Kim . . . Kim . . .".'

The results of all this, continued Gatti, 'speak for themselves', in that sales of Kim rose from 85 million cigarettes in 1975 to 2,275 million cigarettes in 1980. 'Can we say,' he added, 'that there is more than one way to be creative in advertising? Or that sometimes you have to use creativity to find a way to be creative?'

The great irony, of course, is the way agencies and cigarette companies continue to cite Italy as an example of restrictions on cigarette advertising not affecting consumption. In *The Trouble with Advertising*,

John O'Toole, chairman of Foote, Cone and Belding, states that 'experience after experience demonstrates [banning advertising] doesn't work. Cigarette advertising has been banned in Italy since 1962. Cigarette consumption has actually increased since that date.'*

In Britain in 1982, Kim did not have to overcome a situation where cigarette advertising was totally illegal, but it did face restrictions that, among other things, were designed to prevent cigarettes being linked with feminine charm or with health benefits or heroes or heroines. As regards open and overt advertising BAT and its UK agency, Dorland, part of the Saatchi empire, trod a careful tightrope.

Most interesting, though, was the way the Kim logo appeared on the television screens. And not only on the TV screens but associated with a woman (the Kim target market) and a healthy sportswoman at that. Martina Navratilova wore a shirt bearing the logo during the Wimbledon women's final which was televised. In reply to complaints, a BAT public relations man said the shirts had been part of a range of Italian sportswear since 1956 and had nothing to do with the cigarette company – except that BAT had taken out a licence on the Kim logo. The following month, BAT seemingly changed its line when it apologised to the government in a letter from a director to the Sports Minister. The following year, 1983, Navratilova was back at Wimbledon still wearing the Kim logo – this time, BAT claimed later, against the company's wishes.

BAT and its brand Kim are not unique in attempting to get around bans on advertising in such ways. Circumventing restrictions is now an integral part of cigarette promotion. In 1979, BAT executives met together in Germany to discuss precisely the problem of how to deal with growing restrictions. They were concerned about what was going to happen and how, as traditional advertising was banned in more and more markets, other methods could be used. A BAT memorandum written after the conference showed how pessimistic they were about 'straight' advertising: 'Prospects for 1990 are poor. Among the most important BAT markets, the number completely free of all bans and restrictions will have diminished from eight (in 1979) to two, and those with complete bans on all media will have increased from eight to twenty-two. These restrictions primarily affect the "persuasive" nature of advertising.'

A number of suggestions for action emerged. 'As advertising bans tend to fall unevenly on countries, within regions, companies should explore the opportunities to co-operate one with another by beaming

---

* It should also be noted about Italy's 'ban' that it is widely broken in other ways. The industry's own journal, *Tobacco Reporter*, said in its April 1980 issue, 'Cigarette advertising, illegal though it may be, is not uncommon in Italy . . . Ad agencies inside the country protect themselves by requiring their tobacco clients to sign contracts with print and poster media agreeing to pay any fines which they may incur. The cost is included in the budget.'

TV and radio into, for example, a "ban" country. Obviously the political risks of this action must be weighed up and treated with prudence.'

Sponsorship and promotion loomed large in suggestions: 'The great importance of fostering goodwill should be one of the most important criteria by which all promotions and sponsorships are judged. Opportunities should be explored by all companies so as to find non-tobacco products and other services which can be used to communicate the brand or house name, together with their essential visual identifiers. This is likely to be a long term and costly operation, but the principle is, nevertheless, to ensure that cigarette lines can be effectively publicised when all direct forms of communication are denied.'

The cigarette industry has taken such thoughts to heart and acted upon them. What is particularly striking about cigarette promotion today is that in response to advertising restrictions, and in anticipation of more, it has become so comprehensive. Smaller and smaller groups of potential customers are specially targeted. In the US, for example, Hispanics have become an especial target with new brands tailored to fit research findings – in one case, full flavour cigarettes in a pack designed to reflect both status and machismo. Black neighbourhoods are flooded with billboards and sponsored fashion shows in which models smoke on the catwalk to link cigarettes and elegance. Sampling has reached new heights. In the US, Brown and Williamson in launching Barclay gave away cartons of 200 cigarettes on request. In Holland, two packs (forty cigarettes) were given away to telephone callers – 65,000 of them in five days. Special offers have proliferated: flight bags with R. J. Reynolds brands (thus also providing the company with free travelling ads for Camel, Winston, Salem and Vantage brands), a free carton with every four Marlboro cartons bought; $12 coupons back on two cartons of Bright.

Competition prizes have reached ever more dizzy heights. A Marlboro UK competition offered £1 million in total, including six 'fabulous dream cars'. Silk Cut offered that much as its first prize in its promotion. More run-of-the-mill competitions include Embassy's cash bingo with a guaranteed prize every time (from £1 up to £50,000), Dunhill's £500,000 for solving a mystery, and a Volkswagen Golf convertible from Kim. A black Lotus Turbo was on offer at the John Player Roadshow. During the show's tour, John Player dominated the concourse of London's Victoria railway station. The Lotus and the black John Player racing car were part of the set, together with formula one racing on a video screen. Beautiful girls in tight black trousers and jackets with the JPS logo handed out packs – each one contained stickers, brochures for JPS clothes, competition details, a Grand Prix calendar poster, and a book of coupons that could be part exchanged for cigarettes.

The companies have become adept at creating loopholes. To promote its Merit brand, Philip Morris in the US launched a public opinion survey organisation which fed its *Merit Report* 'as an authoritative source of valid information about what people are thinking' to newspapers and broadcasters. R. J. Reynolds began underwriting public broadcast programmes in the US after it was agreed the company could be identified on the air as having 'major interests in tobaccco, foods and beverages'. A small gain, it might be thought, but it is the total of such small gains that counts. The Raffles brand name appeared prominently on the cover of a menu and of a record album in what appeared to be an advertisement for Tia Maria in the UK woman's magazine, *Options*. It emerged, however, that half the cost of the ad was being paid by Raffles' producers, Philip Morris. The setting of the ads – spread over four pages – suggested a couple dining and then going to bed together. There were complaints that in linking cigarettes with sex and elegant surroundings and in not displaying a health warning, the ads broke the industry's code. After a letter from the government's Department of Health and Social Security, Philip Morris apologised. By then, of course, the ad had done its work. In 1988 in the US the same company was behind a campaign against those who wanted to prohibit smoking on commuter trains in the New York area, a fact that the public was not meant to know. It was also identified as the main drive behind a new body, the Leadership Council on Advertising Issues, to fight government infringement on advertiser rights.

Some successes have been shortlived. Benson and Hedges paid to have 100 cabs in London painted gold and with the company's name. After complaints, it was ruled they were ads and had to carry a government health warning.

Cigarette companies have rushed to enter the holiday business, thus encouraging new use of the brand name and linking it – without problems – with youth, fun and excitement. Marlboro's Adventure Travel urges, 'Test yourself . . . your spirit for adventure, for excitement, for freedom.' One holiday involves 'reliving the Old West'. The brochure includes a picture of a cowboy – complete with cigarette. Peter Stuyvesant Travel concentrates on sea and sand, full of illustrations of beautiful young people and exotic places. Gallaher's Silk Cut offers wine study in France and tennis in Portugal. John Player Special offers holidays at Grand Prix events. Almost every page of the very glossy brochure has the JPS logo (the same one as on the cigarette packs) – on cars, on the clothes of glamorous girl greeters and on banners. Of the catalogues, John Player's is the most overtly sexy – in one shot a girl sits on a tyre, naked but for a man's shirt which is unbuttoned and open wide. The holiday link also provides a way of advertising in newspapers and magazines without including health warnings.

Cigarette companies have also gone into clothes and related products thus providing walking ads for their brand names. There are Silk Cut track suits and watches, Kim umbrellas, Camel trousers, Marlboro ski goggles and jeans, John Player jackets. Images are sporting, clean cut, often slightly upmarket – and always young. There are sponsored books (like Peter Stuyvesant's books on windsurfing and waterskiing produced jointly with the *Daily Mail*) and even logo-covered cans of motor oil and car wax (from John Player). John Player also promotes its own cocktail, Black Orchid, a 'sophisticated' blend it claims, but the ingredients again point to a youngish and female target: they are Pernod, Cointreau, blackcurrant and lemonade.

And beyond all this is the enormous field of sponsorship, of both sport and the arts. In the UK, sponsorship has ranged from Glyndebourne to country music, from the National Theatre to rock, from Ballet Rambert to classical records. In the US, Brown and Williamson's Kool Jazz Festivals are attended by over 2 million people each year. Marlboro sponsors country music; Camel, rock. Sport, with its connotations of young people and health, has been an even bigger recipient of tobacco company money in both the US and Britain. In the UK, a list of sports taking tobacco money includes angling, cricket, darts, riding, golf, horse racing, power-boat racing, motorcycling, rugby, snooker and tennis. In 1986 more than 360 hours of sport on TV were sponsored by the tobacco industry. Ninety-eight per cent of this was on the advertising-free BBC. Critics claimed it constituted the equivalent of 700 30-second commercials. Two years earlier the Embassy-sponsored snooker championship provided 100 hours of TV viewing – and brand exposure.

Sponsorship also grinds small. Newspaper ads for the game between Brighton and Hove Albion, my local football club, and Leeds United, promised, 'And there's a special BONUS this week . . . Marlboro cigarettes are jointly promoting the game with Albion . . . If you come to the Goldstone on Saturday Marlboro staff will greet you and offer you the choice to have a cigarette with them . . . Come to the Goldstone this Saturday . . . enjoy your football . . . and enjoy a Marlboro at the same time.'

Not everyone will take tobacco money. The organisers of the 1988 Winter Olympics in Calgary decided not to accept cigarette sponsorship. Individual performers like the Oak Ridge Boys in the US and actors Warren Mitchell and Paul Eddington in the UK (who have founded a pressure group) have refused involvement. However, there have been strong lobbyists for, not least cash-hungry sporting clubs themselves. In the UK, the Association of Business Sponsors of Arts has spoken out strongly in favour of tobacco sponsorship. The tobacco companies BAT, Gallaher, Imperial and Philip Morris are prominent among the association's members.

Some advertising professionals, in support of tobacco advertising, actually argue that tobacco sponsorship with its links with sport, youth and glamour is the fault of the people who have banned or restricted advertising. One, Charles Plouviez, former chairman of the public affairs group of the Advertising Association, has written that 'by obtaining the ban on TV advertising, the anti-smoking lobby has stimulated the monstrous growth of cigarette sponsorship, which, in turn, it now wants banned . . . Nobody, not even the tobacco manufacturers, saw the potential in sponsorship until they were forced to find alternative methods of promotion.' What about banning sponsorship, then? Plouviez has his answer: 'Nobody can foresee what would be the result of banning sponsorship – but the evidence suggests that it wouldn't do much to reduce smoking, while it might lead to even more covert and unregulated forms of promotion.'

Does it matter? In other words, does it all work? Although common sense is frequently a bad judge, it is hard to believe that the cigarette marketers – hardly innocents when it comes to selling – do not know what they are doing.

In public the tobacco companies and admen argue that advertising and promotion of cigarettes does nothing to encourage people to smoke, only to change brand. However, as Bernard Barnett, as editor of *Campaign*, has pointed out, 'It is curious that the only two categories of advertising that the industry suggests do not increase consumption (i.e. tobacco and alcohol) are also those threatened with extinction by legislation in the not too distant future.' David Abbott says, 'I think arguments like shifting brands are just insulting in their shallowness. There is no other category where you can spend £70–100 million and not have an effect in protecting or increasing the market. I think advertising has certainly slowed down the rate of decline. It has certainly helped to introduce new smokers be they women or be they the Third World. The other thing about cigarette advertising, I do think it makes it more difficult for health education in that it makes the government's attitude more ambivalent.'

Abbott's own father, a smoker, died from cancer at the age of fifty-two. He sees cigarettes as 'a unique kind of product in that it can be indulged in in moderation and do you harm . . . In the end it is a moral question. I react against being called an advertising man because I am a man who works in advertising. I think one of the advantages of starting your own company is that you can do what you want to do . . . Everyone in the industry says, "How can you be so prim about cigarettes when you advertise cars that kill people, and alcohol?" Everyone has to draw a line. My line is that you can drink or you can drive and not kill yourself.'

The industry's other great argument, that if a product is legal to sell it should be legal to advertise it, is a more persuasive one. But at the end of the day the greatest argument against cigarette advertising – or sponsorship or other promotions – is simply this:

If tobacco was introduced now, with all we know about its effects on health, society would oppose it in the way it opposes all the illegal drugs. In practical terms it is too late to do anything about that – only the most naïve person would propose a ban on sales because it is totally impractical. However, advertising helps create an environment in which smoking is acceptable, and, as Abbott says, delays its decline.

In truth, everyone concerned – advertising agencies, tobacco companies and (especially) governments – knows this. They indulge in public fictions because they have large and public interests. The government's is one of the largest – huge taxes. Sylvan Barnet, chairman of the Advisory Council of the International Advertising Association, and a fervent opponent of any restrictions, came, I thought, closest to summing up the truth. He said for a government to ban cigarette advertising is 'like shooting yourself in the foot. Why not ban it? They need the business.'

Drinkers

'More and more, it seems the liquor industry has awakened to
the truth. It isn't selling bottles or glasses or even liquor. It's
selling fantasies.'
Carol Nathanson-Mogg, American psychologist
specialising in advertising

Drink is the supreme Image Product. With the persistent skill of the
advertiser, a drink becomes not a taste but an illusion, a glass filled not
with flavour but with dreams. It becomes indelibly linked with social
acceptability, or carefree youth, or glamour or sexiness or sophistication. As David Ogilvy writes in his latest primer, *Ogilvy on Advertising*, 'It isn't the whisky they choose, it's the image. The brand image is
90 per cent of what the distiller has to sell.'

The power of image was well illustrated in research into a drink called
Savannah Gold. Drinkers who tasted it without being told what it was,
liked it. Then other tasters were told it was rum, a product with a very
poor image in the UK. The result: 'It was rejected almost before they
started.' The drink is now described as a 'matured cane spirit'.

Alcohol is a very special product for the advertising industry. Worldwide, the drinks business has a sales turnover of over $170 billion a
year, considerably more, for example, than the gross domestic product
of Mexico. In the UK, Britons spend £42 million on alcohol every day,
more than on clothes or running their cars.

Alcohol is sold in what the marketing men call a 'high turnover
environment'. What this means is that while the market represents
billions of gallons of liquor, it is bought or sold by the bottle or by the
six-pack or by the glass – giving constant opportunities for the successful
advertiser to get someone to change his drink or his brand.

The competing companies are vast conglomerates: Philip Morris,
cigarette makers supreme but also since 1970 owners of Miller, the
second largest selling US beer; Seagram, with its 150 brands of spirits
and 300 brands of wine and champagne; Allied Lyons, 8,000 British
pubs as well as ownership of the giant Canadian Hiram Walker drink
company; Grand Metropolitan, another British company with a giant
foreign drink firm under its wing, in this case the American Heublein.

The products themselves are household words: Jack Daniels, Bacardi, Martini, Schlitz, Martell – most of them as familiar to non-drinkers as to drinkers and as well-known in Oslo and Caracas as in New York and London.

Drink advertising creates and reinforces images. It also does something else. Where necessary (and increasingly) it tries to change images so that yesterday's drink for old ladies becomes today's fashionable accessory for the young swinger.

As for any reservations, the days are long over when J. Walter Thompson would not take hard liquor accounts because its head, though no teetotaller, reputedly believed that if the agency harnessed all its creative skills 'a good many people would start drinking'. That, thought Stanley Resor, might be destructive for some of them. Now, for all agencies, what soul-searching there is concerns whether they have harnessed the right creative skills.

Advertising built vodka into *the* drink of the sixties and seventies, managing to persuade a young public that one brand of an odourless, colourless, tasteless liquid – Smirnoff – was better than other odourless, colourless, tasteless competitors even if it cost a lot more. The higher price – around £1 more a bottle in the UK – was, in fact, part of the process of 'proving' the product was premium and thus superior. More practically, it was also essential to facilitate the huge advertising that persuaded drinkers it was worth paying more in the first place.

In the eighties, advertising made Bailey's Irish Cream the world's largest selling liqueur, and helped it retain its domination with advertising budgets larger than any competitor could match.*

And when one of the world's most famous brewers, Guinness, finally faced up to the fact in the 1980s that its 220-year-old dark stout was in real trouble, it was advertising that was enlisted to save it in the form of a new agency, a new approach and a lot of money.

The drink industry is a business in the throes of problems – changing consumer tastes, a generally static or falling market, an increasing amount of social criticism from outside, and ever more aggressive competition within, much generated by comparative newcomers like Philip Morris who have brought with them tough strategies refined elsewhere.

Ironically, it is when things are bad that the advertising business can make one of its best cases for companies to spend greater and greater amounts on advertising. In the US, the brewing industry in the early eighties experienced its first non-growth year for twenty-five years; in the UK, beer drinkers were sinking nearly one and a half million fewer pints every year. But the message to the industry was, 'Spend! Don't

---

* Despite its name, Bailey's is not an ancient recipe, but a blend put together in London by a small company, Innovation and Development, in the mid 1970s. It was taken up and perfected by International Distillers and Vintners. By 1982 it was selling 2.2 million cases a year.

cut back and watch your market share be eaten away.' So in one year when US liquor sales went down, top companies spent about $6 million more on their advertising. It was 'a sign', said the liquor trade paper *Impact*, 'that distilled spirits marketers are not going to take their stagnant sales performance lying down.'

Such attitudes helped to keep drink as one of the world's largest advertising categories – worldwide more than $3 billion, over 1.5 per cent of all advertising spending. In the US, it topped $1.5 billion in 1987. In the UK, the total amount was a comparatively modest £200 million, though to put that into some context, it was over twice as much as on holidays, travel and transport together, and 100 times as much as spent on advertising pens and all other writing instruments.

For the advertising man, alcohol is a worthy challenge. What is more potent than persuading hundreds of thousands of people, millions even, to call for a drink that touches chords you have placed in their minds? The product is exciting. There's a constant dash of risk. As with tobacco, there are laws and regulations planted like mines to note and, hopefully, to bypass with a cleverly executed strategy. Drink advertising has always been special. Slogans and images endure over the decades: Schlitz's 'The Beer that made Milwaukee Famous' is nearly ninety years old; 'Dubo, Dubon, Dubonnet' dates back to the 1930s. Those originally responsible for creating Guinness advertising became an élite within the already élite copy department of the agency S. H. Benson.

The largest selling spirit brand in the world in the middle of the 1980s was not whisky, nor gin, nor even vodka. But white rum. Bacardi, to be precise.

Its real rise to the top position has taken place only since the mid 1970s. It has benefited from a number of changes in people's tastes, from short to long drinks, from heavy to light, from dark to white, from drinks that taste alcoholic to those reminiscent of liquid confectionery. Such changes have favoured some drinks, such as wine, lager beer, vodka and white rum, while hitting the sales of others including dark beers, fortified wines like sherry and most 'traditional' spirits including whisky.

Bacardi's genius, however, has been in its advertising – by carefully and skilfully targeting the young and making the drink synonymous in their minds with freedom, fun and sophistication.

Today perhaps 60 per cent of all the world's rum sales are Bacardi, frequently mixed with drinks like Coca-Cola that mask its taste. In the UK, four out of every five white rums sold carry the brand's name. Ironically – and perhaps most impressive of all for the dream-makers – many of Bacardi's drinkers have no idea that what they are ordering is even a rum at all. It is a Bacardi. Full point.

Take a look at one ad. Telly Savalas, carefully garbed in blazer and open-neck shirt, sits at a bar planted on a Caribbean beach. He has a glass in one hand. The bottle is Bacardi. Its label is face on to the camera.

The expression is one every kid knows from his TV set. It's easy to imagine the voice clipping the words across the picture. 'Bacardi and lemonade. It makes for one cool customer.'

Robin Ritchie, Bacardi's UK managing director, explained why Savalas was seen as the ideal man to endorse the drink: 'Savalas has the maturity, the potency, and the seriousness to consider a real spirit brand and, at the same time, adds that certain touch of glamour and chic.' The company's international vice-president put it another way: 'His personality appeals to a lot of people and there isn't a recognition problem. He is regarded as a tough guy with a heart of gold.'

The 'right' celebrity is crucial to drink advertising. One major study which was carried out for US government departments found that younger people – the target here – were more impressed by such endorsements than older people. They also felt, 'The finding that famous sources enhance the impact of alcohol ads indicates that the social implications of this practice should be given closer examination. To the extent that celebrity endorsements for beer, wine and liquor encourage under-age youth to have a more favourable disposition toward alcohol, there is a basis for concern by responsible advertisers.'

As an advertiser, Bacardi's philosophy has been described as 'spend, spend, spend'. In one half year, for example, it spent £2.5 million on the Savalas campaign in the UK, an amount claimed to be the biggest for any spirit brand. Such a figure is impressive, but perhaps largely without real meaning to anyone not in the advertising business. But when the money is translated into what it actually bought the picture becomes awesome.

It was said that print ads were seen by eight out of ten of the key young target audience up to ten times each. At the same time the message was continuously on display at nearly 1,100 prime poster sites. And a sixty-second cinema commercial being shown on 1,183 cinema screens was designed to be seen by over half of the target audience more than four times each.

To envisage the scale of Bacardi advertising it is necessary to imagine that repeated throughout the rest of the developed world, and to bear in mind that it is an advertising budget that has risen dramatically over the years – by 250 per cent in the US, for example, in the five years to 1982 – and which continues to rise.

Bacardi, which was founded in Cuba by the family of the same name, moved its operations to Puerto Rico after Castro nationalised all private industry in 1959. The company's grip on the young seems firm, although it needs to keep replacing its youthful drinkers as they age and it must constantly fear that a new, more 'in' drink will come along to win them. To stay on top Bacardi needs to get the young person the moment he or she starts drinking or, more likely perhaps, the moment he or she 'graduates' from beer or wine to their first spirit drink. Talking glowingly of one of the brand's campaigns, the marketing director of Hedges and Butler, the company which distributes Bacardi in the UK, said it did 'persuade lots of new consumers to try the drink . . . we achieved record sales in the pre-Christmas period – the crucial time to attract first-time drinkers to the brand'. He thought that with the campaign Bacardi had reinforced its role as the first-time spirit drink.

Bacardi is not alone in trying to woo the youth of the world. Nor, of course, is the drinks industry. However, for drinks companies, faced with stagnant or declining markets, young people are especially important. It helps that they are impressionable, and thus good targets for an image-laden product. In all, it is seen as a market-place still full of potential, ripe for much greater exploitation.

A 'Case History' of TV advertising in the UK beer market put together by the agency Boase Massimi Pollitt noted, 'The importance of the younger drinkers is fourfold. They tend to consume more bitter (beer) than older men; they represent the market's future and will retain, in later years, the tastes they now develop; and they are more interested in advertising.'

There is, however, one special problem for the drinks marketer – the special nature of the product itself. On one hand, the industry *needs* young drinkers, and that means hitting the group as hard and effectively as he can. On the other, he has to be careful not to stir too many waves: there is a minefield of regulations and do-gooder critics. Not surprisingly, therefore, those involved with drink advertising prefer to keep a low profile about trying to attract the young. One reason is that companies know that targeting can never be precise enough to exclude the under-age drinker. The advertiser may be after only the drinking-age readers of, say, *Rolling Stone* but he can't stop vast numbers of their younger brothers and sisters seeing the same advertising. Nor, not only cynics would add, can he be all that upset that by the time someone can legally drink he or she already knows the best brand to try! Additionally, there is a strident lobby, prominent in the United States, that sees advertising drink to the young as reprehensible in itself.

One advantage of the young is that they have newly-earned money not yet earmarked – although at times it may be a struggle to shift enough of it to drink from, say, hi-tech equipment or clothes. This problem is not a new one. Over fifty years ago Sir Edgar Saunders, director of the UK Brewers' Society, told a private meeting that beer consumption was falling because men were spending their money on such things as the cinema and attending football games. In words that have echoed over the years, he proclaimed, 'We want to get the beer-drinking habit instilled into thousands, almost millions, of young men who do not at present know the taste of beer.' The answer to the problem was seen as a massive advertising campaign that was launched on 1 December 1933. Advertisements divided into four main themes:

beer for health, beer for refreshment, beer for good fellowship, and beer as a staple product vital to British industry, agriculture and revenue. Every month the *Brewers Journal* published a synopsis of the campaign. It reported, for example, that in the month of September 1934 8,500 posters would be displayed, and more than 92 million impressions of the campaign's slogan, 'Beer is Best', would be published in the press.

Methods may have become more sophisticated, society may have imposed some rules, but the basic needs of the drink marketers have not altered. Jess DiPasquale, of PepsiCo Wine and Spirits International. said the goal is 'to get the attention of the entry level consumer'. A marketing executive told two researchers, James R. DeFoe and Warren Breed, 'Let's not forget that getting a freshman (seventeen or eighteen years old) to choose a certain brand of beer may mean that he will maintain his brand loyalty for the next twenty to thirty years. If he turns out to be a big drinker, the beer company has bought itself an annuity.'

Advertisements aimed at the young frequently concentrate on two areas, the 'good life' and sex, approaches they share with much cigarette advertising. This is not surprising: most of the time the two products are chasing the same customers, and, therefore, seek to manipulate the same desires and feelings.

An advertising executive, Charles Sharp, has described in some detail the ingredients of 'lifestyle' ads. He was speaking specifically about cigarette advertising but his words are as relevant to alcohol promotion:

> The ads are rich in thematic imagery and portray the desirability of smoking by associating it with the latest trends in lifestyle, fashion and entertainment, as well as associating smoking with youthful vigor, social, sexual and professional success, intelligence, beauty, sophistication, independence, masculinity and femininity. The ads are filled with exceptionally attractive, healthy looking, vigorous young people who are both worthy of emulation and free of any concerns relating to health and who are living energetic lives filled with sexual, social, and financial success and achievement.

Thus, take a pre-Christmas advertisement for Johnnie Walker Red Label. A young, handsome, happy couple are shown in an open top sportscar. The back of the car is filled with gift-wrapped boxes of the drink, which they are delivering to friends. The picture only needs snow to make the images complete – and snow it has. Or one for Two Fingers Tequila Gold. In this a small group of young people are in a modern bar. All of them look ecstatically happy. The copy reads, 'Wild on the weekend. Crazy in a crowd. Sensational as a shot or in a Sunrise. Make the most of your good times, anytime. Go for the fun of Two Fingers Tequila.'

The examples are legion and international. On American TV, jet planes zoom and couples splash through waves in aid of selling Michelob beer; on European television jets soar again though this time the couples are skiing and the drink is Ballantine's whisky.

In Hong Kong, where brandy is drunk from tall glasses, more or less like softer drinks, the images contain even more wish-fulfilment. In one, for Courvoisier, a Chinese couple dine in a Paris restaurant. He signs the bill. They walk by the Seine, he with a bottle of Courvoisier he has bought in the restaurant. Henry Pomeroy, London-based director of advertising for Hiram Walker International, explains that such ads are on TV every night in the peak season there: 'It's all status and face in the Far East.'

Described baldly, the ads sound simplistic. But a crucial factor with advertising is the execution, the 'rightness' of all the parts. On the printed page, or on the screen, therefore, the ads touch nerves – they have the potency of good pop songs. The young glance and see not just a group of schoolfriends but The Good Times, the way they would like them to be, with themselves at the centre of things. And part of it always, of course, is the drink – the Lowenbrau or the Johnnie Walker or whatever. To paraphrase the Heineken ad, when they succeed drink advertisements reach the parts that other ads often cannot reach.

Not surprisingly, lifestyle and sex often go together, as, for example, in a Japanese ad for Suntory brandy in which the drink is being clutched by a (Western) airline captain in full uniform as he gazes closely (and meaningfully) at a stewardess.

Ads that concentrate on sex are often not very subtle. A number play on double meanings. Two Fingers Tequila shows an attractive woman together with the slogan, 'Two Fingers is all it takes.' Fernandes Distillers rum shows the silhouette of a nude woman seated on the floor, legs splayed wide in a yoga pose, a huge bottle between her thighs.

Campari and St Paul's beer both adopt a similar approach. Campari shows the entertainer Tony Roberts, with the headline, 'Tony Roberts talks about his first time.' The words across the foot of the ad reinforce the point in case the dumb have missed it, 'Campari. The first time is never the best.' St Paul's Brewery is a little less laboured, but the message is equally direct. The label of the beer bottle carries a picture of a woman, and the message reads, 'You never forget your first girl.'

Seagram's gin hardly bothers with double meanings. One ad features a couple on a settee. Her thighs are bare of clothing and his hand is smoothing her leg. The words say, 'They . . . say you should drink it with someone you know very, very well . . . or want to.' In another a black girl lies over a black man, pulling his head into her breast. 'They say it's the number one gin in America . . . They also say it could turn a "maybe" into . . . "again".' Bart Cummins, the veteran American advertising man, protested, 'The ads are very clear. Get the gal loaded, then get the gal.'

Sometimes the sex is adolescent comic-strip fantasy. Ads for Paddington Corp's Rumple Minze peppermint schnapps introduced in 1986 to 'get through' to young men showed a sword-wielding woman astride a giant polar bear. Her breasts are swollen globes encased in shiny armour.

The *quantity* of alcohol advertising and promotion aimed at the young is vast. According to figures put together by a college marketing service, Alan Weston Communications, and the *Wall Street Journal*, college newspapers in the US take $15 million worth of national advertising each year, and about $10 million of this is for alcohol advertising. The sum is much more significant than it seems at first look – college newspaper ad rates are comparatively low and, therefore, $10 million buys a lot of space.

Everywhere, promotions and ads go hand in hand. In the UK, great stress is laid on 'promotional evenings' at colleges, universities and at other places where the young gather, like discos. There are Bacardi Caribbean evenings, High and Dry gin beachcomber parties, Holsten lager old movie nights. In Mecca young people's nightspots, a large three-dimensional hologram of the Babycham deer operates when a laser beam is triggered by music. Apart from giving a setting in which the drinks marketer can implant the image of the drink, the evenings also encourage consumption by selling the particular brand at special low prices.

Although drink advertisers obviously press their own brands, they would rather a youngster started with something – even if it is a rival drink – than did not start at all. In this respect, the spirit advertiser may see beer or wine as the drinker's first rung on the ladder. He will have his opportunity to press his own brand when the man or woman is ready to 'advance'.

In Britain, lager beer is seen as a very important entry drink, a point conceded publicly by Garry Luddington, the marketing director of Guinness. In the process of noting what he hoped was a slight move in popularity towards more full-bodied beers (like Guinness itself), he added: 'Not that lager is running out of steam. The demand for lager among young people, *as a weaning process*, will always be there.' (My italics.)

Abroad, particularly in the United States, Britain is seen as a nation of drinkers of 'traditional' beer – foaming pint mugs of mild and bitter brews. The reality is that Britain is a country of lager drinkers. A great deal of money – over £60 million a year by 1987 – has gone into creating and maintaining that situation. Lager is now so entrenched as a drink that it is easy to forget the part that careful marketing and advertising played in its introductory stages. The first major brand, Bass's Carling Black Label, appeared in the late 1950s when the nation still consisted of 'traditional' beer drinkers.

The advertising then, and for years after, had to convince British beer drinkers that lager was not an effeminate, weak drink. Ads concentrated on getting across a hard, macho image. Caps were taken off lager bottles to the soundtrack accompaniment of thunderclaps; casks were heaved about by men with huge biceps; words like 'strength' were hammered home. It was only later when the influx of women drinkers became more important that advertising sought to widen the image – though usually without ever forgetting the key youth market.

Lager is a near-perfect example of the advertising being the product. The Research Business, a London research company, pointed out in a report that the lager market is one 'where few significant product differences exist, certainly with regard to mainstream lagers. It is primarily advertising-created images that enable drinkers to differentiate between brands.' Today's image of lager is proof that the advertisers and their agencies have worked well. In one survey, lager came across with students as being casual, fun-loving, sporty and with a young age profile.* Advertising has had another effect in the case of two lagers in the UK, Heineken and Carlsberg. They are both comparatively weak in alcohol, but thanks to the advertising, consumers believe them to be at least as strong as competing brands. They therefore can sell at the same price as others. This means in effect a price premium estimated by one expert at £7 million annual profit to each company.

Beer occupies a similarly important position in the United States.† Attracting youth has become more important in a declining market. And in recent years, the way markets are attacked and wooed has been transformed almost beyond recognition.

Regular Budweiser is the biggest selling beer in the world. Its manufacturer, Anheuser-Busch, can call it 'King of Beers' without contradiction despite fierce competition from the nation's second largest beer company, Philip Morris Inc's Miller Brewing Company.

How Anheuser and Miller came to dominate the industry is an object lesson in the role and power of advertising. By the early 1980s they controlled over half of the domestic market. As the gap between them and other brewers widened, the two companies found themselves with yet more money coming in to invest in yet more marketing effort. The general manager of House of Beers, a Bronx beer-wholesaling operation, told the *Wall Street Journal* that he had no doubt what this meant: 'The big dogs will get the big pieces of meat.' It might be added that where the US once had 750 breweries, by the mid 1980s the number had fallen to about fifty, although marketing and advertising were not, of course, the sole reasons.

---

* Other images that emerged in this survey conducted by students at Hatfield Polytechnic were: Wine – pleasant tasting, relaxing and for modern, successful, cultivated people who are pleasure seeking without being self-indulgent. Whisky – pre-eminently the drink for the conventionally successful, extrovert, dominant older man. Gin – for successful career women (but expensive and 'a very unpleasant taste'). And vodka – for younger drinkers than whisky or gin: 'The influence of advertising can be detected in its association with excitement and glamour.'

† American beer is much closer to lager than 'traditional' English beer which is darker and heavier and has a higher alcohol content.

The situation had its roots in the early 1970s. Then, as now, Anheuser led the brewing industry in sales. But Anheuser did so not because it *sold* its products aggressively but because people *bought* them. Enter Philip Morris whose marketing techniques had already turned the cigarette business upside down. In 1970, it took over Miller. Among the modern marketing techniques which it brought to the beer industry was advertising and promotion clearly targeted to specific groups including the young. Miller sales started to rise.

In the second half of the 1970s, Anheuser began to hit back. By now it was under the control of August Busch Jr who had taken over from his highly conservative father. A former Anheuser division manager described the younger Busch's style of leadership in three words – 'attack, attack, attack'.

The battle between the two giants has dominated the industry, and its marketing and advertising techniques, ever since. In a fight to survive, other brewers have changed strategies and produced more and more new ad campaigns. But the onslaught of the leaders took its toll. The *Wall Street Journal* has referred to 'the chilling effect on all their competitors' of the 'national advertising onslaughts' of Anheuser and Miller. Since its takeover Miller had moved from being the seventh largest brewer to number two. The two companies, it said, were now 'the only two truly national brewers. Their huge ad campaigns have rendered nearly all other brewers – and accordingly their distributors – also-rans in most of the country, even in some old strongholds of regional brands.'

The efforts – and the cash expenditure – of the other brewers has been considerable. One company, Pabst, spent $14 million in six months advertising a new beer. But no matter how huge the sums, or the effort, they have paled beside what Anheuser and Miller have made their norm. Anheuser's own Budweiser Light Beer has been backed by over $60 million worth of advertising a year, a sum higher than many brewers put behind the whole of their range. *Business Week* has referred to competitors 'cringing' before huge advertising and promotion campaigns. A Schlitz distributor was quoted as saying, 'We are overwhelmed by Anheuser advertising. It keeps our brands out of the consumer's mind.' To which August Busch replied, 'Miller brought marketing prowess to the industry, and we sure are using it. God bless 'em.'

In common with the tobacco industry, brewers have backed advertising strongly with other youth marketing techniques – sponsoring sports, rock concerts and parties. In sport, Anheuser is linked with golf, horse racing, soccer, boxing, bowling, shooting, the triathlon, automobile racing, lacrosse, skiing and volleyball. Tie-ups range from local college football teams to the Los Angeles Olympics. Miller has shooting, hydroplane, racing, golf, darts, running, sailboat racing and racquetball among other affiliations. There is the Anheuser-Busch Golf Classic, the Miller 500 Stock Car Race, the Coors International Bicycle Classic, the

Stroh Salmon Derby, the Bud Ironman Triathlon World Championship. A Schlitz marketing executive explained, 'People like to identify with sports heroes. If one is wearing your logo, they will buy your product because he does.'

Linking beer with sport is not confined to the United States. In the UK, as part of its attempt to stem declining sales, Guinness signed a three-year £450,000 contract with Queens Park Rangers Football Club. For this the brewery got – among other things – the players wearing its advertising on their shirts and a Guinness-QPR song for the fans to sing. Critics have pointed to the irony of such a situation when drink has been linked with violence at football matches. One critic envisaged a situation in which people would be banned from entering the ground by police for drinking the product that the players were advertising on their shirts.

Perhaps one of the oddest of sport/drink links involved the former world light heavyweight boxing champion, John Conteh. He has promoted beer for the brewers Whitbread and also appeared in advertisements for a London bartending school – despite the fact that he is a 'reformed alcoholic'. He agreed with the London *Evening Standard* that his presence in the bartending ad was 'rather funny', and said that during the Whitbread promotion he had toured their pubs 'without touching a drop'.

Rock music, for the most obvious reason, has been another key area of drink company activity. In the US, Miller's 'Rock Series' sponsors regional bands, and visited seventy-five schools one spring. In the UK, in one year, 1986, Harp Lager sponsored more than 150 pop music concerts given by more than a dozen groups and artists. Simon Mallalieu, a director of Harp, said, 'Since nearly half a million pop fans and potential or existing lager drinkers are expected to attend the concerts around the country, our on and off trade stockists are bound to feel the benefit of Harp Beat.'

The fight to succeed – or augment – beer in the young drinker's repertoire when the time comes is a fiercely fought one. A comparatively recent major target for spirits companies is the man or woman who does not really like the taste of hard liquor. People who, in the words of John Maxwell Jr of Lehman Bros Kuhn Loeb, New York, 'want to chug stuff. They don't want to acquire a taste. They want it to taste like candy the first time going down.'

The answer is a breathtakingly simple one. Make the hard liquor taste like candy. This is what the drinks companies have done, and here new product development and advertising go hand in hand. In some cases, it is hard to be clear which came first: the ad strategy or the new drink itself. Bailey's Irish Cream (developed in the UK), Captain Morgan Spiced Rum (developed in the US) and Malibu (developed in South Africa) are all now major international drinks. There are countless others. The W. V. Elliott company in the US has created such products as Rumpel Minze peppermint schnapps and Schnapple Appeal liqueur, and its chairman says he finds much evidence that Americans 'talk dry but drink sweet. Kids in this country grow up with Coca-Cola and ice cream. We don't know what dry is.' New liqueurs and cordials have poured onto the market. In one year Heublein introduced twelve new flavoured schnapps, including peach, raspberry, blue grass and mint julep.

Traditional liqueurs have rushed to join the bandwagon. After all, there is a strict limit to the amount of 'serious' liqueur that can be sipped after dinner. With ice added, virtually any liqueur can be promoted as an any-time drink. Thus Tia Maria, claimed by its distributors to be the 'biggest traditional liqueur in the UK', turned its eyes towards the young, backing youth-orientated advertising with nearly 1,000 'party nights' in one year.

However, drinks companies cannot afford to attack on only one front. Traditional spirits are so important a part of their range that, to counter falling sales, these, too, need to be retargeted, again towards the young.

An inspiration for many of them is Smirnoff vodka, one of the great advertising successes since the 1950s. It was replaced as the world's best-selling spirit by Bacardi in 1980, but it is still no slouch. A 1960s ad is a classic example of the strategy of linking the drink with youth: three couples, including Woody Allen and Monique Van Dooren, are sitting on a skeleton wooden mule drinking vodka out of mugs and clowning about. Ten years later another shows a parachutist and an attractive girl seemingly skydiving together. She is wearing a snorkeling outfit. Both are clutching vodka martinis. The copy reads, 'Well, they said anything could happen.' Other fantasy ads have shown a woman water ski-ing, with the Loch Ness Monster doing the pulling, and another flying on a magic carpet. Young and Rubicam, the agency responsible, talks of 'stunning visuals' that 'reinforce the exuberance and freedom of the brand's image'.

Perhaps over-optimistically other spirits dream of emulating vodka's winning of the youth market. One is another colourless spirit, gin. This is a drink with an image as old and tired as vodka's is young and swinging, although one firm of analysts provided some grounds for *hope*. It felt that new young drinkers might react against vodka which they saw as their parents' drink. 'Although many drinks are attempting to fill this niche,' reported the analysts, 'we see no reason, given the necessary promotional investment and correct positioning, why this shouldn't be gin. Certainly the success or otherwise of recruiting young people as gin drinkers will determine the long-term future of the UK gin market.'

One such campaign to reach the youth market was that of Gilbey's gin which used the whimsical drawings of the fashionable artist, Glen Baxter. Whole page ads featured drawings aimed at destroying the stuffy image said to be associated with the drink. One illustrated men in a boat that was dangerously close to the edge of a waterfall. The text read, '"I know this sounds scarcely feasible, but I almost believe I can hear a tonic being poured into a gigantic glass of Gilbey's gin . . ." stammered young Rodford.'

One agency, Grey Advertising, New York, believes that it was a gin advertising campaign that broke the mould in the early 1980s. In this, for Gordon's, couples were seen together, one concentrating, the other interrupting. Thus, in one she is painting at an easel on a beach, he is tugging at her clothes. The taglines on all of them read, 'The possibilities are endless.' Dick Karp, Grey's creative director, explained, 'We wanted to concentrate attention on the man and the woman, and especially on what I call "the delicious moment of interruption", in which one of the two – who's perhaps a little bored – distracts the other in a teasing, understatedly sexy kind of way.' Karp believes the campaign shifted the emphasis in drink ads onto people and 'especially on one to one relationships between men and women'.

Pernod, the traditional anis-flavoured drink beloved of the French, also decided in the 1980s that its target had to be the young. Advertising in the UK was directed into the pop music press and the cinema, and this was accompanied by promotions that included dispensing 600,000 sample tots at road shows and discos in one year. The trade magazine, *Drinks Marketing*, commented that Pernod 'has attacked and found a niche within the spirits market, attracting, like vodka, the younger drinker. It has to be asked, therefore, whether there is a possibility that Pernod will ultimately establish itself as the young person's spirit.' The sales director of the brand's UK distributor was in no doubt: 'We do, in fact, measure our performance by vodka and if you were to take vodka fifteen years ago and compare it with Pernod now you might have a good comparison.'

In France itself, Pernod launched an even more direct attack, producing the company's first new product for thirty-two years, Pernod Light, a low-strength version of the brand. André Roch, the director of marketing, described the target as young adults 'who want something new, with a modern image'. The advertising needed to change Pernod's home image – traditionally it is associated with peasants and with games like boules. The use of the word 'Light', spelled in English, was intentional – it is a word much used in France attached to imported drinks and cigarettes and conveys health consciousness. The bottle of the new drink carried a picture of a Mediterranean terrace at sunset. One advertisement was of the bottle emerging from the sea, like the shark in *Jaws*, with the slogan, 'The big new thrill'. The drink was featured in six pages of *Lui*, the magazine for sophisticated young Frenchmen, and offprints were distributed to all drinks outlets.

Cognac, too, has been attempting to change its image by advertising to reach the young (as well as women and, in the US, black and Hispanic groups). Of all drinks it is probably most associated with age and affluence and tradition. The new advertisements, though, urged drinkers to forsake the traditional small measure in the balloon glass for highball glasses with ice and soda. One brand manager explained that what his company, Martell, was seeking was nothing less than creating a 'different drink', one that would have 'more mainstream usage'.

Some Martell ads managed to combine three target groups in one picture: a young, beautiful black woman pours a brandy while gazing at the reader and saying, 'I assume you drink Martell.'

Whisky too, heavily under siege, has rushed to try to embrace the young. Dewar's advertising featured famous personalities in the 1970s, but this was changed to highlight 'achievers', ordinary people who had succeeded. Talking of the strategy, David Small, the company's managing director, said, 'Dewar's profile certainly appeals to the younger elements of the market.' In 1988 both Chivas Regal and Johnnie Walker projected themselves as fashionable yuppie drinks. One Johnnie Walker ad had two bikini-clad women jogging, one saying, 'He loves my mind. And he drinks Johnnie Walker.'

Canadian Club provides a good example of *why* such attempts at repositioning are essential. In the US, the brand is responsible for a third of all the sales of Hiram Walker Inc. In 1984, it was still the country's ninth largest-selling distilled spirit, but with sales falling the future did not look bright. Hiram Walker decided to embark on a new $15 million advertising campaign, said to be the first really different one for the brand since Prohibition. In one ad, a woman stands with a drink in hand in a darkened room. A man is framed in a doorway that leads onto a balcony. The picture has a heavy fantasy quality. It is mystical and sexy. 'We're trying to emulate Calvin Klein and Chanel,' said Stephen Nadelberg, marketing director for Hiram Walker, the brand's importer. 'We believe the liquor business sells image and fashion too.'

The brand had already launched its youth market attempt in the UK, billing itself as 'The Uncommon Spirit' – a way of getting around having to use the word 'whisky' which, of course, is what the drink actually is. Ads were placed in youth-oriented publications such as *Time Out* and *New Musical Express* and *Blitz*. In the third year of the campaign, 80 per cent of the ads went on cinema – the young person's medium. A ninety-second commercial showed a 1984-ish world when the sale of Canadian Club is prohibited by government. The hero and heroine outwit the security police and find an ingenious way of drinking their Canadian Club without being caught. The sets are reminiscent of the movie, *Blade Runner*, and the message is a clear one: young defiance which is successful and pleasurable.

Canadian Club's target was clearcut: young men. Others saw at least part of the hope for their salvation in another 'ripe' market.

As with cigarettes, women are a prime target of growing importance. The fact that they drink substantially less alcohol than men is both a sign of hope and a challenge for the drink companies. A look through one young women's magazine – *Ms* – selected at random, shows how drinks companies are facing that challenge. The October issue contains fourteen drink ads, eleven of them covering full pages. Drink is thus by far the largest single advertising category in the magazine, larger by far than makeup, feminine hygiene products and cigarettes.*

Some tried the pseudo-feminist, new-woman path long trodden by the cigarette companies: 'Break tradition,' urges the ad for Ronrico rum, showing a trendy woman dressed all in black with matching cat; 'Break away from the ordinary,' says the message for Seagram's VO whisky. In Remy Martin ads a suave woman sniffs the bouquet from a balloon glass before handing it to a waiting man. The copy reads, 'The lady has it. The sense of Remy.'

Even marketers of beer, the most male of drinks, began to advertise directly to women. One advertisement for Molson Golden shows two tents, one illuminated to show the silhouette of a man and a woman cosily sharing a beer. 'You really know how to welcome a lady to the neighbourhood,' says the copy.

Some advertisers are not yet quite sure how best to approach women. One school believes that advertising a drink as being specifically female can actually put off women. Some beer companies think that the key factor in what beer a woman will drink is the brand chosen by her husband or boyfriend. Research gathered by Cinzano pointed to a similar conclusion. It indicated that women had a need for a male stamp of approval on what they drink – a pointer, it was said, for the advertiser to take a slightly masculine approach.

Drinks marketers, though, have no reservations about the importance and the potential of the female market. They literally drool over it. An executive of Brown-Forman distillery said, 'We have kept looking for places to find new drinkers . . . women are a big, untapped category for whisky'.

The industry is encouraged by the fact that women are drinking more at business lunches, turn more to alcohol to relieve stress (like men before them), and find drink easier to buy in supermarkets or in more spacious and less dingy liquor stores. Times are changing, the drink advertiser can proclaim happily. Those days (pre-1958) when even using women in ads was proscribed by the Distilled Spirits Council of the US are long gone.

In reaching women, new products are even more important than with the young male market. Here they can be advertised and promoted as new and for women – not just second-hand men's drinks.

With the new cream drinks, stress is often placed on the non-alcoholic part of the liqueur. Thus one for Leroux Blackberry Flavoured Brandy

---

* In fairness, it should be admitted that drinks companies concentrate their advertising in the pre-Christmas period.

carries the headline, 'It tastes like real blackberry. Naturally. Because it's Leroux.' Old-established brands, like Grand Marnier and Myers, stress cream as a mixer – an ad for Kahlua liqueur shows thick cream being poured into a glass.

Crocodillo is a drink that was invented to take advantage of the young woman market in the UK. When it was launched in 1980, trade press commentators called it the biggest new drink launch in the country for ten years. What went into the drink, and its targeting, was later recounted by two researchers involved, Philip Hill and Stephen Woodward, when speaking to fellow professionals at the Market Research Society's annual conference. 'Even without the marketing hyperbole,' the researchers said, 'Crocodillo was certainly the most important "event" ever undertaken by Seagram (UK) Ltd, the British subsidiary of the world's largest wine and spirits corporation.'

The reason for the launch was simple: 'The growth of the drinks business largely depends on young people, who, because of fewer financial commitments, enjoy more disposable income which they generally choose to spend on themselves . . . 18–24 year old girls spend some £600 million per annum on alcoholic beverages. Their repertoires are relatively large. It is significant that a small number of brands have a large share of their repertoire, but a number of the drinks in that repertoire have been around a long time. Young girls are looking for a new drink experience.' And so – 'We developed a new drink for them – Crocodillo – a new product which had been expensively developed, extensively researched, and was to be heavily supported in both advertising and promotional terms'.

The drink itself, described as a 'sparkling white wine aperitif', is a blend of Italian and German white wines. It is low proof and sells in individual 10 cl bottles.

The precise groups of women to target in advertising were defined after depth interviewing research. The researchers divided women into six groups as a result of their interview findings. Two of the groups were judged to be of low interest for the proposed new drink. Women in one of these two groups were those who would drink anything; others were 'volume drinkers'. The researchers gave the first of these groups the name 'Promiscuous Pat' and the second that of 'Boozy Brenda'.

Two further groups were thought likely to 'flirt with the new drink' but then move on to something else, and were thus 'unlikely to provide the backbone with which to sustain the proposed new brand'.

It was the last two groups that were seen as providing the target:

5. Norma – (Wife of sexual Norm) – the big step has been taken, ring on the finger and all that, settled down now, only goes out at weekends. Regular as clockwork, Friday and Saturday night, and Sunday morning if you're lucky – a low volume drinker – likely to be still drinking baby bottle brands but could be Martini, Vodka and

lime. Needing a bit of excitement in her life, Norma could be easily impressed by a *new* heavily-advertised (on TV) drink.

6. Cilla – the archetypal baby bottle drinker. Not yet into her 20s, Cilla has a somewhat limited view of life. 'Gettin' a fella and settlin' down' is what her aspirations are all about. Cilla might have progressed as far as Martini or Cinzano but she still considers spirits to be a bit on the dangerous side. A small thrill is about all that Cilla could cope with.

These 'typologies' said the researchers – without a hint of humour – 'served to profile the target audience in a much more meaningful way than straight demographic data ever could'. With it, the advertising agency had 'something very tangible to run with'. They had no doubt about the importance of getting that advertising right: 'In the drinks market it is generally accepted that the imagery of a brand can be vital to a product's success or failure.' The drink was priced at a relatively high figure; this, it was explained, 'helped contribute to the brand's relatively sophisticated personality'. However, there was another very important reason for the price – 'a premium price was essential to support the advertising spend level'.

The advertising that emerged from this identified the drink with Italy and Italians. With Norma and Cilla in mind, it was 'exotic and slightly naughty'.

It is a pleasure to report that, despite all the 'scientific' research, the drink was not a world beater.

If you haven't a new drink for women you have to 'reposition' the old one. Beer manufacturers have linked light beer with dieting. One for Michelob Light from Anheuser shows two women at a lunch table. They're sipping their beers as they study the menu. The message, 'Omelet? Shrimp salad? Quiche? At least the beer was an easy choice.'

Spirits ads dare women to be different – the female equivalent of macho ads. Or they promote a new way of drinking an old drink. Jack Daniels executives dreamed up one called 'Lynchburg Lemonade', no more than a mixture of the whisky and the soft drink, but apparently very effective as a sales ploy.

If the drinks companies and their agencies are reticent about talking in public about targeting young people and women, they are almost totally silent when it comes to another group – the heavy drinkers. Yet this is a key group without doubt. The importance lies in the fact that it is easier to get a man who drinks to drink more than it is to turn on a new drinker or encourage a light drinker.

David Ogilvy puts it less crudely: 'Thirty-two per cent of beer drinkers drink 80 per cent of all beer . . . Fourteen per cent of the people who drink gin consume 80 per cent of all gin. In anything you do, keep your eye glued to the heavy users.' In the UK, 20 per cent of drinkers are said to drink over 70 per cent of all beer and lager sold.

The question is whether the drinks companies and their agencies – most of whom increasingly pay lip service to 'moderation' – concentrate on this group. Bodies like the American consumer activist organisation, the Center for Science in the Public Interest, are in no doubt: 'Heavy drinkers make up one of the two top target groups for alcohol market-ing.' The group, it believes, is vulnerable to advertising because of its members 'existing or developing psychological commitment and physiological addiction'. Developing its case, CSPI presents a number of ads in which it claims drink is presented as the key to unwinding, coping with problems, and staying ahead. Thus, Southern Comfort – 'Everyone needs a little comfort' and 'Getting comfortable sometimes means getting away from it all'. Seagram's Crown Royal whisky – for 'when you really get it all together'. Heublein's Steel schnapps – with its 'After a hard day's work, pour yourself some Steel' and picture of four shot glasses of the eighty-five-proof ('strong suggestion', says CSPI, of the recommended dose'.

Other ads which it claims are 'highly supportive of a heavy drinker's daily drinking style' include these: Grand Marnier which asks, 'What time today will you say "Grand Marnier"? – 3:06 p.m.' (thus, claims CSPI, encouraging daytime drinking). Anheuser's Michelob with 'Put a little weekend in your week' (allegedly encouraging daily drinking). And Johnnie Walker Red which shows a thirty-one-day calendar and the words, 'Wouldn't it be wonderful if every birthday this month ended with red?' (also, allegedly, supporting drinking every day).

Isn't this, though, a little like the psychiatrist in the jokes who sees a sexual reason for everything? Or the conspiracy theorists who see menace and manipulation and dreaded deeds behind every political event?

A lot, it must be admitted, depends on just where you stand at the beginning of the debate. But there is some evidence to support those who place the most cynical interpretation on the thinking behind some of the ads.

Take a Federal Trade Commission staff memo, dated 23 April 1976, which reached CSPI. Staff had examined an advertisement by Somerset Importers who handle Johnnie Walker in the US. They reported prelimi-nary findings that 'Life style research conducted by Somerset . . . appeared to assist this distributor . . . to target its advertising campaign toward persons who (during market research studies) strongly identified themselves with various attitudes associated with problem drinking (e.g. "I don't know if I could manage without a drink at the end of the day").' According to staff, the studies were used in an advertisement for Johnnie Walker Black Label 'which appeared to offer the product to relieve stress and tension associated with striving for success – "The road to success is paved with rocks: Let us smooth them for you."'

According to the staff memo, FTC concern was voiced at a meeting in November 1975. 'Although the company disputed our interpretation of the ads, it discontinued the ads at the beginning of this year.'

Or examine the detail of a market research study for Anheuser conducted between 1963 and 1974 which was revealed in the spring 1975 issue of MIT's *Sloan Management Review*. Two professors sought to classify drinkers into personality groups and then see how they reacted to various advertisements. Two of four categories developed were said to describe personalities that try to escape problems by drinking. The researchers reported, 'The understanding . . . gained has enabled Anheuser-Busch to develop more effective advertising and other marketing tools at appropriate points before, during and after the introduction of new products into the market.' CSPI believes it is 'quite likely that ads based on the research did run'.

In any event, there can be little argument that one motive of drinks companies in introducing new low-alcohol products onto the market is to extend people's drinking hours and/or keep them in pubs and bars for longer periods.

Thus, a strong marketing point of Pernod Light – twice as light as a deluxe beer – is that it can be drunk throughout the day. Even the cream drinks have tried to use the same strategy: 'Malibu can be drunk any time, straight, on the rocks, or as a long drink. Lace it with cola, soda water, tonic or milk.'

Ironically, perhaps one of the most blatant attempts to increase and extend people's drinking patterns can be seen with a non-alcohol beer product, Barbican, made by Bass, the UK's biggest brewer. From almost nothing, Barbican created from 1980 in the UK a multi-million low and non-alcohol market in the UK of several million pounds. At first, it seemed to the company that the big market for its product would be the occasional drinker. In fact, according to its research, it emerged as the medium to heavy drinker, a man aged over twenty-five who regularly drinks real lager in pubs. These drinkers, it was found, used the non-alcohol product as well as their usual drink. The heavy drinker mixed the two or switched to the non-alcoholic lager temporarily during the evening to slow his alcohol intake.

This, of course, became a key marketing element. Not to consumers, but to the pub keepers who had to be persuaded to stock and 'push' Barbican. Consumer ads showed the beer being drunk in one of those jolly pubs beloved of advertising companies. The ads to the trade got closer to the real message. 'Barbican extends drinking hours,' said the headlines. Underneath, the copy read, 'Normally, customers who feel they have had enough alcohol will leave the pub. But when they stay on with Barbican, they are still in with the crowd and still there to buy their round, so boosting your sales of other drinks too. So *you* get profits you otherwise would have missed.'

One theme that is believed by many to be emphasised especially to heavy drinkers is that of risk-taking and daring. It is one that was singled out by the CSPI in their attack: 'Risk-taking, or the desire to do so, has been cited as a prominent behaviour of many alcoholics and heavy drinkers. As part of living a dangerous life, problem drinkers act recklessly. The best example is driving while drunk. The risk-taking ads not only appeal to such personalities, they may in fact encourage such behaviour.'

Such ads are certainly common. Cutty Sark has used a stuntwoman to endorse its whisky; Budweiser has featured lumberjacks; Lord Calvert whiskey ads have shown a man in a kayak. In a Michelob ad, a couple race horses – 'A ride becomes a race when it's Michelob Light for the winner.' Eclipse Rum links the drink with sailing in a rough sea – 'The tougher the challenge, the sweeter the satisfaction.'

Some of the image-making of drink advertising is directed towards fairly innocuous fantasy. Stress may be laid upon a drink's country of origin, trying to imbue it with desirable (though often fanciful) qualities widely thought to be associated with that place. Burroughs gin, for example, lays great stress on its Englishness in the US market. The director of marketing for its US importers has commented, 'Americans have long admired the unique blend of elegance and sophistication synonymous with the words "Made in England". Names like Burberry, Laura Ashley, Dunhill and Rolls Royce suggest a class apart.' Copy in Ballantine's advertisements in Germany and Holland is kept in English because research shows 'the semi-upmarket consumer tends to be flattered that you believe he has enough knowledge of English for you to do it'.

Equally, in Japan Anheuser has helped to make Budweiser the country's best selling foreign beer by stressing its American origin. Paul Hogan sold the Australian-ness of Foster's lager long before he became an international movie star.

Perhaps the most impressive use of advertising in making a brand synonymous with a place is that of Jack Daniels and Lynchburg, Tennessee (population 361). The ads are like a brilliant conjuring trick. They create an illusion that is breathtakingly effective. By association they create the picture of a brand that is produced in limited amounts in a small distillery in a sleepy little Tennessee hollow. Other images immediately ripple out from this – limited, exclusive, expensive, sought after, traditional, not mass market.

The ads, which have been running for thirty years, are all in black and white by design. A typical one shows a peaceful stream in one picture, and 'the oldest registered distillery in the US' in another. Ducks waddle in front of the building to complete the image. The copy begins, 'At the Jack Daniels distillery, this iron free stream helps make the world's smoothest whiskey'. Other parts of the ad reinforce the picture: a series of gold medal awards, all but one pre-World War I, the reproduction of the bottle with its dated label. Here, you feel is unchanging quality in a changed (and inferior) world.

Readers are invited to send for a booklet. Those who write – and hundreds of thousands do so – will receive a personalised reply on heavy yellow paper decorated with a picture of 'Lem Motlow, Proprietor' and embossed with gold medals. They will also see more photographs of rural Tennessee, of close-ups of hands holding barley, and will read constant references to Mr Daniels himself. Small everywhere is beautiful.

The analogy with a conjuring trick is totally valid. All attention in the ads is focused on a few (true) facts. As for the rest, it is Deception by Omission.

This exclusive whiskey produced in this small place totals a production of 4 million cases a year! In 1986, according to Laidlaw Ansbacher, New York, it was the eighth largest selling liquor brand in the United States. Its sales, in fact, are almost the same as those of an 'ordinary, everyday' whiskey like Jim Beam. Furthermore, the Jack Daniels operation is not only big on its own account. Jack Daniels is part of Brown-Forman Corporation, the US's second largest distiller with sales in 1986 of over $1 billion and on *Advertising Age* estimates a total advertising budget of nearly $99 million. Although in the mid 1980s its sales were down – like the rest of the distilled spirits market – its share was up. That, said insiders, was in large measure due to the loyalty it had won by its unusual advertising.

In any discussion on drink advertising, both the alcohol and advertising industries can claim that society has taken account of the special position alcohol holds by creating often complex systems of regulation. As Bruce Weininger, chief of the trade and consumer affairs division of the Bureau of Alcohol, Tobacco and Firearms, put it, 'It cannot be sold like soda pop or soap powder.'

Certainly none of the more obvious and blatant excesses and advertising claims of even twenty years ago would be possible today in either the US or the UK. Even earlier advertisements would be totally unthinkable.* Health giving properties were frequently claimed. One for Fig Rye, an American whisky, boasted that in it 'science has produced a whiskey which aids digestion instead of retarding, helps the liver to proper action and keeps the kidneys in a state of perfect health'.

In the UK in the 1920s, Guinness distributed samples of its beer to doctors with the suggestion it was worth recommending as a pickup. An early piece of Guinness copy read:

Seven good reasons Why Guinness is Good for You.
1. Builds strong muscles for sports.
2. It is good for the nerves.
3. It is good for the blood (also the complexion).

* Though it is hard to know what the regulators would make of a 19th century advertisement for port wine which claimed the drink was 'Pure as the tears which fall upon a sister's grave'.

4. It is a splendid digestive.
5. It gives a permanent sense of greater health and strength.
6. It is beneficial to the aged.
7. It helps you to sleep.*

One critic of the time, Sir F. Gowland Hopkins, complained that it was 'unfair, and even cruel, that propaganda, subtle, suggestive and intensive, should endeavour to persuade the worker that his beer should make him more robust and increase the power of his muscles; thus tempting him to increase consumption, and helping to salve his conscience when he knows that his expenditure on it is beyond his means'.

Today Britain and the United States are not alone in having controls. The situation changes, but a roundup in the 1980s showed that Ecuador allowed no drink advertising on television before 9 p.m., Switzerland allowed none on TV, India none on TV or radio. Venezuela barred the use of sports activities or athletes in advertising, New Zealand permitted no brand names but only such details as the names and opening hours of retail outlets. Finland allowed no alcohol advertising at all, and Norway restricted it to restaurant trade publications. Canada forbids the use in alcohol advertisements of well-known public figures or look-alikes. In 1985, South Korea joined a growing number of countries prohibiting advertising of spirits on television. The same year, Switzerland extended its controls to all public sites, including sports stadiums. Constraints are 'getting stronger', says Hiram Walker's Henry Pomeroy. 'The first thing that normally happens is that they restrict the hours in which you can advertise on TV. Then they ban advertising on television. They may ban outdoor advertising. Then finally they get to print . . . The percentage of markets where you can't do what you want to is still very much a minor part, but it is growing.'

No country in the world has greater ambivalence and complexity in its regulations than the United States. This is not surprising when you consider that the country which introduced Prohibition also turned drunkenness into a macho art form (witness, for example, many of the John Wayne movies).

US drink regulations are complex – the situation in each state ranges from more or less a free market to a government-controlled monopoly. With advertising, there is a mix of Federal law and industry self-regulation. A division of the Treasury Department, the Bureau of Alcohol, Tobacco and Firearms, has both a regulation and enforcement task. With advertising this means prohibiting false, misleading, obscene

* Contrast with the fact that in the 1980s the UK Advertising Standards Authority ruled against an advertisement that urged 'Drink as much Guinness as you like' after claims it might encourage excessive drinking. But also note that nearly sixty years later Guinness was still telling Nigerians, 'Guinness gives you power', next to a picture of bulging African biceps.

or indecent statements. Additionally the three branches of the industry – beer, wines and spirits – have their own codes. These are voluntary guidelines. The Code of Good Practice of the Distilled Spirits Council of the United States (DISCUS) requests members to present their advertising in a tasteful and dignified manner, to direct it to adult audiences, and to refrain from using broadcast media. The US Brewers' Association Guidelines for Beer Advertising discourage ads that appeal to over-indulgence, link the drink to dangerous or criminal activities, lewd or obscene material and the use of young models. The Wine Institute's Code of Advertising is against ads that suggest excessive drinking and that link wine with 'dangerous activities' and with driving. It also discourages the kind of lifestyle advertisements that are widely used by beer and spirit companies: 'Any attempt to suggest that wine directly contributes to success or achievement is unacceptable.'

In the UK, the system of regulation is less complex though in interpretation and practice it is sometimes as confusing. Attempts to restrict drink advertising have a long history. Two years after the repeal of US Prohibition, a Bill introduced into the House of Lords sought, among other things, to restrict drink advertising to the name of the product and name and address of the manufacturer or seller. It died a quick death. Thirty-five years later, a government committee on liquor licensing felt it would be 'inappropriate to involve ourselves too closely' in advertising which was 'complicated and controversial'. But it did deprecate campaigns directed increasingly at the young, and urged the industry to 'recognise its social responsibilities'.

In 1975, the Advertising Standards Authority decided to formulate rules specially for alcohol advertising for the first time. These rules were basically ones devised by the drink manufacturers themselves who saw that if there was not voluntary restriction, government action was likely.

They were 'updated' in 1988 after mounting public disgust about alcohol and the young. They rule advertisements should not be directed at people under eighteen or feature characters likely to attract their admiration. Ads should not suggest drinking is an essential attribute of masculinity, nor that femininity is enhanced by it 'or by the choice of a particular drink'. Nor should ads suggest drink can resolve personal problems, lead to social acceptance or popularity, or that 'immoderate drinking' is 'sensible, admirable or amusing'.

The ASA Code applies only to print advertising. Three years later, in 1978, the Independent Broadcasting Authority introduced its own. Commentators saw this code as much more rigorous and neither the drinks trade nor advertising agencies were as enthusiastic about it. It too was revised in 1988.

Liquor advertising, it said, must not be addressed particularly at the young, and no one associated with drinking in a commercial should seem to be younger than twenty-five. Advertisements could not imply drinking was essential to social success or acceptance or that refusal was a sign of weakness. Nor must they feature 'immoderate' drinking, claim alcohol has any therapeutic qualities, place 'undue emphasis' on the strength of drinks, or feature daring or toughness to associate drinking with masculinity. Additionally, alcohol advertisements are not allowed during or immediately before or after children's programmes.

The Authority says that the requirements are all 'strictly interpreted' although interpretation is obviously a subjective matter. The brewers Charrington, for example, were stopped from using Dennis Waterman, star of the prime-time television series *Minder*, in radio commercials because use was said to contravene the section forbidding featuring 'any personality who commands the loyalty of the young'. The brewery objected that a rival brewer, Courage, was being allowed to use Chas and Dave, two Cockney pop personalities.

In general, though, drinks advertisers seem happy with the status quo in both the UK and the US. Thus Kenneth Dunjohn, spokesman for the UK Brewers' Society, has said, 'Drink advertising in the UK is probably the best and most responsible in the world. This is very largely because the drink-producing industries willingly acknowledge that their products are capable of misuse and that this necessarily requires them to exercise restraint and awareness of the likely problems.'

Depending on your viewpoint, the liquor industry's opinion could reflect one of two opposite realities. By the test of time, society in both countries has found the right balance between freedom to promote a legal product and the need to protect society. Or, of course, alternatively that the industry has a situation that it is very happy to live with because, in practice, the restrictions are none too onerous and, in any event, far less worrying than any that might be imposed from outside.

The possibility of greater restriction grows, and there's no doubt that the drinks advertiser finds himself with a difficult conundrum. Rance Crain, president and editor-in-chief of *Advertising Age*, and hardly an anti-advertising man, summed it up well: 'The liquor industry finds itself between a rock and a hard place. On the one hand liquor consumption is down, and liquor companies are eyeing new potential drinker groups, such as working women, to bolster sales. On the other hand there's probably more anti-liquor sentiment brewing now than at any time since Prohibition.' He added, 'With liquor sales already in a slump, I really can't imagine the liquor companies avoiding a confrontation by stepping up their "Moderation" ad messages or confining their sales appeals to traditional drinker groups.'

The gulf is wide and widening. The critics of alcohol and alcohol advertising see drink as the 'number one hard drug'. For them the reality of the bottle is drinking and driving, domestic violence and absenteeism, medical conditions from hangover to poisoning. Advertising is a special target. Many of the critics would not oppose the selling of liquor (if only in some cases on pragmatic grounds). But advertising, they claim, spreads the habit, and imbues it with an image that is far, far removed from the (dangerous) facts.

Lord Avebury argued this case at a symposium organised by the United Kingdom Alliance, a temperance body, held at the House of Commons:

> Alcohol causes far more damage to health in Britain than heroin. On the roads, it kills far more people than IRA terrorists do in Northern Ireland. The majority of persistent petty offenders have a serious drink problem, and there is also a connection between major crimes of violence and the abuse of alcohol. Alcohol is responsible for the loss of more working days than strikes. It is a factor in the destruction of marriages and the psychological mutilation of children of an impressionable age . . . How is it that a product which reaps such immense havoc is treated as an ordinary, everyday item of consumption? . . . The drink industry clearly believes that the public can be made to forget the seamy side of drinking, and to see only the folly fun of an English pub, or the wonderful world of imagination. The presentation of alcohol in advertising, particularly on television, concentrates on reinforcing the social acceptability of the product.

As to regulations, many critics would argue that they are worded and policed loosely enough to allow advertisers all the scope they need. There is, for example, an ASA clause which says ads 'should not give the general impression of being inducements to prefer a drink because of its higher alcohol content or intoxicating effect'. How, then, should one view a double-page colour advertisement for a strong beer. It shows an elephant being frightened by a mouse with the copy, 'As any elephant will tell you, size is no guarantee of strength . . . Gold Label Barley Wine is almost two and a half times more concentrated than ordinary beers. It's fermented for at least twice as long. And matured for ten times as long. Consequently, Gold Label should be approached with caution.' It would be a naïve person who didn't get the message that with Gold Label you get loaded more than twice as fast.

Ads can operate on two levels, giving words and phrases and situations which can be held to say one thing but which actually convey another. Carl Hixon, creator and executive producer of *Cameo*, a sponsored in-flight show hosted by David Frost, believes the reason British beer commercials are the world's best is because Britons are 'experts at double meanings'. Thus, while the words in the ads say beer 'tastes good' or is 'refreshing' or 'has few calories', Hixon believes 'the visual is nudging, winking and signalling benefits much closer to the knuckle – *gets you laid, gives you peer status, helps you master situations*.' (His emphasis.)

As to policing, some American critics would claim there is little need for subterfuge. The Center for Science in the Public Interest says that 'Judging from the prevalence of questionable ads and marketing practices, the BATF seems to be asleep at the wheel.' As to the industries' own codes, 'It is clear . . . judging from ads, that many companies don't pay them much heed.'

Calls for tougher restrictions have grown throughout the eighties. *USA Today* pointed out the 'new twist' of what some call the 'born-again temperance movement' – 'Don't cut off the flow of alcohol, cut off the advertising.' A former member of the Federal Communications Commission has called for a ban on all alcohol advertising, and one Congressman (Representative George Brown, California) has attempted to bring an end to Federal Income Tax deductions for drink ads. That same year, twenty-five national organisations asked the Federal Trade Commission to ban all ads aimed at the young and at heavy drinkers. What was significant was less the actual demands than the mainstream support from such bodies as the National Parent-Teacher Association.

The founder of the most successful grassroots group to emerge in the US, Candy Lightner of Mothers Against Drunk Driving, gave her personal endorsement to restrictions, saying that advertisers portrayed drinking as a 'macho thing that appeals to young people'. Light beer commercials promoted the camaraderie of drinking, made it seem romantic: 'They should show what really happens.'

The Health Education Secretary, Otis Bowen, added his weight to those aiming to restrict alcohol promotions on campus. The American Medical Association approved a programme recommending warning labels on alcohol and asking for more research into the relationship between advertising and consumption.

In Britain, the Royal College of Physicians' Faculty of Community Medicine called for an advertising ban. A secret report by the Central Policy Review Staff (the government's Think Tank) was leaked in the pages of *The Doctor*. One of its recommendations was greater control over alcohol advertising. The British Medical Association decided to press for health warnings on bottles and cans and in advertisements. A Home Office working party said it believed huge advertising sums 'help to create a climate in which alcohol is seen as an indispensable adjunct to all social occasions', and concluded TV and cinema alcohol advertising should be banned.

The drink advertising industry, not surprisingly, has fought back. Key words in its armoury have been 'moderation' and 'caution'. In various statements, spokesmen have argued a variant of 'Guinness is Good for You', adding the words 'In Moderation'. Thus Kenneth Dunjohn of the Brewers' Society: 'The modest, sensible consumption of alcohol is in

---

* On a wider front, by the end of 1985 drinking control laws in America were descending in what one commentator described as an 'avalanche'. Fifteen states had for example already ordered bans to end or curtail the 'happy hour', that period when drinks are cheaper or even free. Attitudes were said to be changing everywhere.

no way harmful and for many people is a positive health benefit. Drink contributes greatly to social pleasures and plays a major part in social relaxation. Stress may be relieved and a great deal of companionship is encouraged. The therapy of a modest pint or two in the congenial surroundings of a decent pub is much to be preferred to a regime of pills, as many medical men contend.'

In the US, James Kuras, executive vice-president and general manager of McCann-Erickson, New York, told a Milwaukee Advertising Club meeting: 'There should not be an advertising club or an advertising agency or an advertiser or a professional advertising person in the entire United States unwilling to fight restrictions on what we can and cannot sell.' He believed that 'trying to control drunk drivers by outlawing the advertising of alcohol makes as little sense as trying to control the Ku Klux Klan by outlawing bed linens.' The same year, William Howell, president of Miller Brewing, told the annual National Beer Wholesalers Convention that the entire industry should lobby aggressively against attempts to ban beer commercials. 'If we are going to go down, then, damn it, let's go down fighting.'

In both countries, in common with the tobacco business, the drinks industry made great weight of the argument that the product itself is legal. In power politics, of course, it could also argue cash and jobs: in the UK, the industry employs about 750,000 people, and was the source in 1986–7 of excise and VAT taxes of £6,500 million. Export sales of Scotch whisky alone are over £1 billion. All convincing reasons for the government not to interfere.

The industry also stressed the efforts it was making to persuade people to drink sensibly. The Distilled Spirits Council of the US had started a print advertising campaign in the early 1970s urging, 'If you choose to drink, drink responsibly.' Ten years later, its promotions included sponsoring a New Year message on the electronic outdoor board at Times Square saying, 'Let someone else drive.' It also distributed pre-Christmas service spots to 400 TV stations nationwide featuring Drew Pearson of the Dallas Cowboys inviting viewers to sign a 'Contract for Life' – an agreement between parents and children that neither would drive when drunk nor ride with someone else who had imbibed too much.

The Licensed Beverage Information Council urged 'Friends don't let friends drive drunk' in its campaign that involved outdoor boards, public service radio and TV spots, and point of sale material.* Individual companies ran their own campaigns. Bacardi advertised that it 'mixes with everything – except driving'. A small spirit company in Connecticut, W. V. Elliott Co, includes in its ads the words 'Enjoy in

---

* The slogan was picked up as far away as Africa – an ad in the *Botswana Daily News* showed a picture of car keys being surrendered with the words, 'Friends don't etc . . . A friendly reminder from Kgalagadi Breweries.'

Moderation'. In a pre-Christmas period a Midwest distributor ran a TV commercial in which a bartender mused aloud as he watched an accident report on TV news. At one point, the bartender said, 'The real answer is that you have to respect this stuff,' pointing as he did to liquor on his shelves.

Seagram has been a constant urger of restraint. Soon after the repeal of Prohibition, the company was saying in an ad, 'We who make whisky say "Drink Moderately".' In one famous ad it showed five lines of handwriting, all by the same person. The first was written before drinking, the last after seven drinks. By that time, the line – 'I can drink when I drive' – had become a scrawl. The copy underneath ended, 'When you drink too much you can't handle a car. You can't even handle a pen.'

Seagram's moderation message was taken onto UK television in 1982. A commercial consisted of stills showing the effects of a car crash. The captioned copy read, in part, 'Naturally we like you to take a drink. But always in moderation. And never when driving.' The UK Brewers' Society has also run a poster campaign to discourage under-age drinking. Courage Brewery devoted £500,000 of its £3 million 1987 Christmas promotions budget to a warning about drink and driving. Critics said compared with the £20 million overall alcohol sales hype it was mere tokenism.

In many countries trade-sponsored messages are joined by others, most of them government-financed. Different nations adopt different techniques. New South Wales, Australia, has concentrated its ad messages on trying to arouse fear of arrest. One advertisement, sited in railway stations, shows police leading a man into a police station. The headline says, 'There's one station these trains won't take you to.'

The Swedes have concentrated on the shock effect of portraying road-accident survivors. In one, a man lies in a hospital bed. His head is heavily bandaged, his arm in a plaster cast. The headline says, 'How about a nightcap?' Another shows a one-legged man with crutches, and the line, 'Just have one more for the road.'

A drink/driving campaign running in the UK since 1976 has tried many approaches. Early commercials showed harrowing pictures of road-accident scenes to a soundtrack of jolly drinking songs. Another centred on a young drunk driver who had killed his girlfriend passenger (headline in print ads, 'A few drinks and you're a real lady killer').

The agency concerned, Wasey Campbell-Ewald, claimed that surveys after six years showed drops in drinking and driving and in heavy drinking. The Department of Transport, at a later date, mindful of a wealth of other factors ranging from police activity to weather conditions, was more cautious, saying it believed the advertising probably had a 'limiting effect'.

No one would deny moderation messages are far, far outnumbered by selling ads. It is also true that most of the thrust is directed to one area, drink and driving. It might, of course, be asked why the drink industry, in any event, should get involved in knocking its own product. The reason, of course, is that it is afraid that if it isn't seen to be concerned, it will fare worse.

This doesn't mean that, privately, companies and advertising agencies handling drink do not wish they could hit back harder. One UK agency, Allen Brady and Marsh, did in fact prepare a pro-drink advertising strategy after the Advertising Association considered the possibility of running a national campaign. The campaign was not adopted (the AA obviously thought it was too much of a double-edged sword), but the strategy document – never published – makes fascinating reading. It recommended that 'the industry should go on the attack' with a campaign 'which will set out to proclaim the important and valuable contribution which the alcoholic drinks industry makes to society'.

The target was seen as opinion formers in government, medical profession, pressure groups, the media and other advertising personnel and marketeers; the method was print, using the quality press. 'The major purpose of the campaign will be to remove the initiative from the anti-alcohol lobby and to choose more favourable grounds on which to conduct the debate.' It suggested possible topics for individual ads. These included: alcohol in moderation is good for you; the pub is part of the cultural heritage of the country and an important protection against drunkenness and alcohol addiction; the British are a race of moderate drinkers; alcoholic duty contributes more to the Treasury than the cost of the Health Service and the Army ('or whatever').

The tone, suggested Allen Brady and Marsh, should be 'Confident, socially responsible'. Suggestions for individual ads included one that would argue that moderate drinkers live longer than non-drinkers, with other pro-points being made such as drink relaxes people and breaks down social barriers. Another argued that what was at stake was the 'freedom to market', and under the headline, 'Most of the hard drinkers of the world have never seen a drinks advertisement in their lives', it sought to compare the US and Soviet Union.

One other theme in Allen Brady and Marsh's document could have come straight from the tobacco advertising lobby. It is the claim that advertising does not sell more alcohol. What it does is to persuade people who drink to choose one brand instead of another.

Thus the Distilled Spirits Council of the US in a statement sent to the author said, 'Scientific research and marketing studies repeatedly show that advertising has no noticeable effect on total alcohol sales or consumption. Advertising merely helps the consumer decide which product they want to buy – it's a form of consumer information.'

The response of critics to such claims can be summed up very simply in the words, 'If you believe this, you'll believe anything.' It was an argument tackled in a lengthy and detailed report into alcohol marketing put together for the World Health Organization, but never published (because, it was claimed, of drink industry pressure). Certainly, the report, a copy of which was 'leaked' to me, was damning of the industry. On advertising restrictions, for example, it commented that 'like water confronting a rock [the drinks company] merely flows around it, deploying its prodigious resources by other techniques'. On this particular argument, the report had this to say:

> However incredulous [sic] it may appear, given the billions of dollars that nourish alcohol advertising, there is an important current of opinion (partially fed by corporate capital) which contends that these colossal advertising sums exercise no impact on inducing new consumers into the alcohol market . . . A myriad of ostensibly 'scientific' research monographs, many based on economic techniques, have grappled with the relationship of advertising to consumption in several countries . . . one must scrutinise carefully the source of funding of these studies, since in several cases it is the alcohol power network (at times through their trade associations) that directly or indirectly bankroll these monographs. It should come as no surprise that what was touted as a distinguished study, whose austere conclusions were 'that no scientific evidence exists that beverage alcohol advertising has any significant impact on alcohol abuse', was sponsored and funded by the US Brewers' Association.

And they add, 'Why, it may be asked, should alcohol and tobacco advertisements differ from ads of other products which are blatantly endeavouring to hike both market shares and consumption?'

For alcohol advertisers it is a crucial point: critics claim that if more alcohol is sold in total it must follow that more people will be harmed by drink.* But it goes beyond this. Advertisers and agencies see the attack on drink (just as many saw the attack on tobacco before it) as the forerunner of others on many products. Mike Waterson, the UK Advertising Association's research director, has warned that 'if advertising were to be banned on drink products which are known to harm only a tiny percentage of users . . . there is no logical reason why advertising should not also be banned for a huge range of other products which it is alleged can damage consumers when misused (ranging from dairy products, sugar, sweets, coffee and similar products through to medicines and motor cars). The logical conclusion of a drink advertising ban would therefore be the ending of the freedom to promote products

---

* Thus the report 'Alcohol and Alcoholism' by a special committee of the Royal College of Psychiatrists, 1979: 'What can be asserted is that if the average man or woman begins to drink more (that is, if the national *per capita* alcohol consumption rises), then the number of people who damage themselves by their drinking will also increase.'

accounting for a very large proportion of consumers' expenditure and consequently a massive reduction in the effectiveness of our market system.'

One might well comment that it's all a matter of degree, but it is a great rallying flag. James Kuras, of McCann-Erickson, New York, put it more emotionally. 'After wine and beer, what will be next? No advertising on television for toys, candy, cereals and soft drinks? No advertising on television for movies other than those that are G-rated? No advertising on television for books other than those that are G-rated? Least we forget, my friends, prohibition begins by prohibiting the freedom to advertise.'

Along with the advertisers and the agencies, the last people to want such a prohibition are the mass of the media. A glance through advertising trade publications illustrates how keenly they compete for the liquor industry's money:

People (US) – 'Thank You' spread across the page, and the words, '*People* magazine carried more beverage alcohol ads in 1982 than any other consumer publication.'

Baltimore Sun (US) – 'Welcome to Baltimore – 9th largest liquor market – 1m reach in the *Baltimore Sun*.'

Amalgamated Publishers Inc (US) ('represents 88 of the nation's leading Black newspapers') – 'The Black liquor market is big – and growing bigger. To make sure of your share of it, apply the formula. One call puts you in any combination of our 88 newspapers.'

Parade (US) – 'Every year is a very good year for wine because *Parade* readers drink 23 billion glasses of wine annually.'

Daily Mail (UK) – 'contains more wines and spirits than any other paper'.

Sunday (UK) – '. . . the country's most popular Sunday colour magazine with a readership of over 10 million. So it's not really surprising that we can reach: 24.8 per cent of heavy drinkers of whisky. 32.8 per cent of heavy drinkers of rum. And 33.3 per cent of heavy drinkers of vodka . . . so if you're looking for more drinkers, you can rely on us to get them.'

The examples could be continued for pages. The fact that there is such a vested interest by the media – just as there is with cigarettes – is important. It is not just that publications often take large sums from liquor advertisers. Some, as *Advertising Age*'s editor-in-chief, Rance Crain, has written, are 'practically supported' by the industry. It has been pointed out by one marketing man that in the UK, as Christmas nears each year, the colour supplements of the Sunday newspapers 'start to look like a special issue of *Harper's Wine and Spirit Gazette* . . . the rest of the press is so laden with booze ads, one could be forgiven for thinking it was the end of Prohibition.'

The argument over alcohol and advertising has strengths on both sides. It is surely one that deserves to be debated publicly, but given a situation like this, only a very great optimist would predict that the mass media would ever provide the forum for such a discussion.

Voters

'Of course you sell candidates for political office the same way you sell soap or sealing wax or whatever; because, when you get right down to it, that's the only way anything is sold.'
Sid Bernstein, American advertising commentator

'Give me the writing of a nation's advertising and propaganda, and I care not who governs its politics.'
Professor Hugh MacLennan

One of the most evocative, and poignant, images in the history of political advertising remains that of General Dwight Eisenhower, war hero and now presidential candidate, sitting in a film studio and turning out TV 'spot' commercials with all the weary regularity of a die-stamping machine. Ads were written – as many as twenty-eight in a few hours – then agreed or rejected, prompt cards handwritten, and commercials recorded, one after another. And between takes Eisenhower sat in a hard chair, shook his head, and muttered sadly, 'To think that an old soldier should come to this!'

The year was 1952, the spots all followed the same format. An announcer would say 'Eisenhower answers the nation!', an 'ordinary citizen' would ask a question, Eisenhower would answer ('My wife, Mamie . . .'). One and a half million dollars was spent broadcasting those spots. Six years later, wrote Martin Mayer, 'echoes of the controversy which they caused' could still be heard. They still can – another two decades further on. For better or for worse (and the consensus would probably be, for worse), the Eisenhower campaign changed the face of political advertising. Until then, political advertising had meant buying large blocks of time to accommodate whole speeches.

Two men were responsible for the idea of using spots, Alfred Hollender, head of the television department at Grey Advertising, and Rosser Reeves, of USP fame, the man who was to write the ads. The arguments advanced in favour of the change of approach were threefold: cost, spots would reach the uncommitted, and a few critical states could be especially targeted. The real impact of the change, however, lay in a fourth direction: from this moment on political advertising became not just bought time, but television *commercials*. They became advertisements – just like ads for soaps or coffee or beer. Issues became image, personality became product. By the 1980s the centrepiece of the Reagan re-election campaign was a commercial that was largely indistinguishable from one for Coca-Cola. The Republican strategy, wrote an English adman, Richard Owen, 'appears to be to put Reagan not only above party, but above issues also.' It is also advertising exempt from the usual rules and regulations. An American adwoman, Paula Green, complained, 'Everything politicians decry in commercial advertising is exploited in TV spots for candidates of every stripe: disregard for facts, deliberate misstatements, personal attacks, subliminal insinuations. Very little if any of it does anything to enlighten, inform or persuade anyone who is not already persuaded of his choice.' Spots mean huge amounts of money – by the 1980s the campaigns were said to be costing $1 billion, the greatest part of it being spent on buying television time.

There was another implication, too, one of much greater concern to those outside the United States (although it could well be argued that how America elects its politicians and especially its president is of concern to everyone in the free world). American style politics had spread and was continuing to spread, notably in Latin America and Western Europe, but also elsewhere. In Britain, once seen as being at the opposite end of the spectrum to the US in its approach to political campaigning, the 1979 election (with Saatchi and Saatchi finding public fame or notoriety as Mrs Thatcher's admen) was hailed as the first of its kind. Within four years the other parties, too, were planning similar 'American style' advertising.

Advertising Age in an editorial warned, 'Be wary, Britannia,' and commented, 'We stand at one extreme in the process; they at another. The secret we hope they discover before it is too late is that they can benefit most, not from copying and cultivating our campaign arsenal excesses, but by assiduously ignoring them.' Just four years later, in 1987, the Labour Party had embraced advertising so warmly that its general election broadcasts were outperforming those of the Conservatives for emotion and glossiness.

American political strategists were imported into Venezuela for its elections. Eight candidates stood for the presidency: all spent the maximum amount on advertising allowed by law – four minutes a day per TV station and five minutes radio plus a full page in each newspaper. The government alone spent about $25 million. Former advisers of President Reagan helped Ferdinand Marcos of the Philippines in the election in which he lost power to Corazon Aquino. Mrs Aquino retaliated in advertising-kind. Her radio advertisements were created by volunteers from at least nine agencies. One of them became a focal point – it featured the pop song 'Tie a yellow ribbon round the old oak tree', which is identified with her husband's murder. In Chile, General Pinochet began advertising three years before his term of office was due to end in 1989, in an attempt to ensure he was rechosen as candidate. In newspapers and on television, he was shown shaking hands with smiling workers, embracing mothers and, in one spot, his picture was superimposed on the national flag (image-building that did not, however, help him in October 1988 when a majority of Chileans voted against him remaining in power for a further eight years).

In India, Rajiv Gandhi used a decidedly Americanised approach in his campaign for prime minister. For the first time his party's advertising was developed by an agency, interestingly the Indian affiliate of Ted Bates, the agency of Rosser Reeves. Ads were dramatic, some capitalising on the strife that followed the assassination of Indira Gandhi. One showed threatening crocodiles with the headline, 'Will another war be the last war in the life of free India?' Opponents criticised numerous references the ads made to an 'enemy' within India. By the standards – or lack of standards – that some campaigns had reached in America it was tame stuff. But a line had been crossed.

The growth and the expansion of political advertising has created both opponents and supporters. The ad that one man hates and loathes may quite literally be the one most praised and admired by another. Take one example. To many people the epitome of 'bad' political advertising is a famous commercial used against Barry Goldwater by the Lyndon B. Johnson camp in 1964. It showed a small girl in a field of daisies. She picked the petals from a flower one by one. On the soundtrack a Russian voice intoned a countdown. At the point the count reached zero, the screen erupted in a nuclear explosion, and a voice pointed out the dangers of a nuclear confrontation.

The inferences were obvious. The impact was considerable. The protests ensured that the commercial was shown only once. David Ogilvy in *Ogilvy on Advertising* describes Johnson's commercials as having a 'cynical dishonesty that would never be tolerated in commercials for toothpaste. They gave voters to understand that Goldwater was an irresponsible trigger-happy ogre who would start nuclear wars at the drop of a hat.' This, argues Ogilvy in some detail, was (a) not true and (b) was known not to be true by Johnson.

However, Tim Bell, formerly of Saatchi and Saatchi, now of Lowe Howard Spink, and widely described as Mrs Thatcher's personal ad-man, sees the ad in a totally different light. He commended it to me as an example of 'good' (i.e. effective) political advertising. 'The most effective political advertising,' he mused, 'is that which says the other side is no good. "Labour Isn't Working" (one of the Conservative party election ads) – what's great about that is that it says Labour is no good.

That one with the little girl on the hill with daisies – all that said was that Goldwater is going to kill your child.'

Perhaps the most important point, though, is that even opponents recognise advertising's vote-winning effectiveness. An American survey on how politicians regard political advertising showed that while many of them believed TV advertising plays too large a role, they were likely to use it more in their own re-election campaigns. This was because they saw it as the most effective medium. Governor Bruce Babbitt of Arizona in his bid for the 1988 Democratic presidential nomination started his advertising campaign in Iowa in April 1987 with the hope of taking the state when the time came. Experts said it was believed to be the earliest start to presidential campaigning in history.

Politics is about being first. It is a race in which there is a winner and a number of also-rans. A victor and the losers. A number of professionals who look on political advertising as simply another branch of the craft told me they regarded that as the greatest difference with product advertising. If, as the result of advertising, a toothpaste, say, increased its share of the market from 10 to 12 per cent, the advertising might be rated an unqualified success. 'To strike an analogy with politics,' one volunteered, 'you have to imagine a situation where at the end of the day there would be only one toothpaste – yours – left, and the others all driven out of business. Anything other than that would be a failure.'

It has been argued that the major difference between advertising a product and a politician is that products can be altered to suit the market. With politicians, on the other hand, the advertiser is stuck with what he has got. It is an argument that no longer rings true.

Advertising Age, however, has described how political consultants in the United States are now using polls to structure themes, slogans and personality of political campaigns to suit the public's tastes. Pollsters, reported the magazine, were employing what amounted to a test-marketing technique to assess the strengths and weaknesses of real and hypothetical candidates.* The technique appeared to go under many different names, including 'Q-vignettes' and 'hypothetical candidate polling'. The standard methodology, though, whatever the name, involved getting a potential voter to read a description of Candidate A's personal characteristics and position on various issues. The researcher asked the voter what he liked and didn't like and, sometimes, his reasons. Using the poll results, candidates could then decide which of the candidate's personality traits to play up (or down), which issues to stress (or not stress), and which areas of their opponents to attack.

---

* This is not the same as what might be called the 'acceptable' use of polls. Parties involved in elections continuously commission their own polling: party leaders use the findings to decide which issues are best pursued at any particular stage.

Mary Ruth Martin, a pollster with V. Lance Tarrance Associates, a Houston company working on Republican campaigns, told the magazine that hypothetical polling was also 'a good way to get at touchy' subjects such as whether a candidate's divorced status interests the electorate. Gary Nordimer, a Washington communications consultant working with Democratic campaigns, said, 'The question of whether polling leads a candidate or vice versa is one of the most philosophically difficult in American politics today.' He added it 'depends on the candidate.' In any event, pollsters were dominant in the 1988 Presidential campaign: the candidates each spent $2 million on them.

A further test-marketing technique was described. Increasingly, said Alex Gage, of Market Opinion Research, which works for Republican campaigns, parties were pre-testing how good potential candidates looked on TV. The would-be politicians were videotaped and then watched on TV by people who had no idea who they were.

Changing the product to meet the image-making part way is not confined to the United States, although it may go further there. Britain's prime minister, Mrs Thatcher, was taught to modulate her over-shrill voice for the 1980 election. She also lost weight and had her teeth treated. Neil Kinnock, The Labour Party leader, was also given a change of hairstyle and persuaded into dark blue jackets to give an image of managerial competence. The colour was also judged best to suit his red hair which itself was restyled for the 1987 general election.

In France, adman Jacques Séguéla helped François Mitterrand win the presidency in 1981 with a campaign based on detailed research. It involved posters depicting Mitterrand as *la force tranquille*. Mitterrand co-operated by changing his appearance to fit the image being sold. 'A candidate for the presidency is a brand,' Séguéla later told fellow admen. 'May the president forgive me. I applied to him the method we employ every day for Diners Club credit cards, Fisher Price toys, Citroën cars and Chantelle bras.'

He explained to me later that he was not claiming that anyone packaged and marketed in the right way could become president. 'But I think the political guy needs a strong concept.' When the adman found the concept, it had to be applied to all the selling of the candidate – press releases, advertising, speeches at meetings. 'It makes all the difference. The concept is not the programme of the guy. It is the character of the guy. You vote for a *man*.'

Helmut Kohl, on the other hand, apparently refused to change his appearance in his successful bid to become West German Chancellor. He did, however, co-operate with a strategy that involved the use of huge posters to emphasise his nickname 'the Black Giant'. His image maker, German adman Coordt von Mannstein, said later, 'Our strategy was to make everything about him the greatest and to give him the image of a winner.'

It is the fact that it *is* winner-take-all, plus the absence of rules, that makes political advertising so contentious an area. The decision over whether or not to use knuckle-dusters or to lie or not to lie depends mainly on one thing: which will *work* best? Thus in one ad, for Republican Robin Bear of Tennessee, a lookalike Fidel Castro was used to denigrate Democratic Senator Jim Sasser and his alleged sending of 'millions of your tax dollars' in foreign aid to such places as 'Cambodia, Angola, and Laos. Even Cuba.' The Castro figure lit his cigar with a $100 bill and said, 'Muchissimas gracias, Senor Sasser'. (No US aid goes to Cuba.) Or take another. This was directed at Republican Senator Harrison Schmitt of New Mexico, a strong opponent of the nuclear freeze. The commercial cut back and forth between a mother sending children to school and a computer-filled nuclear-bomb nerve centre. 'Most Americans support a nuclear freeze,' a voice said. 'But not New Mexico's Senator Harrison Schmitt. He opposes the nuclear freeze. That's why we need to oppose Senator Schmitt. To reduce the danger of a nuclear war being started by a computer.' A warning buzzer sounded. 'It could happen.'

The 1986 Congressional elections were described by Leonard Matthews, president of the American Association of Advertising Agencies, as 'the worst I can recall'. In Missouri, one Democrat tried to link his opponent to bank foreclosures; in Maryland, one woman candidate branded her female opponent a 'San Francisco-type liberal', a euphemism not hard for voters to translate. In New York, a Democrat trying to unseat a Republican questioned campaign contributions to alleged organised crime members; in California, a sitting member was accused of vetoing bills to clean up toxic waste because of money received from 'toxic polluters'.

Advertising, and in particular television advertising, is seen as the villain. It would be naïve to believe that before modern advertising, before television, politicians fought on issues and according to rules. They didn't. The dirtiness of the business is nothing new. Nor is the technique of trying to sell an image, a lie that will appeal to the voter, rather than a political stance. William Henry Harrison, the Whig presidential challenger in the 1840 US election, made extensive use of image advertising, the first time it had been used as a technique in political campaigns. In her book, *Packaging the Presidency*, Professor Kathleen Jamieson tells how Harrison supporters presented him as a farmer and backwoodsman. In reality, Harrison was the wealthy son of a governor and the owner of a palatial Georgian mansion and a 2,000-acre estate farmed by tenant farmers. The symbol of a log cabin was carried in parades, used on badges, and featured in songs to identify Harrison with the pioneers and with the rural voters still living in log cabins. The cabins – together with cider and coonskin caps – says Professor Jamieson, enabled voters vicariously to experience Harrison's supposedly hardy, healthy, heroic life. He won the election misrepresenting himself as a cider-loving, log-cabin farmer (though he died soon after).

That campaign also featured the pseudo-event, now so much an ingredient of elections. To ally himself with the 'new Coonskin Whiggery' Daniel Webster camped with Green Mountain boys in a wood before an open fire, paid tribute to log cabins, and challenged to a fist fight anyone who dared to call him an aristocrat. 'The pseudo-event then,' commented Professor Jamieson, 'is not the child of television but the stepchild of image-making itself.'

What television did, though, was move it into a whole new dimension. Of all the forms of communication, television is the one best suited to emotion, to imagery, to instant branding. Furthermore it enables it to happen simultaneously to millions of people.

The last year of 'old time' campaigning in the US was 1948. That year Truman boasted he travelled 31,000 miles, made 356 speeches, shook hands with half a million people, and talked to 15–20 million Americans in person.* 'Today,' commented Barry Day, an adman who has been involved in political campaigns for the Conservatives in Britain, 'no candidate would even attempt it.' Face to face meetings, he says, are not necessary 'and often not desirable': 'The speech is now primarily a "photo opportunity", the origin of a suitable "quote" for the prime-time newscast – and the TV commercial.'

David Ogilvy credits Governor Dewey as being the first politician to use television, in 1950, in his campaign for the governorship of New York. On one programme passers-by were interviewed on 7th Avenue. Dewey watched them on a monitor in the television studio and answered their questions. The day before, writes Ogilvy, the Governor's staff had carefully selected the 'passers-by'. On the final day of the campaign, Dewey was on television from 6 a.m. to midnight. People could telephone the studio and ask him questions. One of his staff spent the day in a telephone booth with a pile of nickels. 'Dewey,' comments Ogilvy, 'the ex-District Attorney, the battler against corruption, the Governor of the State, thought of himself as an honourable man. It never occurred to him that he was involved in deception.'

By the following year, 1951, coast-to-coast television changed the whole complexion of the campaigning although it was not immediately obvious. Then came the Eisenhower victory. The truth, almost certainly, is that advertising was *not* the decisive factor. The important point, though, was that ads of persuasion *had* been used, and Eisenhower *had* won. As the English adman Winston Fletcher points out, politicians learned a simple lesson: 'without advertising, Dewey lost; with advertising, Eisenhower won. Ergo, advertising wins elections.

* Nixon visited every state in 1960, but it was television – notably the first Kennedy-Nixon debate – that was crucial.

The era of high pressure, all singing and dancing, political commercials had arrived, particularly in the US, but on a lower key throughout the western democratic world'.

It was, some might comment, a perfect match. Peter Jay, the former British Ambassador to Washington and political commentator, says, 'Both by their nature are forms of hucksterism, somebody trying to sell something.' One thing advertising was not trying to sell for a few years, however, was Democratic politicians – or rather the best advertising men were not trying to do so. Agencies were too afraid of offending Big Business. That changed in 1960. By then TV had taken a huge hold (nine out of ten of all US households owned one) and John F. Kennedy was the Democratic candidate. Madison Avenue became more afraid of being branded as villains by the nation than of annoying clients.

Television is good not only at presenting image and emotion, but in providing an ideal framework for adversarial advertising. The 1964 election included the famous Lyndon Johnson 'Daisy'/countdown commercial, mentioned earlier. Its creator, Tony Schwartz, defended it later: 'I think it was right on target. It made people aware of the basic differences between the two. If Goldwater said the next morning that "this should be the theme of the presidential campaign, and I'd like to pay for half of it: How do we prevent atomic warfare in our day and age?" he would have killed that commercial. His saying "foul" says the commercial fits; "that's me they're talking about".' Goldwater had once said jokingly that the eastern seaboard of the US should be 'sawn off' and floated out to sea. The Democrats created a commercial showing the US with the East Coast detached. Goldwater's attacks did not have the same bite or venom, though one commercial showed beer cans being thrown from the window of a moving car after reports that Johnson drank beer as he drove. Such ads may be branded as 'dirty', but the argument is that they work. Roger Stone, a consultant to the Republicans, said 'Voters will tell you in focus groups that they don't like negative ads [i.e. ads that attack an opponent's weaknesses], but they retain the information so much better than the positive ones. The point is: People like dirty laundry. Why do tabloids sell?'

The pattern in the years since has been for more and more of the same – more adversarial, more glossy image-building. The only change, perhaps, has been that, like commercials generally, political ads have become more smooth, more glossy, more slick. John O'Toole, an outspoken opponent of political advertising, thought in 1972 that advertising might find for itself a more noble role in the election morass. He was invited to be part of the advisory council of the November Group, the agency formed to promote Nixon. 'Because of the positions I had taken on political advertising, and because friends urged me to put those views into practice, I agreed,' he writes in *The Trouble with Advertising*.

The commercials the group produced for Nixon's campaign were in my view excellent, primarily because they didn't masquerade as spots. They were documentary films in five minute and one minute lengths. They dealt with substantive issues and supported them with actual accomplishments. But they never ran. Other forces in the White House – led, I was told, by Bob Haldeman (an advertising man manqué) – had another group producing thirty second spots that never showed Nixon, or anyone else, on camera. They talked about how vacillating McGovern was while showing a weathervane with George's face flipping back and forth with the wind. They talked about how dangerous his defence policy was while showing a hand disdainfully sweeping warships off a chessboard. They said nothing . . . I left the Nixon campaign sadder but wiser.

Nixon, he continues, was not alone in his approach.

Dwight Eisenhower and John F. Kennedy ran singing commercials with cartoon visuals that said absolutely nothing of substance. James Buckley, campaigning for the Senate in New York in 1970, ran a commercial in which he never appeared.* It featured John Wayne talking about what a good fellow Buckley was. It goes on and on to this day and to our shame. What can be done about it? We have to separate the televised political message from the formats, conventions and techniques with which people have come to associate – and by which they recognise – a commercial for something of far less significance.

America is one of the few countries in the world that allows political candidates to buy time on TV. O'Toole thinks that the United States 'might learn a lesson from our British cousins' in this respect. In Britain, political advertising is banned on TV. Instead, the two networks, the BBC and commercial television, allocate the parties an amount of free airtime, dependent on party size.

The argument is that doing this immediately removes two major villains – short spots which encourage commercial-type ads (free airtime is in blocks of ten minutes) and the domination of the pocket book. Although there is no maximum legal limit in the UK on the amount a party can spend on its campaign, the amount is controlled in practice by the relative shortness of election campaigns and the absence of paid TV advertising.† There is enormous difference between the amount of money spent on political advertising in the UK and in

---

* Henry Cabot Lodge went one better than this in 1964 in the battle for the Republican nomination. Even though he was abroad – as US ambassador in Saigon – he won the New Hampshire primary, using an old commercial that was first aired in 1960.

† There is a limit for the spending of *individual* candidates. It varies slightly depending on the size of the constituency, but in 1987 it was about £5,500 on average.

the US. In one campaign, Jay Rockefeller spent $11 million of his own money to win a second term as Governor of West Virginia. Candidates in the 1986 Congressional elections spent an estimated $450 million. In 1984, Mondale allocated a budget of $30.9 million to win the primary election against the Reverend Jesse Jackson and Gary Hart. Hart spent over $21 million in his unsuccessful attempt and Jackson $5.5 million. Even though he was unopposed in the Republican primary, Reagan reportedly spent over $18 million. In an eight-day opening advertising burst, $2 million was spent on TV.

In the election battle itself, Reagan and Mondale each had $40 million to spend, contributed by the US government from a voluntary levy of $1 from each taxpayer. In addition, however, they received vast advertising support from 'Political Action Committees'. These committees plough in huge sums of additional money and they also enable party hardliners to indulge in the 'dirtier' attacks that mainstream campaigns leave alone. Thus, in 1984, the wealthy right wing National Conservative Political Action Committee earmarked $14 million to campaign for Reagan's re-election. In a commercial attacking Geraldine Ferraro, the Democratic vice-presidential nominee, Mrs Ann Burford, former head of the Environment Protection Agency, referred to the 'real scandal' surrounding Ms Ferraro, a reference to accusations over her financial dealings and those of her property developer husband. She went on, 'Come on, Ms Ferraro, what are you trying to hide?' Early projections for the 1988 presidential battle topped $500 million.

Critics of political advertising are not alone in attacking the situation that has developed. Newspaper owners have voiced dismay, too – though at the fact that print in the US is not getting a bigger slice of the cake. In 1986 Congressional candidates spent $97 million on TV and radio, only $22 million on print. In an attempt to obtain advertising from 1988 Presidential candidates, the Newspaper Advertising Bureau launched a campaign that argued, 'Voters believe newspapers.'

The key point, of course, is not simply that political advertising costs a lot of money or that the money could be better spent in other ways (both of which are true) but that someone has to put up that money. The consequence is that candidates either have to be rich or be backed by rich men and women. With individual Senate campaigns costing $20 million, it is not surprising that cash-laden special interest groups have played an ever-increasing role.

Amounts spent in the UK are of a totally different order. It was estimated that in the 1987 general election the Conservatives spent about £9 million, Labour over £4 million, and the SDP-Liberal Alliance about £2 million. The Conservative Party, traditionally the party of Big Business, finds it easiest to raise money. It also holds another advantage. Posters are widely used as an advertising medium in British general elections. Obtaining good sites at short notice is difficult; the

Conservatives are able to 'borrow' them from brewing and tobacco companies who have long-term leases on such sites.

Despite the difference in the amounts of money spent and the absence of paid-for TV in Britain, the US and the UK share one important similarity. In neither country is political advertising subject to the normal rules of advertising. In the US, it is protected by the First Amendment to the Constitution which covers the freedom of speech. Robert Spero, author of *Duping the American Voter*, has said, 'The sky is the limit on political advertising with regard to what can be said, what can be promised, what accusations can be made, what lies can be told.' The sales director of WBBM-TV, Chicago, said during the 1983 mayoral campaign, 'We have no censorship powers. We can't make a decision to carry or not to carry a political ad, no matter how bad the technical quality and how outrageous the claim. Jane Byrne [the incumbent mayor] could say "Richie Daley [the main challenger] is gay and we don't want any fags in our government," and we would have to run it.'*

The situation in the UK is similar. The industry's self-regulation code, the British Code of Advertising Practice, exempts politics. It specifies that provided the advertiser is named (and an address is given for any correspondence), 'the Code imposes no restrictions, in regard either to expressions of opinion or assertions of fact, upon claims in advertisements concerned with matters of political, religious, social or aesthetic controversy.' In practice, what this means, in the words of Philip Circus, the IPA's legal advisor, is 'there is no need for authors of political advertisements to substantiate their claims, no requirement of them to make fair comparisons, no ban on misleading the consumer, and no restrictions on denigrating competitors.'

As for television, although there is no paid-for advertising, there *is* advertising in the form of space allocated for parties. Here, too, control is minimal. Product advertising is governed by restrictions and scripts have to be cleared in advance. None of this applies in the case of political broadcasts. What they contain is a matter purely for the parties, provided they do not break any laws or use subliminal techniques.

The conditions in Britain, therefore, have long been ripe for 'American style' political advertising campaigns if any party decided to import it. Before television became a real factor in British politics, the advertising agency, Colman, Prentis and Varley, helped the Conservatives to develop clear campaign lines such as 'Life's better under the Tories, don't let Labour ruin it', and the famous or infamous 'You've never had it so good', the foundation of Harold Macmillan's 1959 victory. Barry Day, who was involved, says that the 'first deliberate attempt to apply some of the relevant lessons of US experience – and, therefore

---

* The only control, it would seem, is one under Federal laws that prohibits pornography in all ads, including political ones!

as far as I can determine, the first conscious effort to use the established techniques of commercial marketing on the British political scene,' came in the 1970 elections on behalf of the Conservative Party.

The programme, recalls Day, was controlled by a small group of professional communicators, with political and party representatives, and specialists from advertising and marketing. 'We couldn't buy commercials, but there was nothing that said we couldn't put them into our programmes – the party political broadcasts. The essence of a TV commercial is its single-minded simplicity. One commercial showed a £1 note – shades of (Harold) Wilson's "Pound in Your Pocket" – being brutally attacked by a pair of scissors. As each segment was snipped away, a voice-over stated the date and depleted value of the pound, ending with the inescapable fact that the continuation of Labour policies would lead to the "Ten Bob Pound". Another showed a woman's hand taking a block of ice from a domestic fridge. Embedded in the ice was a frozen wage packet. Labour gave it to you last time. Vote for them "and you'll get it again – in the family economy size".'

Creative advertising, then, had come to British politicking just as it had to the US. The difference here was that the 'commercials' went on longer and airtime was free. Day not withstanding, though, the year US-style campaigning was really seen to have arrived in Britain was 1979. That was the first year that Saatchi and Saatchi handled the Conservative Party (a relationship which lasted until 1987 when, in the nature of many agency-client marriages, the two decided the time had come to part). 'Some people' reported the *Wall Street Journal* later, 'think their advertising campaign put her into office.' The campaign used the techniques that had become standard in the US, including polling to define the issues that should be targeted, and attention-grabbing attacks. In one poster, a queue of the unemployed stretched into infinity. 'Labour isn't working', said the headline. Another read, 'Cheer up! Labour can't hang on for ever.'

Saatchi and Saatchi were back in 1983. One double-page newspaper ad was headlined, 'Putting a Cross in the Labour Box is the same as signing this piece of paper.' Below, a list began, 'I hereby give up the right to choose which school my children go to . . . I am prepared to see the Police Force placed under political control . . .' Another, headed 'Like your manifesto, Comrade' ran eleven items from the Labour Party Manifesto and the Communist Party Manifesto side by side – each of them identical. (The Communist Party duly issued a press release objecting!)

The ads brought criticisms – 'the present campaign . . . seems to have gone down quicker into the gutter than the election campaign last time,' said Michael Foot, the Labour leader – but they also created front-page news, and priceless publicity not least for Saatchi and Saatchi. Perhaps most significantly this election campaign also saw 'creative' ad approaches from the Labour Party. Twenty-four years before, a group of admen sympathetic to Labour had offered their help, and been turned away. A volunteer team of admen was involved in the 1979 campaign, but they were barely tolerated, let alone fully utilised. They were not even allowed to look at the party's private polling. Tim Delaney, head of that team, said later, 'Our problem was the lack of sympathy in the Labour Party for professional advertising people.' Another adman who was involved, Tony Bodinetz, vice-chairman of the agency KMP, described working with Labour on that occasion as 'hell'. He said, 'The general view from the Labour Party was that advertising was a nasty business and life would have been better if they didn't have to deal with us. But if they did, they were going to keep us at arm's length. It was that kind of feeling . . . They wanted turgid propaganda, not what we would call real ads.'

By 1983, however, the Labour Party had an ad agency, Wright and Partners. 'The Labour Party,' said *Campaign* in an editorial, 'must be getting desperate if it is turning to one of capitalism's weapons to put its message across.' Whether Labour's heart was in what they were doing was debatable, as was whether its agency was up to Saatchi and Saatchi. But the campaign was tackled professionally – concepts were researched, just as they would be for any product. The UK had fully entered the new age of political advertising. If there was still any doubt, late in 1983 Saatchi and Saatchi reportedly were approached by the Republicans about involving themselves in the 1984 presidential elections. The impression leaked, at least in London, was that it was Saatchi and Saatchi who decided not to pursue the matter.

The relationship between Saatchi and Saatchi and the Conservative Party illustrates a striking difference between the situation in Britain and that in the United States. In America, political accounts are not highly coveted by agencies, although a number of major individual admen do involve themselves. One reason for this is the antagonism many admen feel towards political advertising. Another is financial: candidates frequently overspend and run out of funds; sometimes advertising bills are not paid until years after elections, sometimes not at all. Many small agencies have gone bankrupt as a result. Another is an agency's desire to be seen – for clients' benefit – as neutral. A fourth is the sheer hard work involved. One adman involved in Reagan's campaign told Jeremy Campbell of the London *Evening Standard* that he would never do it again: 'Admittedly, there is only one product to sell. But there are hundreds of changing strategies and themes that come at you like an express train, with sometimes less than a day to react. You work seven days a week, fourteen hours a day, until the campaign is over.' Campbell wondered whether the low esteem accorded to politics by US agencies was one reason why the Republicans held talks with Saatchi and Saatchi.

The Republicans have, in fact, developed a system that overcomes individual agency reluctance. It was first devised by Peter Dailey, founder chairman of Dailey and Associates, a Los Angeles agency, for President Nixon's re-election campaign. Dailey, later President Reagan's ambassador to Ireland, did not use his own agency to service the campaign, but took leave of absence and organised the November Group, an *ad hoc* 'company' composed of volunteer admen. Dailey did a similar job for Reagan in 1980. He formed an 'agency' of 'all stars' called Campaign 80 with offices in Washington and New York and a $25 million budget. In 1984, his idea survived though Dailey himself was left in the wings. The Tuesday Team, put together by James Travis, president and chief executive officer of Della Femina Travisano, had four creative units, each composed of a writer and an art director. Some of the most prestigious creative names in American advertising were involved, including Marvin Honig, formerly of Doyle Dane Bernbach, and Hal Riney, of Ogilvy and Mather's West Coast operation, regarded by many as the master of the use of emotion in American advertising.

Out of the Team came ads that were slick, ultra-polished – and dripping with emotion. They presented a United States which had more in common with Norman Rockwell's America of the fifties than the reality of the mid 1980s. 'America,' wrote a London *Times* writer, 'is depicted as a land of wide vistas, neat towns, booming factories, inhabited by a wholesome, well-fed populace. There is no poverty, no unemployment. Lebanon, Central America and nuclear weapons are unheard of.' Happy people were accompanied by syrupy background music. Visuals showed American flags, the Statue of Liberty, the Grand Canyon and ethnic groups happy together. The message was patriotic, soothing, optimistic. One commentator thought they were 'so good, they're scary'. Walter Carey, a member of the team on leave from the agency Leber Katz, New York, said they weren't slick but professional. 'I don't think anyone has fully understood the importance of emotion in political advertising,' he said. The Team's commercials 'appeal to people who feel great about being American'.

No one who saw any of the commercials could deny their slickness, nor that Madison Avenue, or at least that part of it that comprised the Tuesday Team, had reigned supreme. They had, commented one respected observer, changed the face of national campaign advertising. 'The Tuesday Team's craftsmen have replaced political discourse with political propaganda in Campaign '84.'

The America that Reagan gave the voters might not have been the America that exists, but there is no doubt it was the one they wanted to exist. In this respect, the ads only did what all political ads seek to do – find out what the audience wants to hear and give it to them. Polling and the advertising message are closely linked in political campaigns. The pollsters tell the politician what the voter wants to hear. Messages can then be devised to appeal to the greatest number. One reason direct mail is so highly regarded by many campaigners is that it enables different voters to be given different assurances at the same time, not all of them necessarily compatible.

Those who seek controls on political advertising include both admen and politicians. They argue, variously, that the present free-for-all gives advantage to the disreputable and to the liar (provided he has skilled admen behind him) and that it brings both politics and advertising into disrepute or into deeper disrepute. 'Political advertising ought to be stopped', David Ogilvy said in a videotape made for the Broadcast Promotion Association. 'It's the only really dishonest kind of advertising that's left. It's totally dishonest.' John O'Toole said in a speech to students, 'Political commercials encourage the deceptive, the destructive and the degrading.' O'Toole is one of the critics who sees the giving of free TV time as a remedy in the US. Other solutions that have been put forward range from the introduction of codes of conduct (although the American Association of Advertising Agencies does have a 'Code of Ethics' covering political campaigns) to outright legislation on the grounds that television is the media with the most impact. Others argue that TV advertising should be banned as in Britain.

Opponents had their worst fears confirmed by the 1988 Presidential contest where an estimated 70 per cent of ads were classed as negative, some outright brutal. One adman described them as the 'worst I can remember – I hope this is the lowest we'll see political advertising sink.'

Polls, however, showed that while voters disliked the ads, they were swayed by them. In this respect, Bush's successful campaign was brilliantly run and ruthlessly effective. Roger Ailes, the guru who produced the 'New Nixon' in 1968, headed a lean team with Sig Rogich, president of R & R Advertising, Las Vegas, as director and Ed Ney, former chairman of Young and Rubicam, as chief adviser. Ailes worked on his declared beliefs that 'television only covers three things: visuals, attacks and mistakes.'

The Bush campaign relentlessly questioned Dukakis's patriotism, softness on crime, weakness on defense. One memorable ad showed convicts walking through a revolving prison gate. A voice intoned, 'Dukakis's revolving door prison policy gave weekend furloughs to first-degree murderers not eligible for parole. While put, many of them committed other crimes like kidnap, rape . . .' One, Willie Horton, kidnapped a white couple, stabbing the husband, raping the wife. Like many ads on both sides, it was full of half-truths: the furloughs were begun by Dukakis's Republican predecessor; Dukakis stopped them after the Horton case; Reagan ran a similar programme while Governor of California.

Dukakis's ad campaign, in contrast, had an amateur-night feel. For a long time, there was talent but no leadership or direction. Failure to buy network time after the Democratic convention was a crucial error.

When Dukakis released his negative ads, they too twisted the facts – but they just weren't as persuasive. And that was a major reason he lost and Bush got to the White House.

Political advertising does have its defenders. Judith Press Brenner, head of a New York agency specialising in politics and public affairs, has written: 'It informs the public on key issues, new ideas and public policy problems. Candidates can't meet every voter. Political advertising conveys their messages, in their own words, unprocessed by the press or other go-betweens. It demonstrates the candidate's personality and character. It enables the public to decide whom they trust, agree with, believe in or just plain like. It points out differences between the candidates. It's fair and necessary for candidates to examine each other's records, ideas and character – just as they did in stump speeches fifty years ago. Candidates are presumed experts until proven otherwise.'

Robert Hinton, the media director of the Tuesday Team, later told the American Newspaper Association that, importantly, political advertising intruded on people. 'And this might even be central to the health of the American election process. Statistics indicate somewhat disturbing levels of voter registration and voter turnout. One might argue that if it does nothing else political advertising raises the noise level, envelops the country in the battle of ideas. If it does nothing more than heighten attention to a campaign and increase voter turnout, it's served a valuable purpose.'

Some advertising men, in fact, argue that the real problem is that not enough advertising professionals are involved – in an ideal world *every* candidate would get the best backup. Robin Wight, who in 1977 co-ordinated a group advising the Conservative Party, has said, 'I believe that in a democratic society *all* political parties should have first-class advertising at their disposal. Rather like the allocation of airtime on party political broadcasts, maybe there should be an allocation of public funds for political advertising.'

All very well, others argue, if the excesses are legislated away. Some American politicians made a bid to ban any political ads that went beyond a candidate speaking straight to camera. Sponsors of a bill argued that their proposed legislation was not a restriction on free speech because it concerned itself only with the manner of presentation. Senator Warren Rudman said the bill's purpose was 'to make television political campaigns less a function of Madison Avenue and more a contest of ideas'.

Many politicians and admen regard that kind of attitude as living in cloud-cuckoo-land. One of them is certainly Tim Bell, the individual adman most closely linked with political advertising in Britain. He has Mrs Thatcher's personal ear, and has been called 'one of her most important manicurists'. I met him a few days after he had moved from

Saatchi and Saatchi, which he co-founded, to another agency, which later became Lowe Howard-Spink and Bell. Pictures and cartoons were still stacked on the floor around him, waiting to be hung. One, however, *was* in place, a photograph of the Prime Minister signed 'Margaret, with love.'

Bell is a perfect example of the Thatcherism which he helps sell. He first entered advertising when poverty forced him to abandon a career as a modern jazz musician (he played trumpet, piano and vibes). An early job was as a time buyer at Colman, Prentis and Varley. After short stays at Ted Bates and Geers Gross, he helped found Saatchi's in the early seventies with Charles and Maurice Saatchi. In the second half of the seventies, as managing director, he steered it into its position of dominance.

When the Tory Party became Saatchi's most famous account, Bell took personal responsibility. After fifteen years at Saatchi, he moved in 1985 to join an old friend, Frank Lowe. At Saatchi's, he said, the brothers had built and he had operated; as group chief executive at Lowe Howard-Spink Campbell-Ewald, 'I'm going to be the builder.'

In his early forties, he is a millionaire several times over and says that his life is not divided into work and non-work – it's 'all a totality'. He exudes tremendous charm and boundless energy. His voice, again in keeping with Thatcher Conservatism, is educated but classless. Occasionally his words become blimpish. You suspect many of them are spoken to provoke effect. He wants the BBC 'to fail because I don't want the system to work. It only works now because it is a monopoly'; he believes that 'the best measure of any entertainment is popularity'. Such statements are often followed by a self-deprecating smile.

A former Saatchi colleague, Ron Leagas, referring to his personal charisma and ability to sell, said, 'If he was found leaning over a dead body with a smoking gun in hand, he would talk his way out of it.' The main thing he wants to talk his way out of today is the belief that politicians – and Mrs Thatcher in particular – rebuild themselves according to the advice of men like him. If politicians are more dress conscious, he argues, it is because they appear on TV more often. As for Mrs Thatcher herself, 'she is a woman so people are interested in how she dresses'. If he tried to advise her on her clothes, 'I would be thrown out of the room in five minutes'. It's not altogether convincing despite the charm. The media, he adds more matter-of-factly than complainingly, has taken to attributing roles to Saatchi's 'and particularly to me'. He dismisses one claim: 'I have never been involved in discussing policies with her. It is a forbidden subject.'

However, when it comes to *advertising* Mrs Thatcher and the Tory Party, Bell drops any coyness. He is in no doubts about either the point or the power of political advertising. With politics, he says, 'you get one shopping day every four to five years. Having bought it, you can't take it back.' He talks excitedly about the importance of ensuring that political advertising is *attacking* advertising.* But regardless of its effectiveness, wouldn't he make any changes to appease critics? 'God, no,' he says with what seems genuine feeling. 'The whole process is based on debate. Politicians say, "Surely you should be putting forward policies [in ads]." But they have the manifesto to do that. This expensive thing [advertising] should be used for doing something that cannot be done other ways.' He pauses. 'Capturing imaginations – it's trite, but that's what it's all about.' As to suggestions that there should be rules or codes of practice, he seems appalled. 'To do that,' he says quickly, 'would be to suggest that there is some authority greater than our political parties.'

Others agree – though sometimes for different reasons. Tom Edmonds is chairman of the ad committee of the American Association of Political Consultants, the group of men largely responsible for the way American campaigning is today. Edmonds, like the rest of the association, was angered by criticisms of political advertising coming from advertising agency professionals: 'Can you imagine,' he asked, 'such a comment coming from the same people who sell junk food to kids, unsafe cars, wine and beer, high price cosmetics that don't live up to their claims or chewing gum to teenagers?'

It is the right that has been most associated with political advertising. It was used in the United States by the Republicans before the Democrats and in Britain by the Conservatives at a time the Labour Party still viewed the approach with disgust.

The left has used it as a weapon, however. The Communist Party in Italy hired a Rome agency DBR & F from 1980, and said that their decision represented no judgment for or against advertising *per se*. One 1986 commercial showed two men balanced on a see-saw in the clouds. Each took out a pistol; one shot the other, the see-saw upended causing the one who fired to plunge. 'Vote Communist,' came the voice-over. 'It is a sign that you want peace.'

What has been striking, however, is how much by the second half of the 1980s the left had embraced political advertising, bringing the process into the mainstream of the political arena. Nowhere was this more marked than in Britain where the general election of 1987 could accurately be described as a 'watershed'. All three parties relied on the image-makers, the Socialists most of all. The party that a few years before had treated political advertising with undisguised contempt be-

---

* Attacking advertisements can have great wit and style. During French municipal elections, huge posters supported Jacques Médécin, the neo-Gaullist, mayor of Nice. The first showed a blonde in a bikini with the promise, in large letters, that she would TAKE IT OFF. A week later new posters arrived – the same blonde but this time without her top. The third posters showed her without top or bottom, with the words AS PROMISED AFTER 21 MONTHS OF SOCIALISM, I'VE GOT NOTHING LEFT.

gan to create commercials reminiscent of those of Reagan. The *Observer* commented, 'Whatever the outcome of the general election, 1987 will go down in political history as the year that Labour beat the Conservatives at their own game.'

A – perhaps *the* – major reason for all this was an advertising campaign that had taken place earlier. Because of its longer-term impact it is worth examining it in some detail.

The campaign was one designed to oppose the plans by Mrs Thatcher and her Conservative government to abolish the Greater London Council, an elected body responsible for a variety of services from housing and refuse disposal to administering the Royal Festival Hall. The government claimed its functions could be handled better and more cheaply by other bodies; it hardly helped the GLC that its image was one of the extreme, even loony, left. The GLC was the stuff that cartoonists draw, not that sane seek to defend.

The man responsible for helping to alter all that – and for changing the view of advertising among Britain's left – cuts an incongruous figure for such a role. Martin Boase is slim, elegant, neatly bearded, and the day we talked he sat draped languidly in his uncluttered working office. He wears a dark blue velvet suit, and answers questions calmly and carefully in a quiet, convincing voice. The corridor wall of his office is all glass, and the door remains open. People pass constantly, but in two hours he is only interrupted once, by a secretary – a striking fact as by now, with advertising men, I'm used to interviews punctuated by the delivery of messages, crisis telephone calls and demands for 'urgent decisions'.

Boase is chairman of Boase Massimi Pollitt, an agency he helped to found in 1968 when he was in his mid thirties. By 1986 it was the ninth largest agency in Britain, with £94 million worth of business, placing it in size between the London operations of the US giants McCann-Erickson (at seven) and Grey (ten). It was solid enough to make it a darling of the City (it went public in 1983) and exciting and trendy enough to be one of the most sought-after homes for would-be admen and women. Its offices reflect the dual virtues – a converted warehouse with a nondescript entrance in an ugly and unfashionable area behind Paddington station, but inside wide corridors, vistas of glass, apple green and red décor, and lots of beautiful people (the secretary who interrupted rustled in black leather).

BMP is the agency other ad agencies in London voted they would most want to represent them if they were clients. It is also the agency that has most involved itself in political 'issue' or advocacy advertising, for the Trades Union Congress, the unions NALGO and CPSA – and, most importantly, for the Greater London Council.

The GLC campaign gave it not just any left-wing client. The GLC and its leader, Ken Livingstone, represented almost everything calculated to make Tories splutter into their cups of afternoon tea or glasses of gin and tonic. It was identified with ladling out voters' money to anti-establishment fringe groups and with sympathy for such organisations as the political wing of the IRA. Livingstone's public and press nickname was 'Red Ken'.

In all, in fact, Livingstone and the GLC might be seen as unlikely candidates for an advertising agency. Livingstone himself was later to volunteer that, 'Labour has tended to view advertising and marketing as areas irreparably "tainted" with capitalism and has therefore kept these skills at arm's length.' The GLC, however, had a major problem. The Conservative government, fresh from its massive 1983 general election victory, was determined to abolish it. The GLC, conscious of the general antagonism of Britain's popular press, saw only one way to get across its message in the way it wanted it communicated – to advertise.

So it turned to Boase Massimi Pollitt. To say the least, the agency found itself with an unpopular client. Early research showed that it would be wrong to feature Livingstone himself in any advertising. He was 'such a hated figure', says David Cowan, a BMP director.

One of the key figures throughout the campaign was Denis Robb, a thirty-year-old Northern Irishman, with a Cambridge PhD in nineteenth-century British political history. He entered advertising 'by accident' in 1978 after a brief stint in academic publishing. He had been at BMP as a planner for just over a year when he heard the agency was to handle the Save the GLC Campaign. He immediately volunteered. Robb's job was co-ordinating and sometimes conducting all the research that helped create the actual advertising. Looking back, he says that the agency had many doubts initially as to how effective advertising could be. On one side, was a government with a massive majority committed to abolition. On the other, was the GLC led by a man whose image was 'largely negative'; at the same time research showed that most people had little idea of what the GLC did anyway. The situation, says Robb, did not look 'very promising'.

The agency decided, though, that there was a way to influence events. The right advertising could influence public opinion and opposition politicians and thus put pressure on Conservatives. That in turn would create media coverage which in itself would mean more pressure. All of this might make the government feel very uncomfortable. It all depended on finding something to say that would excite public opinion and the press.

What BMP wanted, says Robb, was an ideologically disturbing issue that would generate some moral outrage in the press and on TV. In its search for such an issue, the agency went out and talked to GLC electors. Robb himself in the space of the year conducted discussions with eighty separate groups, a gigantic number in terms of normal research feed-in. The BMP team had already dreamed up a number of possible issues. They turned these into mock ads to show to the groups.

The first was: abolition was organisational nonsense; one body was needed to run London. The reaction: 'People were not interested. People are not interested in local government – I challenge you to find a more boring subject to talk about.'

The second was: abolishing the GLC would not save any money. The problem: it was an issue on which people had already made up their minds. The GLC was already identified by some with handing out money to fringe groups (with names like 'Lesbian mothers against the Bomb'). The agency decided that to change people's minds would be impossible.

The third: if the GLC was abolished services would be cut. Some people were concerned – but they were mainly Labour voters. The agency wanted to reach the unconverted and the Tory voters.

The fourth: abolition would lead to remote decision taking. The reaction: people saw it as boring and without interest.

The fifth: it was against the will of Londoners. Reaction: people didn't really feel very strongly at all.

The sixth: abolition plans were motivated by spite. This was widely acknowledged to be true, but where did it lead as far as an ad campaign was concerned?

None of them was promising. However, one area was left, and this turned out to be a streak of pure gold. The seventh issue put to the groups was that in its plan to abolish the GLC, the government was taking away the Londoner's *right* to vote. The reaction, by all accounts, was astonishing. 'The first,' says Robb, 'was "What vote? Did we vote for the GLC?" The second was "My God, the government cannot do that. It is totally undemocratic. It is unBritish. It is Authoritarian. It is not the way we do things in this country." '

The agency had its issue. Ads were devised to fit the strategy and they began running in March 1984. The first showed the Houses of Parliament with the line, 'What kind of place is it that takes away your right to vote and leaves you with no say?' Another had a padlocked dustbin labelled, 'Next year all Londoners' votes go the same way.' Each carried the tagline, 'Say No to No Say.'

Surveys showing public knowledge of the government's abolition plans and of people's attitudes were conducted in January and in June. Before the campaign started, 45 per cent of Londoners were not even aware of the situation. Of those who were, 32 per cent disapproved. By July only 21 per cent were unaware, and the number against had risen to 55 per cent (those for had also increased but only from 13 per cent to 16 per cent).

There were more spectacular signs that the ads were having impact. In late May, the government's first legislative step towards abolition ran into difficulties. The annual poll of representative MPs conducted by the research company MORI in June showed half the Tories who answered thought abolition was a vote loser; every opposition MP questioned agreed. Something else happened. The research, says Robb, showed a profound difference in the way Livingstone was regarded. From being 'the most unpopular man in British politics he became the most popular'. 'It is,' reflects Robb, 'interesting the way people see politics. They see it in terms of individual people. I think people vote very much for politicians whose personality and psychology they can identify with. People suddenly felt great sympathy for Ken Livingstone. He was like Robin Hood. People got to like him. He got a lot of TV coverage, and what people saw was this charming, very reassuring bloke.' Suddenly, it was possible to use a large picture of Livingstone in ads, with the message that 'If you want me out, you should have the right to vote me out.'

At the end of the day the campaign – which cost £11 million overall (including lobbying, PR and direct mail as well as advertising) – was a failure in that abolition finally took place even though polls showed the number of Londoners opposed had soared, and even though, says Robb, there had been legislative concessions. The campaign did have one very tangible effect that could not have been anticipated – the government was so incensed that it brought in legislation that stopped any such 'political propaganda' in the future. The government's subsequent bill banned local authorities from publishing any material which appeared designed to affect, or could be assumed to affect, public support for a political party. The campaign also altered the image – and possibly the whole political future – of Ken Livingstone. He hadn't changed, said cynics, but how people saw him had – and that was what mattered in politics. In 1987, he was elected to Parliament.

The deepest, most important effect, though, must be the way the campaign illustrated to all politicians, especially those of the left, what can be done when political advertising is placed in the hands of the pragmatic professionals. Martin Boase says he believes 'passionately' that the relationship between agencies and clients has much in common with that between barristers and those they represent. Everyone is entitled to professional representation. Not only does the adman not have to believe in the cause, he argues – but it is much better if he does not. 'The best people to work on issue advertising, such as the GLC, are those who are neutral,' says Boase. 'Certainly the people who write the advertisements are uncommitted. Those against won't work on them. The best advertisements are ones that try to argue something coolly and rationally and it is the uncommitted who will do the best.' He reminded me that at the moment we talked the agency was hoping to win the advertising for British Nuclear Fuels ('Certainly some people here would refuse to work on it').*

Robb, as the man at the centre of the strategies of the campaign, never saw himself involved politically. 'I find politics immensely inter-

---

* In any event, BMP's pitch failed.

esting but in an academic way . . . I felt very cynical about it. I felt detached. On balance I thought it was probably a good thing if the GLC stayed – but that's only because the ads persuaded me.'

Robb believes the campaign produced Britain's 'first good political ads'. What remains of interest to him, the campaign over, is what makes a good *political* ad as distinct from a good ad for something else. 'Our ads were most successful when they struck at an emotional chord in people and visualised for people something everyone felt to be latently true whether it was about the nature of democracy or of the civil service. Such ads are immediately disarming and will immediately win people over to your side.' He thinks the fact they were witty was also crucial. 'If they had been banners with slogans they wouldn't have worked. That's what politicians do – they bandy slogans around.'

The campaign made many left-wingers see advertising in a new light. It did not stop them from regarding advertising as a device for manipulating people – but it made them realise it could work for *them* too. And as they happened to be selling the right message, the moral message . . .

The Labour Party took this lesson to heart in the following general election. It was a campaign that produced the most intensive and expensive political advertising ever seen in Britain. There were attacking ads on both sides: the Tories depicted Labour's policy on arms with a photograph of a soldier with his arms in the air, surrendering. Labour showed the Tory education policy as caring only for the privileged.

During the election Saatchi's also came under pressure as the Tories' agency (Bell's Lowe Howard-Spink and Bell and Young and Rubicam both claimed to have played a part in dictating the tone of the concluding week's advertising). But it was the Labour Party's performance that was the most notable feature. The party used a committee of prominent advertising men as advisers. Many remained anonymous, but prominent among them was known to be Chris Powell, the chief executive of BMP, the GLC campaign agency, and the strategy was remarkably similar. An agency observer, John Hegarty, commented, 'As with the GLC, the campaign centres on the individual v the might of the Tory establishment.' Neil Kinnock was promoted presidential style, walking hand in hand with his wife with the sea in the background, punching the air and entering halls to a fanfare.

The team behind the Oscar-winning film, *Chariots of Fire*, director Hugh Hudson and writer Colin Welland, were brought in for one political party broadcast that might have been, as one observer called it, 'a dead ringer' for a Reagan commercial; it was regarded highly enough by the image-makers for it to be given an unprecedented second showing.

The broadcast so inflamed the pro-Conservative *Times* that it urged its readers not to be taken in by this attempt at 'mass deception'. A leader, under the title 'Deceptive images', advised its readers that the strategy for the film had been created by the same men who opposed the end of the GLC. 'Mr Hudson's film has little to say about Labour's problems, about its surrender-first policy on defence, about its promises to flying pickets, inflation addicts and the shop stewards of the closed shops. It has everything to suggest about Mr Kinnock's capacity to deal with life's difficulties with the help of his disarming character, his delightful wife and the respectful advice of his party elders.'

At the end of the day, the majority view was that the Conservative Party and Saatchi's had been outmanoeuvred; in the words of the noted political observer, Brian Walden, Kinnock had become 'a pupil who has excelled his teachers'.

But –

Labour lost the election. Mrs Thatcher won an unprecedented third term with a massive majority. Didn't that prove that political advertising at the end of the day is of little or no significance? Wasn't it all reminiscent, say, of another slick campaign, in the United States this time, when Senator John Glenn made a bid for the presidency? It was generally agreed that Glenn commercials, which showed the ex-astronaut in a space capsule and with John F. Kennedy, had enormous power. But Glenn didn't succeed, and one reason was that it was impossible to disguise the fact that the screen image and the lacklustre Glenn were miles apart from each other.

Some knowledgeable observers have argued that advertising's impact is a marginal ingredient given everything that is involved. In any event, it is added, voters are cynical and prepared for false claims and promises. 'Any time a political commercial goes on the air today,' said Raymond Strother, a leading consultant for Democratic Party candidates, 'little red flags go up in people's minds, and they start to wonder if someone is trying to manipulate them.'

But it would be wrong to draw such a conclusion from the gap between Labour's advertising excellence and its performance at the polls. Labour did emerge with some clear victories. Chris Powell argued that, 'This election was meant to be about the death of the Labour Party.' And the party came out of it remarkably strong and well-placed for future battle. Furthermore, the party that did lamentably badly was the SDP/Liberal Alliance, the one which by general consensus had easily the worst advertising and marketing campaign. Labour emerged as the definitive opposition, no small achievement despite the overall result. It could be argued that given the *content* of what the party was trying to sell, without the advertising there could have been total disaster.

Does political advertising work? 'Of course it does. Some of it, some of the time,' argues Barry Day. In any event there was no doubting that the face of British politics had been changed for ever.

PART THREE

THE
MEDIA

Advertising and the Media

'With no ads, who would pay for the media? The good fairy?'
Samuel Thurm, a senior vice-president of the US Association of
National Advertisers

Advertising is the principal source of revenue for most of the commercial mass media throughout the world. In more and more places, it is now the advertiser who is paying. The trend is relentless and seemingly inexorable.

'The media no longer serve primarily as news producers, but rather as transmitters of commercial messages,' say Noreen Janus and Rafael Roncagliolo, two researchers primarily concerned with Latin America, a claim that, though overstated, contains some truth. Even a newspaper publisher, A. Roy Megary, of the *Toronto Globe and Mail*, has said, 'By 1990, publishers of mass circulation daily newspapers will finally stop kidding themselves that they are in the newspaper business and admit they are primarily in the business of carrying advertising messages.'

The relationship between advertising and the media, whether it is print or television or radio, has long been an incestuous one. Without a medium to contain the message, advertising cannot exist. Equally, and increasingly, that medium is dependent upon the advertiser for its survival. In an ideal balance between the two forces, the television station or newspaper or magazine concentrates upon its job of satisfying its viewers or readers, and the advertiser buys space or time to reach those potential customers. In a less than ideal world, which this is, the media owner may make his priority packaging the readers that the advertiser wants, a classic case of tails wagging dogs.

There are media at each extreme: the *Wall Street Journal* has no need to bend towards advertisers as its readers are precisely the kind of people certain companies need to reach. Contrariwise, huge numbers of glossy magazines exist not just at the approval of the advertiser, but *for* him. American network television is in the business of making money, not by selling programmes to viewers, but by selling parcels of viewers to advertisers, and in such a situation it is the advertiser who rules.

The incestuousness is not new. What is, is that increasing reliance. Advertisers are keen that the media, including the new media, shall turn to them. In a message to advertisers on how to cope with the 'new media', Lawrence Cole, director of media services at Ogilvy and Mather, New York, advised: 'Encourage all new media to accept advertising. Advertising can effectively defray or eliminate costs of these media to the consumer.' That's the bait. Marcel Bleustein-Blanchet, founder of France's largest advertising agency, Publicis, has written:

> Advertising will follow the media's evolution, whatever happens. If media multiply, advertising will extend itself. If shifts take place, advertising will adapt. You see, advertising has a major trump card: *it creates content*. We keep repeating, after McLuhan, that 'the medium is the message', but we forget that a medium without messages is nothing but an empty sock. That's the real problem: what are we going to do with all these new media? Who is going to feed them? Already there is a shortage of programs all over the world. Advertising can help it by financing new programs and by providing its own messages.

Today the various media have to fight fiercely for the advertiser's money. In the UK Rupert Murdoch's newspapers offer special deals to advertisers who agree not to appear in rivals' pages. Television companies operate a system whereby buyers get cheaper rates for guaranteeing them a specified share of their business. Space and time salesmen produce pages of research statistics designed to show that their magazines or networks offer the kind of readers or viewers the advertiser should want at the best rates – and their rivals the worst.

The media are huge advertisers themselves although usually in specialised publications that the public does not see. There is no doubt what they're selling – buyers of goods. *True Story* shows a cartoon family sploshing ketchup everywhere, with the headline, 'Our readers feel that few meals are complete without ketchup.' The text begins, 'By downing it at breakfast, lunch, dinner and for snacks, *True Story* readers last year used 37,837 tons of the red stuff. Which is enough to win the respect of tomato farmers if not gourmet chefs.' What is more, its readers are loyal, not just to the magazine but to brand names. So, 'If ads in *True Story* suggest they buy a particular ketchup, they're likely to do so.'

While *True Story* is busy selling buyers of ketchup and other down-market everyday brand goods, *Life* is reminding its advertisers that its readers like their drink. 'To celebrate their triumphs, quench their thirsts and drown their sorrows, the people who buy *Life* will down almost six million beers next week. Don't you belong in *Life*?'

Christmas for the media is a time for selling. To promote its year-end double issue *New York* sent thirteen singing Santa Clauses round the city to chant to eighty prospective advertisers. 'God bless you, Mr X,' went one line of the lyric, 'from *New York* Magazine, our year-end double issue is an advertiser's dream.'

Media advertisers want their customers to know that whatever image readers or viewers may have of themselves, they, the media owners, know it is their spending power that matters. *Rolling Stone* shows two full-page pictures, one a long-haired hippy, the other a sharp-looking keen-eyed young man. The first is labelled 'Perception', the second 'Reality'. 'If your idea of a *Rolling Stone* reader looks like a holdout from the 60s, welcome to the 80s,' reads the copy. '*Rolling Stone* ranks number one in reaching concentrations of 18–34 readers with household incomes exceeding $25,000. When you buy *Rolling Stone*, you buy an audience that sets the trends and shapes the buying patterns for the most affluent consumers in America. That's the kind of reality you can take to the bank.'

What might seem like limitations become advantages. *Hustler* is a squalid porn monthly that specialises in (to use its own literature) 'open, honest pictorials no other magazine offers'.

HUSTLER, [says its ads] DELIVERS MEN THAT THE OTHERS DON'T. Let's face facts. The average HUSTLER reader doesn't wear designer jeans. Or play racquetball. Or attend the opera. He doesn't even read a lot. So you don't reach him with your advertising in standard magazines. Nor even in the other men's books. But more than four million men read each issue of HUSTLER. Not sophisticates and intellectuals, perhaps. Just hard-working, hard-playing guys who happen to buy a lot of products and services. Isn't that what you want? Well, HUSTLER's the only one who's got 'em. So come and get 'em!

Anyone in competition for the advertiser's dollar or pound is an enemy. 'It was a grey day at *Smithsonian*,' begins a two-page *Life* ad presenting a comparison of readership figures. 'We didn't scare the daylights out of them, *Life* merely rained a bit on their parade.' What *Life* had done was deduce that it was reaching more college-educated readers than the prestigious *Smithsonian*. *Soap Opera Digest* boasts its readers swallow more indigestion aids than those of *Family Circle* or *People*.

It's tame stuff, though, compared with the fighting between different types of media. Television, because it is the rising champ, is a major target. To remind media buyers at advertising agencies that viewers are 'zapping', the *Reader's Digest* sent out toy-ray guns: 'Zap. There go millions of well-planned TV dollars, wasted.'

In Britain the *Daily Mail* refers to falling TV audience figures and asks, 'If people aren't watching the television, what are they doing with it?' It gives the 'answer' – a photograph of a man reading his newspaper by the light of a TV screen. 'Just because a TV set is turned on doesn't necessarily mean someone's watching it,' says the Institute of Outdoor

Advertising, showing a TV set with one viewer – the dog. Radio hits at TV's rising costs: 'Inflation may be slowing to a crawl but the cost of television continues its steep climb,' says the Radio Advertising Bureau. 'Dollar for dollar, radio delivers more than three times as many impressions as prime time television.' Newspapers get the treatment, too: 'Radio is "Vital Growth" Medium, Newspapers in "No Growth" Groove.'

Television retaliates with advertisements like the one that points out the *Daily Mail* has 'spent £26,000 telling you television doesn't work . . . and then £2.5 million advertising on it'. Another asks, 'Take away movement, take away sound and what are you left with?' The answer: 'That's right, a press ad.'

Dependence on advertising varies from media to media and country to country. In most countries the advertiser's choice is restricted by availability – advertising on television may not be allowed or it may be restricted by law to no more than a few minutes a day. The advertiser's money then flows into alternative media. In Germany, strict limits on television advertising have meant advertisers channelling their money into magazines, making possible fat, general interest publications of the kind that long ago died in other countries.* In Saudi Arabia, a sub-industry has developed selling advertisements on pre-recorded video tapes – a way of reaching a wealthy but still largely illiterate population. In Italy, on the other hand, where there has been a proliferation of private TV stations, advertisers rush to spend almost half of all their money in that medium.

Worldwide, print is still the most important medium – according to 1986 figures, it took 54 per cent of the expenditure. Television was second with 31 per cent and radio third at 8 per cent. The rest of the money went to outdoor posters, cinema, direct mail, exhibitions, sales promotion and other forms. However, television is regarded as the most potent of selling tools, and despite variations between countries, the trend is clear: the use of television as an advertising medium continuously increases everywhere. The most important and obvious factor, of course, is the sheer growth of available viewers. According to figures produced for the UN, the rates of growth of television sets in the world from 1960 soared anywhere from twice to 500 times higher than those of population growth.

The United States has a basically free market in advertising outlets. In the United States in the mid eighties, about a third of the advertisers' money goes into TV, 40 per cent into newspapers, 13 per cent into magazines and 11 per cent into radio. In Britain, over 28 per cent of the advertising money goes into television, and 58 per cent into print.

The amount of revenue that the media draws from the advertiser

---

* At the time the three major US networks were carrying 540 minutes of commercials a day, Germany had forty minutes!

varies according to the particular media and the particular part of the world. In the United States, advertisers provide 75 per cent of the income of newspapers, a little over 50 per cent of that of general circulation magazines, and almost 100 per cent of the income of broadcasting.

Torin Douglas, a trade commentator, has provided a detailed breakdown for the UK: free newspapers and controlled circulation magazines, and posters, 100 per cent; commercial radio, 99 per cent; commercial TV, 97 per cent; regional weekly papers, 82 per cent; regional daily, 60 per cent; quality Sunday papers, 68 per cent; popular Sunday, 31 per cent; popular daily, 27 per cent; general interest magazines, 38 per cent; business publications, 62 per cent.

In pure revenue terms, the money derived from advertising can be even more important than it seems from the figures. With magazines, for example, the cost of obtaining additional subscriptions is higher than the cost of attracting additional advertising, and thus, advertising accounts for a higher percentage of operating profits.

Advertising has had a major influence on the growth of the media. 'Advertising . . . is a kind of news,' wrote Denis Thomas in a paper published by J. Walter Thompson. 'So it is not surprising that it and the media have grown up together, profiting in good times and suffering together in bad.'

Early publications, however, took little or no advertising. A 1919 textbook points out that 'in earlier days' periodicals disliked to give up any portion of the paper for advertising, limited the amount of space which could be secured for such advertising, and left it out if the reading matter covered more space than was allowed for. 'As a matter of fact, the publisher in the early days had the advertising forced upon him by the merchant who offered inducements to the publisher which were sufficiently strong to engage him to give up a small portion of his paper to such announcements. It was a very long time after the introduction of advertising into periodicals before the publisher began to see the possibilities of his medium in connection with the business.'

According to Stephen Fox in his detailed history of American advertising, *The Mirror Makers*, it was J. Walter Thompson who realised the potential of advertising in magazines. While working at a one-man agency in New York as a book-keeper and assistant, he was struck by the fact that 'polite magazines' ran only a page or two of ads in each issue. Thompson decided to place an ad for asbestos-roofing in the unlikely medium of two women's journals. The ads sold more roofing than any promotion in the company's history. Thompson began approaching the literary monthlies; by 1876 *Scribner's* was carrying twenty pages of ads per issue. Soon virtually all the 'best' American magazines were under Thompson's exclusive contract for advertising.

Together, the advertising needs of manufacturers and technological developments combined to make magazines the first national media. Towards the end of the nineteenth century, there were a number of new printing inventions. Handprinting methods were made obsolete by the linotype typesetting machine; better presses and binding machines made larger, faster print runs feasible. The effect was that a monthly magazine could be produced more quickly, in greater volume and more cheaply. At the same time, the booming manufacturing industries needed to merchandise themselves nationally. In the United States, one man, Frank Mumsey, saw the implications. In 1891 he launched *Mumsey's Magazine*. After two years, he cut the price from a quarter to a dime. He intended the magazine from then on to live by advertising revenue, not sales.

In 1885, reports Fox, four general magazines claimed 100,000 or more readers, with an aggregate total of 600,000. Two decades later there were twenty such magazines, with a combined circulation of 5.5 million. 'The magazine world had been transformed: a revolution prodded, celebrated, and paid for by advertising.'

In the early days, the relationship between publisher and advertiser was uneasy. Lord Northcliffe set up the advertisement department of the *Daily Mail* in 1900, instructing, 'Don't go out after your advertisers. Wait for them to come to you.' Newspaper profitability, however, depended on the advertiser; by 1904 Northcliffe's Associated Press was taking in £264,000 from advertisers. When there were not enough major advertisers featured in the *Daily Mail*, he ran free advertisements for George Newnes, his rival, to make it look as though even Newnes couldn't afford not to advertise with him.

At the same time it was said that Northcliffe would have done without advertising completely were it possible. Some of his missives show his disquiet:

'Most strongly protest against your injuring my newspaper by use of such type as in OXO advertisements. Please send me written explanation why you disobey my orders.' (Telegram to his advertising director in 1914.)

'Deal firmly with advertising plastering *The Times* with advertisements to the disgust of many readers.' (To Wickham Steed, 1919.)

'Leave out all top-heavy advertisements which ruin the paper, such as the bottle in Johnson's Prepared Wax, and the large heading of Quaker Oats. If you do not leave them out, I shall ask the printer to do so.' (To the *Daily Mail*, 1922.)

In one message to *The Times*, in 1920, he encapsulated his unease:

'It is not pleasant to think that, owing to the gigantic wages paid in newspaper offices and the high price of paper, newspapers are now for the first time in their history, *entirely* subordinate to advertisers.

I see no way out of this impasse, other than by maintaining a great daily net sale and thus keeping the whip hand of the advertiser.'

By 1919, S. H. Behrman complained in the *New Republic*, 'The cornerstone of the most respectable American institutions, the newspapers and magazines depend on him [the advertiser]; literature and journalism are his hand maidens. He is the Fifth Estate.'

Not all publishers were reluctant to embrace the advertiser. In 1909, Condé Nast created *Vogue* (as he said) 'to bait the editorial pages in such a way to lift out of all the millions of Americans just the hundred thousand cultivated persons who can buy these quality goods'. Sixty-three years later, with the magazine owned by the Newhouse newspaper chain, its publisher, Richard Shortway, was equally frank about the editorial/advertising link: 'The cold, hard facts of magazine publishing mean that those who advertise get editorial coverage.'

In both Britain and the United States, the development of print advertising followed similar patterns. Broadcasting, however, was different. In the United States, advertising as part of radio began nervously and haphazardly after World War I. Initially, radio as a medium was largely amateurish – many operators were mainly concerned with selling radio sets; others were educational and religious bodies, newspapers and department stores. From the beginning, there was dispute over whether advertising should be allowed, and if so, in what form, sponsorship or 'spots'.

Commercial radio began when A T & T instituted 'toll broadcasting' at WEAF, its New York station. By paying a fee, it became possible for anyone to enter the station and address the public – not unlike making a telephone call. Perhaps not surprisingly, one advertising man, William H. Rankin, saw possibilities. He bought time and tested using it to advertise. Within six months he had sixteen sponsors. There was no sales message other than the name of the company and its link with the subject-matter. Thus Gillette, for example, would provide a talk on fashions in beards.

Such indirect advertising endured the birth of NBC, the first network, in 1926 but yielded to the pressures of a second network's arrival (CBS) and the Depression. Advertisers began to see there was a new mass public for the exploiting; agencies realised that the new medium gave them access to people who rarely looked at newspapers or magazines.

Sponsors quickly found a formula of light entertainment that people liked; to get it, audiences showed they were prepared to pay the price of some not very heavy salesmanship. Albert Lasker's agency hired talent scouts, built up stars like Bob Hope, produced shows and became a powerful branch of show business. Listeners received talent shows, quizzes, give-away programmes, all at no apparent cost.

'Most serious-minded Americans, watching the give-away programmes grow into a popular frenzy, suspected by now they had been cheated,' wrote E. S. Turner in his *Shocking History of Advertising*. 'The radio industry was firmly in the hands of advertisers, and advertisers were concerned only to reach the largest mass audiences. It followed, therefore, that the great bulk of programmes would be light, popular, and unlikely to inspire thought or controversy. Radio, in short, was only a time-filling interval; between bouts of salesmanship.'

By the 1930s, the advertiser was king. As Llewellyn White wrote in *The American Radio*, 'Like the beleaguered Czechs of ancient Bohemia, the broadcasters had cried out for succour. Like the Hapsburgs, the advertising men who came to rescue remained to rule. And like many a philosophical Slav, the broadcasters accepted the conquerer's tongue.'

What had happened was not just that advertising had become the master of radio, but that a pattern for commercial broadcasting had been established for when TV appeared. In the US, television almost from its invention was being hailed as 'the vacuum cleaner salesman's dream' and 'advertising's third dimension'. When expansion began after the war television was placed firmly in the hands of the advertiser for its finance. In the early days, advertisers sponsored and produced entire programmes, thus giving them complete and direct control of their content. The results were sometimes ludicrous enough to make them legendary.

Camel cigarettes sponsored NBC's news programme from 1947. The company banned the showing of all film of news that happened to take place where a 'No Smoking' sign could be seen. No one was allowed to be shown smoking a cigar with the one exception of Winston Churchill. In another Camel-sponsored programme, the drama series, *Man Against Crime*, no one was allowed to cough.

Car companies in particular were zealous in pursuit of programme 'purity'. John Mantley, who worked as a story consultant on the series *Gunsmoke*, said that the ad agencies read scripts and came to the rough cuts 'to make sure you didn't "ford" a river if you were sponsored by Chevrolet. Honest!' The De Soto car company as sponsors of a Groucho Marx show insisted that the name of one of the assistant producers should be removed from the screen credits – because he was called Ford! On another occasion, Ford actually asked for the Chrysler Building to be painted out of the New York skyline.

Rudyard Kipling's *The Light that Failed* was renamed *The Gathering Night* because one of the sponsors was Westinghouse which made light bulbs. In the most notorious case, the word 'gas' was deleted by an engineer from the soundtrack of *Judgement at Nuremberg*, a dramatisation of the Nazi war crimes tribunal. The American Gas Association was one of the programme's sponsors. There was silent mouthing whenever the words 'gas chamber' occurred. Even more obscenely, the programme was punctuated with commercials extolling gas.

Sponsorship, however, did have its positive side. Individual examples of advertiser-power might have been ludicrous, but, overall, sponsored television delivered a wide range of good programmes. There were popular variety and comedy shows but there were also live dramas by authors like Gore Vidal and Paddy Chayevsky. The period is now widely regarded nostalgically as a 'Golden Age' of American commercial television. Its end was heralded by the enterprise of a small lipstick company called Hazell Bishop. With annual sales of only $50,000, it could not afford to sponsor programmes. It presented a message not attached to a show, and its sales soared. Other companies rushed to follow. Networks instituted the 'spot' ad – short commercials from different sponsors in one programme. They found they could make more money each hour from many sponsors than one large one. Television was never to be the same again. What television had to do from now on was be a medium acceptable to advertising, not just one advertiser who might be worried about someone saying 'Ford' or showing the wrong building. From this moment the whole ambience mattered. What the networks did was create a new kind of programme, one that well fitted the advertiser's message. Programmes that 'jarred' had to go. Erik Barnouw in his history of television, *Tube of Plenty*, says that the live plays fascinated millions and held consistently high ratings. 'But one group hated them: The advertising profession.' The reason was that 'most advertisers were selling magic. Their commercials posed the same problems that Chayevsky drama dealt with: people who feared failure in love and business. But in the commercials there was always a solution as clear cut as the snap of a finger: The problem could be solved by a new pill, deodorant, toothpaste, shampoo, shaving lotion, hair tonic, car, girdle, coffee, muffin recipe, or floor wax.'

Programmes had to be the kind that would put people in the right mood – a buying kind of mood. They also had to reach the greatest possible number of people. Ratings ruled. Shows that did not measure up were killed off swiftly.

In Britain, commercial television also followed the example of radio, but radio developed very differently from the US pattern. Early suppliers of radio in Britain, as in America, were manufacturers seeking to spread the sales of their products. It was businessmen who banded together to form the British Broadcasting Company (now Corporation) in 1922. Its first general manager, John (later Lord) Reith, was, however, a passionate believer in the public service ideal, and the opening paragraph of the corporation's constitution says, 'The Corporation's object is to provide a public service of broadcasting for general reception at home and abroad.'

From the beginning – 1927 – the corporation has drawn its income from a licence fee. In 1927 it was ten shillings; by 1988 it was £58 but with two television networks, four radio networks and thirty-two local radio stations that was not enough.

The BBC launched the world's first high-definition television service in 1936, but, as in the United States, it was from the 1950s that television took hold. Throughout the early fifties campaigning grew for a commercial television network. A Popular Television Association was backed by both the advertising industry and the Conservative Central Office. There was strong opposition to the whole idea. A National Television Council opposing commercial TV was formed by the Labour MP, Christopher Mayhew, and included Bertrand Russell and E. M. Forster. Mayhew, in a pamphlet which sold 60,000 copies, called upon the reader 'to exercise all the influence you have, as a free citizen of the most democratic country in the world, to prevent this barbarous idea being realised'. Reith himself thundered in the House of Lords, 'Somebody introduced Christianity into England and somebody introduced smallpox, bubonic plague, and the Black Death. Somebody is trying now to introduce sponsored broadcasting.' Moral values were at stake.

When commercial television did arrive, in 1955, it came defensively and hedged by restrictions. Sir John Barbirolli, the conductor, announced that no programme in which he appeared with the Hallé Orchestra would have commercial breaks. Commercials could only be shown at the beginning and end of programmes and in 'natural breaks' within them. Today the breaks aren't always 'natural', but there is nothing of the burst of commercials moments after the opening of a programme as in America.

The very name the commercial companies chose to use reflects the defensiveness: *Independent* television. The controlling body was called the Independent Television Authority (later, when independent radio followed in 1973, the Independent Broadcasting Authority). European countries generally have set up television systems with a determination not to follow the American pattern. Stations have been primarily financed by licences, though sometimes augmented by advertising.

In recent years two major developments have taken place that affect the advertiser and the media he uses. Advertising reached its present position as a tool of mass marketing. However, recent years have seen the breaking-up of mass markets into segments. Partly this is because in the developed world the advertisers' traditional target – the 'typical family' – is a vanishing concept. What there is instead is a larger number of smaller households or individuals, wanting different things, having different interests – reachable only through different media.

The mass market 'has splintered and . . . companies can't sell their products the way they used to,' said Laurel Cutler, executive vice-president for market planning at Leber Katz Partners, an advertising agency specialising in new products. 'The largest number of households may fall into the two-wage earner grouping, but that includes everyone from a manicurist to a Wall Street type – and that's really too diverse in lifestyle and income to qualify as a mass market.'

Along with the segmentation of markets – and encouraged by them and made possible by new technology – has come a veritable explosion of media aimed at selective groups of people. It happened first in the magazine world when the huge mass circulation magazines like *Life*, *Paris-Match* and the women's weeklies gave ground to others with more specialist readerships. By 1988, the UK alone had over 3,000 magazine titles on bookstall sale with the number rising literally daily. In the United States, there were more than four times that number. Furthermore, almost one in five of American magazine ads were being directed at a specific segment – that is, they were running in either a regional edition of a magazine or one with a precise 'demographic' readership.

Newspapers, too, began to segment their markets, 'zoning' different editions, thus allowing advertisers to target markets with less wastage. In Britain, for example, the *Express and Star*, a provincial newspaper and an early user of new technology, was producing ten different editions by the mid eighties, making it possible for local advertisers such as retailers and estate agents to reach defined audiences.

With more radio stations and an increasing number of television channels, segmentation became possible there, too. In two-television homes, advertisers could be selling soft drinks on a rock video programme to teenagers in one room and financial services in a news format to their parents in another.

It is largely because it reaches specific, defined audiences that American radio, which seemed to be doomed by the coming of television, has survived – and even thrived. In recent years, there has been a continuing explosion of stations: by the mid eighties there were about 8,500. Americans were listening to radio for three and a half hours a day – on their clock radios, car radios, portable radios. At least a fifth of what they were hearing was advertising.

In Europe, changes in government attitudes to commercial broadcasting have again brought an explosion of stations. By the mid-eighties Belgium and Italy had around 2,000 and 3,000 private stations respectively.

Everywhere there has been a massive explosion of all forms of media, or what John Perriss, media director of Saatchi's in London, calls 'an expansion of media opportunities'. In just the ten years up to the beginning of 1985, he points out, there appeared in the UK two new television stations taking ads – Breakfast TV and Channel 4, two new national newspapers – the *Star* and the *Mail on Sunday*, a third more consumer magazines, the whole (forty-eight station) chain of local commercial radio,* about 750 free newspapers and 180 free magazines.

At the same time there has been a rush to convert almost anything which might attract an audience into a medium for advertising messages. When an eighty-foot catamaran, contender for the world's speed record was launched in Britain, on her sides were the words 'This Space to

* Commercial radio came late to Britain, in 1973.

Let'. The vessel was being promoted as 'the world's biggest, fastest floating poster site'.

Sometimes it seems that the first law of advertising is: if it's visible and you can get away with it, stick an ad on it. Ron de Pear, media director of J. Walter Thompson, London, said, 'Back home (in Australia), we used to have a boxer who was knocked down so many times that people used to joke about selling space on the soles of his boots. These days, someone would probably try it.'

The ingenuity of the advertiser in finding places to display his message has always been awesome. Last century men with sandwich boards marched the London streets in outfits uncannily like British army uniforms, a practice ended by the passing of the 1894 Uniforms Act, although one advertiser overcame this by using men dressed as *German* soldiers. Thomas Lipton, the grocer, produced what looked like Scottish banknotes carrying advertising slogans – one man received twenty days' imprisonment for trying to pass one. Thomas Barratt, of Pears' Soap, made use of actual coins. In the early 1890s, French ten-centime pieces were accepted in Britain as the equivalent of the penny. Barratt imported 250,000, had them stamped 'Pears' and put them into circulation. As a result, Parliament passed an act ending the use of French coins, and the 'Pears' coins were collected and melted down.

Telegrams, indistinguishable from those carrying urgent news, were used for the most routine advertising. An old lady described in a letter to *The Times* in 1896 how she had been awakened by her maid clutching a telegram. When it was opened, the message read, 'Peter Robinson's sale now proceeding.' In 1893, a 'cloud projector' was set up on the roof of the Manufacturers' Building at the Chicago Exhibition. The number of people who had visited the fair during each day was shone onto clouds.

In the 1920s and 1930s, advertising messages were yelled from airborne loudspeakers, sent into homes on unbreakable plastic records, conveyed by moving models who tapped shop windows to attract attention, and were even printed on the back of British dog licences with the express permission of the Treasury.

The ingenuity of the advertiser has not flagged. Today advertisements can be found on ball-washer units at tee positions on US golf courses; on supermarket trolleys; on milk bottles; on street signs in Los Angeles Zoo (under the company 'Adopt a road' scheme); on the backs of toilet stalls in Australian public wash-rooms.

They appear in school exercise books in Strathclyde in Scotland (£8,550 buys an advertiser three pages in 500,000 books, £2,850 one page. The first client was the Bank of Scotland); on give-away plastic rainwear handed out at prestigious outside events, trade shows and promotions ('Now is your chance to capitalise on that most famous of British institutions – the weather'). In hospital waiting-rooms videos deliver a mixture of entertainment and ads, though not including ones for tobacco, drink or branded medicines. ('We have totally overcome initial scepticism and hospitals are now approaching us,' said the company responsible after early trials.)

Ads appear on football videos on oil rigs; on TV monitors hung in railway terminals; over checkout lines; in British pubs (three commercials per twenty minutes of sporting clips); in discos; on carrier bags; on Washington Metro Fare cards; on paperclips; on buses in the north of England (at the time of writing as audio ads only); on football shirts, boxes of matches, rubbish sacks and bins, lamp posts, and on blinds in the rear of car windows. The man who thought of this last one admitted to me that he thought in an ideal world people would rather have no advertising at all – 'Everything would look so clean.' He added, 'But our economy is geared to it. Products have to be promoted and advertising is part of it.'

Compared with the main media, they're all peripheral and often distinctly jokey. But those that survive – and those mentioned have – are all taken seriously by some advertisers whose only criteria has to be: does it work cost effectively? In other words, If I advertise on this, can I sell more goods? 'No one is pretending it is an up-market medium,' said Geoff Cherry who supplies hot-air balloons as an advertising medium. 'You have a pretty difficult job flogging it to the agencies . . . But in the right places, the medium really works.'

John Perriss says that his agency, Saatchi's, is deluged by new ideas. 'Last week I had the Skyrocket Diving Co – their parachutes open fifteen seconds above the ground. They wanted advertisers to sponsor the parachutes, said that the advertisement would get increased attention value because everyone's eyes would be fixed on them. I said, what happens if they don't open? What do you think one of our clients would think of having his advert on a shroud? At the end of the day they all want five–ten minutes of your attention. You may laugh, but you must listen. Meter ads were ingenious – they've been pretty successful.' Advertising on London parking meters, in fact, was considered effective enough to attract 500 advertisers (paying out around £1 million) in its first two years, including names like Coca-Cola, British Telecom, and Imperial Tobacco.

As with all media, research is called into action to provide 'scientific' statistics about audiences and results: clients putting their ads on supermarket trolleys via TrolleyAds were told they gained an audience of 88 per cent of the country's housewives who each received 52.98 exposures of each ad at a cost for a four-week period of £99,192 (or 0.12p per thousand gross such opportunities to see, as they have it in advertising jargon). Kellogg's boosted sales of corn flakes by 17 per cent by advertising on a million milk bottles.

Even advertising men are frequently amazed by the intrusion people are prepared to accept without protest. People do rebel – loud speakers ads at Grand Central Station were stopped after a campaign led by

Harold Ross, the editor of the *New Yorker*. But mostly they mutter and acquiesce, although the recent history of outdoor advertising – the oldest of the advertising media – is a struggle between the advertisers and those trying to control or legislate against billboard blight. Governor Pat Brown of California, scene of some of the most glaringly intrusive boards, said, 'When a man throws an empty cigarette packet from an automobile, he is liable to a fine of $50. When a man throws a billboard across a view, he is richly rewarded.' A view answered by the head of one American billboard company who opined, 'There are times when most people would rather look at posters than scenery.' Advertising men love them. Because outdoor boards usually represent a low proportion of an advertiser's budget, the creative men are likely to be allowed their heads. In doing so, they can argue that a poster has got to *grab* immediate attention. The result is boards pierced with real cars; giant models of inflated dogs; a huge Incredible Hulk lurching through a TV screen . . . A London agency, FCO, promoted Araldite adhesive by sticking a car to a billboard with the words, 'It also sticks handles to teapots.' Billboards utilise moving discs to reflect light and provide the illusion of motion. A new generation of huge video billboards, costing $1.5 million each, loom high. The United States has about 500,000 outdoor boards, Britain a surprising 170,000. Where signs don't exist, 'rolling boards' – boards attached to the side of tractor trailers – fill the gap.

A frustrated sculptor, Robert Keith Vicino, has created a new outdoor form that almost justifies his boast that he turns outdoor promotion into art. Vicino, who trades under the name Robert Keith, produces huge inflated replicas of products and characters. There are twenty and thirty-foot-high Pepsi bottles, Campbells soup cans, cigarette packs, even a five-storey tall Budweiser six-pack that Anheuser-Busch uses as an auditorium. In true inventor fashion, Vicino produced his first in his living room – a thirty-foot-high Windsor Canadian whiskey bottle. Today he has over 150 major clients for his San Diego company, including McDonald's, American Tobacco, and many of the 'name' hard and soft drink manufacturers. What he set out to do, he explained, was 'make the medium the message. I didn't want some kid to say, "Hey, Mommy, look at the big balloon." I wanted him to say, "Hey, Mommy, look at the big can of Coke."'

However, print and television remain the main media, and of all the ways of selling a product or a person or an idea television stands supreme.

The facts about television are awesome. By the 1980s seven out of ten Americans had never known a world without television. Television had become an essential of the developed world and increasingly one of the developing – in India the number of sets rose tenfold between 1975 and 1985. An American survey showed that 72 per cent of Americans over seventeen watched television daily. It has been estimated that by the time Americans leave school each will have watched, on average, 15,000 to 18,000 hours of television, as against the 11,000 hours he or she will have spent in school. During that time the young American will have been subjected to 350,000 commercials.

In 1987, the average person in the UK watched TV for over six hours a day in the winter and more than four and a half in the summer. On television even the 'small' audiences are huge by other standards. One show that ranked near the bottom of the American Nielsen charts with a rating (10.8) that was described by media men as 'lousy', was watched by 18 million people. Ron Kaatz, director of media concepts at J. Walter Thompson, New York, pointed out that this was as many people as had watched *A Chorus Line* (the longest running show in Broadway history) all over the world on stage in ten years.

Of all advertising media, it is television that is subject to the greatest change of all. Once, watching TV meant switching on network television or the one or two government-provided national stations. Today, increasingly, the viewer has access to what has been dubbed AOT – All Other Television. He can tune to programmes provided by cable or even beamed direct by satellite, call up pages of text, or slip a cassette into his video recorder and watch that.

By the mid 1980s video at home was rivalling broadcast TV, cable and the movies as America's preferred entertainment medium. By 1985 one in every three American homes with a TV set also had a VCR, and the number was soaring. This was low compared with some countries, however – in Britain the figure was 45 per cent, in Japan 60 per cent, and in the United Arab Emirates a staggering 83 per cent.

The video recorder brought its own very special problem – viewers in countries as far apart as the US and Australia found they could record programmes and then zap the commercials. (Or they could even allow increasingly sophisticated technology to do the job for them – a $399 device launched onto the US market automatically sensed and obliterated commercials during the recording process.)

The real impact, however, was that in all countries the traditional providers of television have seen their supremacy undermined. What is startling is how quickly it has happened. US commercial television became a significant advertising medium in 1948 and by 1955, the year commercial TV began in Britain, it dominated the scene. Networking was the driving force of those same networks which had developed national radio, ABC, NBC and CBS. American broadcasting is founded on a system of local stations. Some are independent, but most are affiliated to the national peak-hour programming networks. For years television was a carve-up. Between them the three nets controlled 95 per cent and more of the nation's prime time.

As recently as the first half of the seventies there was virtually no competition. The networks basked in surging ratings and profits. In 1975, two events took place; neither attracted much attention, but they were the triggers that were to change television's world. Home Box Office, Time Inc's new pay TV company, bounced a signal off a satellite 22,300 miles above the earth, thus signalling the way for national cable networks. And Sony introduced into the US the first successful video cassette recorder, meaning that future viewers could record what they liked and then put together their own schedules. Two years later, the networks suffered the first erosions in their share of the total audience. As *Time* magazine commented, though, 'Few network people read these tea leaves; they were too busy sipping champagne.' In 1980 the three networks shared 84 per cent of the amount of viewing at prime time. By the last quarter of 1987 it was 77 per cent. Steve Fajen, of Saatchi's in New York, estimated that by 1990 it would be down to 63 per cent and by 2000 to 50 per cent.

As a system of delivering television, cable nullifies all the limitations of airborne broadcasts. Airborne wavelengths are scarce and rationed internationally. For a country like the UK only a handful are available. With cable, the number of television channels is virtually unlimited. For its part, satellite nullifies distance. The two have gone hand in hand, or – perhaps more accurately – like the two halves of unseparated Siamese twins. The satellites transmit the programmes over distances, and the cable systems distribute them through localities. In the United States, nearly all programmes shown on cable television networks have been received by satellite. In Europe, by 1986, a half-dozen channels were being beamed across countries by satellite and being watched in an estimated 12 million cable-linked homes.

Cable television is not new. The first systems were installed in the UK as long ago as 1950. In both the US and Britain, however, the first cable was designed purely to take signals into remote areas where normal airborne signals were weak. As implied by the name, cable television is transmitted via cables, either buried underground or slung on telegraph poles. In the 1970s, the invention of 'optical fibre' cables meant that an almost unlimited number of channels could be carried to a linked home. These cables are made from very thin glass down which signals can be sent as pulses of light. The real growth of cable network dates from the mid 1970s when satellites began to make 'real time' distribution of programming possible. The impact is most easily seen in the United States where viewers in, say, Manhattan had a choice of thirty-five or more channels by the mid 1980s. Cable viewers could tune to channels carrying Spanish programmes or live broadcasts from the UN, or specialising in finance, health, sports, news, entertainment, or rock videos – or even presenting such oddities as Ugly George, in which the self-named presenter persuaded women to strip in front of his camera. By 1988 an estimated 45 million households – over half of all the households with a television – had access to cable, even if the spread was unevenly weighted to the wealthier suburbs.

In Britain, the early responses to cable were indifferent. In the 1980s, the British government decided to encourage the development of new cable systems. In December 1984, two million people in thirty major towns became able to receive up to nine new additional channels. A little more than a year later there were only around 134,000 cable subscribers. A major reason had to be the fact that British viewers already receive a fairly satisfying diet of programming on their existing TV. And even if they find something lacking, it would be hard to argue persuasively that the extra programming available through other channels at the time of writing is very exciting.

The result was that Britain was way down in the European league of cable subscribers, although some insiders were convinced this was only a temporary phenomenon. Elsewhere, however, the situation was very different. Significantly, viewers in continental Europe were less happy with the quality and variety of their national programmes, thus providing a fertile seedbed. Equally important, in many countries cable – operated like gas or electricity by municipal authorities – was relatively advanced.

By 1987, according to estimates from Saatchi and Saatchi Compton, eight out of ten homes in Belgium were cable subscribers, as were more than half in the Netherlands. In Holland, viewers could get in addition to their two national channels: two Dutch cable networks, four Belgian, several German, British forces, BBC 1 and BBC 2 and trans-Europe satellite stations such as Sky and Music Box. One organisation, CIT Research, estimated that nearly 17 per cent of European homes would be linked to what is known as large cable systems by 1995. (There are two cable systems, large cable – CATV, and small cable – Master Antenna Television or MATV). The latter is that in use in hotels and blocks of flats. In countries like West Germany and Scandinavia, with large numbers of apartment blocks, it provides cable to large numbers of people.

It is satellites that made possible the development of cable networks. The idea dates back to 1945 when, in a now famous article in *Wireless World*, the science fiction writer, Arthur C. Clarke, pointed out that if a satellite could be sent into orbit at a height of 22,000 miles, it would revolve at the same speed as the earth. It would, thus, remain stationary, and properly positioned three such satellites could cover the world.

The first satellite used to beam television signals internationally was Telstar I, launched by the United States in 1962. It went into orbit much lower than Clarke's and was only able to transmit signals between the US and Europe for eighteen minutes during each orbit. The first 'stationary orbit' satellite was the US Early Bird three years later. A month after its launch it was used to show the Cassius Clay v Sonny Liston fight live in Europe.

Used domestically, satellites have allowed countries like the USSR and Canada to have national television. The Soviet Union also uses satellites to transmit programmes to its nationals serving abroad in such countries as Afghanistan. Satellites are owned either by governments (as in Russia), by private companies (such as RCA's satellite on which Home Box Office began leasing space in 1975) or by post and telecommunications ministries, like the two satellites which provided first signals to the UK, which were owned by associations of western PTTs.

Sky, which is part of Rupert Murdoch's international media empire, has gone for programmes that are unashamedly downmarket and entertaining on the assumption that most Europeans are starved of such fare. Much material is also visual – like sport, cartoons and rock – because of the variety of first languages of its audience.

It schedules in what is called 'strip programming'. This is based on the concept that different groups of people are more likely to watch television at specific times each day. Thus it screens pop videos for children late afternoon after school, situation comedies in early evening when the whole family is likely to be gathered together, and sport for men late at night.

Programming is often, to an English or American viewer, decidedly ancient: Starsky and Hutch, the Lucy Show, The Untouchables, Mork and Mindy. Stewart Butterfield, media director of McCann-Erickson, London, has attributed its success to 'the fact that it tends to offer bland programming geared to the lowest common denominator'. Sky Channel publicly rejects such criticisms, of course. Richard Platt, head of programming, argues that the phrase 'lowest common denominator' 'smacks of the Old English notion that people should be given what's good for them and not what they want. Our philosophy is that the viewer is King. We have a mission to entertain.'

Although most satellite programmes are dependent on cable for their distribution, it was possible by the 1980s to receive signals direct. In the United States, by 1985 nearly 2 million homes did so. In the UK, circa 1986, it meant having a dish 1.8 metres wide, facing about twenty-seven degrees south, embedded in three 150-pound concrete blocks for stability, and having an unobstructed view of the sky!

All that, however, began to change in the late 1980s with the advent of DBS – Direct Broadcasting by Satellite. Signals from a DBS need only a 50 cm diameter dish (about the size of a fruit bowl) because its transmitters are much more powerful. The crucial turning point came late 1987 with the launch of the first European direct broadcast satellite TV-Sat, described as 'the pioneer for extra-terrestrial broadcasting'. Other satellites – from Luxembourg, France, Scandinavia and the UK – were due to follow within two years. In Britain 1989 was heralded as the first year of this 'new era' in broadcasting. Murdoch, with four satellite-beamed channels on offer, was predicting that by 1992 over 6 million British homes would be receiving such programmes. Forecasters talked of a leap from 1988's total of four UK channels to forty or fifty and of 40 million homes in Europe with receivers by 1990.

Michael Tracey, head of British Film Institute's Broadcasting Research Unit, believed that by 2001 DBS would be the most important source of TV programmes. Comsat, an American corporation, has estimated that by that year there will be room for 110 to 142 satellite-delivered channels for each American time zone. One British expert, John Howkins, has estimated there could be 175 channels utilising the 12 giga hertz (12m kilohertz) range. However, wrote Tracey, 'By the late 1990s a whole new part of the direct broadcast spectrum will have been opened up in the 22.5 to 23 ghz range which could provide another 150 to 300 channels. 2001 may also see the advent of laser-driven, light-wave satellite communications with footprints, the area covered by the beam, no larger than a city block . . . By 2001, satellites will have established themselves as the cheapest, most efficient, most easily maintained way of delivering signals to homes.' Others were estimating that by the 1990s Europe could have a choice of 144 TV channels. 'We may need our home computers to help us programme the evening's viewing,' delegates were told at a congress in Rome.

What's important about all this cable and satellite in the context of advertising is that its growth increases the strength of the advertiser.

It does this in a number of ways. The first, and the most obvious, is that someone has to pay for the programmes. Much of the time it is the advertiser. Of the thirteen channels broadcasting in mid 1985 to head-end cable systems in Europe, eight were accepting advertising or sponsorship. Of twelve channels on the way, ten had said they would do so.

Furthermore, for international advertisers there was the reality of true trans-national advertising, even if it was in its infancy. International agencies looked at prospects and liked what they saw. Jeremy Bullmore, chairman of J. Walter Thompson in London, enthused in a speech, 'For the first time it would seem, we can fulfil the multinational's corporate dream: to establish at a signal moment in time, eyeball-to-eyeball interface with the man in the street on a global scale. What power, what savings, what consistency; what an opportunity!'

Compared with national TV advertising, the amount being spent on satellite was still very small, but the advertisers were the powerful multinational companies – Coke, Levi, British Airways, Canon. The European advertising magazine *Focus* began enthusing that satellite 'provides advertisers with a massive cross-cultural audience which already dwarfs many of Europe's national markets . . . Advertisers see the beginnings of a common "supra culture" emerging across Europe, reflected in the commercials and the programmes now broadcast by satellite TV.'

Much the most striking benefit for advertisers, though, has been that the growth of the new media has put crucial pressure on the old. As at the mid eighties, television advertising in Europe was available in any real sense only in the UK, Luxembourg, Italy, Spain and Portugal. The result, it was claimed, was frustrated advertisers forced to divert money elsewhere (mainly into newspapers and magazines). As the satellite channels began mopping up some of that money, national broadcast systems began to cast envious glances. By the second half of the 1980s the effect was clearly visible. State-owned national broadcast systems were being 'stimulated' into making more advertising time available.

Sweden, by 1987 one of the rare countries holding out against any television advertising, provides an example of what has been happening. Due to cable and satellite, Swedes were able to watch Sky Channel, Superchannel and Screen Sport, three advertiser-supported satellite channels from the UK, as well as programmes from France. Some could also watch Ted Turner's American Cable News Network.

The Swedish authorities have been forced to adopt a pragmatic approach. The director of the Swedish Cable TV Authority said, 'We allow international advertising on the satellite channels as long as it isn't directed specifically at Swedish consumers. But the law says that if a Swedish company buys commercial airtime on Sky Channel, for example, to appeal directly to Swedish viewers, then we shall have to ban that satellite channel from being distributed through the cable networks.'* Or, as one advertising man commented, 'It's all right to say "Drink more Pepsi", but not "Swedes, drink more Pepsi".'

By 1987 many observers thought advertising on the two national networks was only a matter of time. Charles Dawson, director of Horizons Media International, commented, 'Sweden's two ad-free TV networks face mounting costs, and the money has to come from somewhere. Swedish advertisers increasingly seem to be the only logical source, and the authorities are reluctant to sit idly by while Sky and Superchannel siphon off revenue which could be staying in Sweden.'

Throughout Europe, state-dominated TV in the eighties was under siege from its commercial brother. The advertising magazine *Focus* was in no doubt who was winning: 'Commercial TV is emerging triumphant. Its opponents are in the process of being vanquished on all sides. And what the future holds is a Europe in which TV is a continent-wide advertising medium, offering untold opportunities for its marketers.' Instances of the 'slow, but sure, shift towards the new TV advertising era' were coming from all over Europe. More advertising time had recently been made available in France, Germany and the Netherlands. Generic advertising had been permitted on Belgium's French channels, Norway had been experimenting with TV ads on Saturday nights. In Britain, long regarded as the model of independent public broadcasting, agencies pressed for advertising on the BBC. The Peacock Committee was appointed by the government and in 1986 recommended against the idea, reportedly to the chagrin of the Prime Minister, Margaret Thatcher. The committee pinned its hope for future television funding on pay-to-view subscriber methods.

What the advertisers see in more commercial television is not just

---

* With DBS even that unpopular option won't be available – satellite signals are hard to jam, as the Soviet Union has found.

more time in which to sell their wares, but a prospect of a shift in power. Too often, advertisers believe, traditional media uses a monopoly position to enforce unfair conditions – and to impose ludicrously high charges.

Antagonism is not new. In 1930, the book *Is Advertising Today a Burden or – a Boon? A discussion* was a 154-page attack by advertising on the press. 'It is no exaggeration to say that publishers treat advertisers in a way they would not dare treat their own compositors,' complained the foreword. One section thundered, 'An advertiser is compelled to "buy" his place in the market at an amazingly high price. No wonder so many of them can't "keep it up" when they find the pace so fast. Nowadays sums like £5,000 and £10,000 are less than a mere bagatelle in the buying of newspaper space for anything like a worth-while campaign directed even to winning a foothold in the market.'

Over fifty years later the sums were different, but the complaint was still cost. In New York, a media director juggled with his rate cards to explain to me why, if I were an advertiser, I wouldn't be able to get 'too much exposure' for $10 million. There, according to one agency's calculations, the cost of a TV commercial had soared 230 per cent in 12 years.* In the UK, too, the *real* cost of buying media has soared. In 1988, ten minutes of UK airtime cost roughly £4 million. To justify that money, a brand needed to sell anything from £75–£200 millions depending on the specific product and the amount of competition, according to Tony Stead, a director of J. Walter Thompson.

Advertisers unwilling to buy network TV time could, of course, shift some of their money to magazines, radio, or independent stations, and some did. However, scream as they might, network TV was where most of them needed to be, even with its declining share of the audiences. They had no doubt that media monopoly was the reason why costs were soaring. In Britain, for example, television contractors hold different regions of the country under government franchise. None of them, except in London, where there are separate contractors for weekday and weekend programmes, has any competition.

If, as seems likely, more advertising time does lead eventually to cheaper advertising, there will certainly be changes in the type of commercials seen, particularly in the UK and Europe. At present, because cost is so high, television advertising there is largely a rich man's way of selling. Rich men can also afford to put up large sums to produce commercials. This has always been less true in the United States where much of the advertising that so repels visitors is *local* television advertising – arm-waving car salesmen, crude come-ons from retail stores.

* As an example, a thirty-second spot of *Moonlighting* in the 1987-8 season cost around $249,000; the average cost for a prime-time spot in October 1987 was $121,860, 8 per cent more than a year before.

What a future with more available, cheaper advertising time means is more cheaply-made commercials. In one sense, it is to be hailed – it democratises advertising. However, it may not be pleasing to watch. If British commercials on the whole are more 'creative', less offensive, more entertaining than America's, the major reason is probably not that the practitioners are better but that the medium is more élitist.

Many advertisers would not deny that advertising can be irritating – but they would argue that the alternative is far worse for the media and its readers and viewers. Their argument, which on the surface can be persuasive, is that advertisers equal freedom. The claim is that, in the main, revenue cannot be drawn exclusively from subscribers (because they would be unwilling to pay the amounts involved) and, therefore, the alternative is direct subsidies from governments who will demand their pound of flesh in return.

A paper by J. Walter Thompson, published as part of a series extolling the role of advertising in society, looked back to the tax the British government imposed on all advertisements at the beginning of the eighteenth century:

> The tax was directed not against advertisers as such but against the press, which had become, in political terms, inconveniently popular and independent . . . At that time, five of London's nine daily newspapers were primarily advertising sheets. Most of these quickly succumbed to the tax. The survivors, in their economically weakened state, were forced to accept subsidies, or more accurately bribes, from political factions in return for conformity or support. Before long, some papers, including *The Times*, were receiving a regular allowance from the government itself.

And to reinforce its point, it went on to quote Francis Williams, the press historian: 'Only through the growth of advertising did the press achieve independence.'

It is further argued that advertisers, unlike governments and political parties, are rarely concerned about editorial policies, and in any event interests of one advertiser counterbalance those of another. Many go further. Not only do advertisers keep the media 'free', but they also ensure that the end product is democratic in content. Thus Gary Davey, head of television services for Sky Channel, argues, 'The economics of modern commercial television instil a discipline that represents the ultimate in media democracy. If the viewer does not like what we offer, we go broke . . . The TV viewer casts a vote every day at the touch of a button. The viewer's the customer and yes, dammit, he's always right!'

The advertising industry paints a bleak picture of a world without advertising, not least as far as the media is concerned. Harold Lind, an economist, wrote:

The effect on media would be devastating. Nearly all quality national newspapers and most regional newspapers would become economically unviable. A continuation of the present level of television programmes would require a licence fee increase of some 60 to 70 per cent. Those media which survived would be more expensive and much less comprehensive, and any government subsidy to overcome those losses would, in economic terms, count as a real cost on the community in a way which media's income from advertisers does not, because the payment from advertisers is not a subsidy, but a method of improving their efficiency . . . Besides the general loss of efficiency in business and the loss of media, the general public would also be cut off from a variety of information, from entertainment guides to job opportunities, which are useful to them.

Harold Fellows, the president of the US National Association of Radio and Television Broadcasters, speaking in the late fifties, gave his forecast of what would happen if advertising stopped suddenly. There would be the closure of 2,700 radio stations and over 400 TV stations; the bankruptcy of many newspapers and journals, with a reduction in size and a doubling in price of most others; a spread of unemployment moving out to embrace all manufacturing and transport; the collapse of the Stock Exchange; and steeply rising prices. It would reduce the United States to 'a shambles faster than a thousand atom or hydrogen bombs'.

None of the advertisers' claims should obscure one paramount fact, however: as holders of the purse strings, they are holders of power. What they have, as we have noted before is that 'power to *prevail* – prevail in our magazines, newspapers; prevail in our radio and television programs; prevail on the shelves, and in the store windows; ultimately, prevail in our priorities'.

At a New York conference of advertising men, one of them openly made a rare admission. Advertisers and their agencies were much to blame for the woes and the failures of hard-pressed media, said John Reidy, of Drexel Burnham Lambert: 'Agencies want to go with the winning media.'

Advertisers can – and do – of course, advertise where they believe they will reach the best mix of potential product buyers at the best price. But what Reidy was conceding, albeit to other advertising men, was that because of advertising vast numbers of newspapers have been forced to close. It is true that there have been other factors, not least Luddite labour unions and poor management. But what advertising has done is selectively to wipe out the competing newspaper in each town and city. Ironically, as a group, neither advertisers nor agencies want media monopolies, but that is what results as a consequence of neither group backing losers. And in this context 'loser' means all but the leader. Advertising budgets have no place for second runners.

Because of this, mass advertising has been, to use the words of Professor Ben Bagdikian, the noted American media observer, 'deadly and inexorable'. There are no longer towns in the UK where local daily newspapers compete for readers and advertising; the best mix is a morning paper and an evening paper, invariably owned by the same company. Ninety-eight per cent of US cities are in the same situation. Professor Bagdikian has detailed one example of how it happened. Until the 1970s Washington DC had three newspapers, the *Washington Post*, the Washington *Star*, and the Washington *Daily News*. In 1970, the circulations were respectively 500,000, 300,000 and 200,000 and the advertising rates for an equivalent amount of space were $16,676, $12,634 and $9,676. Calculated in cost per thousand – the amount it costs to reach 1,000 readers – the *Post*'s (higher) initial rate worked out at 3.34 cents per household and the *News* 4.84 cents per household. It requires no media buying skill to see which of the two provides a better buy. More advertising money, therefore, went into the *Post*. This sets off a spiral. More revenue means a newspaper can spend more on editorial and on sales-people to sell more ads. The winning paper widens its lead even more. The result was that the *Daily News* died in 1972, the *Star* followed in 1981.

It could be argued that the advertisers, though saving money initially, were being short-sighted. A monopoly newspaper gives advertisers one choice – take it or leave it. Professor Bagdikian points out that two years after the *Star* folded, the *Post* increased its advertising rate by 58 per cent: 'For the winner, victory is sweet. But there is only one survivor.' Rupert Murdoch, who tends to know about such things, said that running a monopoly newspaper was a 'licence to steal money forever'. Today with their monopolies, newspapers constitute one of the most profitable businesses in America.

Given that the economics of newspapers are now based firmly on advertising not subscription, it also follows that a publication with readers that aren't attractive to advertisers has very real problems. The best known example in Britain is that of the *Daily Herald* which died in the 1960s. It still had a circulation of nearly 1.5 million – three times the size of the triumphant *Washington Post*, it might be noted. But its readers were precisely the mix that advertisers do NOT want – male, ageing, and belonging to the lower socio-economic groups C2 and DE. In other words, though they might want to go on buying the *Daily Herald*, they were unlikely to buy anything they saw advertised in its pages. When the *Herald* closed it was being read by over twice as many people as the *Guardian*, *The Times* and the *Financial Times* (all papers, though, with precisely the adman's kind of readers).

It is not the individual advertisers who can be blamed. It is the system. What has happened is an inevitable result of an ad-dominated newspaper industry. The newspapers, however have hardly been passive figures in their dealings with advertisers. Advertisers have been taken more into account in devising the finished newspaper. Today's newspaper publishers and executives have come a long way from Northcliffe and his messages to *The Times* and the *Daily Mail*.

When, in 1986, Britain's first national 'new technology' daily newspaper *Today* was launched, it was widely believed in both the newspaper and advertising business that the first front page was determined not by the editor but by the media director of the paper's advertising agency, Wight Collins Rutherford and Scott. (Not, it might be added, that it did the paper much good. It was soon struggling for its life). Any new newspaper – or any established one contemplating a change of direction – routinely brings in the advertising agency for advice at an early stage.

This is not the same as the claim, sometimes made, that newspapers knuckle in to individual advertisers. From time to time minor scandals have arisen when an individual advertiser has attempted to influence a newspaper's policies. Sometimes, reasons verge on the eccentric. In October 1959, the managing director of Sutherland's Paste withdrew advertising from Granada TV because the company did not play the National Anthem at the end of the evening's transmissions. Twenty-three years later the grocery chain Sainsbury's withdrew its advertising from the *Sun* and the *Daily Star* for a week in protest against the newspapers carrying 'snatched' pictures of Charles and Diana frolicking in the surf on holiday, pictures said to have made the Queen angry. Car advertisers refused to advertise in the Zürich daily *Tages Anzeiger* after an editorial charged that cars were the major source of pollution in the country.

G. K. Chesterton complained many years ago:

Twice in my time, I have attempted to write to an excellent country paper, certainly among the more honourable papers, an article showing that the big shops and stores . . . are not anything like so convenient and satisfactory as the small shops that used to exist in old London, and do still exist in inland towns and villages . . . On both these occasions and in varying degrees of irony the same editor of this excellent paper has written back to say he cannot publish an attack upon the big shops because 'we would lose the advertisement'.

Such attempts by advertisers to exert direct pressure may still work; one suspects that most of them do not, even if advertisers are naïve enough to try. As a newspaperman for two decades, my experience is that major papers are good at resisting direct approaches.* Advertiser pressure, though, even on many of the biggest and best of our newspapers and magazines is real. It is simply more insidious.

* Although it is also my experience that newspapers are then more cautious in their future reporting.

Whole sections of newspapers now consist of what has been dubbed 'revenue related reading matter'. Increasingly newspapers have created special sections to cover such subjects as fashion, food, property, computers, travel, primarily as bait to the advertisers. This does not mean that they are not read, although the percentage of a paper's total audience reading the section may be small. But the driving force is the advertising. The areas have been chosen because they are ones of high advertiser activity.

More important, perhaps, is the editorial material that fills the spaces between the ads in these sections. In the words of one advertisement manager, it is designed to be 'sympathetic'. Some, undeniably, is genuinely useful. Much, however, is a mix of syndicated articles and of rephrased press releases from the suppliers of the products in the ads.

An American study, by the Housing Research Group of the Center for Responsive Law, found 'Articles that appear as "news" (in property sections) frequently are promotional pieces for developers, real estate agents or industry associations.' The same could well be said of the property sections of the vast majority of English national and local newspapers. Further, another survey showed that 94 per cent of food editors used food company releases for recipes.

Professor Bagdikian points out that the advertising department of the *Houston Chronicle* provides all the 'news' for home, townhouse, apartments, travel, technology, livestock and swimming pools. The vice-president of sales and marketing said, 'We do nothing controversial. We're not in the investigative business. Our only concern is giving additional editorial support to our ad projects.'

It is salutary to work carefully through the articles in a special section, noting where the material originated. Chances are that the piece on makeup or on hair care came from a company that makes cosmetics or shampoos, that the recipes come courtesy of the promoters of butter or milk, that the advice on what food to serve at a party is from someone who is pushing bread or canned fish, that the piece on what to look for in a house improvement comes from a builders' organisation. As for the business pages of any newspaper – even the most prestigious ones – many columns would be blank if they removed the articles that emanated from public relations companies pushing clients. This applies especially on those days of the week when the papers concentrate on 'personal finance', and when editorial is surrounded by ads for insurance, unit trusts, mortgages and various other investment schemes.

Revenue Related Reading Matter – or 'fluff' as Professor Bagdikian calls it – can be seen at its most extreme in the ever-growing number of free newspapers and magazines. A very quick glance through one reveals in addition to the obvious product-linked advice features a prominent 'news story' on what to do if you are unhappy with the quality of dry-cleaning, full of reassuring quotes from local companies, and an article that argues the advantages of having your home repainted more often – detail courtesy of the Paintmakers' Association.

Free newspapers have had a large impact on the whole industry. They began in the United States and spread to the UK in the second half of the sixties. Their great advantage to the advertiser is that as they are delivered door to door, they give him total coverage in a locality. They boomed on a plethora of classified advertising that the paid-for papers were proving unable to handle. They also, one publisher argued with me, arrived at a time when people were becoming more divorced from traditional local newspapers. People, more mobile, identified less with a particular locality, and no longer wanted the old-style local news with its coverage of courts and council affairs.

If that is true, free newspapers have certainly given readers what they want. In those that contain editorial, 'news' relies heavily on 'fluff' and uncritical announcements whether it is about restaurants or films. It just so happens, too, that this kind of editorial material is the cheapest to supply – a free newspaper can literally be put together by a man and a boy. Those 'outdated' news items that people do not want call for larger staffs and expensive commitments.

The free-paper market is huge. The United States has over 3,000 of them. In Britain, there were almost 950 by 1988, compared with less than 200 no more than a dozen years before. In 1984, free newspapers in the UK took in more advertising revenue than paid-for papers for the first time. In addition there were over 400 free magazines with a total 'circulation' of 49 million copies. Some were delivered door to door but others were handed out at stations, by cab drivers, or in hotels or planes.

At one level any war being waged between free and paid-for papers is a phoney one: over half the free papers in the UK are produced by paid-for publishers. The war, however, *is* a real one in that one side provides a real threat to the other. In Britain, paid-for papers are converted into free ones; in the US, the free pose an increasingly serious threat to local dailies. However much the free papers improve themselves by increasing editorial content, at the end of the day they are handmaidens of the advertising men, and 'sympathetic' editorial is an essential part of the product.

Newspaper advertising departments, not surprisingly, are keen to take ads. Each paper does have advertisements that it will not take – either because they're precluded by law or codes of practice, or more rarely because they err against the newspaper's own standards. 'Taste' is usually the stopper here. The *Daily Mail* refused to show the back view of a nude man (in an ad for Burton's Menswear) unless he was given a pair of underpants; the *Reader's Digest* stipulated it would only run a picture of a boy (back view shown) peeing into the sea if it were retouched (prompting one wag to say that it proved 'you can take the piss out of your own ads'). Some newspapers won't accept ads for rivals – *The Times* and the *Daily Telegraph* refused to carry a notice from the *Financial Times* explaining its side of a dispute with printers; the *Mail* and the *Telegraph* would not take an advertisement for Thames Television on the grounds that it might damage their business. Women's magazines sometimes crack down on what they see as sexist advertising: *Woman's Own* refused one for Aquasun showing two naked girls lying in the water. Television stations in the United States have refused to show South African Tourist Board commercials. Less politically, some American stations turned down an advertisement for the film, *The Secret Policeman's Other Ball*. The commercial began with Graham Chapman sitting at a desk with the American flag hanging behind him. 'I'm from the Oral Majority. I wish to complain strongly about this disgusting new comedy movie *The Secret Policeman's Other Ball*. It is easily the most depraved, foul, filthy, lewd, rotten, tasteless movie since *The Sound of Music*. This movie must be banned before it turns us all into a nation of perverts.' The Monty Python star then stood to reveal that below his grey suit jacket he wore a pink ballet tu-tu, black fishnet stockings and a suspender belt.

In the main, though, the internal pressure is to accept advertisements. In practice, it can mean that products or services that readers are being warned off on the editorial pages are wooing the same readers in the ads.

It is not a new situation. The authors of a book in 1915 said

> We have seen in New York City papers advertisements of the sale of stock by promoters who were afterwards pictured on the first page of the same papers as on trial for their criminal actions . . . It has long been known and must be recognised by the newspaper publishers themselves, that most newspapers have taken practically any advertising which came along without much attempt to investigate. Were this practice confined to the country weeklies of doubtful value, it might be easily taken care of, but it obtains with some of the largest newspapers in the country and there is apparently neither a tendency nor a desire materially to change their attitude.

The abuses, though less obvious, are not all of the past. In 1983, *Advertising Age* was complaining that 'for "back of the book" advertisers – even in respectable media – almost anything goes'. Most newspapers and magazines felt a reasonable amount of pride about keeping their ad columns clean. 'But somehow or other they find it painfully difficult to say no when an order comes over the transom.'

The following year, the magazine was bemoaning the publishing of ads for medical quack cures. Law enforcement agencies, it said, would continue to be hopelessly outnumbered 'until there are effective mechanisms to keep the quacks from getting their phoney appeals into print and on the air'. The problem wasn't a minor one: unproven cures for chronic diseases were said to make $10 billion a year. 'Quacks flourish in part because media sales executives, quite rightly, don't want to be in the position of judging scientific questions.'

The day I read that editorial I picked up the *New York Post* and flipped some ads there, all given big display treatment. One pill promised, 'you can turn from Fat to Firm while you sleep' with 'amazingly' no dieting and no strenuous exercises . . . Another for Thera Man's Stimulant promised 'extra surge of vitality, extra performance . . . You'll get a charge out of it.' Yet another promised protein and vitamins for the hair on the dubious proposition that they were needed because 'hair grows seven times faster than your body cells'. 'Scientific questions' would hardly seem to come into it.

At the same time in the UK a rash of money-lending ads – most secured on houses – were selling loans with weasel words: 'low monthly repayments', for example. If they were compared with other credit sources they were far from low, but as no comparisons were made they were considered all right. One city journalist took space on the editorial pages to warn his readers 'Beware this advert.'

The situation, as I know from experience, is basically that an ad that is offered is innocent until proved guilty. And that guilt has to be 10,000 per cent certain. I remember, as an investigative journalist, being asked to advise on a new international organisation that wished to advertise for members. After some inquiries, I advised that the organisation was run by naïve but ambitious individuals and that subscribers would certainly lose their money. Under questioning, I agreed, however, that the instigators were not fraudulent, just incapable. 'Ah, that's all right, then,' said the ad manager with relief. The ad was published.*

The influence on magazines has been greater than on newspapers. Professor Bagdikian sees three stages in advertiser influence. First, it reached a point where editors began selecting articles not only on the basis of readers but for their influence on advertisements. Then, in the mid twentieth century, came articles that were specially commissioned to please the advertiser. More recently, in the 1970s, magazines were developed for identifiable special audiences, 'often created solely to carry ads to a target audience'.

The influence of the advertiser is self-evident in almost any consumer, women's interest or special interest magazine that is picked up from the bookstall. 'We considered the needs of advertisers and agencies when we designed *Chat*,' said the trade ad for a new mass circulation weekly for women in the UK. The specialist magazine, *Marketing Week*, commenting on the colour supplements that form part of many British Sunday newspapers pointed out that there had been a 'move to Identikit publishing' that had been 'accelerated by steadily shifting advertising

---

* The organisation failed.

to editorial ratio and management demands for glamour'. Trevor Grove, editor of one of the magazines, that of the *Observer*, was quoted as saying, 'A lot of the staff of colour magazines come under considerable pressure to bear the prejudices of advertisers in mind as well as what they see as suitable material. At least two out of the four covers we do would generally be considered glamorous but we also did a cover on a Lebanese soldier in Beirut – considered not glamorous enough by our advertising department. The advertising department has been able to call the tune more than it should because of economic pressures.' Two years later Grove was replaced, reputedly because the product he was producing wasn't glamorous enough for those advertisers.

Perhaps the most obvious sign of advertiser impact comes in the 'special sections' and advertorials. Special sections and supplements usually contain material prepared by a magazine's staff or by freelances; ads are then sold against those features which, theoretically at least, are not directly influenced by the advertisers. Advertorials are sections in which advertisers buy the editorial content too.

The borderline can be hazy. The London *Observer* has produced separate magazines such as 'Technology Extra' and 'Travel Extra' and 'Photography Extra' as well as ones on Zambia and on trade with China. The *Sunday Times* has published 'House and Home' (in association with the Halifax Building Society), 'Holiday Plus' (with Pickfords travel agency) and 'Road and Car' (with the RAC). One writer to *Campaign* complained of the 'new tendency to disguise advertising as editorial'. Of the holiday supplement, he commented that it was 'nothing more than a puff for Pickfords. Even an article on sunburn gets in a Pickfords subsidiary while the "Holiday Questions and Answers" is pure Pickfords publicity. My complaint is against the *Sunday Times*, not Pickfords which has brought off a substantial coup. The ultimate loser is the reader, who now finds it difficult to distinguish between advertising and paid-for editorial.'

Time has its special sections on subjects from football to duty-free goods (though it does carefully label them 'A TIME special *advertising* section') as does *Business Week*. They are large money earners. The *New York Times* (which carefully labels its sections as Advertising) took in over $14 million from advertorials in 1983.

Some of the world's most prestigious publications have come to depend on regular special sections and advertorials on foreign countries – apparently widely regarded as 'the pits' by some of those involved in the business. Thus, for example, the *Telegraph* magazine carried an eighteen-page 'special edition' on Hong Kong and Singapore, replete with ads from such as the Hong Kong Police, travel agencies and airlines, the Hong Kong Development Council and the Hong Kong Government Industrial Promotion Office. The question to be asked, not just of this particular example but of all such, is: how objective can editorials be if you are not to alienate the agencies from whom you will be soliciting more ads for the next supplement? In what must be one of the most bizarre examples of a special supplement being forced to take account of realities, the *Financial Times* ran one on the Lebanon at a time when papers were full of the massacre of Druze villagers. The supplement was headed 'Crisis in the Lebanon' but was suitably stuffed with ads from such as the Beirut Riyadh Bank.

Advertisers and agencies like supplements and advertorials. Robert O'Donnell, head of a company that produces business advertorials in the US, said, 'They're attractive because they look like news. No law says advertising has to look like advertising.' Peter Verbeck, executive creative director at Ogilvy and Mather, said, 'People are five times more likely to read editorial than ads. So the idea of advertorials is probably a pretty good one.'

Condé Nast are masters of the advertorial. Freddie Beech, UK group advertising director, pioneered them in *Vogue* and in *House and Garden*, and in 1983 he described to *Campaign* how he developed them:

> We gradually built up what we called a promotion department which was like an advertising agency in the sense that it has its own art room, its own copywriters and executives who do the advertising . . . The whole idea was to create something that wasn't run of the mill. We bring two or three companies together, like a fashion house, a beauty house and a jeweller and wrap them all up into one package. The object is to think up the ideas, sell them, bring the people together, create the pages and get the retailers to merchandise. We have a considerable department and a very great volume of this business and it is exclusive to our magazines. We don't allow the pages to appear elsewhere. They're created for our magazines, they are in the spirit and have the same copywriting as the magazines and we tie the power of the title to the High Street. We do windows, we sell hundreds of thousands of shelfcards which say 'as seen in *Vogue* or *House and Garden*' and you see them everywhere. But the reason why the ad volume in our magazines is bigger than it is in other magazines is because all these promotion pages are extra and no one else gets them. I don't like to boast, but we are experts at this kind of thing. We use all the top photographers, the top models, the finest of interior decorators.

Beech estimated that as much as 15 per cent of the two magazines' advertising revenues came from the advertorials.

There is little doubt that providing editorial themes that advertisers like does bring in the advertising revenue. *Esquire*, the American men's magazine, is a case in point. It was first published in 1933; Hemingway's *The Snows of Kilimanjaro* and Fitzgerald's *The Crack-Up* were first published in its pages. By the seventies, it was losing money. By the eighties, it was back in profit. It did it by shifting its emphasis to 'service' journalism, running themed editorial issues on such subjects as fashion, fitness, and travel. *Advertising Age* commented, 'The themes have helped *Esquire* dramatically boost ad pages, particularly to attract marketers whose messages match the themes of a particular issue. While some have criticised the approach, contending it is more like marketing a magazine than editing it, others believe it to be a key ingredient in keeping *Esquire* afloat.'

Increasingly 'service' journalism is what magazines are about. James Autry, general manager of the Meredith Publishing Group, publishers of *Better Homes and Gardens* and *Metropolitan Home*, defends such journalism with a crusading fervour:

> Picture if you will this image – the hard driving, soft spoken but aggressive young man walking the streets in rumpled, threadbare clothes and rundown shoes, ferreting out corruption in high places. Romantic – but it is largely a contrivance of the entertainment media. I say largely because there are quite a few of these dedicated news people still alive and well in our profession. Woodward and Bernstein and other reporters of the Watergate mess proved that – and I thank God for those guys. But few of us are involved in that type of journalism . . . which does *not* mean we are involved in a less important or less ethical journalism. Indeed we are in a field of professional journalism that is becoming more vital every day – let's call it *service* journalism . . .
>
> Service journalism [Autry later says rather grandly] is journalism that goes beyond the delivery of pure information, to include the expectation that the reader will *do* something as a result of the reading. In some cases, that means making something that will somehow enhance the reader's life; it could be using a product to better advantage; or trying a different approach in the rearing of children or in the day to day relationship with the spouse; it could be trying harder on the job because of a new pride gained or a new understanding felt; it could be voting more knowledgeably at the next stockholders' meeting or credit union meeting. I could go on, but you get the idea Service journalism is action journalism. *Not because of the terrific award-winning actions of the journalist* – but because of the *action we expect from the reader*. (Autry's emphasis.)

He went on:

> Let's look at the editor's role in dealing with the advertising director, and by extension, with the advertisers. This always seems to give people a lot of hang-ups, but I believe the contemporary editor must involve himself with the advertising department. He does this both to the benefit of the advertiser and of the reader. *I'm not talking about selling advertising*. That's the advertising department's problem. And

I *am not* talking about the rather unworthy practice of *pre-selling editorial or pre-announcing editorial articles*. I am talking about interpreting to the advertising department the editorial rationale for every article you publish . . . On the rare occasions, make a call with one of their people, to help out with a particular tough account. In that case you simply extend your role as interpreter. Often you would be amazed how much good a simple conversation with the right guy can do for your publication. No giveaways. No whoring. Just a good explanation job.

Autry believes the editor must represent the readers against practices that can work against his benefit. 'That includes pre-selling, the disguising of advertising as editorial material, and the acceptance of advertising which you the editor feel does not fit the goals of your magazine.' The problem is that in many magazines ads *are* pre-sold against editorial, editorial and advertising *is* purposely made indistinguishable, and editorial material is either drawn from advertisers or presents a view of 'truth' as the advertiser would have it. An English journalist, Sandra Barwick, recounted in the *Independent* how she once began an article for a glossy magazine with the words, 'No beauty treatment, however expensive, is as good for the skin as the cheap benefits of a sensible lifestyle: a healthy diet, little alcohol, no smoking and staying out of strong sunshine.' Striking her pen through it, the magazine's assistant editor told her, 'I don't think that the advertisers would like it.'

All this pales beside the co-operation some Italian magazines have given Ragno, an underwear manufacturer. Its advertising agency, Foote Cone and Belding, Milan, arranges to be present at the shooting of the magazine covers. The agency then shoots its Ragno ad, using the same model. The result, as seen by readers, is first an ordinary magazine cover shot. But then on the inside cover there is a near-identical copy – the same model in the same pose as part of the same layout. The difference is that the title of the magazine is replaced by the word 'Ragno' (in the same place, type and size, however) and the model who was clothed on the cover is now in her underwear.

Advertisers may also help determine what does *not* get into magazines. In most general terms, this may be the move away from 'realistic' subjects to more glamorous ones better suited to providing the right ambience for selling. It can also be specific. Coverage of cigarette smoking provides a chilling example.

Ever since cigarette advertising was taken off television in the US and in Britain, tobacco companies have ploughed a disproportionate amount of their advertising millions into print. For some magazines tobacco company income makes the difference between profit and loss, perhaps even of survival or closure. The big question is whether this affects what happens – or doesn't happen – on the editorial pages. Critics of cigarette advertising say it does. The claim is not that the tobacco companies apply direct pressure but that magazines and newspapers tread very warily, toning down or killing stories so as not to antagonise them.

There is a deal of evidence to support that view. The *Wall Street Journal* in an article examining the claims commented, 'A publication that fre-. quently crusaded against smoking could hardly hope to attract tobacco advertising. For cigarette makers – like liquor companies – are among the most pernickety about the editorial environment in which their ads appear. Says the advertising manager at a major Texas daily: "One is a poison and the other causes cancer, so they're very sensitive about it."'

The *Wall Street Journal* pointed out that because cigarettes exist in a perpetually negative environment, tobacco companies take special pains to see that their ads don't call undue attention to that fact. 'They stipulate that cigarette ads can't run near obituaries, for example, or near news stories "antithetical" to smoking or tobacco . . . Until recently Reynolds went even further: Outraging many editors, it asked to be notified in advance if a publication planned to run a negative story about smoking. Reynolds dropped its policy after it received critical scrutiny from the *Columbia Journalism Review* and after this newspaper inquired about it.'

The *Columbia Journalism Review* in an article by R. C. Smith surveyed the coverage of the link between cancer and cigarettes in the leading American national magazines during the period between 1971 and 1978. Smith found a 'striking and disturbing' pattern. He wrote that in magazines which accepted cigarette advertising, 'I was unable to find a single article in seven years of publication, that would have given readers any clear notion of the nature and extent of the medical and social havoc being wreaked by the cigarette-smoking habit.'

Some magazines do ban cigarette ads. The most notable example is the *Reader's Digest*, but there are also the *New Yorker*, *Good Housekeeping*, the porn publication *Hustler* (since publisher Larry Flynt became a born-again Christian) and the *Saturday Evening Post* which introduced its ban in 1984 because it felt ads were 'inconsistent' with the message that the parent organisation, the Benjamin Franklin Literary and Medical Society, was trying to give. However, they are very much the minority. Two studies by the American Council on Science and Health have looked especially at women's magazines.

In a survey, the organisation considered the record of eighteen magazines picked because they normally covered a wide variety of health issues and had large circulations. It concluded that while a third reported the hazards of smoking frequently and accurately, 'The majority confused and obfuscated the facts, or neglected to mention them at all.' The 'good' included *Reader's Digest*, *Good Housekeeping* and *Time*. At the other end of the scale were *Redbook* and *Ms* which between 1970 and 1981 and 1972 and 1981 respectively, had never discussed the subject.

ACSH's comments on five are worth reproducing:

Parade, estimated income from cigarette ads in 1981, $36m (25.4 per cent of all ad income): 'Articles on smoking were few and, when present, almost encouraged the smoking habit.' On one occasion, for example, the magazine, 'Noted that "Jack Nicklaus smokes two packs a day", and that smokers tend to be confident, unemotional people.'

Redbook, $7.5m (16.1 per cent). 'Not a single mention of smoking between 1970 and 1981. Other health topics like breast cancer, VD, stress, hysterectomies, drugs, alcohol and radiation were discussed.'

Ms, $500,000 (14.8 per cent). 'The complete absence of articles on the hazards of smoking is particularly striking in this magazine which covers many other important issues in women's health.'

Mademoiselle, $1m (7.3 per cent). 'Unreliable source of information about the hazards of smoking. Used editorial ploys to de-emphasise smoking, gave misinformation, and excluded smoking from mention in articles on relevant health topics altogether. One of the worst.'

Cosmopolitan, $5.5m (9.4 per cent). 'Although smoking was noted as a risk factor in heart disease, it was never mentioned in preventive health articles or in reference to lung cancer. The ordinary subject of smoking has a hard time competing with such extraordinary topics as dysentery and crushed testicles, which seem part of *Cosmo*'s style of health coverage.'

Individual examples do surface. One involved Paul Maccabee, a young reporter at the *Twin Cities Reader*, Minneapolis. Reporting a press conference on the annual Kool Jazz Festival, he included a list of great jazz men who had died of lung cancer. He was fired the next day. Mark Hopp, the publisher, later conceded that he feared losing the paper's cigarette ads, and the paper's national sales manager wrote to all cigarette advertisers apologising for the story and saying the twenty-six-year-old reporter had been sacked. In another, the name of a freelance writer, Carol Wheeler, was removed from the masthead of a New York magazine called *Savvy* after her review of an anti-smoking book. The editor told the *Wall Street Journal* that she neglected to read the review before it appeared and afterwards was afraid its tone might offend cigarette advertisers. In neither case, it should be noted, was there any pressure from tobacco companies: the publications acted because of what they feared *might* happen.

ACSH cites a third case, involving one of its own staff who was asked by *Harper's Bazaar* for an article called 'Protect your man from cancer'. The author was paid in full, but the article was not used because 'in the words of the editor, "it focused too much on tobacco" and "the magazine is running three full-page, colour ads (for tobacco) this month"'.

The influence of the advertiser on radio today is a different case, stemming from that medium's need to produce endless hours of broadcasting at low cost. Jeremy Tunstall who examined American radio for

his book *Communications Deregulation* (Blackwell, 1986) describes it
as the best example to date of a deregulated mass medium. The number
of stations in the US is now around 10,000 – ten times that of 1946.
More than half of the content is music. At least a fifth of the time is
devoted to advertising. Radio is also the most pervasive source of news.
Tunstall points out, however, that the medium jumbles everything up
so that listeners have difficulty separating music, news, views and
advertising. 'The music and talk tend to be free publicity for rock bands,
authors and other self promoters. The views aired tend to be rabid, the
phone-ins voyeuristic excursions into unstable minds. The news itself is
suspect. What presents itself as news may also be a plug for a particular
company. Even the fast, genuine news is often undiluted mayhem and
murder.'

It is easy to recognise early stages of that situation in Britain's still
closely regulated radio, both commercial and public – again because it
is a cheap way of filling time. It is not just 'plugs' for books and records,
but 'experts' from manufacturers appear endlessly to give seemingly
impartial advice. Thus on a local BBC station a woman guest expert is
advising on pastry-making. We've been told at the beginning that she
comes courtesy of Cookeen, a cooking fat manufactured by Van den
Berghs. The interviewer confesses she is not good at making shortcrust
pastry. 'That's where Cookeen is so good . . . you can use it straight
from the fridge,' interjects the nimble expert. A few seconds later she
launches into a description of what Cookeen is and how it is made and
extols her product as the 'only one' specially made for pastry-making.
It is commercial as editorial, and the justification can only be that the
woman expert delivers by being professional and sounding good and
that her presence costs nothing.

That, however, is by no means an isolated example. By the mid-1980s
about 1,000 hours a year of local radio in the UK were coming from
bodies and groups with a vested interest. One commercial company,
UNS Radio Services, specialises in producing tape 'news stories' for
companies and trade associations – over 500 of them a year. PR divisions
of large companies like Yardley, Birdseye and Sterling Health do the
same thing for their own organisations. The tapes are mailed out to
radio stations. Then, in the words of the *Guardian*, 'Every day their
own sophisticated tape "news stories" are being played on the air by
hard-up local radio stations desperate for cheap editorial material.' The
Guardian reported:

The system is very simple. If you're a company or an organisation
with a product, event or point of view to promote you go to UNS,
who advise you how best to give it a 'news angle'. Then, using an
experienced radio journalist to give the item an authentic feel, your
representative or carefully chosen 'expert' is interviewed along pre-
arranged lines. But, of course, if he/she fluffs his line, or sounds less

than convincing, the interview can be restaged, and later re-edited in your favour. And awkward, probing questions contrary to your point of view will be avoided.

UNS, it reported, claim that they get ten transmissions for every twenty-five tapes sent out. Typical clients include the Abbey National Building Society, with an item on house prices, a Kestrel rally-team driver giving winter driving tips, advice to farmers on improvement grants from the Cement and Concrete Association, and the Chemical Industries Association explaining how healthy food additives are. The article's own comment was that this was 'not what local radio was designed for'.

What is the effect of the advertiser on television?

To viewers, a television network is a galaxy of stars, notes one group of observers: to its managers, on the other hand, the programmes are just 'something they give away'. American television, points out the commentator Russell Davies, 'is not there to inform and educate and entertain, it is there strictly to sell advertising products. That's what it's about.' The majority of Americans accept it as an unchangeable fact of life, much as the British regard the weather or queueing. John O'Toole, chairman of Foote, Cone and Belding, bemoans the fact that the system means television going for 'the lowest common denominator' in order to get the biggest ratings to charge the highest ad rates, but continues, 'Well, we can't change the basic nature of the medium, and we can't turn the clock back thirty years and redirect the course of commercial television and television commercials.'

Americans are so hardened to the advertiser domination of their television that what strikes others as almost unbelievable excesses have long been taken for granted. 'Not one half-second is wasted,' writes one observer. 'The commercials come at furious speed. There is no decorous End of Part One caption between programme and advertisement – too wasteful. There is a sudden jump from Ben Hur into a bowl of crunchies . . . Because they call the tune they hamstring programme structure. They not only force interruptions, but in news and news magazine programmes, for example, they oblige presenters to speak the trailers that hint at the exciting things to come in the next segment; so that programmes often consist of advertisements and trailers and not much programme.* And commercials make the watching of films on television maddening. Towards the denouement the commercials come smashing in increasingly frequently, so that you feel as angry as a baby snatched from the teat. And, suddenly, in a news magazine, an

---

* Ironically perhaps, the advertisers also complain about the 'clutter' of trailers, arguing they try the patience of those watching the commercials. Many advertisers also regard as 'clutter' the credits given at the end of programmes and believe they, too, should be dispensed with, so action leaps straight to ads!

interviewer will turn from the person he is interviewing and say to the camera: "And now a commercial I recently recorded." And there he is, large as life and twice as blatant, selling you Bloppo.' Sid Bernstein, the *Advertising Age* columnist, wrote, 'I'm still the only person, I guess, who objects to station newscasters reading the commercials in between reading news items.'

The insidiousness of the commercials is one thing; the effect on the programmes themselves is another. 'Whenever a country has considered introducing commercial television,' wrote Francis Wheen in *Television*, 'there has always been a powerful lobby to argue that the demands of advertisers will somehow "infect" the programmes and reduce their quality. This lobby has seldom been successful in preventing the arrival of commercial television, but its predictions have often come true.'

There are very few countries that have television with no advertising at all. Even the Soviet Union has allowed it a toehold. One country, Indonesia, banned ads in 1981 to 'encourage development without presenting the picture of goods and services that were out of reach of the majority of viewers'. At the other extreme there are those countries, which include most of Latin America, where television is completely dependent on advertising or sponsorship. Others, such as the UK and Japan, offer a mix of public and commercial. The United States, because it has public television, theoretically falls into this group, although the vast majority of US TV is commercial.

Public Broadcasting, the alternative to the commercial channels in the US, occupies a curious and somewhat uneasy position. It was founded in 1967, and it survives on a mixture of government funding (always inadequate but more so under the Reagan administration), gifts from corporations and foundations, and contributions from viewers. It shows a great deal of British drama and dramatic series. Its 300 or so stations throughout the country supplement the national output with a variety of locally-made programmes. Public Television is a minority channel, but its audience is upscale, precisely the kind of viewers that many big advertisers want – and for that reason Public TV has been an ad industry target. A rigidly circumscribed form of sponsoring is allowed. Companies can 'underwrite' programmes. Messages before or after programmes are allowed to say, for example, 'This programme was made possible by a grant by X Corporation.' Traditionally, the oil companies – seeking prestige advertising – have been the heaviest underwriters, so much so that it became known as the Petroleum Broadcasting Service.

Oil companies not only plough in money for programmes but promote to bring in viewers. Thus Gulf Oil spent $1.7 million a year underwriting 'National Geographic Specials' and a further $2.5 million a season on support ads and promotion. They and other large companies see it as the best way to enhance an image. AT & T has found it worthwhile to put up $10 million a year as half the budget for the MacNeil/Lehrer *News Hour* in return for a mention. These underwriters have opposed lobbying from many companies wanting to open PBS to 'ordinary' advertising. They have included Kraft, Hallmark, Eastern Airlines and J. Walter Thompson and Foote Cone and Belding. One of these argued, 'We believe that limited advertising, which would involve such things as clustering of commercials between programmes, is an effective way to raise more much needed funds for public TV without being a detriment to the character of public broadcasting.'

In 1984, the pro-advertising lobbyists had partial success. The FCC relaxed rules so that underwriters could also give a brief message about their products though without actually trying to sell them. Some advertisers produced messages that seemed almost identical with normal commercials. One public broadcaster tried to explain what was considered all right and what was over the borderline: 'It's perfectly legitimate for United Airlines to identify themselves as the carrier that flies the friendly skies, but they can't promote a special $419 fare to Hawaii.' In 1988 a further blurring of the line with commercial TV occurred. Guidelines were relaxed to allow sponsors to use theme music, corporate mascots and even show some products in motion.

Where the advertiser is king, as on American network TV and in Latin America, the impact on programmes is profound. It affects the actual style; they need to be fast to grip from the first second, stopping people switching over before the first commercial. Because of that it encourages TV that is jerky and sensationalist: in its own jargon, it has to deliver lots of 'Jolts per minute'.

It determines the *length* of programmes. American television is organised into shows of thirty minutes or multiples of that time. There are no 'odd' lengths of programme, such as forty minutes, as in the UK. Thus, every programme has direct time competitors.

Because of the crucial importance of audience size – a one per cent rating point drop in 1987 could cost a loss of about $90 million in advertising revenue – shows, like the ads that pay for them, are pretested.* They are shown to 'representative' audiences who decide whether they live or die. The three networks unveil their programme plans to advertisers before they do so to their own affiliates (each network can own no more than twelve stations but also has about 200 others bound to it by loose contractual agreements). Each May, for example, the networks sell the 'Fall Schedule' to an audience of advertisers. There is a day-long presentation from a network executive,

---

* Measuring audience size is big business. The Nielsen Company, virtually synonymous with US TV audience measuring, had worldwide TV research revenues of $75 million in 1985. Increasingly audiences are measured by 'people meters' a device pioneered by the UK AGB Research. With this, members of each household have buttons assigned to them to push while watching TV. The meter then records what channel was watched by whom and for how long

including trailers, extracts from shows, and appearances by actors and actresses. Each show is 'justified' slot by slot.

The criterion for judging programmes is not just numbers. It is *product-buying* numbers. Programmes, including *Gunsmoke*, *The Virginian*, *The Beverley Hillbillies*, have all in their time been dropped by the networks in spite of good ratings. The audience was the wrong one – too old, too rural, not moneyed enough. The advertisers also want 'safe' programmes. They do not want to alienate potential buyers of their products, which means blandness is in, controversy is out. No network produces a programme without considering the views of advertisers. Major advertisers are usually consulted over prospective shows at an early stage.

As to actual content, advertisers can have strong views. The general advertising manager of Procter and Gamble, America's largest and most powerful advertiser, testified before FCC hearings in 1965 that the company had directives for programmes in which it would advertise. For example, as far as the presentation of business or businessmen was concerned, 'There will be no material on any of our programmes which could in any way further the concept of business as cold, ruthless, and lacking all sentiment or spiritual motivation. If a businessman is cast in the role of villain, it must be made clear that he is not typical but is as much despised by his fellow businessmen as he is by other members of society.'

Today the company insists on previewing all the programmes in which its near 28,000 commercials a year may appear. If P & G then finds anything about the programme objectionable the commercial is withdrawn. The company's attitude to what it likes and doesn't like might be thought to have an indirect, though real, effect on what a lot of people ultimately see.

Robert Goldstein, P & G's vice-president in charge of advertising, chose his words carefully when I raised this with him. 'We are not censors, and cannot be and we are not broadcasters or publishers, but basically we have got two kinds of responsibility in this area.' The first was that 'as people and Corporate citizens we feel a responsibility to associate our products with a context that is suitable for our brands . . . wholesome (in some cases family entertainment) which is not an unwelcome or an offensive guest in the household. We don't claim responsibility for what the station or publisher puts out, but we have to accept the responsibility for it once we're in.' There were several print and programme 'situations' the company would not go into, said Goldstein. If ads were scheduled, the company would pull out. 'There are several reasons I wouldn't want to be associated with something: sex, violence, gratuitous material, filthy material.'

The second reason was that the company chose an environment in order to sell products. It would not, therefore, want to advertise during 'a particularly grisly true story about a highly controversial subject –

something dealing with abortion or the end of the world. Do you really want to see people singing about peanut butter if the next thing you see is a nuclear holocaust?'

Goldstein went on to say he believed that there was also a 'responsibility to make TV a better place. That's the reason why you will find *AD* last night, and *Marco Polo* and several award winning shows. I feel it important to demonstrate that with good family shows you can crack the family audience, that you don't have to have puerile violence.' *AD* and *Marco Polo*, both mini-series, are among 1,000 hours of programmes the company makes each year. In making programmes, he added, Procter's invested a lot of money and took risks: 'If we judged them solely on economic grounds we wouldn't do many of them. The profitability isn't worth the risk.'

He expanded on the kind of programme the company wouldn't associate with: 'a gang war movie, a controversial subject like abortion where you know half the people who see it are going to be mad with you, programmes with excessive sex – girls in T-shirts, breasts bouncing up and down. Incest would be another subject. I am not saying we are Victorian. The story of the holocaust is violent, but we sponsored *The Holocaust*. There, in the context of what it was trying to do, there had to be a lot of violence.'

Other companies have testified to programming concerns. An executive of Whitehall Laboratories, for example, has said that the company demanded from networks that if a scene showed someone committing suicide by taking tablets, 'we would not want this to be on the air'. Holiday Inns refused to pay for a commercial shown during a programme which it considered to be anti-Reagan 'propaganda' even though it had been led to believe it would be 'balanced'. To date British advertisers have had appreciably less influence on programmes, although there are early signs of change. Certainly there's no doubt some advertisers and their agencies would like more. Wilfred Greatorex, the scriptwriter, in a letter to *The Times* told of an event while he was writer-producer of a drama series called *Hine* for ATV. 'As we were recording the first episode I noticed three elegant young men in the studio gallery. I found they came from an advertising agency: their task was to report on the kind of content that might "improve" the programme. I explained that while I was aware that scenes of hanky-panky in a hayrick or the odd bottlefight *might* "improve" the ratings, there was no place for them in *Hine*. Neither would I ever be persuaded to add a cute child or cuddly pet to the cast. I then told the interloping admen to leave. The programme controller backed me up, and I heard no more of the matter.'

The story of the UK commercial breakfast time station TV-AM provides a salutary example. The franchise was won by a consortium led by Peter Jay, the journalist and former ambassador to Washington, noted for his belief that television news should have a 'mission to explain'. Viewers were promised a new style of visual pioneering

journalism. The contract, as handed out by the IBA, was for programmes primarily of news, information and current affairs.

The station began broadcasting in February 1983. Ratings were poor;
the channel was unattractive to advertisers. Within three months Jay
and his co-founders were out. In came straightforward entertainment
led by a puppet called Roland Rat and such fare as recipes and rock
videos.

It was the chairman of an advertising agency, Roger Mavity, who
commented, 'Whatever you think of TV-AM now, it's got precious
little to do with the TV-AM we were promised when the IBA gave it
the contract.' The reason, in fact, why the high-minded IBA didn't
intervene was because it feared that the alternative to letting the station
have its way, and thus attracting advertisers, was that it would close.
But as Mavity added, 'If the IBA has the power to launch TV-AM, it
has the responsibility to keep it on course. It may think that it must let
TV-AM be populist in order to be profitable. But surely the original
idea of TV-AM was that broadcasting could be financially solvent
without being creatively bankrupt. It's a good ambition. If the IBA
stood by it then, why not now?'

Advertisers in their turn have no desire to alienate, which makes
them highly susceptible to concerted lobbying or threats. This then
affects their own attitudes to programming.

Hard-line conservative lobby groups have had their impact. After the
Coalition for Better Television was set up in the United States in 1981
with the backing of fundamentalist Christian churches, a number of
major advertisers rushed to assure the chairman, the Rev. Donald
Wildmon, that they shared his concerns. The organisation called off a
threatened boycott of companies that advertised on programmes it
deemed offensive after several major advertisers gave assurances they
would be more selective in future. One of the companies under pressure,
Procter and Gamble, made a point of announcing that it had withdrawn
about fifty commercials from programmes which the company felt
contained too much sex, violence and bad language.

The following year *Advertising Age* sent a questionnaire to the chief
executive officers of the 100 largest US advertisers. Twenty-eight of
them replied, and all but five said they had reviewed their policy for
buying time and sponsorship within the past year, twelve because of
the Coalition for Better Television and/or the National Coalition on
Television Violence. Eleven of the companies said they bought time on
all types of programmes but screened and reviewed the scripts of any
that were potentially 'offensive'. Three replied that they only bought
time on programmes whose contents would not be questioned.

The Coalition's 'monitoring reports' list 'top sponsors of sex, violence
and profanity'. One I have before me details the top ten 'offenders',
led by the Mennen Company followed by Ciba Geigy. Each company
has a number against it, 20.54 in the case of Mennen. This, the report

explains, represents 'the average number of violent, sex and profanity incidents per commercial unit [thirty-second ad] run'. The report also explains how it defines its terms:

Violence: A violent incident is defined as an attempt to do bodily harm to a person or bodily harm actually done. Cartoon and comic violence were not included.

Sex: A sex incident is defined as a scene of suggested sexual intercourse, a sexually suggestive comment, or a skin scene (undue and unnecessary emphasis on the human anatomy).

Profanity: A profanity incident includes the following words used by the networks during the monitoring period – damn, hell, God, Christ, Jesus, as-, sh-, bast-, son-of-a-bi-, god-, bitch.

Names and addresses of 'offending' companies, with the list of products and the names of chairmen, are listed for protest or boycott.

The National Coalition on Television Violence, an organisation directed to 'reversing the massive amounts of glorified violence' on television, also had no doubt as to where the power lay and where to attack. Its campaign received wide attention, but seemed to be making little real impact. 'This is because these commercial information channels usually leave out the names of the advertisers, the people who provide the money to bring this entertainment to the American public,' wrote its chairman to its members. 'I am asking you to help correct this problem by carrying the enclosed column in your organisational newspaper, newsletter or bulletin. The most important element is to include the advertiser addresses.' The companies earmarked as offenders include Wrigley's Gum, Kellogg, Hershey and McDonald's.

In the UK, Channel 4 used a red triangle symbol to signify a film that might shock for a trial period. Mrs Mary Whitehouse of the National Viewers and Listeners Association, another lobby group, wrote to advertisers whose spots appeared with one of the films. As a result, five instructed their agencies that their products should no longer be advertised within red triangle films: Lloyds Bank, Sainsbury's, Kellogg, the Bank of Scotland and Hill Samuel bankers.

In denying the effectiveness of advertiser pressures, many broadcasters point to instances when networks have been seen to adopt a strong stance. ABC's decision in 1983 to show *The Day After*, a made-for-television film about a nuclear holocaust, is given as the prime example. The Rev. Jerry Falwell, head of the hardline religious lobby, Moral Majority, later renamed Liberty Federation, threatened a consumer boycott against advertisers who bought time during the programme. He later withdrew the threat, but letters were sent to over a hundred major advertisers. Falwell said, 'We didn't threaten anyone. We simply stated that American industries who have earned their money from American consumers in the free market system should be careful not to spend that money in a way that threatens this country's security.' It must be conceded that a programme about the nuclear holocaust hardly looks the best forum for persuading people to buy goods anyway. In the event advertisers were so nervous that thirty-second spots were selling for as low as $60,000, giving them about 1,000 viewers for every sixty cents. The important point, though, says the network, is that the programme *was* shown, that it was watched (by about 100 million people), and that research showed that there was no 'negative fallout' to those who did advertise.

ABC, which followed with a TV drama about incestuous child abuse (which also drew a large audience), complained about a dichotomy between what audiences want and what advertisers were willing to accept. 'The consumer expects TV on certain occasions to deal with sensitive issues,' Alan Wurtzel, ABC's vice-president in charge of Broadcast Standards and Practises told me. Many advertisers, though, looked at such ideas and felt 'they would not be acceptable as programming and would damage the credibility of their advertising'. Research, he said, had shown this to be untrue. 'There were still some advertisers on hearing what the programme [on incest] was about didn't want to get onto the show. All we were saying was, Look at the show, see how it's handled. However, a number of advertisers didn't even want to see – they felt we would offend our audience.'

Robert Silverbert, ABC's general manager, sales, reckoned the network was 'getting there' with a policy of approaching advertisers and convincing them that a subject like incest was being treated 'tactfully'. He explained advertisers were torn two ways: 'If they get a letter of complaint from a couple in Missouri they get worried. At the same time, audiences *are* watching and so they want to be in it.' He added, 'What advertisers are concerned about is having any kind of negative rub off.'

It can be argued that sooner or later advertisers will go where the audiences are. Jeff Greenfield, media analyst of ABC TV, has said, 'If a company objected to, say, JR of Dallas because he's too anti-social, CBS would just say, fine, "see you around later, and who's next?"' It could also be said – with absolute justification – that an advertiser who is paying over his money has the right to advertise where he wishes. And, as we've seen, a network can argue that whatever the advertiser response, it will go ahead with a programme like *The Day After*.

These three arguments, however, add up to only a partial truth. The first – that advertisers will go where the big audiences go – only means that there will always be a few big crowd pullers that will force some advertisers to relax their moral rules temporarily. Advertisers do have the right to place their ads where they wish – but this, surely, does not alter the fact that a *system* that means this can determine what is shown or not shown is wrong. And, as for the third, there are few *The Day After*'s. The networks may stand firm on the big, highly visible battles, but this does not mean that they won't co-operate the rest of the time. It may, in fact, mean they're *more* co-operative on other occasions.

None of this is to claim, either, that American television produces only bad programmes, or that British TV is not often awful. That would be rubbish. As Christopher Dunkley, television critic of the *Financial Times*, has pointed out, the US gave the UK *Bilko*, *I Love Lucy*, *Rhoda* and *Cheers*; we give them Benny Hill: 'Which way does that suggest the rubbish was travelling?' Nor is it to claim that advertiser pressure is the only pressure. The BBC suppressed its nuclear holocaust film, *The War Game*, for nearly twenty years.

What it does claim is that advertiser-dominated television means television that the advertiser wants – mainly bland, uncontroversial, certainly not likely to alienate any potential customers. It may even be that what the advertiser wants some of the time coincides with what we should all want – television, for example, might be better with less violence. But the question surely is: why should the advertiser have the right to decide? It is an important question because as more and more media emerge – more television channels, more magazines, more newspapers – the advertisers' power to affect content will grow.

Italy is a warning of what can happen when the advertisers' interest rules. In a judgment in 1976, the Constitutional Court decided that RAI, the public service broadcaster, did not have a monopoly at local level. Hundreds of commercial television stations came into operation as a consequence, all able to exist within a legal vacuum. The big operators moved in, chasing the riches of advertisers. One, Silvio Berlusconi, a Milanese entrepreneur, succeeded in winning control of three principal private networks. The staple fare is imported soaps, variety spectaculars and quiz shows. The great diversity held out as the promise of free broadcasting has meant more and more of the same. RAI in turn, has been pushed towards more and more entertainment.

On some stations the line between advertising and editorial has become invisible. A breakfast show features a furrier talking about his furs. Nothing odd in that – except that he has paid for his 'editorial' spot just as he would for an ad. Similarly in the United States the glut of channels has brought advertiser-produced shows that look like ordinary programmes but are actually a new form of commercial advertising. The Home Shopping Show is a prime example. This is a half-hour programme with 'guests' who in reality are company sponsors who have paid for nine minutes of time. The MTV channel routinely uses videos of music taken from films. The advertising department for Orion Pictures had a bright idea for taking this further: they would put together a video featuring a number of rock stars, extracts from their own music videos and clips from the film *Amadeus* as a commercial *for* the film. Because of its music content, however, MTV agreed to air it free as part of its non-advertising content.

At least, it is argued, advertiser-paid-for media are either free to the customer or cheaper than they would be without ads. It is an argument made not only to advance the spread of new commercial outlets, but also in a bid by some agencies and advertisers to press advertising onto public networks like the BBC.

The 'free-TV' is almost an article of faith. Thus, the Television Information Office in the US hired the Roper Organisation to conduct research which then found that 74 per cent agreed that 'having commercials is a fair price to pay for being able to watch television programs' without charge. Commercial TV, however, is *not* free in the sense that viewers don't pay anything for it. What they do is pay the cash in an indirect way as part of the added cost of the products that are advertised. A few argue that this is not so: that advertising means bigger sales which means lower manufacturing costs which means lower prices. But even the majority of people I talked to in agencies or advertisers accepted this was a specious argument for the majority of goods and services advertised.

A paper published by J. Walter Thompson made no attempt to fudge the reality:

There was a time, in ITV's early days, when one of the major programme companies took to announcing themselves as 'Your free television service'. The Independent Television Authority (as the IBA then was) asked them to stop it, on the grounds that it was not true. For one thing, the television licence is not free. Less obviously, perhaps, the cost of commercials is included, in however minute fractions of a penny, in the price of goods and services advertised. Advertising is a built in cost, which is passed to the consumer. He, or more probably she, pays in the local shop or supermarket for having a choice of channels – but on the easiest of easy terms.

The advantage of commercial television, therefore, is not that it's free, but that it *seems* free. Its revenue collection system is an inconspicuous one, while that of licence collection is not. Christopher Dunkley has commented, 'Though we pay more for ITV nobody ever complains; it is the size of the BBC's lump sum which offends politicians and pensioners alike.'

But what of newspapers and magazines. If not free, at least they come heavily subsidised by the advertiser. Professor Bagdikian has shown how this is not so.

In 1940 daily newspapers averaged thirty-one pages, of which advertisers occupied 40 per cent, or twelve and a half pages. Consumers paid 2 cents for the whole paper and got eighteen and a half pages of editorial matter for it. In 1980, papers averaged sixty-six pages, of which 65 per cent or forty-three pages, was advertising. By this time readers were paying 20 cents for the whole paper, out of which they got twenty-three pages of editorial matter. Applying price indices from 1940 to 1980 brings the cost of a 1940-size paper to 5.7 cents in 1980. The reader got 24 per cent more editorial matter in 1980, which brings the price to 7 cents. If another cent were added to give the publisher an extravagant profit beyond the 1940 margin, the price would be 8 cents, four times the 1940 price. But the price in 1980 was 20 cents, ten times the 1940 price. The difference is mainly the money charged to readers for the added advertising pages delivered to their homes. Readers in 1980 were not getting the paper for less than cost; they were paying for the advertising.

The developments in media and the preoccupation of advertisers with the soaring costs have given the specialists in agencies a new importance. Media men say that their day has finally dawned. Some believe, perhaps over-optimistically, that the next decade will see them as the most important single group within the agency.

The departments in agencies which handle media planning and buying are updated versions of what was once the whole agency. Its specialists analyse the media, calculate costs, recommend a plan, and then buy at the best price. They work out, for example, the best – and cheapest – way to reach young teenage girls about to buy their first lipstick. How well – or how badly – they do their job is measurable in one crucial area – whether they paid more or less for TV time than rival agencies. Big advertisers may have a dozen agencies buying time or space for different brands, giving them continuous comparison of who buys well and who buys badly.

Media men are a race apart – the buyers, one suspects, would be as at home calculating trade-in prices on motor cars or negotiating coffee or pork belly futures. The planners could be analysts in almost any industry. Media men come complete with uniforms (smart salesmen's suits or shirt sleeves, tie loose for telephone deals), tool kits (computers, slide rules and American Express gold cards), and – in the UK where these things matter – fast and sporty cars. In 1986, a twenty-two-year-old in a London agency was probably getting around £25,000 plus perks including a company car, with the prospect of doubling that by the time he was twenty-seven. If he achieved media stardom, rewards could be glittering: one asked for – and got – a Rolls Royce to move to Doyle Dane Bernbach's London office. Probably the agency hardly hesitated – they had recently lost three accounts, reportedly because of poor media buying.

In the early days of modern advertising, buying media was an agency's sole function. A 1905 book published by the agency S. H. Benson, *Facts for Advertisers*, has 374 pages with sections on postal rates, populations, early closing days and market days of towns and cities, and a map showing the location of the main newspapers. There are vast lists of general weeklies and monthlies, long since gone – the Graphic, the Pall Mall Magazine, the Strand magazine – and a page and a quarter of temperance papers.

Traditionally media has been a low status and low pay department. John Perriss, worldwide media director of Saatchi's, said that when he moved to the agency world from newspapers in 1968 'media was really backroom, below stairs. It had no status at all compared with the account handlers and the creatives.' The media explosion and rising costs have changed that: 'Media can lose you an account nowadays. If the media is bad, the client will move it.'

Buying space and time – particularly time – is big business with big risks and rewards. Television time, not surprisingly, is where the real action is. Television time is a perishable commodity, sold on supply and demand. How much is paid for a 'spot' (thirty seconds is the most common length) depends on just what is being bought (what programme), when, and the skill and clout of the negotiator.

Media men deny it is all about buying cheap: they want the money to go where it will buy the best advertising prospects for the particular product and the skill is buying precisely the right mix of audience. That said, the buyers are the people continuously being judged. Mostly, they're young, ambitious, have heads for figures and tough nerves. 'A buyer is only as good as his last buying result,' said Rodney Harris, media director of D'Arcy Masius Benton and Bowles in London. 'The archetypal buyer is someone who has grown up in the East End where he's gone to market with his parents who run a vegetable shop. He's got this whole buying thing at his fingertips. They're people who're very active streetwise. A trainee can come in and move very fast if he's good. Because it is the only bit of business in an agency that can be measured, you are a winner or a loser.' Many burn themselves out quickly, he says. He adds, apparently only half jokingly: 'They run into problems when they're twenty-two. You have your spotty youth leaning against his Porsche and wondering what to do next.'

Steve Fajen, Saatchi's media director in New York, explained 'there are many ways of buying. You can buy up front – gamble that you'll probably get a good price. Or you can wait until most others have done that, husband your money and go into the "scatter market", that's buying on a scatter basis. Or you can husband your money even further and buy at the last moment. Say it's now 5 p.m. and I've got $50,000 I've kept for an advert. I'd just let it be known at the networks that we have some opportunistic money. They will let us buy at 50 per cent of the rate – just so that they're making some money. They're selling distressed merchandise. It would cost me say $50,000 for a $90,000 spot.' He adds, somewhat regretfully, that it is, however, 'rather difficult to buy everything opportunistically'. Experts say that the difference between good and bad buying can be horrendous. A poor buyer might spend 125,000 dollars or pounds for a spot that the best operator might get for 70,000.

Whatever the merits and demerits of television commercials, it's obvious they are advertisements. There is a form of advertising that not so much blurs the line with editorial, but destroys it by design. It is one that even many advertising men find dishonest.

In a review of a forgettable film called *Little Treasure*, Vincent Canby of the *New York Times* noted, 'The containers of Coke don't actually receive more closeups than Miss (Margot) Kidder, but their closeups seem more lingering and loving.' What Canby had seen was one of the latest forms of pseudo-advertising. It began, as a professionally organised business, in the late 1970s. By the mid eighties there were about thirty companies operating in Hollywood to 'place' goods in television programmes and movies. A number of advertising agencies, including Chiat/Day, Ogilvy and Mather and Ted Bates, had also become involved; Coke and Pepsi both had fulltime employees scouting out movies; in Britain a growing number of London 'placement' offices had signed up such big advertisers as Vauxhall Motors, Watney Mann and Truman, DHL and the Distillers Company.

It had become an established quasi-advertising medium, and its practitioners could look back on such successes as: Gene Wilder spending a long time in a Cadillac in *Woman in Red*, Clint Eastwood drinking Budweiser, with appropriate contented noises, in *Sudden Impact*, Richard Prior showering friends with Dom Perignon champagne in *Brewster's Millions*, Madonna clicking away with a Polaroid camera in *Desperately Seeking Susan*, and the characters in *Prizzi's Honour* flying United Airlines – not once but many times.

The list could fill several pages. In one year alone, one 'placement' company managed to get goods into 156 American-made films. The same company, Associated Film Promotions, boasts over 100 top clients, including General Motors and Procter and Gamble, and says that in one year client products appeared in nine of the twenty top grossing films in UK cinemas.

Movie directors have long included products in their films, to create impressions or to contribute to authenticity. What is new is the practice as a business. Associated Film Promotions was set up in 1978. It was started by an ex-advertising man Robert Kovoloff – he entered the business as a result of seeing the film *The Hucksters!* a movie most ad men hate for the scheming way it depicts them.

Its trade ads today ask, 'How did Lay's Potato Chips get in *Poltergeist*? How did Wheaties get in *Rocky III*? How did Budweiser get in *Tootsie*? How did Milk Duds and Zagnut get in *48 Hours*? How does *any* product get in the movies?'

Kovoloff assures clients, 'We meet with studio staff members to determine the most effective way to use a client's product. And our executives go on location to ensure products appear to their best advantage.' In return for their money – which may be up to hundreds of thousands of dollars – clients are guaranteed 'placement in a minimum of five motion pictures annually'. AFP's literature boasts, justifiably, that 'In most cases, it is the stars who will use the product – always in a positive and memorable manner.'

The movie makers co-operate partly for the cash, partly for the free supply of sometimes expensive products (like cars or computers), but even more so for promotional help which can be massive. *Santa Claus – The Movie* was set in a specially constructed McDonald's. The hamburger company gave $1 million to the film makers – but also spent $18 million on promotion and network advertising.

Kovoloff talks darkly of individuals from 'as high as the president of the studio to the husband of the leading lady in the picture' being involved in setting up the deals. 'He [the husband] could be an agent, a theatrical manager, and he might say that his wife will appear in the film if, and only if, product X also appears.' In *Fame*, a dance sequence involved kids carrying boxes of Tide detergent. According to Kovoloff, Walter Mondale, in some unspecified way, helped to arrange that.

Products are not simply dropped into movies. It has gone way beyond that. Scripts are altered to fit products into the action. Thus *Rocky III* was amended so that Sylvester Stallone could advise his young son to eat Wheaties – the 'breakfast of champions'. The beer being promoted will be drunk by the hero; the villain will drink another brand. 'Great care is taken to prevent a product being used by "villains" or in a disparaging way,' says one piece of promotional literature.

It can even be a way of getting some link with an actor who won't ordinarily involve himself with advertising. Thus Marlon Brando in *The Formula* was seen offering Milk Duds to George C. Scott. The film, doesn't have to be 'light' or easy entertainment. In *Missing*, Jack Lemmon, the fraught father, pauses in a Chilean bar to drink Coca-Cola courtesy of product placers. Nor is it only movies, although this is where most of the action is. Ford was placed in *Dallas*, Grant's whisky into both *Dallas* and *Dynasty*, Royal Crown Cola into the *A Team*.

Companies obviously believe it works. Many point to what is still regarded as the prime example. Hershey Chocolate Co's Reese Pieces appeared in *ET* and sales of the coloured candy reportedly soared 85 per cent. There is also, ad-wise, research of a kind – movie-goers are asked for their names and telephone numbers as they enter theatres, and are telephoned days afterwards to ask what products they can recall. Companies are obviously appreciative. Bob Harvey, an executive of General Mills, wrote glowingly to AFP: 'The Wheaties dialogue with Sylvester Stallone in *Rocky III* was outstanding and the placing of our Yoplait Yoghurt in *ET* was a real coup.'

Kovoloff says, 'Seeing a product, even for a second, in a realistic dramatic setting in which the viewer is already emotionally involved leaves an invaluable impression.' Peter Thomas, marketing manager for the Perrier operation in the UK, says, 'This sort of exposure is very important to us because it's all part of getting Perrier into the fabric of society. It's a very subtle way of selling.'

There are other blurry areas. In the mid eighties, game shows were so popular on American television that there was an explosion of new ones: two-thirds of the new shows for syndication introduced in January 1986 at the convention of the National Association of Television Program Executives were game shows. The major feature of such shows, of course, is that things get given away. And the programme makers and product makers came to a neat agreement. The companies supply the prizes (plus a cash fee of around $600–700 at 1985 figures) and in return the programme producers give the product a few seconds in close-up and a few words of sales pitch (some even allow the companies 10 seconds of their own taped commercial message). Products on offer ranged from books to boats, electrical appliances to $25 worth of cough syrup, allowing winners to go away with armfuls. One programme, CBS's *The Price is Right*, made use of fifty products a day. Payment from manufacturers was bringing in $1 million a year which was used for buying prizes bigger and better than ones advertisers were willing to give away. Enthusiasts saw it as a 'great equaliser' in giving mass TV time for companies with budgets normally too small.

Latin America goes further. From the 1970s the dominant TV programmes throughout the region have come to be *novelas*, or soap operas, each one running for several months. Products are incorporated into the scripts. Characters 'plug' Atari video games, Braun mixers, Johnson's wax polish, Ford cars. In one *novela* from Brazil's TV Globo, Honda motorcycles appeared in almost every episode. In one show a doctor prescribes a drug to a patient suffering from sclerosis. The drug is not named, but the camera halts in close-up on the distinctive 'S' logo of the drug manufacturer Sandoz. In another, women's plastic shoes are worn to get across the image for the manufacturer that the rich wear them. In yet another, a wealthy banker commits himself to helping prisoners; this series was part-funded by a bank keen to improve the image of the business. In what may be the ultimate in built-in advertising one *novela* used as part of its storyline the actual advertising campaign (with close ups of the ads) for Brazil's main panties maker. Synopses of new serials are sent routinely to advertisers and agencies. A typical contract might then give the advertiser twenty 'secondary' appearances (where the product is shown only) and twelve main ones (where it actually features in the action or dialogue). For this an advertiser might pay anything up to around $500,000. Globo reckoned to cover 25–30 per cent of the cost of its serials by inserting the products of a dozen or more major advertisers into each one.

There is also straight sponsorship – even though here the biggest objective is often getting the sponsored product's name on television. One of Britain's leading brass bands changed its name. Wingates *Temperance* Band of Bolton dropped the word 'temperance' after 107 years. What's more it became *Bass* Wingates Band, taking on the name of one of the country's leading brewers in return for much-needed sponsorship.

Sponsorship, like advertising, is a way of getting a message across to people who might be induced to buy a company's product. Its users see it as a way of establishing goodwill, of creating an aura of excellence that, hopefully, will be reflected in longterm sales, and – not infrequently – as a backdoor advertising method for products like tobacco banned from television. It is increasingly regarded as a sophisticated marketing tool. Outsiders may see it as company patronage, but its purpose is strictly commercial. The sponsor wants to reach a certain audience and he decides that sponsoring a concert or a golf tournament is the best way. The joint managing director of Saatchi's in London has said, 'We regard sponsorship simply as one of the marketing tools at our disposal. We don't differentiate sponsorship from advertising or any other form of communication we might use on behalf of our clients.'

Audiences are targeted just as they are in conventional advertising. Thus Tesco puts money into a music school for young people because it is 'naturally very concerned about tomorrow's generation of shoppers' and because it is trying to move upmarket in image. Many of the sponsors are from industries hoping that the aura of what they are backing will rub off on their own frequently less than spotless auras – banks with high profits, oil companies and tobacco firms.

Sponsors thrive in both sports and the arts because bodies from tennis organisers to museums are faced with rising costs and decreasing public funds from government.

The 1984 Olympic Games in Los Angeles became the first to be supported entirely by commercial sponsorship. The Games, traditionally funded (at a loss) by governments, turned to private industry and made a profit. Major corporations paid for everything in return for sponsorship. In its wake, the *Financial Times* commented, 'One by one the world's greatest sporting events are turning seriously to sponsorship for their funding.' Nine worldwide sponsors each put up millions for the 1988 Olympics in return for exclusive rights to use Olympic rings and logos across the world. One, Visa, for example spent an estimated $25 million on buying its rights and or its marketing effort.

Television exposure for the sponsors is, of course, a key factor. One observer, the critic Peter Lennon, has called sponsorship 'indirect selling, which evades worldwide television advertising fees'. American networks actively peddle the opportunity for companies to add their brand names to the official titles of televised sport. In Britain, it is usually seen as part of the price television has to pay for the existence of the sports that are screened – although occasionally there is a reaction against the blatancy involved: the BBC made a decision not to give the names of horses competing in showjumping events which had been named after tobacco companies.

By 1986 nearly 1,600 companies in the UK were sponsoring sport to the total tune of about £129 million. Over 170 got themselves onto network TV. Not surprisingly the great draws for sponsors are those sports that do fill TV time regularly – snooker, cricket, horse racing, tennis, golf and football. Thus, tennis, for example, was receiving sponsorship in one year from Barratt's the building firm, Benson and Hedges, Carlsberg, Pretty Polly, the Refuge Assurance, Stella Artois beer, Sunbeam, and – from further afield – Nippon, Volvo and Nabisco. It was estimated that a company sponsoring tennis would be obtaining television 'exposure' for around £17,000 an hour, a trifling sum in promotion terms.

Ironically much of the hidden advertising is on commercial-free BBC. The satirical programme *Spitting Image* presented its own version of an evening's schedule for BBC1: 'Now a look ahead to programmes on BBC1. At 7 p.m. highlights of the Embassy World Snooker Championship, which is followed by cricket, including the Benson and Hedges Cup final and highlights of the Cornhill test. In Match of the Day, at 10.15 p.m., action from the Canon League and the Milk Cup fifth round replay. And finally, Profile: BBC Chairman Stuart Young explains why he will never allow advertising on the BBC.'

Isn't it, though, just a question of two groups that need each other coming together for the betterment of both and for everyone else? Sport needs money; advertisers have it and want what sport has to give; sports fans benefit.

Up to a point, that is true. The problem lies, first, in the blurring yet again between what's editorial and what's advertising. Then there is a second one – the degree of reliance. Companies sponsor because they – rightly – expect to gain something in return. What they want, however, is not necessarily what others might want. The two may be incompatible. Government sports subsidy, for example, which it increasingly replaces, has tended to go to sports that will have a health-creating benefit. Two lecturers in economics writing in the National Westminster Bank's quarterly review pointed out that much business sponsorship on the other hand has gone into sports like darts and snooker. Additionally, business sponsors tend to focus on top-class professional events and do little to provide sports facilities.

There is another danger: business sponsors can start calling the tune, deciding not just what they will back but making it shape itself to their own wants and needs. The sport itself can become secondary. There are signs of this happening in a smaller, but growing, area of sponsorship – that of the arts. In the US, the Reagan policy was to try to shift the burden of the arts away from the public to the private sector. The UK government, too, has cut back on arts funding. In both countries, business sponsorship has been rising – in the US it had probably reached about $1,800 million by the mid eighties including marketing and advertising support. In 1987, around £30 million worth of business sponsorship was going into the arts in Britain.

Thus, American Express supports museums and jazz bands, Philip Morris dance companies, Time-Life plays and exhibitions, Salem and Silk Cut country and western music, and Kool jazz festivals. The Philharmonia Orchestra plays easy with the help of £400,000 from Nissan, and the Welsh National Opera is able to get on with its singing thanks to Amoco. The Segovia guitar competition comes courtesy of the Sherry Producers of Spain.

The Victoria and Albert Museum, seeking a sponsor for its new theatre museum, offered not just a name link but also artistic control for two seasons a year in the museum's theatre, together with the use of the building for trade and private functions. Britain's arts festivals by the mid 1980s were being sponsored commercially to about 40 per cent of their costs.

The problem arises, of course, in what the sponsors want for their money. Do they simply want to be associated with museums or orchestras or festivals? Or do they also want to have some say in exhibitions that are organised, or musical works that are chosen, or plays that are presented? By the mid eighties there was no doubt that they were having a real and growing influence on determining artistic policy.

The parallel with advertiser influence on TV (sometimes by the very same companies) was clear. Just as on television they want programmes that appeal to Middle America or its equivalent, in the arts they prefer the tried, tested and sure – Mozart, say, rather than some modern composer. What they don't want as a general rule is innovation and daring.

Again, it is the advertiser as arbiter. We get what he pays for.

THE FUTURE

Advertising has always aroused fierce passions.

It is 'an evil service', believed Aneurin Bevan. It 'degrades the people it appeals to; it deprives them of their will to choose', thought C. P. Snow. Arnold Toynbee could not 'think of any circumstances in which advertising would not be an evil'.

Malcolm Muggeridge prophesies that history will see it 'as one of the real evil things of our time. It is stimulating people constantly to want things, want this, want that.' Pope John Paul II has warned young people they are 'threatened . . . by the evil use of advertising techniques that stimulate the natural inclination to avoid hard work by promising the immediate satisfaction of every desire'. As for advertisers, 'They exploit human inadequacy', holds Richard Hoggart.

Advertising may be a key ingredient of a competitive economy, but as advertising budgets become ever more mega it is also increasingly a weapon that benefits the large at the expense of the small. To join, and remain, in the big league takes more and more advertising pounds. In Britain, Lever Brothers and Procter and Gamble dominate washing-powder advertising and between them they share nearly 90 per cent of the total market; the two facts are not unrelated.

Advertising may also, as some claim, help reduce costs by stimulating high volumes of production – but that does not necessarily mean goods cost less to the customer. It may mean higher profits; it may simply mean that high volume is bought at an advertising cost that more than cancels out any other savings.

Advertisers, and their agencies, have always argued that advertising can neither sell poor products nor persuade people to act against their own real wishes. Such an argument rings increasingly hollow in days when the advertising often *is* the product. Advertising sells patent medicines that are at best no more than placebos, branded goods that are identical to cheaper, non-branded products – not only 'image' items like jeans, but mundane goods such as bleach. One hundred million dollars of advertising sells mouthwashes that, in the words of the National Academy of Sciences, have no 'therapeutic advantage over . . . salt water or even water'.

This is proclaimed as the Age of Marketing – a time in which businesses concentrate on giving people what *they* want rather than what business decides to produce. But advertising, a major part of the marketing package, encourages makers of goods and suppliers of services to try to change perceptions rather than the products themselves.

It can even be argued that advertising encourages manufacturers to downgrade quality from the start. The editors of the *New American*, Paul Vail and Alexander Genis, two Latvian émigrés living in the United States, asked themselves why Americans seem to prefer foreign goods. They concluded that advertising was the villain: 'Instead of improving the quality, the larger companies rely on a different method – advertisement. It is simpler and cheaper to run commercials than introduce quality control.'

It is sometimes possible to stand back and see two products or services – the one presented in advertisements, the other in reality. Airlines, hotels, banks, car makers all provide obvious examples. Very rarely does the advertiser feel shamed enough by the quality of his product to drop the advertising – as British Rail finally did with its 'We Are Getting There' claim, when it so obviously was not.

At one level, of course, it is a joke: we don't expect life to be exactly as it is in commercials. But it goes far beyond that: these are advertisements devised with seemingly no reference to what is actually on offer. They do not involve a bending of the truth; they are out and out lies.

Advertisers claim that their offerings are simply mirrors of ourselves. To a degree that must be true. But in that itself lie dangers. It can delay change: whether or not advertising actively encourages people to smoke, there can surely be no argument that it delays the demise of a potentially lethal habit.

Commercials speak of people and situations in a visual shorthand – Americans are brash and philistine, Soviets mindless and grim, Orientals gibberish or sinister, the Irish thick, Australians uncouth, Germans corpulent corporate groupies. Women in advertisements directed at doctors are usually drivelling, snivelling wrecks who need drugs to turn them into normal functioning adults. Advertising may not create the stereotypes – but it polishes and helps perpetuate them.

However, even if we accept that advertising has no virtues (which certainly I do not), there remains one overriding fact: advertising exists and, short of world-changing upheaval, will continue to exist. A world without it is now inconceivable. Furthermore, advertising will continue to grow, both in quantity and in the impact it has upon our lives: a host of factors from the explosion of media to the increasing globalisation of markets will ensure this.

Simply to condemn is to allow the power of the advertiser to continue its growth by stealth. What we must do is learn to live with advertising more intelligently.

Dealing with advertising intelligently means control and education. There are already restrictions, of course, but too often, because society always lags behind the reality of advertising development, such restrictions are too heavily biased in favour of the advertiser: they represent what he is forced to concede at any given time, and no more. In a year or three or five he'll agree grudgingly to another limitation or two, but only when he has to do so and only when it is clear that the alternative, forced control or totally unacceptable adverse public reaction, is much worse.

What we must always remember is that the advertiser's purpose is to sell more goods in order to increase his own wealth. There is nothing wrong in that *per se*. But we forget it is not just at our peril but at our children's peril, too. There is one key phrase we must have held in front of us, larger than the largest advertisement: *advertisers advertise in the way they can get away with*. Advertisers justify themselves in the name of need (to compete on behalf of their shareholders, their workers) and the agency professionals by claiming they have a duty to provide the best possible work for their client.

More control over advertising is vital, at the risk even of the great evil, bureaucracy. Self-regulation, conceded inch by inch by a reluctant industry, is not enough. Advertisers chase us wherever we go, making it almost impossible for us to avoid them, giving us no opportunity to respond or react except at the moment of buying. The target, the consumer, must play a real part in what advertising is and is not allowed to be and do.

But if more control is necessary so is education. One of the major problems with advertising is that the contest between the seller and the buyer is so unequal. This is true of almost all advertising, but most so with vulnerable groups – heavy drinkers, those in debt, old people bewildered by today's advertising 'overkill', or people in the Third World.

Even the good Dr Ernest Dichter who has devoted so much of his life trying to make people buy is in agreement. 'I think it would be a good idea to teach youngsters to recognise their own gullibility, their readiness to be fooled, simply because they want to believe something. I can see students being asked to analyse advertising, to bring in merchandise which they or their parents have bought and which has turned out to be faulty and falsely represented. This kind of training will be a better guard than even a self-imposed code of ethics among advertisers or a control by the FTC.'

Denys Thompson, writing in *Voice of Civilisation*, argued, 'We train our children in road-sense, and we should with equal application bring them up in such a way that they will not be run over by juggernaut advertising.'

Some researchers have concluded, 'it is clear . . . that it is possible to "arm" children against commercials, to use various education strategies to reduce their vulnerability to commercial appeals'.

It is touched on in some education, but not much more. Organisations such as the Consumers' Union have devised films showing, for example, how celebrity endorsers are used to link a product with success and what can be achieved by using tricks of cameras and lighting. The British

Film Institute has a teaching pack. One part raises questions about how advertising images convey their messages. A wholesome, half-cheeky red-haired schoolboy in uniform is shown sneakily munching a Harvest Crunch bar. Children are asked such questions as, 'Why do you think a ginger-haired boy was chosen?'

But it is peripheral, whereas advertising itself and certainly persuasion techniques generally are central to much of our life. Although school curriculums are already crowded, it cries out to be included. In any event, in showing us how advertisers research and manoeuvre to tap our hopes, fears and dreams it teaches us much more – it tells us about ourselves and the positive benefits that could emerge from understanding those motivations.

It might be argued that any teaching that considers advertising could only be an outpouring against capitalism and a free economy, the kind of thing we have seen so often in recent years in education areas controlled by the far left.

It need be nothing of the sort. First, there are enough businessmen concerned about advertising to demonstrate that it is not just a concern of the left. Second, to educate a society to understand advertising in order to face it on equal terms can only make advertising more responsible, more responsive, and help in the creation of a more genuinely competitive society.

With a mixture of controls and education at home, it remains our duty to see that the advertisers do not simply export more of their illegal or discredited practices to countries less able to handle them. In Thailand, international companies like Colgate-Palmolive have been accused of spending disproportionately large amounts on advertising in order to gain domination of the market. According to Ministry of Commerce figures, up to 32 per cent of the price of soap and 40 per cent of the cost of toothpaste was being earmarked for advertising and marketing. A government source claimed that small, local firms could not compete with the big marketers 'who will do anything to boost their market share'.

It is not only additives banned in Europe and the US that abound; so, too, do discredited advertising and marketing practices. Thus, although there is a World Health Organization Code covering the selling of infant formula, it does not include claims for other baby products.

There remains one cause of concern which, I believe, should involve us above all at this moment. It is inherent in the advertiser's ever-growing role as the picker-up of bills. In most areas of life, it is the piper who calls the tune – if not at first, certainly at some later stage. With advertising, this is increasingly the case with television, newspapers and magazines; with sport; with the arts; and in a number of smaller areas. Without action, the advertiser's power is likely to become ever greater.

The invasion is sometimes obvious, occasionally ludicrous: a Toronto soccer referee, equipped with a concealed electronic bleeper, calls eleven fouls so that CBS can fit in commercials; English press photographers covering cricket are reminded they can take up positions on the boundary only on the understanding they do not obscure the advertisement hoardings from the cameras of the BBC, ironically at that time fighting off having to run ads.

Mostly, however, it happens stealthily and goes largely unnoticed. With the media, it is not only dependence on advertisers – but on a remarkably small number of big ones. By 1981, for example, two-thirds of the advertising revenues of the Latin American press came from just thirty multinational corporations, most of them American. It is just conceivable that all advertisers are benevolent, neutral, disinterested in policy, oblivious to programme or editorial page content, but it is surely a most unwise society that allows its communications to rely on such a gamble.

Most advertisers and their agencies know exactly what they want from the media even if they are not stupid enough to proclaim it publicly. Often, it's far from what readers or viewers would desire – or what society should tolerate.

Take a speech by Gerrold Rubin, president of the American agency Needham, Harper and Steers, Los Angeles, delivered to the California Broadcasters' Association. He told them that if they want to sell more retail advertising they should be willing to give their customers more exposure, even if that meant doing news stories on big advertisers. He gave them examples of where this was already happening. According to reports of the speech, his proposal 'was well received by the broadcasters in attendance'.

Or consider the views of a UK advertising man on what the new media explosion should mean. Sean McCormick, deputy managing director of SJIP/BBDO, believes, 'Given that even blocks of commercials, let alone breaks, have to be surrounded by programming, and that competition will increase in a manner currently only experienced by the American networks, the opportunities for agencies to influence the content of each station will be there . . . We believe that agencies can only gain from having more control over the carrier, previously known as the media owner. We believe consumers will respond more effectively to programme (or editorial) association, when it is in keeping with the desired product image.'

This would be less of a problem were the media standing vigilant, ready to cry 'Rape' at the first attempt of over-familiarity. Unfortunately, the increasing trend is for it to lie back with a fixed smile, ready and eager to be seduced.

In the United States, advertisers have long influenced broadcasters to the point of dictation. By 1987 there were worrying, though not unexpected, signs that some stations in Britain were taking the first perilous steps. Television companies have been under great pressure from advertisers angry about the soaring cost of airtime and the decline in the number of viewers. Thames TV decided to call a meeting to allow advertisers a chance to express their views about programmes, a hitherto unimaginable gathering. According to reports they gave the director of programmes 'a roasting'.

More significant, though, was the way the other London station, London Weekend, launched its new Night Network, a programme service aimed at eighteen to thirty-four-year-olds and beginning at 1 a.m. on Friday, Saturday and Sunday nights.

The station's Controller of Entertainment explained that the service 'will break new ground in that production and sales will be working closely together'. The aim was to ensure that 'advertising becomes more of a part of the viewing experience than would normally be the case', according to Night Network's sales manager. He volunteered, 'We're selling product television. So there has to be a cross flow (between the production and sales area) as in magazines.'

The printed media should, of course, keep a watching brief on what is happening in such an important area as broadcasting. But it, too, has a vested interest – print and TV companies interlock. A British newspaper may be pro the status quo of the present system of commercial television because it owns part of a station; alternatively, like Murdoch's *Times* or *Sunday Times* it may be against it because the boss is into satellite in a big way and wants to burst the TV world wide open.

Not infrequently the time arrives when even if advertiser domination of a medium is so obviously and glaringly bad there may be no real way of tackling the problem; it has been allowed to drift too far by a toothless watchdog. TV-AM was born on the promise of illuminating TV; when it couldn't supply the viewers the advertisers wanted, it became cheap, downmarket TV to survive. The number of viewers, and advertisers, rose. But even then it only survived economically because of a staggering number of children's TV ads – a barrage surely infinitely greater than any body with wider interests would have tolerated if the alternative did not look like possible disaster for the station.

Advertising is *not* the only way of paying for television. Nor, as we've seen, is advertiser-supported television genuinely free TV. The fact that it is an easy option does not mean it should be allowed to prevail and dominate. It is an easy way out for governments. It saves any need for real initiatives over alternative methods of paying for TV and, in any event, in political terms, advertiser-led TV emerges as being as 'safe' for politicians as it is for the advertisers.

There are alternative ways of funding; they may present difficulties, but that does not mean they are impossible.

The truth is that with more channels and more stations in the offing only a system with some order, some regulation and control can be genuinely free. The alternative is the monopoly and lack of variety we now see in Italy. In Britain, a Ministry of Communications needs to be set up. Given the importance of the subject and complexity of constant developments, the present situation whereby responsibilities are shared between the Department of Trade and the Home Office is ludicrous.

Print is a separate problem. Vincent P. Norris wrote in the *Journal of Advertising History*, 'The role of the publisher . . . has changed from seller of a product to consumers, to gatherer of consumers for advertisers . . . The role of the reader changes from sovereign consumer to advertiser bait.' This is not universally true yet – but we are frighteningly far along the road.

Modern newspaper technology could provide an answer, used in the right way. To date in the UK the new technology has been seen simply as a way of continuing the old at lower cost and, thus, hopefully of higher profit. It could, however, go a long way to restoring power to the reader at the expense of the advertiser. What it calls for is publications using the new technology but at low cost throughout the system. Given this, newspapers would be economically viable at very low circulations with little or no advertising.

There is already a curious precedent for this. Of the four new titles born of the newspaper revolution by 1987 only one had prospered, the very downmarket, soft-porn weekly *Sunday Sport*. The obvious reason was that it was further living proof no one goes broke underestimating the market. But there was another, more important lesson: alone among the four, the paper had been started on a ridiculously low budget (£150,000) and had incredibly low costs. Because of that it was making profits on a circulation of no more than 500,000 and with hardly any advertisements.

Our vigilance must extend to other areas of increasing domination such as sponsorship where more and more it is the advertiser who calls the shots. ('Eleven years ago corporations gave to the arts out of a general feeling of goodwill. Now businesses want a return' – Colin Tweedy, of the Association of Business Sponsorship of the Arts in 1987.)

As for hidden advertising, there should be the most stringent control. More and more school material comes courtesy of banks and food manufacturers and detergent makers. A random check of such material by the National Consumer Council showed a third was inaccurate and over half was biased in favour of the commercial company that was responsible for it. One guide for children, from Lever Brothers, was entitled, 'How to tell the difference between a good quality dishwashing liquid (like Sunlight Lemon Liquid) and a cheaper dishwashing liquid.' A booklet from Kellogg's contained the company's name ninety-six times. A leaflet from the Butter Information Council was headed 'Butter v Margarine: THE FACTS'. Surprise, surprise, butter emerged rather well.

Advertising has many positive features. It is needed to spread useful information. It has energy and extravagance. It can be fun – most of us have favourite ads that actually engender affection.

But it is also a big, powerful, highly talented and immensely wealthy industry.

We are on the threshold of a new advertising explosion, and that is why we must be eternally vigilant.

Its target is us.

SOURCES

Introduction

11 Edgar Allan Poe short story, *The Purloined Letter*. The letter is finally found by Poe's amateur detective, C. Auguste Dupin.

11 'As *The Times*': *The Times*, 6 June 1987.

12 'America's advertising expenditure has': Daniel Oliver, chairman of the FTC, 1987.

12 'the typical American has': *International Herald Tribune*, 5 June 1986.

12 'the film *Superman* was': Professor Kim Rotzoll, paper.

12 'A visual equivalent of Muzak': *Advertising Age*, 28 February 1985.

13 'Truman W. Eustis III, senior attorney': *Virginian Pilot and Ledger*, 15 January 1984.

13 *Business* list: 'The Business 500' in *Business*, October 1987.

13 *Business Week* list: *Business Week*, 21 April 1986.

14 'David Bernstein, one of': David Bernstein, *Creative Advertising*.

15 'in America and other': *Advertising Age*, 22 April 1985.

16 'There's "all natural" spray': *Time*, 11 October 1982.

Chapter 1

23 'All to sell a carbonated soft drink': Cola drinkers are measured in tens of millions. The magazine *Which?* tested colas on 'fifty discriminating cola drinkers' in 1985, and reported in its January 1986 issue that when given new Coke and Pepsi 'nine testers couldn't tell a difference'.

24 'Mike Detsiny is managing': Article in *Campaign*, 1 August 1986.

27 'By 1985 the average': Association of National Advertisers, New York.

27 'If they spent money': *Sunday Telegraph*, 15 June 1980.

27 'Miner Raymond tells of': *New York Times*, 6 May 1985.

28 'Peter Levelle, head of': *Sunday Telegraph*, 15 June, 1980.

28 'In an attempt to': *Design and Art Direction*, September 1983.

29 'Eighty-seven of America's': Saatchi and Saatchi Compton Worldwide, Review of Advertising Operations 1984.

30 'So does the Dow': *Evening Argus*, Brighton, 20 February 1986.

30 'In its attempt to': *International Herald Tribune*, 15 August 1985.

30 'In spring 1986, Britain's': *The Times*, 3 March 1986.

30 'Even the BBC in': Advertisement in *The Times*, 26 September 1985.

30 'The range of those': *Advertising Age*, 9 September 1985.

30 'The unlikeliest products are': Advertisement in *Defence* magazine, March 1987.

31 'In the three-years period': Spanish Advertising Agencies Association.

32 'In the words of': *Eyes on Tomorrow*.

32 'By the beginning of': *Advertising Age*, 22 June 1981.

34 'Gordon Wade, a management': *Cincinnati Enquirer*, 4 October 1982.

34 'Outside, staff are warned': *Advertising Age*, 21 February 1983.

36 'Five of P & G's': *Advertising Age*, 20 October 1986.

38 'As for individuals': *Financial Times*, 29 May 1986.

38 'In England, Malcolm Parkinson': *Marketing*, 28 July 1983.

38 Figures of agency numbers: US Census Bureau 1984, *Advertising Age*, *Brad Advertiser and Agency List*, January 1987.

39 'Until that time advertising': *The Trouble with Advertising*.

40 'As with the advertisers': *Advertising Age*, 25 May 1987.

40 Lists: *Advertising Age*, 11 May 1987.

43 'In Taiwan, Pepsi's': *Media International*, March 1984.

44 'Erik Elinder argued': Erik Elinder, 'How International can European advertising be?' *Journal of Marketing*, April 1965.

45 'Hallmark Cards, in 1984': *Advertising Age*, 14 May 1984.

45 'At 2.4 per cent of': Simon Lloyd, managing director, Foote, Cone and Belding, London.

46 'If Wall Street is': *Advertising, The Uneasy Persuasion*.

47 'Jay Chiat, of Chiat/Day': *Adweek*, 24 January 1983.

47 'As an advertising market': Fuji Bank estimates.

52 'An anonymous agency chairman': *Campaign*, 27 February 1987.

53 'Neil Patterson, as creative': *Design and Art Direction*, 10 May 1985.

53 'Bob Pritikin, a San Francisco': *Advertising Age*, 6 September 1982.

54 'In the 1930s, an': Jerry Cowle in *Advertising Age*, 21 March 1983.

54 'More recently, Ian Potter': *Design and Art Direction*, September 1984.

56 'The men at the corporate': *The Gallagher Report* newsletter, New York, 1988.

56 'In the UK, 1988': *Campaign*, 19 February 1988, and 17 June 1988.

56 'In the US, *Adweek*': *Adweek*, 3 June 1985.

56 'Winston Fletcher said': *Campaign*, 11 April 1986.

57 'An anonymous creative head': *Design and Art Direction*, 19 April 1984.

57 'In 1976, a paper': Quoted in *Campaign*, 21 May 1976.

58 Shepherd Mead, author of': *Campaign*, 7 May 1976.

58 'Joe Bensman, a sociologist': *Dollars and Sense*, Macmillan, New York, 1987.

58 'Or as Jerry della Femina': della Femina speaking on Public Television in January 1975.

Chapter 2

62 'There was a similar': Graham Poulter, *Marketing*, 14 November 1985.

62 'Research carried out in': *Admap*, February 1982.

63 'Overall, the amount spent': Eileen Cole, chief executive, Research International, London.

64 'A little unnecessary but': *The Persuasion Industry*.

64 'Albert Lasker, who has': *Advertising, The Uneasy Persuasion*.

64 'After thousands of experiences': *The Trouble with Advertising*.

64 'Bill Bernbach's view': *Madison Avenue USA*.

64 'John O'Toole, chairman': *The Trouble with Advertising*.
64 'Or what of a paragraph': Paul E. Green and Catherine M. Schaffer, 'Ad Copy Testing', *Journal of Advertising Research*, Vol 23, No 5, October–November 1983.
65 'Iain Murray, an English': *Marketing Week*, 1 February 1985.
65 'Viewed that way': Herbert Zeltner in *Advertising Age*, 26 July 1982.
65 'The New York agency': Ayer company history.
66 'Around the same time': *Madison Avenue USA*.
67 'More than sixty years': *Advertising Age*, 30 January 1984.
69 'By the mid 1970s': Alan Resnik and Bruce L. Stern, 'An Analysis of information Content in Television Advertising', *Journal of Marketing*, January 1977.
69 'By the same criteria': Bruce L. Stern, Dean M. Krugman, Alan Resnik, 'Magazine Advertising: An Analysis of its Information Content', *Journal of Advertising Research*, April 1981.
69 'Advertising, believes Marcel': *The Rage to Persuade*.
69 'Professor Hugh Rank': *The Pitch*.
69 'David Bernstein, a well-known': *Creative Advertising*.
74 'He told the British': *The Persuasion Industry*.
75 'He illustrates the difference': *Research in Marketing*, Vol 1, 1978.
76 'Another client, an oil': *Research in Marketing*, Vol 1, 1978.
77 'Dichter argues that': *Research in Marketing*, Vol 1, 1978.
77 'Is it moral to': *The Strategy of Desire*.
78 'The central point': *Strategic Ad Campaigns*.
79 'Sue Robson, managing director': *Campaign*, 15 July 1983.
79 'In Britain, the London': *Creative Review*, July 1982.
80 'According to Cooper and': Cooper and Lannon, 'Humanistic Advertising, A Cultural Perspective', *International Journal of Advertising*, 1983, 2.
80 'in a paper co-authored': Cooper and Lannon, 'Humanistic Advertising, A Cultural Perspective', *International Journal of Advertising*, 1983, 2.
81 'In a political research': Lunn, Cooper, Murphy, 'The Fluctuating Fortunes of the UK Social Democratic Party: An Application of Creative Qualitative Research'.
83 Planmetric projects – *Wall Street Journal*, 7 July 1983; *Adweek*, 5 September; *Advertising Age*, 14 January 1985.
87 'She says that she': *Campaign*, 7 December 1984.
87 'Within six months': *Fortune*, 23 July 1984.

Chapter 3

94 'Incorporating both emotional and': *Psychology and Marketing*, Vol 1, No 1, spring 1984.
94 'Y & R, he adds': *Advertising Age*, 31 October 1983.
95 'The cover which does best': *Sunday Times Magazine*, 30 October 1983.
95 'At least one British': *Marketing Week*, 18 May 1984.
95 'Such a device is': *The Times*, 31 May 1986.
96 'ARC makes play of': *Advertising Age*, 24 November 1986.
96 'Barry Day, recalling a': *And You Call That Creative . . .?*

97 'In one such test': *Journal of Advertising Research*, Vol 23, No 5, October/November 1983.

97 'One comparatively cheap system': *Marketing*, 29 March 1984.

98 'If replacing the interviewer': *Marketing*, 20 September 1984.

98 'Studies published in the': James MacLachlan and Michael Siegal, 'Reducing the costs of TV commercials by use of time compression,' *Journal of Marketing Research*, Vol 17, No 1, February 1980.

99 'Additionally, Time-compression': James MacLachlan, 'Listener perception of time-compressed spokespersons', *Journal of Advertising Research*, Vol 22, No 2, April/May 1982.

99 'However, D. J. R. Coulson': Letter, 13 February 1986.

100 'Leonard Matthews, president of': *Wall Street Journal*, 10 February 1984.

100 'Al Ries and Jack Trout': *Advertising Age*, 14 March 1983.

101 'Three researchers, including the': Robert C. Grass, Wallace H. Wallace and Wayne G. Robertshaw, 'The NOLAD Concept,' *Journal of Advertising Research*, Vol 23, No 1, February/March 1983.

102 'For example, Dr Herbert Krugman': *Journal of Advertising Research*, Vol 23, No 1, February/March 1983.

102 'Two of them, David': David A. Aaker and Donald E. Bruzzone, 'Viewer perceptions of prime-time television advertising', *Journal of Advertising Research*, Vol 21, No 5, October 1981.

103 'Jerry Jontry, eastern manager': *Advertising Age*, 8 August 1983.

105 'In the *Harvard Business*': *Harvard Business Review*, July–August 1982.

106 'Helmut Sihler, of the': *Financial Times*, 20 October 1980.

107 'Without recall there is': Letter in *Advertising Age*, 13 February 1984.

107 'One of the most': *Harvard Business Review*, March–April 1975.

108 'Agencies generally were reported': *Campaign*, 22 February 1985.

108 'Adrian Hosford, BT's head': *Marketing*, 7 March 1985.

109 'In the UK in': *Advertising Inside Out*.

109 'By 1987 over 90': *Focus*, March 1987.

110 'Laurence Gold, of ERIM': *Advertising Age*, 6 September 1984.

111 'William D. Wells, director': *Journal of Advertising Research*, Vol 22, No 1, February/March 1982.

111 'Sir Hedley le Bas': 'Advertising for an Army' in *The Lord Kitchener Memorial Book*.

112 'Denys Thompson in his': *Voice of Civilisation*.

113 'One research team concluded': I. L. Janis, 'Effects of Fear Arousal on Attitude Change, Recent Developments in Theory and Experimental Research,' *Advances in Experimental Psychology*, Vol 3, Academic Press, New York, 1967.

113 '"In fact," reported': *Tobacco Reporter*, June 1982.

113 'Barry Day, of McCann': *Campaign*, 1 March 1985.

114 'Is everything going': *Advertising Age*, 7 May 1984.

114 'A young English creative in': *Cosmopolitan*, July 1983.

114 'The following examples are': 'Naked Ape', *Guardian*.

115 'A 1983 study': Davis and Welsch, *International Journal of Advertising*.

115 'Another piece of research': Chestnut, LaChance and Lubitz, 'The Decorative Female Model: Sexual Stimuli and the Recognition of Advertisements', *Journal of Advertising*, 6, 1977.

115 'Two other researchers concluded': Baker and Churchill, 'The Impact of

Physically Attractive Models on Advertising Evaluations,' *Journal of Marketing Research*, November 1977.

115 'More recently, in 1987': *Guardian*, 19 January 1987.
117 'In Argentina, television': *Advertising Age*, 9 December 1985.
118 'Wilson Bryan Key, who': *Subliminal Seduction*.
119 'Walter Weir, an associate': Weir, 'Another Look at Subliminal Facts', *Advertising Age*, 15 October 1984.
119 'Claims that the Welsh': *Advertising in a Free Society*.
121 'Dr Stephen Kelly, a': *Journal of Advertising*, Vol 8, No 3, 1979.
121 'Six years later a': *Advertising Age*, 26 August 1985.
122 'Three researchers interviewed': Zanot, Pincus, Lamp, 'Public Perceptions of Subliminal Advertising', *Journal of Advertising*, Vol 12, No 1, 1983.
122 'Thus in January 1986': *The Times*, 17 January 1986.
122 'Wallace LaBenne, a psychotherapist': Grand Rapids Press, 1983.
123 'The US magazine, *New Woman*': *New Woman* press release, 30 September 1983.
123 'I note with interest': UPI, 11 May 1978.

Chapter 4

126 'Even in Brazil': *Advertising Age*, 1 April 1985.
127 'In one case the': *Marketing*, 3 June 1983.
127 'In another, at the': *Evening Argus*, Brighton, 16 February 1984.
127 'In the United States': *Consumer Behavior*.
127 'Formal FTC proceedings': *The Trouble with Advertising*.
128 'Stanley E. Cohen': *Advertising Age*, 5 March 1984.
128 'In 1983, the FTC': *Advertising Age*, 6 February 1984.
128 'Three years later': *Advertising Age*, 17 November 1986.
128 'In one case the': *Advertising Age*, 3 June 1985.
130 'Peter Rennie, chairman': *Admap* Seminar, London, 29 October 1981.
130 'Between 2 and 3 per cent': 'Advertising Control', the IBA.
130 '"Taste and decency"': *Campaign*, 4 December 1981.
130 Salesman and lager scripts: *Design and Art Direction*, September 1985.
131 'Another, for Heineken lager': *Campaign*, 4 December 1981.
131 'The word "lefty" was': *Campaign*, 2 October 1981.
131 'An ad that would . . .': *Guardian*, 10 March 1983.
131 Various complaints: BA, *Campaign*, 23 September 1983; Russia, wig, *Campaign*, 25 January 1985; rock, *The Times*, 16 March 1983; Holy, *Campaign*, 15 June 1984; Quavers, *Campaign*, 5 October 1984; frog, *The Times*, 9 July 1983.
132 'The committee's responsibility': Speech to *Admap* Seminar, London, 29 October 1981.
133 'Leonard Matthews, president of': *Advertising Age*, 25 June 1984.
133 'In addition, the ASA': *Campaign*, 16 September 1983.
135 'The Oxford dictionary'; *Marketing Week*, 9 September 1983.
135 'Beecham was prevented from': *Financial Times*, 27 October 1983.
135 'The MFI furniture chain': *Marketing*, 15 April 1981.
137 Continental Baking Company case: *Consumer Behavior*.

137 Listerine mouthwash ad – *Advertising Age*, December 1980 and *Campaign*, 13 November 1981.

137 'Albert Lasker said allowing': *The Mirror Makers*.

138 'The Buckingham Company was': *Advertising Age*, 15 June 1987.

139 'Leonard Matthews, president of': *Advertising Age*, 11 June 1983.

140 'Robin Wight, of': *Campaign*, 2 August 1985.

140 'Richard Glitter, vice-president': *Wall Street Journal*, 16 January 1984.

141 'Professor J. J. Boddewyn': *Journal of International Marketing*, Vol 1, No 1, 1982.

142 'Advertising, argued a United': 'Transnational Corporations in Advertising'. UN, NY.

142 'Wealth is used to': Noreene Janus and Rafael Roncaglioli, 'Advertising entry, Mass Media and Dependency', Development Dialogue, Latin American Institute for Transnational Studies, 1979.

142 'Advertisers at the American': *Advertising Age*, 23 June 1986.

143 'One consultant has suggested': Richard K. Manoff, a social marketing and communications consultant in *Advertising Age*, 13 February 1984.

144 'Philip J. Circus, legal': *Advertising Age*, 30 August 1984.

144 'In the United States': Professor J. J. Boddewyn, *Journal of International Marketing*, Vol 1, No 1, 1982.

145 'Peter Rennie, chairman of': *Admap* Seminar, London, 29 August 1981.

146 'In Washington he': *Campaign*, 28 May 1982.

146 'In Australia he has': *Campaign*, 8 April 1983.

146 'Thus Waterson wrote': *Campaign*, 23 November 1984.

149 'It is *not* the case': *Admap* Seminar, 29 October 1981.

149 First Amendment protection: Versfelt, *Advertising Age*, 7 July 1986; Luken, *Advertising Age*, 13 April 1987.

150 'Philip Circus enthused': *Marketing*, 21 March 1985.

150 'The authors of a paper': Bruce, Keller, Cunard etc, 'Worldwide Restrictions on Advertising: An Outline of Principles, Problems and Solutions', IAA, 1984.

152 'An ad showing a': *Advertising Age*, 4 November 1985.

152 Depression years examples: *The Shocking History of Advertising*.

154 'In the United States': *Washington Post* service in *Adweek*, 21 January 1985.

154 AIDS campaign examples: *Advertising Age*, 9 March 1987, and *Focus*, February 1987.

156 Harry Theobalds, IBA's: *Marketing*, 13 June, 1985.

156 'One was broken in 1985': *Advertising Age*, 11 March 1985.

157 Cemetery ads: *Wall Street Journal*, 27 January 1984.

158 Surveys of professional advertising: *Focus*, October 1984, and *Advertising Age*, 24 September 1984.

158 '"The only thing worse"': *The Times*, 30 September 1983.

159 'In Australia, the firm': *Financial Times*, 19 July 1984.

159 'The screen shows a': *Wall Street Journal*, 14 March 1984.

Chapter 5

164 'Thus, Midway Airlines': *Advertising Age*, 7 February 1985.

165 British social grade groups: JICNARS, National Readership Survey, 1979.

166 US social grade groups: the Warner Social Class Hierarchy, quoted in *Contemporary Marketing*.

166 'By 1982 *Time* in an ad': *Advertising Age*, 16 August 1982.

168 'The agency Benton and Bowles': *The Atlantic Monthly*, October 1984.

168 'Questrel, the qualitative': *Marketing*, 2 April 1987.

168 'One marketing professional': *Time*, 20 April 1987.

168 'Yankelovich, Clancy and Schulman': Research prepared for *People* magazine, 1986.

169 'Yet another grouping': *Marketing*, 12 June 1986.

169 Timex advertising: *Ad Forum*, September 1984.

169 VALS history and categories: *Principles of the VALS Classification System*, SRI.

171 'One critic told *Ad Forum*': *Ad Forum*, September 1984.

172 'Plummer, an executive': SRI literature.

172 Merrill Lynch ad campaign: *Insight*, 19 September 1984; *Advertising Age*, 9 November 1982; *The Atlantic Monthly*, October 1984.

177 'Another, ClusterPlus, from': Ad in *Advertising Age*, 19 September 1983.

179 'Harold Lind, a British': *Campaign*, 6 May 1983.

179 'Today it is hard': *International Herald Tribune*, 15 August 1985.

179 'In France, Michel Suquet': *Focus*, November 1984.

180 'Carbonated soft drinks are': research by Goldring and Co, Chicago, 1987.

180 'Mo Drake, a creative': *Campaign*, 29 June 1984.

180 'One company, Ramada Inns': *Wall Street Journal*, 31 August 1984.

181 '*The Economist* began': *The Economist*, 23 January 1982.

181 'Peter Frisch, publisher of': *Sunday Telegraph*, 14 November 1982.

181 'Another is Seagram': *Advertising Age*, 26 March 1984.

182 Film advertising examples: *Sunday Telegraph*, 14 November 1982.

182 'One gay advertising executive': *Advertising Age*, 26 March 1984.

183 '"Black people are not"': *Advertising Age*, 19 November 1984.

184 '"In many black households"': *Crain's Chicago Business*, 21 May 1984.

184 'It is not surprising that': *Wall Street Journal*, 23 March 1982.

185 'A 1985 survey of': Carrick James Market Research.

185 'Teenagers in the US': Rand Youth Poll, New York, 1985.

185 'Yankelovich studies for': Advertisements for *Seventeen* magazine.

186 'Heather Auton, the company's': *Marketing*, 22 July 1982.

186 'Selina S. Guber': *Advertising Age*, 23 December 1985.

186 'Budgets are big: in': *Financial Times*, 7 February 1985.

186 'Kool-Aid soft drinks . . .': *New York Post*, 2 April 1985.

187 'Don Blundell, UK': *Marketing*, 7 June 1984.

187 'Thus, this extract': *The Shocking History of Advertising*.

188 'Yet the following remark': *Boston Globe*, 14 February 1985.

188 'Thus Selina Guber': *Advertising Age*, 23 December 1985.

189 '"Role playing," David Brown': *Marketing*, 6 September 1984.

189 'Children don't think or': ad in *Advertising Age*, 5 March 1984.
191 'Other survey material claimed': ad for *Seventeen*, 1983.
191 'They choose between': *Advertising Age*, 14 November 1985.
191 'Perhaps most stunning': *Fortune*, 30 March 1987.
192 'Sid Bernstein, the advertising': *Advertising Age*, 4 June 1984.
192 Rules regarding confectionery: *Here's Health*, July 1983.
193 'In the US and the': *Campaign*, 16 October 1981.
194 'The staff, in a': *Advertising Age*, 6 April 1981.
194 'Action for Children's Television attempted': *Advertising Age*, 27 June 1983.
194 '*Advertising Age*'s reporter': *Advertising Age*, 8 October 1984.
194 Programmes built on toys: *Advertising Age*, 3 November 1986; *The Listener*, 9 October 1986.
195 'Chris Wicks of Zodiac': *Marketing*, 5 February 1987.
196 'Peter Brown, UK managing': *Marketing*, 5 February 1987.
196 'A British toy retailer': *Marketing*, 5 February 1987.
197 'George F. Schweitzer': *Business Week*, 25 March 1985.
197 'In 1987, the emergence': *Observer*, 3 May 1987; *Advertising Age*, 9 February 1987.
197 Euromonitor Report: Report on the Toy Industry, 1987.
199 'Thus Action for Children's Television': *Fighting TV Stereotypes*, an ACT Handbook.
200 'Glen Smith, managing director': paper given to IPA, edited version published *Advertising* magazine, spring 1981.
200 'In reviewing it in 1983': Roberts, 'Children and commercials: Issues, Evidence, Intervention', 1983.

Chapter 6

203 GP prescribing figures. Year 1985–6, from the Chartered Institute of Public Finance and Accountancy
204 'Routinely, 1,000 tablets': *Marketing*, 19 September 1985.
204 'Research and development cost': Association of the British Pharmaceutical Industry.
204 'Thanks to astute promotion': *Time*, 27 September 1982.
205 'By 1984 there were': *The Economist*, 18 August 1984.
205 'Hans-Peter Hauser': *Wall Street Journal*, 9 February 1983.
206 'Two doctors from the': *Marketing Week*, 25 February 1983.
206 Ad spend in US journals: *Medical Marketing and Media*, CRS Communications, Florida.
207 'Wyeth Laboratories is another': *Wall Street Journal*, 28 December 1981.
207 'Indeed this proved': A. Braithwaite and P. Cooper, Analgesic Effects of Branding in Treatment of Headaches, *British Medical Journal*, 1981.
208 'That is to say': Lannon and Cooper in *International Journal of Advertising*, 2, 1983.
208 'You might *expect* the': *Which?*, February 1982.
208 'Stephen King, the creative': *Advertising Age*, 8 July 1985.
209 'The Public Citizen Health': *Stopping Valium*.

210 'In 1984 Professor Rawlings': *The Times*, 3 August 1984.
211 'With commendable disinterest': *Pharmaceutical Executive*, March 1985.
211 'Lloyd Millstein, director of': *Pharmaceutical Executive*, March 1985.
212 '"They're labelling it"': *Medical Marketing and Media*, March 1985.
212 '"This," commented Paul Vine': *Campaign*, 16 July 1982.
213 'The putting together': *GP*, 4 December 1981.
213 '"Few," wrote Jenny Bryan': *GP*, 4 December 1981.
215 'One company alone': ESOMAR Seminar, Zürich, September 1981.
216 'In 1985, a Direct': Direct Marketing Awards, 1985.
217 'George Teeling-Smith': Green College Lecture, Oxford, 25 January 1982.
218 'John J. Fisher, president': *Advertising Age*, 28 January 1985.
218 'In the UK there': *Marketing*, 19 September 1985.
218 'The televised scene, said': *Guardian*, 2 February 1983.
219 'in the words of one FDA': *Time*, 27 September 1982.
219 'If that was not enough': *Time*, 27 September 1982.
219 'The following year an experiment': *Sunday Times*, 15 January 1984.
219 'The same year Pfizer's': *Guardian*, 10 September 1984.
220 'The *Sunday Times* again': *Sunday Times*, 13 May 1984.
220 'Then Bayer, the UK': *World in Action*, Granada TV, 18 May 1987.
221 'Between 1977 and 1980': *The Economist*, 12 March 1983.
221 'An Indian campaign': *Insult or Injury*.
221 'Oxfam found that': *Bitter Pills: Medicine and the Third World Poor*.
221 'In East Africa': *Africa Now*, October 1984.
222 'An eight-year study': M. Silverman, M. Lydecker and Dr P. Lee, *Prescriptions for Death*, 1982.
222 '"It's an alarming thought"': *Sunday Express*, 24 January 1982.
225 'A congressional sub-committee': *Pharmaceutical Executive*, March 1985.
226 'Merck, for example, made': *Advertising Age*, 15 October 1984.
226 'A Roche spokesman told': *Medical Advertising News*, 15 March 1985.
227 'One analyst, Dr John': *Advertising Age*, 27 September 1982.
227 'The most striking single': *Wall Street Journal*, 22 July 1982.
227 'In Britain, where the drug': *Private Eye*.
227 'Dr Robert Temple, director': *Financial Times*, 29 December 1983.
228 'In Britain, in a twelve': *Marketing*, 12 April 1984.
228 'Lydia E. Pinkhams': *This Fabulous Century*, Time-Life Books.
228 Holloway's Pills detail: *Sunday Times Magazine*, 18 February 1968.
229 Maclean, Phaylex, Eno's examples: Brian Cleeve, *A World Vanishing*, Buchan and Enright, 1982.
230 '*Marketing* magazine spoke to': *Marketing*, 12 April 1984.
230 US figures: Proprietary Association, Washington DC. Figures are for end 1986.
230 UK figures: *The British Pharmaceutical Industry*, Jordan and Sons (Surveys), 1980.
230 'A Sterling Health product': *Marketing*, 16 September 1981.
230 'Sterling's Panadol, already': *Wall Street Journal*, 6 May 1983.
231 'American Home Products ran': *Wall Street Journal*, 19 October 1983.
231 'Ad approaches vary': *Advertising Age*, 3 June 1985.
231 'Ronald A. Ahrens': *Wall Street Journal*, 17 December 1981.
231 'The *Observer*, London, obtained': The *Observer*, 8 April 1984.
232 'Imodium is a prescription': *Marketing*, 9 May 1985.

Chapter 7

234 'British-American Tobacco': *The Smoke Ring.*
234 'Six multinational companies dominate': *The Smoke Ring.*
234 'In England, Saatchi and': *Campaign*, 20 February 1970.
235 'A publication like': *Advertising Age*, 16 December 1985.
237 'Until the 1880s': *The Making of Modern Advertising* and *The Smoke Ring.*
237 'Player's cigarettes adopted': *The Shocking History of Advertising.*
238 'Advertisers of other': Museum of Broadcasting.
238 'In 1904 a young woman': *This Fabulous Century*, Time-Life Books.
238 'Organisations including temperance': *Advertising: The Uneasy Persuasion.*
238 'Philip H. Dougherty': *New York Times*, 26 February 1982.
239 'John Doorley, creative': *Advertising Age*, 12 September 1983.
240 'For Camel, this meant': *Advertising Age*, 31 December 1984.
244 'Barry Day, worldwide creative': *And You Call That Creative . . .?*
244 'Two researchers, a sociologist': 'Forging an Identity for the Non-smoker: The Use of Myth in Health Promotion', Simon Chapman, Gary Egger, *International Journal of Health Education*, July–September 1980.
  245 Camel campaign: *BBDO Magazine*, July 1981.
246 'Brazilians, it seemed': *Advertising Age*, 31 December 1984.
246 'The Marlboro cowboy': *Campaign*, 27 April 1984.
250 'Grey/Kim in Italy': *Grey View*, No 3, 1981.
251 'Edward A. Horrigan': *Business Week*, 7 December 1981.
253 'And not only on': *Campaign*, 9 July 1982.
253 'The following month BAT': *Campaign*, 27 August 1982.
253 'The following year': *Campaign*, 3 September 1983.
256 'One, Charles Plouviez': *Marketing*, 7 February 1985.
257 'Bernard Barnett, the editor': *Marketing*, 10 March 1983.

Chapter 8

262 'One major study which': Charles Atkin and Martin Block, 'The Problem of Alcohol Advertisements in College Newspapers,' *The Journal of American College Health Association*, February 1979, and 'Effectiveness of Celebrity Endorsers', *Journal of Advertising Research*, February/March 1983.
262 'It was said that': *Drinks Marketing*, June 1983.
262 'To envisage the scale of': leading national advertisers.
263 'A "Case History"' BMP Case History No 1, 'The Big John Campaign: A Study of TV Advertising in the Beer Market (Courage)', 1982.
264 'An advertising executive, Charles Sharp': statement to the US Senate committee hearing on smoking, 10 May 1982.
265 'Bart Cummins, the veteran': letter to *Advertising Age*, 29 July 1985.
267 'This means in effect': Mike Detsiny in *Campaign*, 1 August 1986.

267 'The general manager of': *Wall Street Journal*, 5 January 1982.
268 'A former Anheuser division': *Business Week*, 12 July 1982.
268 'Anheuser's own Budweiser': *Business Week*, 12 July 1982.
269 'A Schlitz marketing executive': Quoted in the *Los Angeles Times*.
269 'Simon Mallalieu, a director': *Marketing*, 28 November 1985.
270 'This is a drink': report by Phillips Russell Ltd., published in *Drinks Marketing*, September 1983.
271 'Karp believes the': *Hot Shoe*, No 38, 1984.
271 'In France itself, Pernod': *Focus*, November 1983.
272 'Dewar's advertising featured': *Marketing*, 29 April 1982.
272 '"We're trying to emulate"': *Wall Street Journal*, 28 June 1984.
273 'An executive of Brown-Forman': *Advertising Age*, 27 July 1981.
275 'David Ogilvy puts it': *Ogilvy on Advertising*.
275 'In the UK, 20': Wyman-Harris Research Organisation.
277 'It is one that': *The Booze Merchants*.
279 'As Bruce Weininger, chief': *Advertising Age*, 16 August 1982.
280 'One critic of the time': *Voice of Civilisation*.
280 'The situation changes, but': *The Booze Merchants*.
281 'Thirty-five years later': report of the Department Committee on Liquor Licensing, UK, 1972.
281 'Commentators saw this as': Williams and Brake, *Drink in Great Britain*.
283 'Carl Hixon, creator and': *Focus*, September 1983.
284 'The Center for Science': *The Booze Merchants*.
285 'in the UK, the industry': Alcohol Studies Centre, Paisley College of Technology, Scotland; Wine and Spirit Association; Scotch Whisky Association.

Chapter 9

292 'An American adwoman': *Advertising Age*, 5 November 1984.
292 '*Advertising Age* in a': *Advertising Age*, 16 May 1983.
292 'Eight candidates stood': *Advertising Age*, 5 December 1983.
292 'Mrs Aquino retaliated': *Advertising Age*, 24 February 1986.
292 'In Chile, General': *Advertising Age*, 9 September 1986.
293 'An American survey in': Vitt Media International and St John University Survey, *Advertising Age*, 6 August 1984.
294 'Experts said it was': *Advertising Age*, 11 May 1987.
294 'In 1985, *Advertising Age*': *Advertising Age*, 28 February 1985.
295 'The colour was also': *The Listener*, 3 October 1985.
296 1986 Congressional elections: *Advertising Age*, 10 November 1986.
297 'David Ogilvy credits': *Ogilvy on Advertising*.
297 'As the English adman': *Financial Times*, 15 March 1979.
297 'Peter Jay, the former': *Design and Art Direction*, April 1985.
298 'Agencies were too afraid': *A Walk Through the 20th Century*, PBS, 8 August 1984.
298 'Its creator, Tony Schwartz': PBS, as above.
298 'Goldwater had once said': *Television*.
298 'Roger Stone, a consultant': *Advertising Age*, 10 November 1986.

298 'John O'Toole, an outspoken': *The Trouble with Advertising*.
299 'Henry Cabot Lodge': *Television*.
299 'In one campaign': *Ogilvy on Advertising*.
299 1984 elections: *Campaign*, 24 August 1984, and *Ad Age*, May 1984.
300 'In a commercial attacking': *The Times*, 18 August 1984.
300 'In an attempt': *Advertising Age*, 1 February 1988.
300 'One estimate for the': *Observer*, 1 May 1984.
301 'Robert Spero, author': *Evening Standard*, 4 April 1984.
301 'The sales director of': *Advertising Age*, 17 January 1983.
301 'In practice, what this': *Campaign*, 27 May 1983.
301 'Before television became a': *And You Call That . . .*
302 'Some people, reported': *Wall Street Journal*, 26 May 1983.
302 'Tim Delaney, head of': *Wall Street Journal*, 26 May 1983.
303 'One adman involved in': *Evening Standard*, 4 April 1984.
305 'Judith Press Brenner': *Advertising Age*, 12 July 1984.
305 'Robin Wight, who': *Campaign*, 18 May, 1979.
306 'He wants the BBC': *Media Week*, 26 July 1985.
306 'A former Saatchi colleague': *Campaign*, 25 January 1985.
307 'During the 1983': *Time*, 21 February 1983.
307 'The Communist Party in Italy': *Advertising Age*, 9 June 1986.
308 'The *Observer* commented': *Observer*, 31 May 1987.
308 'BMP is the agency': *Campaign*, 6 June 1980.
309 'Livingstone himself was': *Marketing*, 28 June 1984.
313 'A leader, under the': *The Times*, 6 June 1987.
314 'Any time a political': *Advertising Age*, 12 March 1984.

Chapter 10

317 'The media no longer': Janus and Roncagliolo, 'Advertising Entry, Mass Media and Dependency,' Latin American Institute for Transnational Studies, 1979.
317 'Even a newspaper': *The Media Monopoly*.
318 'In a message to advertisers': *Advertising Age Yearbook*, 1981.
318 'Marcel Bleustein-Blanchet': *The Rage to Persuade*.
318 'To promote its year-end': *Advertising Age*, 5 December 1983.
320 'Worldwide, print is': Figures compiled by Saatchi and Saatchi
320 'According to 1976 figures': *Transnational Corporations in Advertising*.
320 'In the United States': JWT, Unilever Co-ordination Group.
320 'In Britain, over 28': AA European Advertising and Media Forecast.
321 'Torin Douglas, a trade': *The Complete Guide to Advertising*.
321 'With magazines, for example': Marvin Grapp, vice-president, Magazine Publishers Association, *New York Times* Service, 1985.
321 'A 1919 textbook': *Advertising: Its Principles and Practice*.
321 'According to Stephen Fox': *The Mirror Makers*.
322 Northcliffe missives: *Advertising in Britain*.
323 'Sixty-three years later': *The Media Monopoly*.
323 'Perhaps not surprisingly': *The Trouble with Advertising*.
324 'In another Camel-sponsored : *The Media Monopoly* and *Television*.

324 'The De Soto car': *Television*
324 'On another occasion': Russell Davies, 'Hype and Hard Sell', *The Listener*, 24 October 1985.
324 'Even more obscenely': *Television*.
326 'Mayhew, in a pamphlet': *Television*.
326 'Reith himself thundered': *Television Today and Tomorrow*.
326 'European countries generally': Anthony Sampson, *The New Europeans*, Hodder and Stoughton, 1968.
326 'The mass market "has"', *Business Week*, 21 November 1983.
327 'Furthermore, almost one': Magazine Publishers Association, 1983.
327 'In 1985 an eighty': *Marketing*, 2 May 1985.
328 'Ron de Pear': *Marketing*, 27 September 1984.
328 Sandwich boards, Lipton, Barratt: *History of Advertising*.
328 Telegrams, cloud projectors: *The Shocking History of Advertising*.
328 'In the 1920s and': *The History of Advertising*.
328 'The first client': *Campaign*, 2 August 1985.
329 'We have totally': *Marketing*, 8 November 1984.
329 'No one is pretending': *Campaign*, 11 February 1983.
330 'The head of one': *Ogilvy on Advertising*.
330 'An American survey': *Where Does the Time Go?* A study by United Media Enterprises, New York, 1982.
330 'It has been estimated': Edmund Fawcett, *America, Americans*, Collins, 1983.
331 'In 1987, the average': BARB/AGB Trends in Television.
331 'Ron Kaatz, director of': *Advertising Age*, 10 February 1986.
334 'Stewart Butterfield, media': *Focus*, November 1984.
334 'Two years later a survey': *New Electronic Media*, Euromonitor Reports.
334 'Michael Tracey, head of': *The Times*, 8 November 1983.
335 'Jeremy Bullmore, chairman': *Wall Street Journal*, 22 March 1982.
336 'Sweden, by 1987': *Campaign*, 22 November 1985; *Advertising Age*, 31 March 1986.
336 'By 1987 most observers': *Campaign*, 8 May 1987.
336 'More advertising time had': *Focus*, April 1985.
337 'There, according to': *Wall Street Journal*, 27 January 1983.
337 'As an example': *Advertising Age*, 4 January 1988.
338 'A paper by J. Walter': 'Advertising and the Media', Number 5 in a series of JWT papers, 1975.
338 'Harold Lind, an economist': 'Advertising and Economics', Number 2 in a series of JWT papers, 1976.
339 'Harold Fellows, the president': 'If Advertising Stopped at Ten O'clock this Morning', quoted in *Advertising in a Free Society*.
339 'In 1982, at a': *Advertising Age*, 10 May 1982.
340 'Rupert Murdoch, who': *Everybody's Business*.
341 'In October 1959, the': *The Tuppenny Punch and Judy Show*.
341 'Twenty-three years later': *Daily Mirror*, 26 February 1982.
343 'The United States': *Advertising Age*, 7 November 1985.
344 'The Monty Python': *Evening Argus*, Brighton, 16 July 1982.
344 'In 1983, *Advertising Age*': *Advertising Age*, 29 August 1983.
344 'The following year, the': *Advertising Age*, 11 June 1984.
345 'One city journalist took': *Observer*, 22 April 1984.

345 'Trevor Grove, editor': *Marketing Week*, 6 April 1984.

346 'One writer to *Campaign*': *Campaign*, 3 February 1984.

347 'Peter Verbeck, executive creative': *Advertising Age*, 30 April 1984.

347 'Freddie Beech, UK': *Campaign*, 23 December 1983.

348 James Autry quotes: speech at a seminar at the Center for Communication, New York, 1 November 1984.

349 'An English journalist, Sandra': *Independent*, 9 December 1986.

349 'All this pales beside': *Advertising Age*, 3 October 1985.

350 'The *Wall Street Journal*': *Wall Street Journal*, 22 November 1982.

351 'ACSH's comments on five': *ACSH News and Views*, Vol 3, No 3, May/June 1982.

351 'One involved Paul Maccabee': *Wall Street Journal*, 22 November 1982.

351 'ACSH cites a third': *ACSH News and Views*, Vol 3, No 3, May/June 1982.

352 'By the mid 1980s': *Guardian*, 17 February 1986.

353 'American television, points out': *The Listener*, 24 October 1985.

353 'John O'Toole, chairman of': *The Trouble with Advertising*.

353 'Not one half second': *America and the Americans*.

354 'Sid Bernstein, the *Advertising Age*': *Advertising Age*, 27 August 1984.

354 'A T & T has found': *Campaign*, 20 July 1984.

355 'One argued, "We believe"': *Advertising Age*, 3 October 1983.

355 'One public broadcaster': *Advertising Age*, 21 October 1985.

355 'Each May, for example': *The Listener*, 24 October 1985.

356 'The audience was': *Television*.

357 'Holiday Inns refused': *Wall Street Journal*, 29 June 1982.

357 'Wilfred Greatorex, the scriptwriter': letter to *The Times*, 27 March 1986.

358 'It was the chairman': *Campaign*, 31 August 1984.

358 'The following year *Advertising Age*': *Advertising Age*, 8 March 1982.

358 'One I have before': report of the spring 1982 Television Monitoring Program of The Coalition for Better Television.

359 'The National Coalition on': letter dated 14 May 1982.

359 'As a result, five': *Independent*, 5 November 1986.

359 'The Rev. Jerry Falwell': *Advertising Age*, 21 November 1983.

360 'Jeff Greenfield, media': *The Listener*, 24 October 1985.

361 'Italy is a warning': *The Television Explosion*, BBC TV, 11 November 1986.

361 'The Home Shopping Show': BEUC, 'The Impact of Satellite and Cable Television on Advertising'.

362 'A paper published by': 'Advertising and the Media,' a JWT paper.

366 'He [the husband] could: *Campaign*, 3 May 1985.

366 'Bob Harvey, an executive': letter dated 13 April 1983.

366 'Kovoloff says, "Seeing"': *New York Times*, 15 November 1982.

368 'The joint managing director': *Campaign*, 19 July 1985.

368 'Thus Tesco puts': *Campaign*, 19 July 1985.

368 'In Britain, it is': *Evening Argus*, Brighton, 31 May 1986.

369 'The satirical programme': *Spitting Image*, 13 January 1985.

370 'The Victoria and Albert': *The Times*, 23 October 1985.

370 'Britain's arts festivals': *Sunday Times*, 25 May 1986.

The Future

371 'Malcolm Muggeridge prophesies': *Advertising Age*, 7 April 1986.
371 'Pope John Paul II has': Apostolic Letter, March 1985.
371 'In Britain Lever Brothers': *Marketing*, 26 July 1984.
374 'In Thailand': *Advertising Age*, 20 August 1984.
374 'A Toronto soccer referee': *Evening Standard*, 15 May 1967.
375 'English press photographers': *Focus*, September 1985.
375 'By 1981 . . . two-thirds of': Roncaglioli and Janus, 'Advertising and the Democratisation of Communications', Development Dialogue, Sweden, 1981: 2.
375 'Take a speech by': *Advertising Age*, 13 August 1984.
375 'Or consider the views': *Campaign* Media Report, 14 October 1983.
376 'The station's Controller of': *The Listener*, 20 August 1987.
377 'Eleven years ago corporations': *The Listener*, 27 August 1987.
377 'As for hidden advertising': National Consumer Council, 'Classroom Commercials', 1986.

BIBLIOGRAPHY

AA, *Speaking up for Advertising*, Advertising Association, 1983.

AAAA, *A Practical Solution to Client-Agency Account Conflicts*, American Association of Advertising Agencies, 1979.

ACA, *Processed Food: A Pain in the Belly*, Australian Consumers' Association, 1982.

Adams, Robert (ed), *Creativity in Communications*, Studio Vista, 1971.

Adamson, Colin, *Consumers in Business*, National Consumer Council, 1982.

Allison, J. Murray, *Second Essays on Advertising*, Ernest Benn, 1929.

Arlen, Michael J., *Thirty Seconds*, Farrar, Straus and Giroux, N.Y., 1980.

Bagdikian, Ben H., *The Media Monopoly*, Beacon Press, 1983.

Bargmann, Eve, and others, *Stopping Valium*, Warner Books, 1983.

Bartos, Rena, and Dunn, Theodore F., *Advertising and Consumers – New Perspectives*, American Association of Advertising Agencies, 1975.

Beardshaw, Virginia, *Prescription for Change*, International Organisation of Consumers Unions, The Hague, 1983.

Benson, S. H., *Facts for Advertisers, 1905-6*, Compiled and published by S. H. Benson, Advertisers' Agent.

Bernstein, David, *Creative Advertising*, The Creative Business, London.

BEUC, *The Impact of Satellite and Cable Television on Advertising*, Bureau Européen des Unions de Consommateurs, Brussels, 1984.

Bleustein-Blanchet, Marcel, *The Rage to Persuade. Memoirs of a French Advertising Man*, Chelsea House, N.Y., 1982.

Bruce, *et al.*, *Worldwide Restrictions on Advertising: An Outline of Principles, Problems and Solutions*, Robert R. Bruce, Bruce P. Keller, Jeffrey P. Cunard, Debevoise Plimpton, International Advertising Association, N.Y., 28 December 1984.

Bullmore, J. J. D., and Waterson, M. J., *The Advertising Association Handbook*, Holt, Rinehart and Winston, N.Y., 1983.

Caples, John, *How to Make Your Advertising Make Money*, Prentice-Hall, New Jersey, 1983.

Casson, Herbert N., *Ads and Sales – A study of advertising and selling from the standpoint of the new principles of scientific management*, Pitman, 1913.

Chapman, Simon, *The Lung Goodbye*, Consumer Interpol, 1983.

Cole, G. D. H. and others, *Is Advertising Today a Burden or a Boon? A discussion*, New Advertisers' Press, 1930.

Day, Barry, *And You Call That Creative . . .?*, McCann-Erickson, 1984.

De Groot, G., *The Persuaders Exposed*, Associated Business Press, 1980.

Diamant, Lincoln, *Television's Classic Commercials*, Hastings House, N.Y., 1971.

Dichter, Ernest, *The Strategy of Desire*, T. V. Boardman and Co, 1960.

Douglas, Torin, *The Complete Guide to Advertising*, Macmillan, 1984.

Doyal, Leslie, *Picture of Health*, Broadcasting Support Services, 1983.

Dunkley, Christopher, *Television Today and Tomorrow. Wall-to-wall Dallas?*, Penguin, 1985.

Engel, James F., Blackwell, Roger and Kottat, David T., *Consumer Behavior*, Dryden Press, Illinois, third edition, 1978.

ESOMAR, *International Pharmaceutical Marketing Research*, report of a seminar, 1981.

Fletcher, Winston, *Advertising*, Teach Yourself Books, Hodder and Stoughton, 1978.

Fox, Stephen, *The Mirror Makers*, William Morrow, N.Y., 1984.

Freeman, William M., *The Big Name*, Printers' Ink Books, N.Y., 1957.

Fryburger, Vernon (ed), *The New World of Advertising*, Crain Books, Chicago, 1975.

Gable, Jo, *The Tuppenny Punch and Judy Show – 25 Years of TV Commercials* Michael Joseph, 1980.

Galbraith, J. K., *The Affluent Society*, Hamish Hamilton, third edition, 1978.

Ghertman, Michel, and Allen, Margaret, *An Introduction to the multinationals*, Macmillan, 1984.

Gill, Leslie E., *Advertising and Psychology*, Hutchinson's University Library, 1954.

Harris, Ralph, and Seldon, Arthur, *Advertising in a Free Society*, Institute of Economic Affairs, 1959.

Hart, Norman A. (ed), *The Director's Guide to Choosing and Using an Advertising Agency*, Director Publications, 1985.

Holme, Bryan, *Advertising – Reflections of a Century*, Heinemann, 1982.

IAA, *Global Marketing, From Now to the Twenty-First Century*, International Advertising Association Global Media Commission, 1985.

Jacobson, Bobbie, *The Ladykillers*, Pluto Press, 1981.

Jacobson, Michael, Hacker, George, and Atkins, Robert, *The Booze Merchants*, CSPI Books, Washington, DC, 1983.

Katz, Judith A., *The Ad Game*, Barnes and Noble Books, 1984.

Key, Bryan Wilson, *Media Sexploitation*, Signet, 1977.

Key, Bryan Wilson, *Subliminal Seduction*, Signet, 1974.

King, Stephen, *Advertising as a Barrier to Market Entry*, Advertising Association, 1980.

Kleinman, Philip, *Advertising Inside Out*, W. H. Allen, 1977.

Littlechild, Stephen, *The Relationship between Advertising and Price*, Advertising Association, 1982.

Marks, John, *The Search for the Manchurian Candidate – The Story of the CIA's secret efforts to control human behaviour*, Allen Lane, 1979.

Mayer, Martin, *Madison Avenue USA*, Bodley Head, 1958.

Mayle, Peter, *Thirsty Work. Ten Years of Heineken Advertising*, Macmillan, 1983.

Medawar, Charles, *Insult or Injury*, Social Audit, 1979.

Meyers, William, *The Image Makers*, Times Books, 1984.

Mitchell, Arnold, *The Nine American Lifestyles*, Warner Books, 1984.

Moskovitz, Milton, Katz, Michael, and Levering, Robert, *Everybody's Business, An Almanac*, Harper and Row, N.Y., 1980.

Muller, Mike, *Tobacco and the Third World: Tomorrow's Epidemic*, War on Want, 1978.

Nevett, T.R., *Advertising in Britain, A History*, Heinemann (for the History of Advertising Trust), 1982.

Ogilvy, David, *Ogilvy on Advertising*, Pan Books, 1983.

Ogilvy, David, *Confessions of an Advertising Man*, Longmans Green, 1963.

O'Toole, John, *The Trouble with Advertising*, Chelsea House, 1981.

Packard, Vance, *The Hidden Persuaders*, Longmans Green, 1957.

Pearson, John, and Turner, Graham, *The Persuasion Industry*, Eyre and Spottiswoode, 1965.

Pope, Daniel, *The Making of Modern Advertising*, Basic Books, N.Y., 1983.

Rank, Hugh, *The Pitch – How to Analyze Ads*, Counter-Propaganda Press, Illinois, 1982.

Reekie, W. Duncan, *Advertising and Price*, Advertising Association, 1979.

Ries, Al, and Trout, Jack, *Positioning: The Battle for Your Mind*, McGraw-Hill, N.Y., 1981.

Schisgall, Oscar, *Eyes on Tomorrow*, Doubleday/Ferguson, N.Y., 1981.

Schudson, Michael, *Advertising, The Uneasy Persuasion*, Basic Books, N.Y., 1984.

Schultz, Don E., and Martin, Dennis G., *Strategic Advertising Campaigns*, Crain Books, Chicago, 1979.

Taylor, Peter, *Smoke Ring – The Politics of Tobacco*, Bodley Head, 1984.

Thompson, Denys, *Voice of Civilisation – An Enquiry into Advertising*, Frederick Muller, 1944.

Tipper, Harry, Hollingsworth, Harry L., Hotchkiss, George Burton, and Parsons, Frank Alvah, *Advertising: Its principles and practice*, Ronald Press, N.Y., second edition, 1919.

Toffler, Alvin, *Future Shock*, Bodley Head, 1970.

Tuck, Mary, *How do we choose? A study in consumer behaviour*, Methuen, 1976.

Tunstall, Jeremy, *Communications Deregulation, The Unleashing of America's Communications Industry*, Basil Blackwell, 1986.

Turner, E. S., *The Shocking History of Advertising*, revised edition, Penguin Books, 1965.

UN, *Transnational Corporations in Advertising*, Technical Paper, United Nations, N.Y., 1979.

UNCTAD, *Marketing and Distribution of Tobacco*, Study prepared by the secretariat of the UN Conference on Trade and Development, United Nations, 1978.

Veitch, Andrew (ed), *Naked Ape*, Duckworth, 1981.

Waterson, M. J., *Advertising, Brands and Markets*, Advertising Association, 1984.

Waterson, M. J., *Advertising and Cigarette Consumption*, Advertising Association, second edition, 1982.

Wheen, Francis, *Television*, Century Publishing, 1985.

White, Roderick, *Advertising: What it is and how to do it*, McGraw-Hill, N.Y., 1980.

Wickström, Bo, *Cigarette Marketing in the Third World*, University of Gothenburg, 1979.

Williams, G. P. and Brake, G. T., *Drink in Great Britain 1900–1979*, Edsall, London, 1980.

Williams, Keith C., *Behavioural Aspects of Marketing*, Heinemann, 1981.

Williamson, Judith, *Decoding Advertisements*, Marion Boyars, 1978.

Wilson, Alexander (ed), *Advertising and the Community*, Manchester University Press, 1968.

Young, James Webb, *How to Become an Advertising Man*, Advertising Publications Inc., Chicago, 1963.

INDEX

FOR THE BEST IN PAPERBACKS, LOOK FOR THE 🐧

In every corner of the world, on every subject under the sun, Penguin represents quality and variety—the very best in publishing today.

For complete information about books available from Penguin—including Pelicans, Puffins, Peregrines, and Penguin Classics—and how to order them, write to us at the appropriate address below. Please note that for copyright reasons the selection of books varies from country to country.

In the United Kingdom: For a complete list of books available from Penguin in the U.K., please write to *Dept E.P., Penguin Books Ltd, Harmondsworth, Middlesex, UB7 0DA.*

In the United States: For a complete list of books available from Penguin in the U.S., please write to *Dept BA, Penguin*, Box 120, Bergenfield, New Jersey 07621-0120.

In Canada: For a complete list of books available from Penguin in Canada, please write to *Penguin Books Ltd, 2801 John Street, Markham, Ontario L3R 1B4.*

In Australia: For a complete list of books available from Penguin in Australia, please write to the *Marketing Department, Penguin Books Ltd, P.O. Box 257, Ringwood, Victoria 3134.*

In New Zealand: For a complete list of books available from Penguin in New Zealand, please write to the *Marketing Department, Penguin Books (NZ) Ltd, Private Bag, Takapuna, Auckland 9.*

In India: For a complete list of books available from Penguin, please write to *Penguin Overseas Ltd, 706 Eros Apartments, 56 Nehru Place, New Delhi, 110019.*

In Holland: For a complete list of books available from Penguin in Holland, please write to *Penguin Books Nederland B.V., Postbus 195, NL-1380AD Weesp, Netherlands.*

In Germany: For a complete list of books available from Penguin, please write to *Penguin Books Ltd, Friedrichstrasse 10-12, D-6000 Frankfurt Main I, Federal Republic of Germany.*

In Spain: For a complete list of books available from Penguin in Spain, please write to *Longman, Penguin España, Calle San Nicolas 15, E-28013 Madrid, Spain.*

In Japan: For a complete list of books available from Penguin in Japan, please write to *Longman Penguin Japan Co Ltd, Yamaguchi Building, 2-12-9 Kanda Jimbocho, Chiyoda-Ku, Tokyo 101, Japan.*